Ethical Investigations

General Editor

Lawrence C. Becker
Professor Emeritus
College of William & Mary

A ROUTLEDGE SERIES

Contents of the Collection

Volume 1
Conceptual Analyses of Rights and Duties

Volume 2
Rational Foundations of Rights and Duties

Volume 3
Possible Bearers of Rights and Duties

Volume 4
Human rights and Universal Duties

Volume 5
Welfare Rights and Duties of Charity

Volume 6
Property Rights and Duties of Redistribution

Rights and Duties

Volume 3

Possible Bearers of Rights and Duties

Edited with introductions by

Carl Wellman

University of Washington, St. Louis

ROUTLEDGE

New York/London

Published in 2002 by
Routledge
29 West 35th Street
New York, NY 10001

Published in Great Britain by
Routledge
11 New Fetter Lane
London EC4P 4EE

Routledge is an imprint of the Taylor & Francis Group.

Printed in the United States of America on acid-free paper.

10 9 8 7 6 5 4 3 2 1

Library of Congress Cataloging-in-Publication Data

Rights and duties / edited with introductions by Carl Wellman.
p. cm. — (Ethical Investigations)
Includes bibliographical references.
Contents: v. 1. The concept of a right and a duty — v. 2. The rational foundation of rights and duties — v. 3. Natural rights and duties—v. 4. Against rights and duties—v. 5. Duties and obligations to others—v. 6. Property as a right, distribution as a duty.
ISBN 0-415-93982-8 (set : alk paper) — ISBN 0-415-93983-6 (vol. 1 : alk. paper) — ISBN 0-415-93984-4 (vol. 2 : alk. paper) — ISBN 0-415-93985-2 (vol. 3 : alk. paper)—ISBN 0-415-93986-0 (vol. 4 : alk. paper)—ISBN 0-415-93987-9 (vol. 5 : alk. paper)—ISBN 0-415-93988-7 (vol. 6 : alk. paper)
1. Natural law. .2. Obedience (Law) .3. Duty. 4. Law and ethics I. Wellman, Carl II. Series.
K460.R46 2002
340'.112—dc21 2002020621

Contents

vii Series Introduction
ix Volume Introduction

Right-Holders

1 Abortion and Infanticide
Michael Tooley
31 On the Moral and Legal Status of Abortion
Mary Anne Warren
51 The Rights of Animals and Unborn Generations
Joel Feinberg
77 Potentiality in the Abortion Discussion
Francis C. Wade
95 Children's Rights: a Test-Case for Theories of Right
Neil MacCormick
108 Animal Rights
R. G. Frey
112 Rights and Borderline Cases
Jeffrie G. Murphy
127 Moral Rights and Animals
H. J. McCloskey
159 The Rights of Past and Future Persons
Annette Baier
172 Justice and Equality
Tom Regan
207 The Growth of Children's Rights
Carl Wellman
221 Moral Autonomy, Self-Determination, and Animal Rights
Robert Elliot

237 Individuals, Groups, and Rights to Public Goods
Denise Réaume

Duty-Bearers

264 Obligation and Moral Agency
Lucius Garvin

272 Responsibility, Understanding, and Psychopathology
Michael S. Prichard

289 Collective Actions and Secondary Actions
David Copp

299 The Corporation as a Moral Person
Peter A. French

309 Are Animals Moral Beings?
S. F. Sapontzis

317 The Psychopath as Moral Agent
Robert J. Smith

335 Ascriptions of Responsibility
Marina A. L. Oshana

349 Moral Agency, Individual Responsibility, and Human Psychology
N. Ann Davis

377 Kant on Duties Regarding Nonrational Nature.
Onora O'Neill

395 Acknowledgments

Series Introduction

This volume is part of an ambitious series designed to collect English language journal articles and book chapters of enduring philosophical interest in the field of ethics. The articles are published here in their original formats and pagination, without editorial changes of any sort. They are thus primary bibliographic documents as well as philosophical ones.

The series is organized into multivolume collections. The first of these is the six-volume collection called *Rights and Duties*, edited by Carl Wellman, of which this volume is a part. Future collections, with their projected publication dates, include *Justice and Equality* (2002); *Ethics and Public Policy Issues* (2003); *Environmental Ethics* (2003); *Moral Responsibility* (2004); and *Feminist Ethics* (2004).

For obvious reasons the series cannot reasonably aim to be comprehensive. The English language journal literature in ethics is vast, and although the common wisdom is that much of it is ephemeral, a good deal of it is clearly better than that—and there is more of that than we can possibly republish here. Moreover, we have not chosen articles simply because they are, or are likely to be, of interest to historians of philosophy. Rather, we have confined ourselves to topics of continuing philosophical interest, and articles on those topics that are either of continuing importance in themselves or of special use in orienting readers with respect to the wider literature. In addition, we have included some material from serials published in book form, and in unusual cases, we have included chapters from monographs. The focus, however, has been on the journal and serial literature, not monographs.

In an ideal world, all important journal articles in ethics would effortlessly enter into the institutional memory of professional philosophers. Our world falls short of that ideal, of course. For one thing, Anglo-American philosophers are notoriously stingy with citations, and many, on principle, resist attempts to create anything that might be misused as a closed, canonical list of worthy philosophical texts or topics. Those traits, combined with a propensity for closely focused argument on tightly defined problems, can induce a form of professional negligence in which, say, a young philosopher working on property rights in the final third of the twentieth century, circulating drafts of his manuscripts widely, can easily fail to come across Morris Cohen's useful articles on the subject. Moreover, literature searches are of limited use if the literature is difficult to access or too large to survey effectively—especially if one is unconsciously convinced of the false proposition that "If it is important, and if I don't know about it already, one of my critics will point it out to me soon." One of the aims of this series is to address the problem of professional amnesia, by pointing some things out.

Lawrence C. Becker

Volume Introduction

This is one of six volumes of collected articles and chapters on rights and duties. The others are *Conceptual Analyses of Rights and Duties*, *Rational Foundations of Rights and Duties*, *Human Rights and Universal Duties*, *Welfare Rights and Duties of Charity*, and *Property Rights and Duties of Redistribution*. Each is intended to be a coherent collection that presents a set of closely related debates concerning rights and duties. Together they represent the most important themes in the twentieth century theory of rights and duties. In addition to the articles and chapters that had to be omitted from each volume to hold them down to publishable size, there are other important publications that are not included because they do not fit neatly into any of these volumes. As I have attempted to fulfil my duties as an editor, I hope that I have not violated any right of authors I have reluctantly excluded from my selections.

What kinds of beings are possible duty-bearers? The twentieth century literature on this subject is not extensive, partly because this question has not been clearly distinguished from other questions concerning moral responsibility, but even more because the answer has been assumed to be obvious. Only moral agents could have any moral obligations. What capacities, then, are normally required for moral agency? Although Onora O'Neill does not endorse Immanuel Kant's strong notion of what it is to be free and rational, she does insist that only rational beings could be agents and that only agents could have moral duties. Does this imply that only beings capable of moral reflection, able to recognize the moral value of their contemplated acts, possess moral obligations? Lucius Garvin denies this because he accepts G. E. Moore's definition of duty as the act which, of all those open to the agent, will produce the most value. Hence moral agency requires only that one be capable of performing the best act possible under the circumstances. Marina A. L. Oshana builds both epistemic and control conditions into her conception of responsible moral agency. A responsible agent must be self-aware, rational, not ignorant of the circumstances in which she acts, and responsive to reasons to adjust her behavior in light of the relevant moral guidelines. In addition, she must be capable of deliberate intentional behavior free of coercion, manipulation or intimidation. N. Ann Davis adds an explicitly emotional component to her conception of a moral agent as an effective, rational, sympathetic actor. Moral agency requires cognitive skills such as the abilities to make reasonably informed projections of the consequences of acting or not acting in various ways, to compare alternative means to achieve one's ends, and to recognize the impact of one's actions on other human beings. But it also requires sympathetic affective responses sufficient to enable one to modify one's actions in the light of the needs of other people. Finally, a moral agent must have sufficient fixity of purpose to generally follow through on her deliberations and act on the basis of her projections, values and assessments in a significant range of circumstances. According to each of these theories of moral agency, normal adult human beings are paradigms of moral duty-bearers.

There remain, however, more problematic categories of beings. Michael S. Pritchard holds that moral agents must have at least a minimal understanding of the moral concepts applicable to them and must experience moral sentiments such as the feelings of guilt, remorse, shame as well as a concern to treat others with fellow-feeling. Therefore, he takes it for granted, as do many moral philosophers, that very small children and nonhuman animals cannot possess any moral duties. More problematic are psychopaths because, unlike small children, they can carry on intelligent moral conversations and are capable of feigning feelings of guilt and intentions to fulfill responsibilities. Nevertheless, Prichard argues that they lack moral agency. Although psychopaths might seem to possess moral understanding and lack only moral sentiments, this is not so because in order to be practically relevant to moral agency, moral understanding must involve the moral sentiments, especially caring about the way in which moral concepts apply to one's actions. Hence, psychopaths are not possible moral duty-bearers. Robert J. Smith rejects this conclusion both because he sees no clinical evidence that psychopaths are a distinct type of persons and because he can find no justification for distinguishing between normal and psychopathic values. The psychopath acts on the basis of egoistic values aiming at self aggrandizement, values accepted to some degree in every society and by most moral agents. Nonhuman animals constitute another problematic category of beings. S. F. Sapontzis argues that many animals are sufficiently rational to act virtuously but not to act morally. This is because their actions are not part of an attempt to fulfill an ideal way of life. Thus, animals, like holy wills in the philosophy of Kant, may be virtuous but are not possible possessors of moral obligations. Finally, there is considerable debate about whether groups are possible duty-bearers. Although individual members of a group are presumably morally responsible for their actions, it is not clear that a group can act as a collective. Peter A. French adopts Donald Davidson's conception of agency defined in terms of intentionality and argues that because some of the things that corporations do are intended by the corporation itself, corporations are moral agents in precisely the same sense as normal human beings. Hence, they can and do have moral duties. David Copp tries to explain how even relatively unorganized groups as well as corporations can perform secondary actions that fulfill or violate some moral obligation. This is because some act of another agent or actions of other agents are, under specified circumstances, correctly attributable to the group.

There is considerably more debate about the kinds of beings that are possible right-holders. Moral philosophers generally take it for granted that normal adult human beings can and do possess moral rights. But what about dead persons? A corpse is not a person, and the person who has died no longer exists. How, then, can someone who does not now exist have any right now that her last will and testament be respected? Annette Baier explains that to say that someone has a right is to say both that at least one other person has an obligation to the right-holder and that there is or should be a socially recognized means for the right-holder or her proxy to take appropriate action should that obligation be neglected. Now we do recognize that living persons have obligations to deceased persons and there are social practices by which their living proxies can claim performance of these obligations. Thus, dead persons can and do have rights. She then proposes an analogous explanation of how it is possible for future generations of persons to have rights. We might well have obligations to preserve natural resources for their use and it would be entirely possible to institute socially recognized means for persons living now to claim performance of our obligations to future persons.

H. L. A. Hart, who held that moral rights concern the proper distribution of free choice, once suggested that it is idle and misleading to say that very young children and animals incapable of choice have rights. Neil MacCormick regards the denial that even newborn children have a moral right to be nurtured and cared for as a clear case of moral blindness. Therefore, he rejects Hart's will theory of rights and argues that the function of any right is to protect some interest of the right-holder. Because infants do have an interest in being nurtured and cared for, they can and do possess a corresponding right. Jeffrie G. Murphy accepts something like Hart's option theory of rights as part of the truth, but argues that in addition to autonomy rights there are social contract rights concerned to provide morally justified legal guarantees. Although very young children are incapable of possessing any option rights because they are not yet fully rational and autonomous, they could possess social contract rights because it would be rational for adult human beings to adopt certain legal protections of children in their Rawlsian social contract. Although Carl Wellman rejects Hart's option theory of rights, he defends a different sort of will theory that makes autonomy, freedom and control, essential to any right. Because infants are incapable of either acting freely in the morally relevant sense or exercising control, he denies that very young children are possible right-holders.

Although Michael Tooley also denies that infants could possess any moral right to life and suggests that animals might have a right to life, his primary concern is whether abortion violates the right to life of the human fetus. He suggests that an individual has a right to something whenever if she wants that thing, it would be wrong for others to deprive her of that thing. Now a human fetus is incapable of desiring to continue living because a fetus cannot have any concept of itself as a self that is a continuing subject of experiences and other mental states. Hence, a fetus could not possess any serious moral right to life. Mary Anne Warren reaches the same conclusion by a different route. What is it about normal adult human beings that makes them members of the moral community of right-holders? It is not that they are members of the biological species of human organisms but that they are persons. Personhood involves traits such as consciousness, reasoning, self-motivated activity, the capacity to communicate and self-awareness. Although one might question some details in this explication of our concept of a person, it is clear that human fetuses are not persons because they possess none of these traits. Therefore, fetuses are incapable of possessing any moral rights. At this point, opponents of abortion often point out that human fetuses potentially possess personhood or moral agency or rationality or whatever qualifies one to possess moral rights. But does this mean more than that under normal circumstances the fetus could and probably will at some future time become a child that will then acquire moral rights? If not, then the appeal to potentiality cannot explain how the human fetus is now capable of possessing rights. Francis C. Wade argues that potentiality is more than a promise of some future actuality; it is something that already exists in a being. If an acorn has the potentiality to become an oak tree but not a pine tree, this is because there is already in the acorn a tendency to become an oak. Therefore, it might be possible to explain how a human fetus can now possess moral rights because it now possesses in potentiality the qualifications for being an adult right-holder.

Next to the abortion debate, the animal rights debate has attracted the most attention. Joel Feinberg conceives of a moral right as a moral claim and defines a claim in terms of the activity of claiming. This seems to imply that only beings capable of demanding something as their due could be right-holders, but he takes it as clear that infants do have rights. How is this possible? It is because even tiny babies can be represented by adults who claim their rights in their behalf. However, not every kind of being could be represented by another; it would make no sense to claim the right of a stick not to be burnt in a bonfire. All and only beings with interests, with a good of their own, can be represented. Because children and even nonhuman animals do have interests, they are possible right-holders. R. G. Frey questions whether it is so clear that babies do have moral rights. He insists that this requires further argument and criticizes the usual arguments that are alleged to support this conclusion. He thereby undercuts the reasoning that rejects those criteria for the possession of rights that exclude animals on the ground that they also exclude infants who presumably do possess moral rights. Although at one time H. J. McCloskey accepted having interests as sufficient to qualify one for the possession of rights, he later rejected this view. The paradigm possessor of a right is someone who can act as she is entitled to act or can act by demanding or claiming what she is entitled to demand or claim. And one ought to insist on or forgo one's rights only as so acting would be morally justified. Hence, only moral agents could possess moral rights. Because animals lack full moral agency, they are not possible right-holders. Robert Elliot gives examples of some ways in which adult human beings can exercise their rights to show that the possession of a right may require considerably less than full autonomy or moral agency. If so, then nonhuman animals might well possess sufficient agency to have some moral rights. Although Sapontzis denies that animals are possible duty-bearers, he argues that their capacity to act virtuously makes them worthy of moral respect and, thereby, possible possessors of moral rights. Tom Regan adopts the Kantian thesis that it is because human beings have inherent value that they possess moral rights commanding our respect, but he rejects the Kantian view that this inherent value is grounded on pure rationality. Any being that is the subject-of-a-life has inherent value. Because at least the higher species of animals have beliefs and desires, perception, memory and a sense of the future, preferences and welfare-interests, the ability to initiate action in pursuit of their goals and a psychophysical identity over time, they are subjects of a life. Therefore, at least these animals have an inherent value that confers upon them some moral rights.

For those who hold a will theory of rights, the explanations of French and Copp of how groups can and do act could justify the conclusion that groups are possible right-holders as well as duty-bearers. Denise Réaume, who accepts an interest theory of rights, also concludes that some groups could possess rights. There are some participatory public goods, such as the existence of a French school system in a predominantly English province in Canada, that could benefit the entire French community in a way that is not beneficial for everyone else. Hence, the minority group of Francophones could have an important interest sufficient to ground a group right that the society as a whole maintain a bilingual educational system.

A Short List of Related Articles

Christopher D. Stone, "Should Trees Have Standing?—Toward Legal Rights for Natural Objects," *Southern California Law Review* 45 (1972), pp. 450–501.

James Rachels, "Do Animals Have a Right to Liberty?" in *Animal Rights and Human Obligations*, Tom Regan & Peter Singer (eds.), Englewood Cliffs, NJ: Prentice-Hall, 1976.

R. G. Frey, "Interests and Animal Rights," *Philosophical Quarterly* 27 (1977), pp. 254–259.

Loren E. Lomasky, "Being a Person—Does It Matter," *Philosophical Topics* 12 (1981), pp. 139–152.

Aaron Ben-Zeev, "Who Is a Rational Agent?" *Canadian Journal of Philosophy* 12 (1982), pp. 647–661.

Peter A. French, "Crowds and Corporations," *American Philosophical Quarterly* 19 (1982), pp. 271–277.

Vernon Van Dyke, "Collective Entities and Moral Rights," *Journal of Politics* 44 (1982), pp. 21–40.

T. L. S. Sprigge, "Non-human Rights: An Idealist Perspective," *Inquiry* 27 (1984), pp. 439–461.

Tom Regan, "The Case for Animal Rights," in *In Defense of Animals*, Peter Singer (ed.), Oxford: Blackwells, 1985, pp. 13–26.

R. G. Frey, "Autonomy and the Value of Animal Life," *The Monist* 70 (1987), pp. 50–63.

Larry May, "Common Interests and Group Rights," in Larry May, *The Morality of Groups*, Notre Dame IN: University of Notre Dame Press, 1987, pp. 112–134.

Paul W. Taylor, "Inherent Value and Moral Rights," *The Monist* 70 (1987), pp. 15–30.

Michael Hartney, "Some Confusions Concerning Collective Rights," *Canadian Journal of Law and Jurisprudence* 4 (1991), pp. 293–314.

Robert E. Goodin and Diane Gibson, "Rights, Young and Old," *Oxford Journal of Legal Studies* 17 (1997), pp. 185–203.

George E. Panichas, "The Rights-Ascription Problem," *Social Theory and Practice* 23 (1997), pp. 365–398.

Mary Anne Warren "Personhood and Moral Rights" in Mary Anne Warren, *Moral Status: Obligations to Persons and Other Living Things*, Oxford: Clarendon Press, 1997, pp. 90–121.

Christopher Heath Wellman, "Liberalism, Communitarianism, and Group Rights," *Law and Philosophy* 18 (1999), pp. 13–40.

Derrick Darby, "Two Conceptions of Rights Possession," *Social Theory and Practice* 27 (2001), pp. 387–417.

George Rainbolt, "What Are Group Rights?" in *Groups and Group Rights*, Christine Sistare, Larry May & Leslie Francis (eds.), Lawrence KS: University of Kansas Press, 2001, pp. 71–81.

MICHAEL TOOLEY

Abortion and Infanticide[1]

This essay deals with the question of the morality of abortion and infanticide. The fundamental ethical objection traditionally advanced against these practices rests on the contention that human fetuses and infants have a right to life. It is this claim which will be the focus of attention here. The basic issue to be discussed, then, is what properties a thing must possess in order to have a serious right to life. My approach will be to set out and defend a basic moral principle specifying a condition an organism must satisfy if it is to have a serious right to life. It will be seen that this condition is not satisfied by human fetuses and infants, and thus that they do not have a right to life. So unless there are other substantial objections to abortion and infanticide, one is forced to conclude that these practices are morally acceptable ones. In contrast, it may turn out that our treatment of adult members of other species—cats, dogs, polar bears—is morally indefensible. For it is quite possible that such animals do possess properties that endow them with a right to life.

I. ABORTION AND INFANTICIDE

One reason the question of the morality of infanticide is worth examining is that it seems very difficult to formulate a completely satisfactory liberal position on abortion without coming to grips with the

1. I am grateful to a number of people, particularly the Editors of *Philosophy & Public Affairs*, Rodelia Hapke, and Walter Kaufmann, for their helpful comments. It should not, of course, be inferred that they share the views expressed in this paper.

infanticide issue. The problem the liberal encounters is essentially that of specifying a cutoff point which is not arbitrary: at what stage in the development of a human being does it cease to be morally permissible to destroy it? It is important to be clear about the difficulty here. The conservative's objection is not that since there is a continuous line of development from a zygote to a newborn baby, one must conclude that if it is seriously wrong to destroy a newborn baby it is also seriously wrong to destroy a zygote or any intermediate stage in the development of a human being. His point is rather that if one says it is wrong to destroy a newborn baby but not a zygote or some intermediate stage in the development of a human being, one should be prepared to point to a *morally relevant* difference between a newborn baby and the earlier stage in the development of a human being.

Precisely the same difficulty can, of course, be raised for a person who holds that infanticide is morally permissible. The conservative will ask what morally relevant differences there are between an adult human being and a newborn baby. What makes it morally permissible to destroy a baby, but wrong to kill an adult? So the challenge remains. But I will argue that in this case there is an extremely plausible answer.

Reflecting on the morality of infanticide forces one to face up to this challenge. In the case of abortion a number of events—quickening or viability, for instance—might be taken as cutoff points, and it is easy to overlook the fact that none of these events involves any morally significant change in the developing human. In contrast, if one is going to defend infanticide, one has to get very clear about what makes something a person, what gives something a right to life.

One of the interesting ways in which the abortion issue differs from most other moral issues is that the plausible positions on abortion appear to be extreme positions. For if a human fetus is a person, one is inclined to say that, in general, one would be justified in killing it only to save the life of the mother.[2] Such is the extreme conservative

2. Judith Jarvis Thomson, in her article "A Defense of Abortion," *Philosophy & Public Affairs* 1, no. 1 (Fall 1971): 47-66, has argued with great force and ingenuity that this conclusion is mistaken. I will comment on her argument later in this paper.

position.[3] On the other hand, if the fetus is not a person, how can it be seriously wrong to destroy it? Why would one need to point to special circumstances to justify such action? The upshot is that there is no room for a moderate position on the issue of abortion such as one finds, for example, in the Model Penal Code recommendations.[4]

Aside from the light it may shed on the abortion question, the issue of infanticide is both interesting and important in its own right. The theoretical interest has been mentioned: it forces one to face up to the question of what makes something a person. The practical importance need not be labored. Most people would prefer to raise children who do not suffer from gross deformities or from severe physical, emotional, or intellectual handicaps. If it could be shown that there is no moral objection to infanticide the happiness of society could be significantly and justifiably increased.

Infanticide is also of interest because of the strong emotions it arouses. The typical reaction to infanticide is like the reaction to incest or cannibalism, or the reaction of previous generations to masturbation or oral sex. The response, rather than appealing to carefully formulated moral principles, is primarily visceral. When philosophers

3. While this is the position conservatives tend to hold, it is not clear that it is the position they ought to hold. For if the fetus is a person it is far from clear that it is permissible to destroy it to save the mother. Two moral principles lend support to the view that it is the fetus which should live. First, other things being equal, should not one give something to a person who has had less rather than to a person who has had more? The mother has had a chance to live, while the fetus has not. The choice is thus between giving the mother more of an opportunity to live while giving the fetus none at all and giving the fetus an opportunity to enjoy life while not giving the mother a further opportunity to do so. Surely fairness requires the latter. Secondly, since the fetus has a greater life expectancy than the mother, one is in effect distributing more goods by choosing the life of the fetus over the life of the mother.

The position I am here recommending to the conservative should not be confused with the official Catholic position. The Catholic Church holds that it is seriously wrong to kill a fetus directly even if failure to do so will result in the death of *both* the mother and the fetus. This perverse value judgment is not part of the conservative's position.

4. Section 230.3 of the American Law Institute's *Model Penal Code* (Philadelphia, 1962). There is some interesting, though at time confused, discussion of the proposed code in *Model Penal Code–Tentative Draft No. 9* (Philadelphia, 1959), pp. 146-162.

themselves respond in this way, offering no arguments, and dismissing infanticide out of hand, it is reasonable to suspect that one is dealing with a taboo rather than with a rational prohibition.[5] I shall attempt to show that this is in fact the case.

II. TERMINOLOGY: "PERSON" VERSUS "HUMAN BEING"

How is the term "person" to be interpreted? I shall treat the concept of a person as a purely moral concept, free of all descriptive content. Specifically, in my usage the sentence "X is a person" will be synonymous with the sentence "X has a (serious) moral right to life."

This usage diverges slightly from what is perhaps the more common way of interpreting the term "person" when it is employed as a purely moral term, where to say that X is a person is to say that X has rights. If everything that had rights had a right to life, these interpretations would be extensionally equivalent. But I am inclined to think that it does not follow from acceptable moral principles that whatever has any rights at all has a right to life. My reason is this. Given the choice between being killed and being tortured for an hour, most adult humans would surely choose the latter. So it seems plausible to say it is worse to kill an adult human being than it is to torture him for an hour. In contrast, it seems to me that while it is not seriously wrong to kill a newborn kitten, it is seriously wrong to torture one for an hour. This *suggests* that newborn kittens may have a right not to be tortured without having a serious right to life. For it seems to be true that an individual has a right to something whenever it is the case that, if he wants that thing, it would be wrong for others to deprive him of it. Then if it is wrong to inflict a certain sensation upon a kitten if it doesn't want to experience that sensation, it will follow that the kitten has a right not to have sensation inflicted upon it.[6] I shall re-

5. A clear example of such an unwillingness to entertain seriously the possibility that moral judgments widely accepted in one's own society may nevertheless be incorrect is provided by Roger Wertheimer's superficial dismissal of infanticide on pages 69-70 of his article "Understanding the Abortion Argument," *Philosophy & Public Affairs* 1, no. 1 (Fall 1971): 67-95.

6. Compare the discussion of the concept of a right offered by Richard B. Brandt in his *Ethical Theory* (Englewood Cliffs, N.J., 1959), pp. 434-441. As Brandt points out, some philosophers have maintained that only things that can *claim* rights can have rights. I agree with Brandt's view that "inability to claim does not destroy the right" (p. 440).

turn to this example later. My point here is merely that it provides some reason for holding that it does not follow from acceptable moral principles that if something has any rights at all, it has a serious right to life.

There has been a tendency in recent discussions of abortion to use expressions such as "person" and "human being" interchangeably. B. A. Brody, for example, refers to the difficulty of determining "whether destroying the foetus constitutes the taking of a human life," and suggests it is very plausible that "the taking of a human life is an action that has bad consequences for him whose life is being taken."[7] When Brody refers to something as a human life he apparently construes this as entailing that the thing is a person. For if every living organism belonging to the species homo sapiens counted as a human life, there would be no difficulty in determining whether a fetus inside a human mother was a human life.

The same tendency is found in Judith Jarvis Thomson's article, which opens with the statement: "Most opposition to abortion relies on the premise that the fetus is a human being, a person, from the moment of conception."[8] The same is true of Roger Wertheimer, who explicitly says: "First off I should note that the expressions 'a human life,' 'a human being,' 'a person' are virtually interchangeable in this context."[9]

The tendency to use expressions like "person" and "human being" interchangeably is an unfortunate one. For one thing, it tends to lend covert support to antiabortionist positions. Given such usage, one who holds a liberal view of abortion is put in the position of maintaining that fetuses, at least up to a certain point, are not human beings. Even philosophers are led astray by this usage. Thus Wertheimer says that "except for monstrosities, every member of our species is indubitably a person, a human being, at the very latest at birth."[10] Is it really *indubitable* that newborn babies are persons? Surely this is a wild contention. Wertheimer is falling prey to the confusion naturally

7. B. A. Brody, "Abortion and the Law," *Journal of Philosophy*, LXVIII, no. 12 (17 June 1971): 357-369. See pp. 357-358.

8. Thomson, "A Defense of Abortion," p. 47.

9. Wertheimer, "Understanding the Abortion Argument," p. 69.

10. *Ibid.*

engendered by the practice of using "person" and "human being" interchangeably. Another example of this is provided by Thomson: "I am inclined to think also that we shall probably have to agree that the fetus has already become a human person well before birth. Indeed, it comes as a surprise when one first learns how early in its life it begins to acquire human characteristics. By the tenth week, for example, it already has a face, arms and legs, fingers and toes; it has internal organs, and brain activity is detectable."[11] But what do such physiological characteristics have to do with the question of whether the organism is a person? Thomson, partly, I think, because of the unfortunate use of terminology, does not even raise this question. As a result she virtually takes it for granted that there are some cases in which abortion is "positively indecent."[12]

There is a second reason why using "person" and "human being" interchangeably is unhappy philosophically. If one says that the dispute between pro- and anti-abortionists centers on whether the fetus is a human, it is natural to conclude that it is essentially a disagreement about certain facts, a disagreement about what properties a fetus possesses. Thus Wertheimer says that "if one insists on using the raggy fact-value distinction, then one ought to say that the dispute is over a matter of fact in the sense in which it is a fact that the Negro slaves were human beings."[13] I shall argue that the two cases are not parallel, and that in the case of abortion what is primarily at stake is what moral principles one should accept. If one says that the central issue between conservatives and liberals in the abortion question is whether the fetus is a person, it is clear that the dispute may be either about what properties a thing must have in order to be a person, in order to have a right to life—a moral question—or about whether a fetus at a given stage of development as a matter of fact possesses the properties in question. The temptation to suppose that the disagreement must be a factual one is removed.

It should now be clear why the common practice of using expressions such as "person" and "human being" interchangeably in discussions of abortion is unfortunate. It would perhaps be best to avoid

11. Thomson, "A Defense of Abortion," pp. 47-48.
12. *Ibid.*, p. 65.
13. Wertheimer, "Understanding the Abortion Argument," p. 78.

the term "human" altogether, employing instead some expression that is more naturally interpreted as referring to a certain type of biological organism characterized in physiological terms, such as "member of the species Homo sapiens." My own approach will be to use the term "human" only in contexts where it is not philosophically dangerous.

III. THE BASIC ISSUE: WHEN IS A MEMBER OF THE SPECIES HOMO SAPIENS A PERSON?

Settling the issue of the morality of abortion and infanticide will involve answering the following questions: What properties must something have to be a person, i.e., to have a serious right to life? At what point in the development of a member of the species Homo sapiens does the organism possess the properties that make it a person? The first question raises a moral issue. To answer it is to decide what basic[14] moral principles involving the ascription of a right to life one ought to accept. The second question raises a purely factual issue, since the properties in question are properties of a purely descriptive sort.

Some writers seem quite pessimistic about the possibility of resolving the question of the morality of abortion. Indeed, some have gone so far as to suggest that the question of whether the fetus is a person is in principle unanswerable: "we seem to be stuck with the indeterminateness of the fetus' humanity."[15] An understanding of some of the sources of this pessimism will, I think, help us to tackle the problem. Let us begin by considering the similarity a number of people have noted between the issue of abortion and the issue of Negro slavery. The question here is why it should be more difficult to decide whether abortion and infanticide are acceptable than it was to decide whether slavery was acceptable. The answer seems to be that in the case of slavery there are moral principles of a quite uncontroversial sort that settle the issue. Thus most people would agree to some such principle as the following: No organism that has experiences, that is capable of thought and of using language, and that has harmed no one, should

14. A moral principle accepted by a person is *basic for him* if and only if his acceptance of it is not dependent upon any of his (nonmoral) factual beliefs. That is, no change in his factual beliefs would cause him to abandon the principle in question.

15. Wertheimer, "Understanding the Abortion Argument," p. 88.

be made a slave. In the case of abortion, on the other hand, conditions that are generally agreed to be sufficient grounds for ascribing a right to life to something do not suffice to settle the issue. It is easy to specify other, purportedly sufficient conditions that will settle the issue, but no one has been successful in putting forward considerations that will convince others to accept those additional moral principles.

I do not share the general pessimism about the possibility of resolving the issue of abortion and infanticide because I believe it is possible to point to a very plausible moral principle dealing with the question of *necessary* conditions for something's having a right to life, where the conditions in question will provide an answer to the question of the permissibility of abortion and infanticide.

There is a second cause of pessimism that should be noted before proceeding. It is tied up with the fact that the development of an organism is one of gradual and continuous change. Given this continuity, how is one to draw a line at one point and declare it permissible to destroy a member of Homo sapiens up to, but not beyond, that point? Won't there be an arbitrariness about any point that is chosen? I will return to this worry shortly. It does not present a serious difficulty once the basic moral principles relevant to the ascription of a right to life to an individual are established.

Let us turn now to the first and most fundamental question: What properties must something have in order to be a person, i.e., to have a serious right to life? The claim I wish to defend is this: An organism possesses a serious right to life only if it possesses the concept of a self as a continuing subject of experiences and other mental states, and believes that it is itself such a continuing entity.

My basic argument in support of this claim, which I will call the self-consciousness requirement, will be clearest, I think, if I first offer a simplified version of the argument, and then consider a modification that seems desirable. The simplified version of my argument is this. To ascribe a right to an individual is to assert something about the prima facie obligations of other individuals to act, or to refrain from acting, in certain ways. However, the obligations in question are conditional ones, being dependent upon the existence of certain desires of the individual to whom the right is ascribed. Thus if an individual asks one to destroy something to which he has a right, one does not violate his right to that thing if one proceeds to destroy it. This suggests the following analysis: "A has a right to X" is roughly synonymous with "If A desires X, then others are under a prima facie obligation to refrain from actions that would deprive him of it."[16]

Although this analysis is initially plausible, there are reasons for thinking it not entirely correct. I will consider these later. Even here, however, some expansion is necessary, since there are features of the concept of a right that are important in the present context, and that ought to be dealt with more explicitly. In particular, it seems to be a conceptual truth that things that lack consciousness, such as ordinary machines, cannot have rights. Does this conceptual truth follow from the above analysis of the concept of a right? The answer depends on how the term "desire" is interpreted. If one adopts a completely behavioristic interpretation of "desire," so that a machine that searches for an electrical outlet in order to get its batteries recharged is described as having a desire to be recharged, then it will not follow from this analysis that objects that lack consciousness cannot have rights. On the other hand, if "desire" is interpreted in such a way that desires are states necessarily standing in some sort of relationship to states of consciousness, it will follow from the analysis that a machine that is not capable of being conscious, and consequently of having desires, cannot have any rights. I think those who defend analyses of the concept of a right along the lines of this one do have in mind an interpretation of the term "desire" that involves reference to something more than behavioral dispositions. However, rather than relying on this, it seems preferable to make such an interpretation explicit. The following analysis is a natural way of doing that: "A has a right to X" is roughly synonymous with "A is the sort of thing that is a subject of experiences and other mental states, A is capable of desiring X, and if A does desire X, then others are under a prima facie obligation to refrain from actions that would deprive him of it."

The next step in the argument is basically a matter of applying this analysis to the concept of a right to life. Unfortunately the expression

16. Again, compare the analysis defended by Brandt in *Ethical Theory*, pp. 434-441.

"right to life" is not entirely a happy one, since it suggests that the right in question concerns the continued existence of a biological organism. That this is incorrect can be brought out by considering possible ways of violating an individual's right to life. Suppose, for example, that by some technology of the future the brain of an adult human were to be completely reprogrammed, so that the organism wound up with memories (or rather, apparent memories), beliefs, attitudes, and personality traits completely different from those associated with it before it was subjected to reprogramming. In such a case one would surely say that an individual had been destroyed, that an adult human's right to life had been violated, even though no biological organism had been killed. This example shows that the expression "right to life" is misleading, since what one is really concerned about is not just the continued existence of a biological organism, but the right of a subject of experiences and other mental states to continue to exist.

Given this more precise description of the right with which we are here concerned, we are now in a position to apply the analysis of the concept of a right stated above. When we do so we find that the statement "A has a right to continue to exist as a subject of experiences and other mental states" is roughly synonymous with the statement "A is a subject of experiences and other mental states, A is capable of desiring to continue to exist as a subject of experiences and other mental states, and if A does desire to continue to exist as such an entity, then others are under a prima facie obligation not to prevent him from doing so."

The final stage in the argument is simply a matter of asking what must be the case if something is to be capable of having a desire to continue existing as a subject of experiences and other mental states. The basic point here is that the desires a thing can have are limited by the concepts it possesses. For the fundamental way of describing a given desire is as a desire that a certain proposition be true.[17] Then,

17. In everyday life one often speaks of desiring things, such as an apple or a newspaper. Such talk is elliptical, the context together with one's ordinary beliefs serving to make it clear that one wants to eat the apple and read the newspaper. To say that what one desires is that a certain proposition be true should not be construed as involving any particular ontological commitment. The point is merely that it is sentences such as "John wants it to be the case

since one cannot desire that a certain proposition be true unless one understands it, and since one cannot understand it without possessing the concepts involved in it, it follows that the desires one can have are limited by the concepts one possesses. Applying this to the present case results in the conclusion that an entity cannot be the sort of thing that can desire that a subject of experiences and other mental states exist unless it possesses the concept of such a subject. Moreover, an entity cannot desire that it itself *continue* existing as a subject of experiences and other mental states unless it believes that it is now such a subject. This completes the justification of the claim that it is a necessary condition of something's having a serious right to life that it possess the concept of a self as a continuing subject of experiences, and that it believe that it is itself such an entity.

Let us now consider a modification in the above argument that seems desirable. This modification concerns the crucial conceptual claim advanced about the relationship between ascription of rights and ascription of the corresponding desires. Certain situations suggest that there may be exceptions to the claim that if a person doesn't desire something, one cannot violate his right to it. There are three types of situations that call this claim into question: (i) situations in which an individual's desires reflect a state of emotional disturbance; (ii) situations in which a previously conscious individual is temporarily unconscious; (iii) situations in which an individual's desires have been distorted by conditioning or by indoctrination.

As an example of the first, consider a case in which an adult human falls into a state of depression which his psychiatrist recognizes as temporary. While in the state he tells people he wishes he were dead. His psychiatrist, accepting the view that there can be no violation of an individual's right to life unless the individual has a desire to live, decides to let his patient have his way and kills him. Or consider a related case in which one person gives another a drug that produces a state of temporary depression; the recipient expresses a wish that he were dead. The person who administered the drug then kills him. Doesn't one want to say in both these cases that the agent did some-

---

that he is eating an apple in the next few minutes" that provide a completely explicit description of a person's desires. If one fails to use such sentences one can be badly misled about what concepts are presupposed by a particular desire.

thing seriously wrong in killing the other person? And isn't the reason the action was seriously wrong in each case the fact that it violated the individual's right to life? If so, the right to life cannot be linked with a desire to live in the way claimed above.

The second set of situations are ones in which an individual is unconscious for some reason—that is, he is sleeping, or drugged, or in a temporary coma. Does an individual in such a state have any desires? People do sometimes say that an unconscious individual wants something, but it might be argued that if such talk is not to be simply false it must be interpreted as actually referring to the desires the individual *would* have if he were now conscious. Consequently, if the analysis of the concept of a right proposed above were correct, it would follow that one does not violate an individual's right if one takes his car, or kills him, while he is asleep.

Finally, consider situations in which an individual's desires have been distorted, either by inculcation of irrational beliefs or by direct conditioning. Thus an individual may permit someone to kill him because he has been convinced that if he allows himself to be sacrificed to the gods he will be gloriously rewarded in a life to come. Or an individual may be enslaved after first having been conditioned to desire a life of slavery. Doesn't one want to say that in the former case an individual's right to life has been violated, and in the latter his right to freedom?

Situations such as these strongly suggest that even if an individual doesn't want something, it is still possible to violate his right to it. Some modification of the earlier account of the concept of a right thus seems in order. The analysis given covers, I believe, the paradigmatic cases of violation of an individual's rights, but there are other, secondary cases where one also wants to say that someone's right has been violated which are not included.

Precisely how the revised analysis should be formulated is unclear. Here it will be sufficient merely to say that, in view of the above, an individual's right to X can be violated not only when he desires X, but also when he *would* now desire X were it not for one of the following: (i) he is in an emotionally unbalanced state; (ii) he is temporarily unconscious; (iii) he has been conditioned to desire the absence of X.

The critical point now is that, even given this extension of the conditions under which an individual's right to something can be violated, it is still true that one's right to something can be violated only when one has the conceptual capability of desiring the thing in question. For example, an individual who would now desire not to be a slave if he weren't emotionally unbalanced, or if he weren't temporarily unconscious, or if he hadn't previously been conditioned to want to be a slave, must possess the concepts involved in the desire not to be a slave. Since it is really only the conceptual capability presupposed by the desire to continue existing as a subject of experiences and other mental states, and not the desire itself, that enters into the above argument, the modification required in the account of the conditions under which an individual's rights can be violated does not undercut my defense of the self-consciousness requirement.[18]

To sum up, my argument has been that having a right to life presupposes that one is capable of desiring to continue existing as a subject of experiences and other mental states. This in turn presupposes both that one has the concept of such a continuing entity and that one believes that one is oneself such an entity. So an entity that lacks such a consciousness of itself as a continuing subject of mental states does not have a right to life.

It would be natural to ask at this point whether satisfaction of this requirement is not only necessary but also sufficient to ensure that a thing has a right to life. I am inclined to an affirmative answer. However, the issue is not urgent in the present context, since as long as the requirement is in fact a necessary one we have the basis of an adequate defense of abortion and infanticide. If an organism must satisfy some other condition before it has a serious right to life, the result

18. There are, however, situations other than those discussed here which might seem to count against the claim that a person cannot have a right unless he is conceptually capable of having the corresponding desire. Can't a young child, for example, have a right to an estate, even though he may not be conceptually capable of wanting the estate? It is clear that such situations have to be carefully considered if one is to arrive at a satisfactory account of the concept of a right. My inclination is to say that the correct description is not that the child now has a right to the estate, but that he will come to have such a right when he is mature, and that in the meantime no one else has a right to the estate. My reason for saying that the child does not now have a right to the estate is that he cannot now do things with the estate, such as selling it or giving it away, that he will be able to do later on.

will merely be that the interval during which infanticide is morally permissible may be somewhat longer. Although the point at which an organism first achieves self-consciousness and hence the capacity of desiring to continue existing as a subject of experiences and other mental states may be a theoretically incorrect cutoff point, it is at least a morally safe one: any error it involves is on the side of caution.

IV. SOME CRITICAL COMMENTS ON ALTERNATIVE PROPOSALS

I now want to compare the line of demarcation I am proposing with the cutoff points traditionally advanced in discussions of abortion. My fundamental claim will be that none of these cutoff points can be defended by appeal to plausible, basic moral principles. The main suggestions as to the point past which it is seriously wrong to destroy something that will develop into an adult member of the species Homo sapiens are these: (a) conception; (b) the attainment of human form; (c) the achievement of the ability to move about spontaneously; (d) viability; (e) birth.[19] The corresponding moral principles suggested by these cutoff points are as follows: (1) It is seriously wrong to kill an organism, from a zygote on, that belongs to the species Homo sapiens. (2) It is seriously wrong to kill an organism that belongs to Homo sapiens and that has achieved human form. (3) It is seriously wrong to kill an organism that is a member of Homo sapiens and that is capable of spontaneous movement. (4) It is seriously wrong to kill an organism that belongs to Homo sapiens and that is capable of existing outside the womb. (5) It is seriously wrong to kill an organism that is a member of Homo sapiens that is no longer in the womb.

My first comment is that it would not do *simply* to omit the reference to membership in the species Homo sapiens from the above principles, with the exception of principle (2). For then the principles would be applicable to animals in general, and one would be forced to conclude that it was seriously wrong to abort a cat fetus, or that it was seriously wrong to abort a motile cat fetus, and so on.

The second and crucial comment is that none of the five principles

19. Another frequent suggestion as to the cutoff point not listed here is quickening. I omit it because it seems clear that if abortion after quickening is wrong, its wrongness must be tied up with the motility of the fetus, not with the mother's awareness of the fetus' ability to move about.

given above can plausibly be viewed as a *basic* moral principle. To accept any of them as such would be akin to accepting as a basic moral principle the proposition that it is morally permissible to enslave black members of the species Homo sapiens but not white members. Why should it be seriously wrong to kill an unborn member of the species Homo sapiens but not seriously wrong to kill an unborn kitten? Difference in species is not per se a morally relevant difference. If one holds that it is seriously wrong to kill an unborn member of the species Homo sapiens but not an unborn kitten, one should be prepared to point to some property that is morally significant and that is possessed by unborn members of Homo sapiens but not by unborn kittens. Similarly, such a property must be identified if one believes it seriously wrong to kill unborn members of Homo sapiens that have achieved viability but not seriously wrong to kill unborn kittens that have achieved that state.

What property might account for such a difference? That is to say, what *basic* moral principles might a person who accepts one of these five principles appeal to in support of his secondary moral judgment? Why should events such as the achievement of human form, or the achievement of the ability to move about, or the achievement of viability, or birth serve to endow something with a right to life? What the liberal must do is to show that these events involve changes, or are associated with changes, that are morally relevant.

Let us now consider reasons why the events involved in cutoff points (b) through (e) are not morally relevant, beginning with the last two: viability and birth. The fact that an organism is not physiologically dependent upon another organism, or is capable of such physiological independence, is surely irrelevant to whether the organism has a right to life. In defense of this contention, consider a speculative case where a fetus is able to learn a language while in the womb. One would surely not say that the fetus had no right to life until it emerged from the womb, or until it was capable of existing outside the womb. A less speculative example is the case of Siamese twins who have learned to speak. One doesn't want to say that since one of the twins would die were the two to be separated, it therefore has no right to life. Consequently it seems difficult to disagree with the conservative's claim that an organism which lacks a right to life before birth or before becoming viable cannot acquire this right immediately upon birth or upon becoming viable.

This does not, however, completely rule out viability as a line of demarcation. For instead of defending viability as a cutoff point on the ground that only then does a fetus acquire a right to life, it is possible to argue rather that when one organism is physiologically dependent upon another, the former's right to life may conflict with the latter's right to use its body as it will, and moreover, that the latter's right to do what it wants with its body may often take precedence over the other organism's right to life. Thomson has defended this view: "I am arguing only that having a right to life does not guarantee having either a right to the use of or a right to be allowed continued use of another person's body—even if one needs it for life itself. So the right to life will not serve the opponents of abortion in the very simple and clear way in which they seem to have thought it would."[20] I believe that Thomson is right in contending that philosophers have been altogether too casual in assuming that if one grants the fetus a serious right to life, one must accept a conservative position on abortion.[21] I also think the only defense of viability as a cutoff point which has any hope of success at all is one based on the considerations she advances. I doubt very much, however, that this defense of abortion is ultimately tenable. I think that one can grant even stronger assumptions than those made by Thomson and still argue persuasively for a semiconservative view. What I have in mind is this. Let it be granted, for the sake of argument, that a woman's right to free her body of parasites which will inhibit her freedom of action and possibly impair her health is stronger than the parasite's right to life, and is so even if the parasite has as much right to life as an adult human. One can still argue that abortion ought not to be permitted. For if A's right is stronger than B's, and it is impossible to satisfy both, it does not follow that A's should be satisfied rather than B's. It may be possible to compensate A if his right isn't satisfied, but impossible to compensate B if his right isn't satisfied. In such a case the best thing

20. Thomson, "A Defense of Abortion," p. 56.

21. A good example of a failure to probe this issue is provided by Brody's "Abortion and the Law."

to do may be to satisfy B's claim and to compensate A. Abortion may be a case in point. If the fetus has a right to life and the right is not satisfied, there is certainly no way the fetus can be compensated. On the other hand, if the woman's right to rid her body of harmful and annoying parasites is not satisfied, she can be compensated. Thus it would seem that the just thing to do would be to prohibit abortion, but to compensate women for the burden of carrying a parasite to term. Then, however, we are back at a (modified) conservative position.[22] Our conclusion must be that it appears unlikely there is any satisfactory defense either of viability or of birth as cutoff points.

Let us now consider the third suggested line of demarcation, the achievement of the power to move about spontaneously. It might be argued that acquiring this power is a morally relevant event on the grounds that there is a connection between the concept of an agent and the concept of a person, and being motile is an indication that a thing is an agent.[23]

It is difficult to respond to this suggestion unless it is made more specific. Given that one's interest here is in defending a certain cutoff point, it is natural to interpret the proposal as suggesting that motility is a necessary condition of an organism's having a right to life. But this won't do, because one certainly wants to ascribe a right to life to adult humans who are completely paralyzed. Maybe the suggestion is rather that motility is a sufficient condition of something's having a right to life. However, it is clear that motility alone is not sufficient, since this would imply that all animals, and also certain machines, have a right to life. Perhaps, then, the most reasonable interpretation of the claim is that motility together with some other property is a sufficient condition of something's having a right to life, where the other property will have to be a property possessed by unborn members of the species Homo sapiens but not by unborn members of other familiar species.

The central question, then, is what this other property is. Until one

22. Admittedly the modification is a substantial one, since given a society that refused to compensate women, a woman who had an abortion would not be doing anything wrong.

23. Compare Wertheimer's remarks, "Understanding the Abortion Argument," p. 79.

is told, it is very difficult to evaluate either the moral claim that motility together with that property is a sufficient basis for ascribing to an organism a right to life or the factual claim that a motile human fetus possesses that property while a motile fetus belonging to some other species does not. A conservative would presumably reject motility as a cutoff point by arguing that whether an organism has a right to life depends only upon its potentialities, which are of course not changed by its becoming motile. If, on the other hand, one favors a liberal view of abortion, I think that one can attack this third suggested cutoff point, in its unspecified form, only by determining what properties are necessary, or what properties sufficient, for an individual to have a right to life. Thus I would base my rejection of motility as a cutoff point on my claim, defended above, that a necessary condition of an organism's possessing a right to life is that it conceive of itself as a continuing subject of experiences and other mental states.

The second suggested cutoff point—the development of a recognizably human form—can be dismissed fairly quickly. I have already remarked that membership in a particular species is not itself a morally relevant property. For it is obvious that if we encountered other "rational animals," such as Martians, the fact that their physiological makeup was very different from our own would not be grounds for denying them a right to life.[24] Similarly, it is clear that the development of human form is not in itself a morally relevant event. Nor do there seem to be any grounds for holding that there is some other change, associated with this event, that is morally relevant. The appeal of this second cutoff point is, I think, purely emotional.

The overall conclusion seems to be that it is very difficult to defend the cutoff points traditionally advanced by those who advocate either a moderate or a liberal position on abortion. The reason is that there do not seem to be any basic moral principles one can appeal to in support of the cutoff points in question. We must now consider whether the conservative is any better off.

24. This requires qualification. If their central nervous systems were radically different from ours, it might be thought that one would not be justified in ascribing to them mental states of an experiential sort. And then, since it seems to be a conceptual truth that only things having experiential states can have rights, one would be forced to conclude that one was not justified in ascribing any rights to them.

V. REFUTATION OF THE CONSERVATIVE POSITION

Many have felt that the conservative's position is more defensible than the liberal's because the conservative can point to the gradual and continuous development of an organism as it changes from a zygote to an adult human being. He is then in a position to argue that it is morally arbitrary for the liberal to draw a line at some point in this continuous process and to say that abortion is permissible before, but not after, that particular point. The liberal's reply would presumably be that the emphasis upon the continuity of the process is misleading. What the conservative is really doing is simply challenging the liberal to specify the properties a thing must have in order to be a person, and to show that the developing organism does acquire the properties at the point selected by the liberal. The liberal may then reply that the difficulty he has meeting this challenge should not be taken as grounds for rejecting his position. For the conservative cannot meet this challenge either; the conservative is equally unable to say what properties something must have if it is to have a right to life.

Although this rejoinder does not dispose of the conservative's argument, it is not without bite. For defenders of the view that abortion is always wrong have failed to face up to the question of the basic moral principles on which their position rests. They have been content to assert the wrongness of killing any organism, from a zygote on, if that organism is a member of the species Homo sapiens. But they have overlooked the point that this cannot be an acceptable *basic* moral principle, since difference in species is not in itself a morally relevant difference. The conservative can reply, however, that it is possible to defend his position—but not the liberal's—*without* getting clear about the properties a thing must possess if it is to have a right to life. The conservative's defense will rest upon the following two claims: first, that there is a property, even if one is unable to specify what it is, that (i) is possessed by adult humans, and (ii) endows any organism possessing it with a serious right to life. Second, that if there are properties which satisfy (i) and (ii) above, at least one of those properties will be such that any organism potentially possessing that property has a serious right to life even now, simply by virtue of that potentiality, where an organism possesses a property potentially if it will come to have that property in the normal course of its development. The second claim—which I shall refer to as the potentiality principle—is critical to the conservative's defense. Because of it he is able to defend his position without deciding what properties a thing must possess in order to have a right to life. It is enough to know that adult members of Homo sapiens do have such a right. For then one can conclude that any organism which belongs to the species Homo sapiens, from a zygote on, must also have a right to life by virtue of the potentiality principle.

The liberal, by contrast, cannot mount a comparable argument. He cannot defend his position without offering at least a partial answer to the question of what properties a thing must possess in order to have a right to life.

The importance of the potentiality principle, however, goes beyond the fact that it provides support for the conservative's position. If the principle is unacceptable, then so is his position. For if the conservative cannot defend the view that an organism's having certain potentialities is sufficient grounds for ascribing to it a right to life, his claim that a fetus which is a member of Homo sapiens has a right to life can be attacked as follows. The reason an adult member of Homo sapiens has a right to life, but an infant ape does not, is that there are certain psychological properties which the former possesses and the latter lacks. Now, even if one is unsure exactly what these psychological properties are, it is clear that an organism in the early stages of development from a zygote into an adult member of Homo sapiens does not possess these properties. One need merely compare a human fetus with an ape fetus. What mental states does the former enjoy that the latter does not? Surely it is reasonable to hold that there are no significant differences in their respective mental lives—assuming that one wishes to ascribe any mental states at all to such organisms. (Does a zygote have a mental life? Does it have experiences? Or beliefs? Or desires?) There are, of course, physiological differences, but these are not in themselves morally significant. *If* one held that potentialities were relevant to the ascription of a right to life, one could argue that the physiological differences, though not morally significant in themselves, are morally significant by virtue of their causal consequences: they will lead to later psychological differences that are morally relevant, and for this reason the physiological differences are themselves morally significant. But if the potentiality principle is not available, this line of argument cannot be used, and there will then be no differences between a human fetus and an ape fetus that the conservative can use as grounds for ascribing a serious right to life to the former but not to the latter.

It is therefore tempting to conclude that the conservative view of abortion is acceptable if and only if the potentiality principle is acceptable. But to say that the conservative position can be defended if the potentiality principle is acceptable is to assume that the argument is over once it is granted that the fetus has a right to life, and, as was noted above, Thomson has shown that there are serious grounds for questioning this assumption. In any case, the important point here is that the conservative position on abortion is acceptable *only if* the potentiality principle is sound.

One way to attack the potentiality principle is simply to argue in support of the self-consciousness requirement—the claim that only an organism that conceives of itself as a continuing subject of experiences has a right to life. For this requirement, when taken together with the claim that there is at least one property, possessed by adult humans, such that any organism possessing it has a serious right to life, entails the denial of the potentiality principle. Or at least this is so if we add the uncontroversial empirical claim that an organism that will in the normal course of events develop into an adult human does not from the very beginning of its existence possess a concept of a continuing subject of experiences together with a belief that it is itself such an entity.

I think it best, however, to scrutinize the potentiality principle itself, and not to base one's case against it simply on the self-consciousness requirement. Perhaps the first point to note is that the potentiality principle should not be confused with principles such as the following: the value of an object is related to the value of the things into which it can develop. This "valuation principle" is rather vague. There are ways of making it more precise, but we need not consider these here. Suppose now that one were to speak not of a right to life, but of the value of life. It would then be easy to make the mistake of thinking that the valuation principle was relevant to the potentiality principle—indeed, that it entailed it. But an individual's right to life is not based on the value of his life. To say that the world would be better off if it contained fewer people is not to say that it would be right to achieve such a better world by killing some of the present inhabitants. *If* having a right to life were a matter of a thing's value, then a thing's potentialities, being connected with its expected value, would clearly be relevant to the question of what rights it had. Conversely, once one realizes that a thing's rights are not a matter of its value, I think it becomes clear that an organism's potentialities are irrelevant to the question of whether it has a right to life.

But let us now turn to the task of finding a direct refutation of the potentiality principle. The basic issue is this. Is there any property J which satisfies the following conditions: (1) There is a property K such that any individual possessing property K has a right to life, and there is a scientific law L to the effect that any organism possessing property J will in the normal course of events come to possess property K at some later time. (2) Given the relationship between property J and property K just described, anything possessing property J has a right to life. (3) If property J were not related to property K in the way indicated, it would not be the case that anything possessing property J thereby had a right to life. In short, the question is whether there is a property J that bestows a right to life on an organism *only because* J stands in a certain causal relationship to a second property K, which is such that anything possessing that property ipso facto has a right to life.

My argument turns upon the following critical principle: Let C be a causal process that normally leads to outcome E. Let A be an action that initiates process C, and B be an action involving a minimal expenditure of energy that stops process C before outcome E occurs. Assume further that actions A and B do not have any other consequences, and that E is the only morally significant outcome of process C. Then there is no moral difference between intentionally performing action B and intentionally refraining from performing action A, assuming identical motivation in both cases. This principle, which I shall refer to as the moral symmetry principle with respect to action and inaction, would be rejected by some philosophers. They would argue that there is an important distinction to be drawn between "what we owe people in the form of aid and what we owe them in the way of non-interference,"[25] and that the latter, "negative duties," are duties that it is more serious to neglect than the former, "positive" ones. This view arises from an intuitive response to examples such as the following. Even if it is wrong not to send food to starving people in other parts of the world, it is more wrong still to kill someone. And isn't the conclusion, then, that one's obligation to refrain from killing someone is a more serious obligation than one's obligation to save lives?

I want to argue that this is not the correct conclusion. I think it is tempting to draw this conclusion if one fails to consider the motivation that is likely to be associated with the respective actions. If someone performs an action he knows will kill someone else, this will usually be grounds for concluding that he wanted to kill the person in question. In contrast, failing to help someone may indicate only apathy, laziness, selfishness, or an amoral outlook: the fact that a person knowingly allows another to die will not normally be grounds for concluding that he desired that person's death. Someone who knowingly kills another is more likely to be seriously defective from a moral point of view than someone who fails to save another's life.

If we are not to be led to false conclusions by our intuitions about certain cases, we must explicitly assume identical motivations in the two situations. Compare, for example, the following: (1) Jones sees that Smith will be killed by a bomb unless he warns him. Jones's reaction is: "How lucky, it will save me the trouble of killing Smith myself." So Jones allows Smith to be killed by the bomb, even though he could easily have warned him. (2) Jones wants Smith dead, and therefore shoots him. Is one to say there is a significant difference between the wrongness of Jones's behavior in these two cases? Surely not. This shows the mistake of drawing a distinction between positive duties and negative duties and holding that the latter impose stricter obligations than the former. The difference in our intuitions about situations that involve giving aid to others and corresponding situations that involve not interfering with others is to be explained by reference to probable differences in the motivations operating in the

25. Philippa Foot, "The Problem of Abortion and the Doctrine of the Double Effect," *The Oxford Review* 5 (1967): 5-15. See the discussion on pp. 11ff.

two situations, and not by reference to a distinction between positive and negative duties. For once it is specified that the motivation is the same in the two situations, we realize that inaction is as wrong in the one case as action is in the other.

There is another point that may be relevant. Action involves effort, while inaction usually does not. It usually does not require any effort on my part to refrain from killing someone, but saving someone's life will require an expenditure of energy. One must then ask how large a sacrifice a person is morally required to make to save the life of another. If the sacrifice of time and energy is quite large it may be that one is not morally obliged to save the life of another in that situation. Superficial reflection upon such cases might easily lead us to introduce the distinction between positive and negative duties, but again it is clear that this would be a mistake. The point is not that one has a greater duty to refrain from killing others than to perform positive actions that will save them. It is rather that positive actions require effort, and this means that in deciding what to do a person has to take into account his own right to do what he wants with his life, and not only the other person's right to life. To avoid this confusion, we should confine ourselves to comparisons between situations in which the positive action involves minimal effort.

The moral symmetry principle, as formulated above, explicitly takes these two factors into account. It applies only to pairs of situations in which the motivations are identical and the positive action involves minimal effort. Without these restrictions, the principle would be open to serious objection; with them, it seems perfectly acceptable. For the central objection to it rests on the claim that we must distinguish positive from negative duties and recognize that negative duties impose stronger obligations than positive ones. I have tried to show how this claim derives from an unsound account of our moral intuitions about certain situations.

My argument against the potentiality principle can now be stated. Suppose at some future time a chemical were to be discovered which when injected into the brain of a kitten would cause the kitten to develop into a cat possessing a brain of the sort possessed by humans, and consequently into a cat having all the psychological capabilities characteristic of adult humans. Such cats would be able to think, to use language, and so on. Now it would surely be morally indefensible in such a situation to ascribe a serious right to life to members of the species Homo sapiens without also ascribing it to cats that have undergone such a process of development: there would be no morally significant differences.

Secondly, it would not be seriously wrong to refain from injecting a newborn kitten with the special chemical, and to kill it instead. The fact that one could initiate a causal process that would transform a kitten into an entity that would eventually possess properties such that anything possessing them ipso facto has a serious right to life does not mean that the kitten has a serious right to life even before it has been subjected to the process of injection and transformation. The possibility of transforming kittens into persons will not make it any more wrong to kill newborn kittens than it is now.

Thirdly, in view of the symmetry principle, if it is not seriously wrong to refrain from initiating such a causal process, neither is it seriously wrong to interfere with such a process. Suppose a kitten is accidentally injected with the chemical. As long as it has not yet developed those properties that in themselves endow something with a right to life, there cannot be anything wrong with interfering with the causal process and preventing the development of the properties in question. Such interference might be accomplished either by injecting the kitten with some "neutralizing" chemical or simply by killing it.

But if it is not seriously wrong to destroy an injected kitten which will naturally develop the properties that bestow a right to life, neither can it be seriously wrong to destroy a member of Homo sapiens which lacks such properties, but will naturally come to have them. The potentialities are the same in both cases. The only difference is that in the case of a human fetus the potentialities have been present from the beginning of the organism's development, while in the case of the kitten they have been present only from the time it was injected with the special chemical. This difference in the time at which the potentialities were acquired is a morally irrelevant difference.

It should be emphasized that I am not here assuming that a human fetus does not possess properties which in themselves, and irrespective of their causal relationships to other properties, provide grounds for ascribing a right to life to whatever possesses them. The point is merely that if it is seriously wrong to kill something, the reason cannot be that the thing will later acquire properties that in themselves provide something with a right to life.

Finally, it is reasonable to believe that there are properties possessed by adult members of Homo sapiens which establish their right to life, and also that any normal human fetus will come to possess those properties shared by adult humans. But it has just been shown that if it is wrong to kill a human fetus, it cannot be because of its potentialities. One is therefore forced to conclude that the conservative's potentiality principle is false.

In short, anyone who wants to defend the potentiality principle must either argue against the moral symmetry principle or hold that in a world in which kittens could be transformed into "rational animals" it would be seriously wrong to kill newborn kittens. It is hard to believe there is much to be said for the latter moral claim. Consequently one expects the conservative's rejoinder to be directed against the symmetry principle. While I have not attempted to provide a thorough defense of that principle, I have tried to show that what seems to be the most important objection to it—the one that appeals to a distinction between positive and negative duties—is based on a superficial analysis of our moral intuitions. I believe that a more thorough examination of the symmetry principle would show it to be sound. If so, we should reject the potentiality principle, and the conservative position on abortion as well.

VI. SUMMARY AND CONCLUSIONS

Let us return now to my basic claim, the self-consciousness requirement: An organism possesses a serious right to life only if it possesses the concept of a self as a continuing subject of experiences and other mental states, and believes that it is itself such a continuing entity. My defense of this claim has been twofold. I have offered a direct argument in support of it, and I have tried to show that traditional conservative and liberal views on abortion and infanticide, which involve a rejection of it, are unsound. I now want to mention one final reason why my claim should be accepted. Consider the example mentioned in section II—that of killing, as opposed to torturing, newborn kittens. I suggested there that while in the case of adult humans most people would consider it worse to kill an individual than to torture him for an hour, we do not usually view the killing of a newborn kitten as morally outrageous, although we would regard someone who tortured a newborn kitten for an hour as heinously evil. I pointed out that a possible conclusion that might be drawn from this is that newborn kittens have a right not to be tortured, but do not have a serious right to life. If this is the correct conclusion, how is one to explain it? One merit of the self-consciousness requirement is that it provides an explanation of this situation. The reason a newborn kitten does not have a right to life is explained by the fact that it does not possess the concept of a self. But how is one to explain the kitten's having a right not to be tortured? The answer is that a desire not to suffer pain can be ascribed to something without assuming that it has any concept of a continuing self. For while something that lacks the concept of a self cannot desire that a self not suffer, it can desire that a given sensation not exist. The state desired–the absence of a particular sensation, or of sensations of a certain sort–can be described in a purely phenomenalistic language, and hence without the concept of a continuing self. So long as the newborn kitten possesses the relevant phenomenal concepts, it can truly be said to desire that a certain sensation not exist. So we can ascribe to it a right not to be tortured even though, since it lacks the concept of a continuing self, we cannot ascribe to it a right to life.

This completes my discussion of the basic moral principles involved in the issue of abortion and infanticide. But I want to comment upon an important factual question, namely, at what point an organism comes to possess the concept of a self as a continuing subject of experiences and other mental states, together with the belief that it is itself such a continuing entity. This is obviously a matter for detailed psychological investigation, but everyday observation makes it perfectly clear, I believe, that a newborn baby does not possess the concept of a continuing self, any more than a newborn kitten possesses such a concept. If so, infanticide during a time interval shortly after birth must be morally acceptable.

But where is the line to be drawn? What is the cutoff point? If one maintained, as some philosophers have, that an individual possesses concepts only if he can express these concepts in language, it would be a matter of everyday observation whether or not a given organism possessed the concept of a continuing self. Infanticide would then be permissible up to the time an organism learned how to use certain expressions. However, I think the claim that acquisition of concepts is dependent on acquisition of language is mistaken. For example, one wants to ascribe mental states of a conceptual sort–such as beliefs and desires–to organisms that are incapable of learning a language. This issue of prelinguistic understanding is clearly outside the scope of this discussion. My point is simply that *if* an organism can acquire concepts without thereby acquiring a way of expressing those concepts linguistically, the question of whether a given organism possesses the concept of a self as a continuing subject of experiences and other mental states, together with the belief that it is itself such a continuing entity, may be a question that requires fairly subtle experimental techniques to answer.

If this view of the matter is roughly correct, there are two worries one is left with at the level of practical moral decisions, one of which may turn out to be deeply disturbing. The lesser worry is where the line is to be drawn in the case of infanticide. It is not troubling because there is no serious need to know the exact point at which a human infant acquires a right to life. For in the vast majority of cases in which infanticide is desirable, its desirability will be apparent within a short time after birth. Since it is virtually certain that an infant at such a stage of its development does not possess the concept of a continuing self, and thus does not possess a serious right to life, there is excellent reason to believe that infanticide is morally permissible in most cases where it is otherwise desirable. The practical moral problem can thus be satisfactorily handled by choosing some period of time, such as a week after birth, as the interval during which infanticide will be permitted. This interval could then be modified once psychologists have established the point at which a human organism comes to believe that it is a continuing subject of experiences and other mental states.

The troubling worry is whether adult animals belonging to species other than Homo sapiens may not also possess a serious right to life. For once one says that an organism can possess the concept of a continuing self, together with the belief that it is itself such an entity, without having any way of expressing that concept and that belief linguistically, one has to face up to the question of whether animals may not possess properties that bestow a serious right to life upon them. The suggestion itself is a familiar one, and one that most of us are accustomed to dismiss very casually. The line of thought advanced here suggests that this attitude may turn out to be tragically mistaken. Once one reflects upon the question of the *basic* moral principles involved in the ascription of a right to life to organisms, one may find himself driven to conclude that our everyday treatment of animals is morally indefensible, and that we are in fact murdering innocent persons.

ON THE MORAL AND LEGAL STATUS OF ABORTION

We will be concerned with both the moral status of abortion, which for our purposes we may define as the act which a woman performs in voluntarily terminating, or allowing another person to terminate, her pregnancy, and the legal status which is appropriate for this act. I will argue that, while it is not possible to produce a satisfactory defense of a woman's right to obtain an abortion without showing that a fetus is not a human being, in the morally relevant sense of that term, we ought not to conclude that the difficulties involved in determining whether or not a fetus is human make it impossible to produce any satisfactory solution to the problem of the moral status of abortion. For it is possible to show that, on the basis of intuitions which we may expect even the opponents of abortion to share, a fetus is not a person, and hence not the sort of entity to which it is proper to ascribe full moral rights.

Of course, while some philosophers would deny the possibility of any such proof,[1] others will deny that there is any need for it, since the moral permissibility of abortion appears to them to be too obvious to require proof. But the inadequacy of this attitude should be evident from the fact that both the friends and the foes of abortion consider their position to be morally self-evident. Because pro-abortionists have never adequately come to grips with the conceptual issues surrounding abortion, most if not all, of the arguments which they advance in opposition to laws restricting access to abortion fail to refute or even weaken the traditional antiabortion argument, i.e., that a fetus is a human being, and therefore abortion is murder.

These arguments are typically of one of two sorts. Either they point to the terrible side effects of the restrictive laws, e.g., the deaths due to illegal abortions, and the fact that it is poor women

1. For example, Roger Wertheimer, who in "Understanding the Abortion Argument" (*Philosophy and Public Affairs,* 1, No. 1 [Fall, 1971], 67-95), argues that the problem of the moral status of abortion is insoluble, in that the dispute over the status of the fetus is not a question of fact at all, but only a question of how one responds to the facts.

who suffer the most as a result of these laws, or else they state that to deny a woman access to abortion is to deprive her of her right to control her own body. Unfortunately, however, the fact that restricting access to abortion has tragic side effects does not, in itself, show that the restrictions are unjustified, since murder is wrong regardless of the consequences of prohibiting it; and the appeal to the right to control one's body, which is generally construed as a property right, is at best a rather feeble argument for the permissibility of abortion. Mere ownership does not give me the right to kill innocent people whom I find on my property, and indeed I am apt to be held responsible if such people injure themselves while on my property. It is equally unclear that I have any moral right to expel an innocent person from my property when I know that doing so will result in his death.

Furthermore, it is probably inappropriate to describe a woman's body as her property, since it seems natural to hold that a person is something distinct from her property, but not from her body. Even those who would object to the identification of a person with his body, or with the conjunction of his body and his mind, must admit that it would be very odd to describe, say, breaking a leg, as damaging one's property, and much more appropriate to describe it as injuring one*self*. Thus it is probably a mistake to argue that the right to obtain an abortion is in any way derived from the right to own and regulate property.

But however we wish to construe the right to abortion, we cannot hope to convince those who consider abortion a form of murder of the existence of any such right unless we are able to produce a clear and convincing refutation of the traditional antiabortion argument, and this has not, to my knowledge, been done. With respect to the two most vital issues which that argument involves, i.e., the humanity of the fetus and its implication for the moral status of abortion, confusion has prevailed on both sides of the dispute.

Thus, both proabortionists and antiabortionists have tended to abstract the question of whether abortion is wrong to that of whether it is wrong to destroy a fetus, just as though the rights of another person were not necessarily involved. This mistaken abstraction has led to the almost universal assumption that if a fetus is a human being, with a right to life, then it follows immediately that abortion is wrong (except perhaps when necessary to save the woman's life), and that it ought to be prohibited. It has also been generally assumed that unless the question about the status of the fetus is answered, the moral status of abortion cannot possibly be determined.

Two recent papers, one by B. A. Brody,[2] and one by Judith Thomson,[3] have attempted to settle the question of whether abortion ought to be prohibited apart from the question of whether or not the fetus is human. Brody examines the possibility that the following two statements are compatible: (1) that abortion is the taking of innocent human life, and therefore wrong; and (2) that nevertheless it ought not to be prohibited by law, at least under the present circumstances.[4] Not surprisingly, Brody finds it impossible to reconcile these two statements, since, as he rightly argues, none of the unfortunate side effects of the prohibition of abortion is bad enough to justify legalizing the *wrongful* taking of human life. He is mistaken, however, in concluding that the incompatibility of (1) and (2), in itself, shows that "the legal problem about abortion cannot be resolved independently of the status of the fetus problem" (p. 369).

What Brody fails to realize is that (1) embodies the questionable assumption that if a fetus is a human being, then of course abortion is morally wrong, and that an attack on *this* assumption is more promising, as a way of reconciling the humanity of the fetus with the claim that laws prohibiting abortion are unjustified, than is an attack on the assumption that if abortion is the wrongful killing of innocent human beings then it ought to be prohibited. He thus overlooks the possibility that a fetus may have a right to life and abortion still be morally permissible, in that the right of a woman to terminate an unwanted pregnancy might override the right of the fetus to be kept alive. The immorality of abortion is no more demonstrated by the humanity of the fetus, in itself, than the immorality of killing in self-defense is demonstrated by the fact that the as-

2. B. A. Brody, "Abortion and the Law," *The Journal of Philosophy,* 68, No. 12 (June 17, 1971), 357-69.

3. Judith Thomson, "A Defense of Abortion," *Philosophy and Public Affairs,* 1, No. 1 (Fall, 1971), 47-66.

4. I have abbreviated these statements somewhat, but not in a way which affects the argument.

sailant is a human being. Neither is it demonstrated by the *innocence* of the fetus, since there may be situations in which the killing of innocent human beings is justified.

It is perhaps not surprising that Brody fails to spot this assumption, since it has been accepted with little or no argument by nearly everyone who has written on the morality of abortion. John Noonan is correct in saying that "the fundamental question in the long history of abortion is, How do you determine the humanity of a being?" [5] He summarizes his own antiabortion argument, which is a version of the official position of the Catholic Church, as follows:

> . . . it is wrong to kill humans, however poor, weak, defenseless, and lacking in opportunity to develop their potential they may be. It is therefore morally wrong to kill Biafrans. Similarly, it is morally wrong to kill embryos.[6]

Noonan bases his claim that fetuses are human upon what he calls the theologians' criterion of humanity: that whoever is conceived of human beings is human. But although he argues at length for the appropriateness of this criterion, he never questions the assumption that if a fetus is human then abortion is wrong for exactly the same reason that murder is wrong.

Judith Thomson is, in fact, the only writer I am aware of who has seriously questioned this assumption; she has argued that, even if we grant the antiabortionist his claim that a fetus is a human being, with the same right to life as any other human being, we can still demonstrate that, in at least some and perhaps most cases, a woman is under no moral obligation to complete an unwanted pregnancy.[7] Her argument is worth examining, since if it holds up it may enable us to establish the moral permissibility of abortion without becoming involved in problems about what entitles an entity to be considered human, and accorded full moral rights. To be able to do this would be a great gain in the power and simplicity of the proabortion position, since, although I will argue that these problems can be solved at least as decisively as can any other moral problem,

5. John Noonan, "Abortion and the Catholic Church: A Summary History," *Natural Law Forum*, **12** (1967), 125.

6. John Noonan, "Deciding Who is Human," *Natural Law Forum*, **13** (1968), 134.

7. "A Defense of Abortion."

we should certainly be pleased to be able to avoid having to solve them as part of the justification of abortion.

On the other hand, even if Thomson's argument does not hold up, her insight, i.e., that it requires *argument* to show that if fetuses are human then abortion is properly classified as murder, is an extremely valuable one. The assumption she attacks is particularly invidious, for it amounts to the decision that it is appropriate, in deciding the moral status of abortion, to leave the rights of the pregnant woman out of consideration entirely, except possibly when her life is threatened. Obviously, this will not do; determining what moral rights, if any, a fetus possesses is only the first step in determining the moral status of abortion. Step two, which is at least equally essential, is finding a just solution to the conflict between whatever rights the fetus may have, and the rights of the woman who is unwillingly pregnant. While the historical error has been to pay far too little attention to the second step, Ms. Thomson's suggestion is that if we look at the second step first we may find that a woman has a right to obtain an abortion *regardless* of what rights the fetus has.

Our own inquiry will also have two stages. In Section I, we will consider whether or not it is possible to establish that abortion is morally permissible even on the assumption that a fetus is an entity with a full-fledged right to life. I will argue that in fact this cannot be established, at least not with the conclusiveness which is essential to our hopes of convincing those who are skeptical about the morality of abortion, and that we therefore cannot avoid dealing with the question of whether or not a fetus really does have the same right to life as a (more fully developed) human being.

In Section II, I will propose an answer to this question, namely, that a fetus cannot be considered a member of the moral community, the set of beings with full and equal moral rights, for the simple reason that it is not a person, and that it is personhood, and not genetic humanity, i.e., humanity as defined by Noonan, which is the basis for membership in this community. I will argue that a fetus, whatever its stage of development, satisfies none of the basic criteria of personhood, and is not even enough *like* a person to be accorded even some of the same rights on the basis of this resemblance. Nor, as we will see, is a fetus's *potential* personhood a threat to the morality of abortion, since, whatever the rights of potential people may be, they are invariably overridden in any conflict with the moral rights of actual people.

I

We turn now to Professor Thomson's case for the claim that even if a fetus has full moral rights, abortion is still morally permissible, at least sometimes, and for some reasons other than to save the woman's life. Her argument is based upon a clever, but I think faulty, analogy. She asks us to picture ourselves waking up one day, in bed with a famous violinist. Imagine that you have been kidnapped, and your bloodstream hooked up to that of the violinist, who happens to have an ailment which will certainly kill him unless he is permitted to share your kidneys for a period of nine months. No one else can save him, since you alone have the right type of blood. He will be unconscious all that time, and you will have to stay in bed with him, but after the nine months are over he may be unplugged, completely cured, that is provided that you have cooperated.

Now then, she continues, what are your obligations in this situation? The antiabortionist, if he is consistent, will have to say that you are obligated to stay in bed with the violinist: for all people have a right to life, and violinists are people, and therefore it would be murder for you to disconnect yourself from him and let him die (p. 49). But this is outrageous, and so there must be something wrong with the same argument when it is applied to abortion. It would certainly be commendable of you to agree to save the violinist, but it is absurd to suggest that your refusal to do so would be murder. His right to life does not obligate you to do whatever is required to keep him alive; nor does it justify anyone else in forcing you to do so. A law which required you to stay in bed with the violinist would clearly be an unjust law, since it is no proper function of the law to force unwilling people to make huge sacrifices for the sake of other people toward whom they have no such prior obligation.

Thomson concludes that, if this analogy is an apt one, then we can grant the antiabortionist his claim that a fetus is a human being, and still hold that it is at least sometimes the case that a pregnant woman has the right to refuse to be a Good Samaritan towards the fetus, i.e., to obtain an abortion. For there is a great gap between the claim that x has a right to life, and the claim that y is obligated to do whatever is necessary to keep x alive, let alone that he ought to be forced to do so. It is y's duty to keep x alive only if he has somehow contracted a *special* obligation to do so; and a woman who is unwillingly pregnant, e.g., who was raped, has done nothing which obligates her to make the enormous sacrifice which is necessary to preserve the conceptus.

This argument is initially quite plausible, and in the extreme case of pregnancy due to rape it is probably conclusive. Difficulties arise, however, when we try to specify more exactly the range of cases in which abortion is clearly justifiable even on the assumption that the fetus is human. Professor Thomson considers it a virtue of her argument that it does not enable us to conclude that abortion is *always* permissible. It would, she says, be "indecent" for a woman in her seventh month to obtain an abortion just to avoid having to postpone a trip to Europe. On the other hand, her argument enables us to see that "a sick and desperately frightened schoolgirl pregnant due to rape may *of course* choose abortion, and that any law which rules this out is an insane law" (p. 65). So far, so good; but what are we to say about the woman who becomes pregnant not through rape but as a result of her own carelessness, or because of contraceptive failure, or who gets pregnant intentionally and then changes her mind about wanting a child? With respect to such cases, the violinist analogy is of much less use to the defender of the woman's right to obtain an abortion.

Indeed, the choice of a pregnancy due to rape, as an example of a case in which abortion is permissible even if a fetus is considered a human being, is extremely significant; for it is only in the case of pregnancy due to rape that the woman's situation is adequately analogous to the violinist case for our intuitions about the latter to transfer convincingly. The crucial difference between a pregnancy due to rape and the *normal* case of an unwanted pregnancy is that in the normal case we cannot claim that the woman is in no way responsible for her predicament; she could have remained chaste, or taken her pills more faithfully, or abstained on dangerous days, and so on. If, on the other hand, you are kidnapped by strangers, and hooked up to a strange violinist, then you are free of any shred of responsibility for the situation, on the basis of which it could be argued that you are obligated to keep the violinist alive. Only when her pregnancy is due to rape is a woman clearly just as nonresponsible.[8]

Consequently, there is room for the antiabortionist to argue that in the normal case of unwanted pregnancy a woman has, by her own actions, assumed responsibility for the fetus. For if *x* behaves in a way which he could have avoided, and which he knows involves, let us say, a 1 percent chance of bringing into existence a human being, with a right to life, and does so knowing that if this should happen then that human being will perish unless *x* does certain things to keep him alive, then it is by no means clear that when it does happen *x* is free of any obligation to what he knew in advance would be required to keep that human being alive.

The plausibility of such an argument is enough to show that the Thomson analogy can provide a clear and persuasive defense of a woman's right to obtain an abortion only with respect to those cases in which the woman is in no way responsible for her pregnancy, e.g., where it is due to rape. In all other cases, we would almost certainly conclude that it was necessary to look carefully at the particular circumstances in order to determine the extent of the woman's responsibility, and hence the extent of her obligation. This is an extremely unsatisfactory outcome, from the viewpoint of the opponents of restrictive abortion laws, most of whom are convinced that a woman has a right to obtain an abortion regardless of how and why she got pregnant.

Of course a supporter of the violinist analogy might point out that it is absurd to suggest that forgetting her pill one day might be sufficient to obligate a woman to complete an unwanted pregnancy. And indeed it *is* absurd to suggest this. As we will see, the moral right to obtain an abortion is not in the least dependent upon the extent to which the woman is responsible for her pregnancy. But unfortunately, once we allow the assumption that a fetus has full moral rights, we cannot avoid taking this absurd suggestion seriously.

8. We may safely ignore the fact that she might have avoided getting raped, e.g., by carrying a gun, since by similar means you might likewise have avoided getting kidnapped, and in neither case does the victim's failure to take all possible precautions against a highly unlikely event (as opposed to reasonable precautions against a rather likely event) mean that he is morally responsible for what happens.

Perhaps we can make this point more clear by altering the violinist story just enough to make it more analogous to a normal unwanted pregnancy and less to a pregnancy due to rape, and then seeing whether it is still obvious that you are not obligated to stay in bed with the fellow.

Suppose, then, that violinists are peculiarly prone to the sort of illness the only cure for which is the use of someone else's bloodstream for nine months, and that because of this there has been formed a society of music lovers who agree that whenever a violinist is stricken they will draw lots and the loser will, by some means, be made the one and only person capable of saving him. Now then, would you be obligated to cooperate in curing the violinist if you had voluntarily joined this society, knowing the possible consequences, and then your name had been drawn and you had been kidnapped? Admittedly, you did not promise ahead of time that you would, but you did deliberately place yourself in a position in which it might happen that a human life would be lost if you did not. Surely this is at least a prima facie reason for supposing that you have an obligation to stay in bed with the violinist. Suppose that you had gotten your name drawn deliberately; surely *that* would be quite a strong reason for thinking that you had such an obligation.

It might be suggested that there is one important disanalogy between the modified violinist case and the case of an unwanted pregnancy, which makes the woman's responsibility significantly less, namely, the fact that the fetus *comes into existence* as the result of the result of the woman's actions. This fact might give her a right to refuse to keep it alive, whereas she would not have had this right had it existed previously, independently, and then as a result of her actions become dependent upon her for its survival.

My own intuition, however, is that x has no more right to bring into existence, either deliberately or as a foreseeable result of actions he could have avoided, a being with full moral rights (y), and then refuse to do what he knew beforehand would be required to keep that being alive, than he has to enter into an agreement with an existing person, whereby he may be called upon to save that person's life, and then refuse to do so when so called upon. Thus, x's responsibility for y's existence does not seem to lessen his obligation to keep y alive, if he is also responsible for y's being in a situation in which only he can save him.

Whether or not this intuition is entirely correct, it brings us back once again to the conclusion that once we allow the assumption that a fetus has full moral rights it becomes an extremely complex and difficult question whether and when abortion is justifiable. Thus the Thomson analogy cannot help us produce a clear and persuasive proof of the moral permissibility of abortion. Nor will the opponents of the restrictive laws thank us for anything less; for their conviction (for the most part) is that abortion is obviously *not* a morally serious and extremely unfortunate, even though sometimes justified act, comparable to killing in self-defense or to letting the violinist die, but rather is closer to being a morally neutral act, like cutting one's hair.

The basis of this conviction, I believe, is the realization that a fetus is not a person, and thus does not have a full-fledged right to life. Perhaps the reason why this claim has been so inadequately defended is that it seems self-evident to those who accept it. And so it is, insofar as it follows from what I take to be perfectly obvious claims about the nature of personhood, and about the proper grounds for ascribing moral rights, claims which ought, indeed, to be obvious to both the friends and foes of abortion. Nevertheless, it is worth examining these claims, and showing how they demonstrate the moral innocuousness of abortion, since this apparently has not been adequately done before.

II

The question which we must answer in order to produce a satisfactory solution to the problem of the moral status of abortion is this: How are we to define the moral community, the set of beings with full and equal moral rights, such that we can decide whether a human fetus is a member of this community or not? What sort of entity, exactly, has the inalienable rights to life, liberty, and the pursuit of happiness? Jefferson attributed these rights to all *men,* and it may or may not be fair to suggest that he intended to attribute them *only* to men. Perhaps he ought to have attributed them to all human beings. If so, then we arrive, first, at Noonan's problem of defining what makes a being human, and, second, at the equally vital question which Noonan does not consider, namely, What reason is there for identifying the moral community with the set of all human beings, in whatever way we have chosen to define that term?

1. *On the Definition of 'Human'*

One reason why this vital second question is so frequently overlooked in the debate over the moral status of abortion is that the term 'human' has two distinct, but not often distinguished, senses. This fact results in a slide of meaning, which serves to conceal the fallaciousness of the traditional argument that since (1) it is wrong to kill innocent human beings, and (2) fetuses are innocent human beings, then (3) it is wrong to kill fetuses. For if 'human' is used in the same sense in both (1) and (2) then, whichever of the two senses is meant, one of these premises is question-begging. And if it is used in two different senses then of course the conclusion doesn't follow.

Thus, (1) is a self-evident moral truth,[9] and avoids begging the question about abortion, only if 'human being' is used to mean something like "a full-fledged member of the moral community." (It may or may not also be meant to refer exclusively to members of the species *Homo sapiens*.) We may call this the *moral* sense of 'human'. It is not to be confused with what we will call the *genetic* sense, i.e., the sense in which *any* member of the species is a human being, and no member of any other species could be. If (1) is acceptable only if the moral sense is intended, (2) is non-question-begging only if what is intended is the genetic sense.

In "Deciding Who is Human," Noonan argues for the classification of fetuses with human beings by pointing to the presence of the full genetic code, and the potential capacity for rational thought (p. 135). It is clear that what he needs to show, for his version of the traditional argument to be valid, is that fetuses are human in the moral sense, the sense in which it is analytically true that all human beings have full moral rights. But, in the absence of any argument showing that whatever is genetically human is also morally human, and he gives none, nothing more than genetic humanity can be demonstrated by the presence of the human genetic code. And, as we will see, the *potential* capacity for rational thought can at most show that an entity has the potential for *becoming* human in the moral sense.

9. Of course, the principle that it is (always) wrong to kill innocent human beings is in need of many other modifications, e.g., that it may be permissible to do so to save a greater number of other innocent human beings, but we may safely ignore these complications here.

2. *Defining the Moral Community*

Can it be established that genetic humanity is sufficient for moral humanity? I think that there are very good reasons for not defining the moral community in this way. I would like to suggest an alternative way of defining the moral community, which I will argue for only to the extent of explaining why it is, or should be, self-evident. The suggestion is simply that the moral community consists of all and only *people,* rather than all and only human beings;[10] and probably the best way of demonstrating its self-evidence is by considering the concept of personhood, to see what sorts of entity are and are not persons, and what the decision that a being is or is not a person implies about its moral rights.

What characteristics entitle an entity to be considered a person? This is obviously not the place to attempt a complete analysis of the concept of personhood, but we do not need such a fully adequate analysis just to determine whether and why a fetus is or isn't a person. All we need is a rough and approximate list of the most basic criteria of personhood, and some idea of which, or how many, of these an entity must satisfy in order to properly be considered a person.

In searching for such criteria, it is useful to look beyond the set of people with whom we are acquainted, and ask how we would decide whether a totally alien being was a person or not. (For we have no right to assume that genetic humanity is necessary for personhood.) Imagine a space traveler who lands on an unknown planet and encounters a race of beings utterly unlike any he has ever seen or heard of. If he wants to be sure of behaving morally toward these beings, he has to somehow decide whether they are people, and hence have full moral rights, or whether they are the sort of thing which he need not feel guilty about treating as, for example, a source of food.

How should he go about making this decision? If he has some anthropological background, he might look for such things as religion, art, and the manufacturing of tools, weapons, or shelters, since these factors have been used to distinguish our human from

10. From here on, we will use 'human' to mean genetically human, since the moral sense seems closely connected to, and perhaps derived from, the assumption that genetic humanity is sufficient for membership in the moral community.

our prehuman ancestors, in what seems to be closer to the moral than the genetic sense of 'human'. And no doubt he would be right to consider the presence of such factors as good evidence that the alien beings were people, and morally human. It would, however, be overly anthropocentric of him to take the absence of these things as adequate evidence that they were not, since we can imagine people who have progressed beyond, or evolved without ever developing, these cultural characteristics.

I suggest that the traits which are most central to the concept of personhood, or humanity in the moral sense, are, very roughly, the following:

(1) consciousness (of objects and events external and/or internal to the being), and in particular the capacity to feel pain;
(2) reasoning (the *developed* capacity to solve new and relatively complex problems);
(3) self-motivated activity (activity which is relatively independent of either genetic or direct external control);
(4) the capacity to communicate, by whatever means, messages of an indefinite variety of types, that is, not just with an indefinite number of possible contents, but on indefinitely many possible topics;
(5) the presence of self-concepts, and self-awareness, either individual or racial, or both.

Admittedly, there are apt to be a great many problems involved in formulating precise definitions of these criteria, let alone in developing universally valid behavioral criteria for deciding when they apply. But I will assume that both we and our explorer know approximately what (1)-(5) mean, and that he is also able to determine whether or not they apply. How, then, should he use his findings to decide whether or not the alien beings are people? We needn't suppose that an entity must have *all* of these attributes to be properly considered a person; (1) and (2) alone may well be sufficient for personhood, and quite probably (1)-(3) are sufficient. Neither do we need to insist that any one of these criteria is *necessary* for personhood, although once again (1) and (2) look like fairly good candidates for necessary conditions, as does (3), if 'activity' is construed so as to include the activity of reasoning.

All we need to claim, to demonstrate that a fetus is not a person, is that any being which satisfies *none* of (1)-(5) is certainly not a person. I consider this claim to be so obvious that I think anyone who denied it, and claimed that a being which satisfied none of (1)-(5) was a person all the same, would thereby demonstrate that he had no notion at all of what a person is—perhaps because he had confused the concept of a person with that of genetic humanity. If the opponents of abortion were to deny the appropriateness of these five criteria, I do not know what further arguments would convince them. We would probably have to admit that our conceptual schemes were indeed irreconcilably different, and that our dispute could not be settled objectively.

I do not expect this to happen, however, since I think that the concept of a person is one which is very nearly universal (to people), and that it is common to both proabortionists and antiabortionists, even though neither group has fully realized the relevance of this concept to the resolution of their dispute. Furthermore, I think that on reflection even the antiabortionists ought to agree not only that (1)-(5) are central to the concept of personhood, but also that it is a part of this concept that all and only people have full moral rights. The concept of a person is in part a moral concept; once we have admitted that *x* is a person we have recognized, even if we have not agreed to respect, *x*'s right to be treated as a member of the moral community. It is true that the claim that *x* is a *human being* is more commonly voiced as part of an appeal to treat *x* decently than is the claim that *x* is a person, but this is either because 'human being' is here used in the sense which implies personhood, or because the genetic and moral senses of 'human' have been confused.

Now if (1)-(5) are indeed the primary criteria of personhood, then it is clear that genetic humanity is neither necessary nor sufficient for establishing that an entity is a person. Some human beings are not people, and there may well be people who are not human beings. A man or woman whose consciousness has been permanently obliterated but who remains alive is a human being which is no longer a person; defective human beings, with no appreciable mental capacity, are not and presumably never will be people; and a fetus is a human being which is not yet a person, and which therefore cannot coherently be said to have full moral rights. Citizens of the next century should be prepared to recognize highly advanced, self-aware robots or computers, should such be developed, and intelligent inhabitants of other worlds, should such be found, as people in the fullest sense, and to respect their moral rights. But to ascribe full moral rights to an entity which is not a person is as absurd as to ascribe moral obligations and responsibilities to such an entity.

3. *Fetal Development and the Right to Life*

Two problems arise in the application of these suggestions for the definition of the moral community to the determination of the precise moral status of a human fetus. Given that the paradigm example of a person is a normal adult human being, then (1) How like this paradigm, in particular how far advanced since conception, does a human being need to be before it begins to have a right to life by virtue, not of being fully a person as of yet, but of being *like* a person? and (2) To what extent, if any, does the fact that a fetus has the *potential* for becoming a person endow it with some of the same rights? Each of these questions requires some comment.

In answering the first question, we need not attempt a detailed consideration of the moral rights of organisms which are not developed enough, aware enough, intelligent enough, etc., to be considered people, but which resemble people in some respects. It does seem reasonable to suggest that the more like a person, in the relevant respects, a being is, the stronger is the case for regarding it as having a right to life, and indeed the stronger its right to life is. Thus we ought to take seriously the suggestion that, insofar as "the human individual develops biologically in a continuous fashion . . . the rights of a human person might develop in the same way." [11] But we must keep in mind that the attributes which are relevant in determining whether or not an entity is enough like a person to be regarded as having some of the same moral rights are no different from those which are relevant to determining whether or not it is fully a person—i.e., are no different from (1)-(5)—and that being genetically human, or having recognizably human facial and other physical features, or detectable brain activity, or the capacity to survive outside the uterus, are simply not among these relevant attributes.

11. Thomas L. Hayes, "A Biological View," *Commonweal*, 85 (March 17, 1967), 677-78; quoted by Daniel Callahan, in *Abortion, Law, Choice, and Morality* (London: Macmillan & Co., 1970).

Thus it is clear that even though a seven- or eight-month fetus has features which make it apt to arouse in us almost the same powerful protective instinct as is commonly aroused by a small infant, nevertheless it is not significantly more personlike than is a very small embryo. It is *somewhat* more personlike; it can apparently feel and respond to pain, and it may even have a rudimentary form of consciousness, insofar as its brain is quite active. Nevertheless, it seems safe to say that it is not fully conscious, in the way that an infant of a few months is, and that it cannot reason, or communicate messages of indefinitely many sorts, does not engage in self-motivated activity, and has no self-awareness. Thus, in the *relevant* respects, a fetus, even a fully developed one, is considerably less personlike than is the average mature mammal, indeed the average fish. And I think that a rational person must conclude that if the right to life of a fetus is to be based upon its resemblance to a person, then it cannot be said to have any more right to life than, let us say, a newborn guppy (which also seems to be capable of feeling pain), and that a right of that magnitude could never override a woman's right to obtain an abortion, at any stage of her pregnancy.

There may, of course, be other arguments in favor of placing legal limits upon the stage of pregnancy in which an abortion may be performed. Given the relative safety of the new techniques of artifically inducing labor during the third trimester, the danger to the woman's life or health is no longer such an argument. Neither is the fact that people tend to respond to the thought of abortion in the later stages of pregnancy with emotional repulsion, since mere emotional responses cannot take the place of moral reasoning in determining what ought to be permitted. Nor, finally, is the frequently heard argument that legalizing abortion, especially late in the pregnancy, may erode the level of respect for human life, leading, perhaps, to an increase in unjustified euthanasia and other crimes. For this threat, if it is a threat, can be better met by educating people to the kinds of moral distinctions which we are making here than by limiting access to abortion (which limitation may, in its disregard for the rights of women, be just as damaging to the level of respect for human rights).

Thus, since the fact that even a fully developed fetus is not personlike enough to have any significant right to life on the basis of its personlikeness shows that no legal restrictions upon the stage of pregnancy in which an abortion may be performed can be justified on the grounds that we should protect the rights of the older fetus; and since there is no other apparent justification for such restrictions, we may conclude that they are entirely unjustified. Whether or not it would be *indecent* (whatever that means) for a woman in her seventh month to obtain an abortion just to avoid having to postpone a trip to Europe, it would not, in itself, be *immoral,* and therefore it ought to be permitted.

4. *Potential Personhood and the Right to Life*

We have seen that a fetus does not resemble a person in any way which can support the claim that it has even some of the same rights. But what about its *potential,* the fact that if nurtured and allowed to develop naturally it will very probably become a person? Doesn't that alone give it at least some right to life? It is hard to deny that the fact that an entity is a potential person is a strong prima facie reason for not destroying it; but we need not conclude from this that a potential person has a right to life, by virtue of that potential. It may be that our feeling that it is better, other things being equal, not to destroy a potential person is better explained by the fact that potential people are still (felt to be) an invaluable resource, not to be lightly squandered. Surely, if every speck of dust were a potential person, we would be much less apt to conclude that every potential person has a right to become actual.

Still, we do not need to insist that a potential person has no right to life whatever. There may well be something immoral, and not just imprudent, about wantonly destroying potential people, when doing so isn't necessary to protect anyone's rights. But even if a potential person does have some prima facie right to life, such a right could not possibly outweigh the right of a woman to obtain an abortion, since the rights of any actual person invariably outweigh those of any potential person, whenever the two conflict. Since this may not be immediately obvious in the case of a human fetus, let us look at another case.

Suppose that our space explorer falls into the hands of an alien culture, whose scientists decide to create a few hundred thousand or more human beings, by breaking his body into its component cells, and using these to create fully developed human beings, with, of course, his genetic code. We may imagine that each of these newly created men will have all of the original man's abilities, skills, knowledge, and so on, and also have an individual self-concept, in short that each of them will be a bona fide (though hardly unique) person. Imagine that the whole project will take only seconds, and that its chances of success are extremely high, and that our explorer knows all of this, and also knows that these people will be treated fairly. I maintain that in such a situation he would have every right to escape if he could, and thus to deprive all of these potential people of their potential lives; for his right to life outweighs all of theirs together, in spite of the fact that they are all genetically human, all innocent, and all have a very high probability of becoming people very soon, if only he refrains from acting.

Indeed, I think he would have a right to escape even if it were not his life which the alien scientists planned to take, but only a year of his freedom, or, indeed, only a day. Nor would he be obligated to stay if he had gotten captured (thus bringing all these people-potentials into existence) because of his own carelessness, or even if he had done so deliberately, knowing the consequences. Regardless of how he got captured, he is not morally obligated to remain in captivity for *any* period of time for the sake of permitting any number of potential people to come into actuality, so great is the margin by which one actual person's right to liberty outweighs whatever right to life even a hundred thousand potential people have. And it seems reasonable to conclude that the rights of a woman will outweigh by a similar margin whatever right to life a fetus may have by virtue of its potential personhood.

Thus, neither a fetus's resemblance to a person, nor its potential for becoming a person provides any basis whatever for the claim that it has any significant right to life. Consequently, a woman's right to protect her health, happiness, freedom, and even her life,[12] by terminating an unwanted pregnancy, will always override whatever right to life it may be appropriate to ascribe to a fetus, even a fully developed one. And thus, in the absence of any overwhelming social need for every possible child, the laws which restrict the right to obtain an abortion, or limit the period of pregnancy during which

12. That is, insofar as the death rate, for the woman, is higher for childbirth than for early abortion.

an abortion may be performed, are a wholly unjustified violation of a woman's most basic moral and constitutional rights.[13]

MARY ANNE WARREN

SONOMA STATE COLLEGE,
CALIFORNIA

13. My thanks to the following people, who were kind enough to read and criticize an earlier version of this paper: Herbert Gold, Gene Glass, Anne Lauterbach, Judith Thomson, Mary Mothersill, and Timothy Binkley.

The Rights of Animals and Unborn Generations

JOEL FEINBERG

EVERY PHILOSOPHICAL PAPER must begin with an unproved assumption. Mine is the assumption that there will still be a world five hundred years from now, and that it will contain human beings who are very much like us. We have it within our power now, clearly, to affect the lives of these creatures for better or worse by contributing to the conservation or corruption of the environment in which they must live. I shall assume furthermore that it is psychologically possible for us to care about our remote descendants, that many of us in fact do care, and indeed that we ought to care. My main concern then will be to show that it makes sense to speak of the rights of unborn generations against us, and that given the moral judgment that we ought to conserve our environmental inheritance for them, and its grounds, we might well say that future generations *do* have rights correlative to our present duties toward them. Protecting our environment now is also a matter of elementary prudence, and insofar as we do it for the next generation already here in the persons of our children, it is a matter of love. But from the perspective of our remote descendants it is basically a matter of justice, of respect for their rights. My main concern here will be to examine the concept of a right to better understand how that can be.

THE PROBLEM

To have a right is to have a claim[1] *to* something and *against* someone, the recognition of which is called for by legal rules or, in the case of moral rights, by the principles of an enlightened

1. I shall leave the concept of a claim unanalyzed here, but for a detailed discussion, see my "The Nature and Value of Rights," *Journal of Value Inquiry* 4 (Winter 1971): 263–277.

conscience. In the familiar cases of rights, the claimant is a competent adult human being, and the claimee is an officeholder in an institution or else a private individual, in either case, another competent adult human being. Normal adult human beings, then, are obviously the sorts of beings of whom rights can meaningfully be predicated. Everyone would agree to that, even extreme misanthropes who deny that anyone in fact has rights. On the other hand, it is absurd to say that rocks can have rights, not because rocks are morally inferior things unworthy of rights (that statement makes no sense either), but because rocks belong to a category of entities of whom rights cannot be meaningfully predicated. That is not to say that there are no circumstances in which we ought to treat rocks carefully, but only that the rocks themselves cannot validly claim good treatment from us. In between the clear cases of rocks and normal human beings, however, is a spectrum of less obvious cases, including some bewildering borderline ones. Is it meaningful or conceptually possible to ascribe rights to our dead ancestors? to individual animals? to whole species of animals? to plants? to idiots and madmen? to fetuses? to generations yet unborn? Until we know how to settle these puzzling cases, we cannot claim fully to grasp the concept of a right, or to know the shape of its logical boundaries.

One way to approach these riddles is to turn one's attention first to the most familiar and unproblematic instances of rights, note their most salient characteristics, and then compare the borderline cases with them, measuring as closely as possible the points of similarity and difference. In the end, the way we classify the borderline cases may depend on whether we are more impressed with the similarities or the differences between them and the cases in which we have the most confidence.

It will be useful to consider the problem of individual animals first because their case is the one that has already been debated with the most thoroughness by philosophers so that the dialectic of claim and rejoinder has now unfolded to the point where disputants can get to the end game quickly and isolate the crucial point at issue. When we understand precisely what *is* at issue in the debate over animal rights, I think we will have the key to the solution of all the other riddles about rights.

INDIVIDUAL ANIMALS

Almost all modern writers agree that we ought to be kind to animals, but that is quite another thing from holding that animals can claim kind treatment from us as their due. Statutes making cruelty to animals a crime are now very common, and these, of course, impose legal duties on people not to mistreat animals; but that still leaves open the question whether the animals, as beneficiaries of those duties, possess rights correlative to them. We may very well have duties *regarding* animals that are not at the same time duties *to* animals, just as we may have duties regarding rocks, or buildings, or lawns, that are not duties *to* the rocks, buildings, or lawns. Some legal writers have taken the still more extreme position that animals themselves are not even the directly intended beneficiaries of statutes prohibiting cruelty to animals. During the nineteenth century, for example, it was commonly said that such statutes were designed to protect human beings by preventing the growth of cruel habits that could later threaten human beings with harm too. Prof. Louis B. Schwartz finds the rationale of the cruelty-to-animals prohibition in its protection of animal lovers from affronts to their sensibilities. "It is not the mistreated dog who is the ultimate object of concern," he writes. "Our concern is for the feelings of other human beings, a large proportion of whom, although accustomed to the slaughter of animals for food, readily identify themselves with a tortured dog or horse and respond with great sensitivity to its sufferings."[2] This seems to me to be factitious. How much more natural it is to say with John Chipman Gray that the true purpose of cruelty-to-animals statutes is "to preserve the dumb brutes from suffering."[3] The very people whose sensibilities are invoked in the alternative explanation, a group that no doubt now includes most of us, are precisely those who would insist that the protection belongs primarily to the animals themselves, not merely to their own tender feelings. Indeed, it would be difficult even to account for the existence of such

2. Louis B. Schwartz, "Morals, Offenses and the Model Penal Code," *Columbia Law Review* 63 (1963): 673.

3. John Chipman Gray, *The Nature and Sources of the Law*, 2d ed. (Boston: Beacon Press, 1963), p. 43.

feelings in the absence of a belief that the animals deserve the protection in their own right and for their own sakes.

Even if we allow, as I think we must, that animals are the intended direct beneficiaries of legislation forbidding cruelty to animals, it does not follow directly that animals have legal rights, and Gray himself, for one,[4] refused to draw this further inference. Animals cannot have rights, he thought, for the same reason they cannot have duties, namely, that they are not genuine "moral agents." Now, it is relatively easy to see why animals cannot have duties, and this matter is largely beyond controversy. Animals cannot be "reasoned with" or instructed in their responsibilities; they are inflexible and unadaptable to future contingencies; they are subject to fits of instinctive passion which they are incapable of repressing or controlling, postponing or sublimating. Hence, they cannot enter into contractual agreements, or make promises; they cannot be trusted; and they cannot (except within very narrow limits and for purposes of conditioning) be blamed for what would be called "moral failures" in a human being. They are therefore incapable of being moral subjects, of acting rightly or wrongly in the moral sense, of having, discharging, or breeching duties and obligations.

But what is there about the intellectual incompetence of animals (which admittedly disqualifies them for duties) that makes them logically unsuitable for rights? The most common reply to this question is that animals are incapable of *claiming* rights on their own. They cannot make motion, on their own, to courts to have their claims recognized or enforced; they cannot initiate, on their own, any kind of legal proceedings; nor are they capable of even understanding when their rights are being violated, of distinguishing harm from wrongful injury, and responding with indignation and an outraged sense of justice instead of mere anger or fear.

No one can deny any of these allegations, but to the claim that they are the grounds for disqualification of rights of animals, philosophers on the other side of this controversy have made con-

4. And W. D. Ross for another. See *The Right and the Good* (Oxford: Clarendon Press, 1930), app. 1, pp. 48–56.

vincing rejoinders. It is simply not true, says W. D. Lamont,[5] that the ability to understand what a right is and the ability to set legal machinery in motion by one's own initiative are necessary for the possession of rights. If that were the case, then neither human idiots nor wee babies would have any legal rights at all. Yet it is manifest that both of these classes of intellectual incompetents have legal rights recognized and easily enforced by the courts. Children and idiots start legal proceedings, not on their own direct initiative, but rather through the actions of proxies or attorneys who are empowered to speak in their names. If there is no conceptual absurdity in this situation, why should there be in the case where a proxy makes a claim on behalf of an animal? People commonly enough make wills leaving money to trustees for the care of animals. Is it not natural to speak of the animal's right to his inheritance in cases of this kind? If a trustee embezzles money from the animal's account,[6] and a proxy speaking in the dumb brute's behalf presses the animal's claim, can he not be described as asserting the animal's *rights?* More exactly, the animal itself claims its rights through the vicarious actions of a human proxy speaking in its name and in its behalf. There appears to be no reason why we should require the animal to understand what is going on (so the argument concludes) as a condition for regarding it as a possessor of rights.

Some writers protest at this point that the legal relation between a principal and an agent cannot hold between animals and human beings. Between humans, the relation of agency can take two very different forms, depending upon the degree of discretion granted to the agent, and there is a continuum of combinations between the extremes. On the one hand, there is the agent who is the mere "mouthpiece" of his principal. He is a "tool" in much the same sense as is a typewriter or telephone; he simply transmits the instructions of his principal. Human beings could hardly be the agents or representatives of animals in this sense, since the dumb brutes could no more use human "tools" than mechanical ones.

5. W. D. Lamont, *Principles of Moral Judgment* (Oxford: Clarendon Press, 1946), pp. 83–85.

6. Cf. H. J. McCloskey, "Rights," *Philosophical Quarterly* 15 (1965): 121, 124.

On the other hand, an agent may be some sort of expert hired to exercise his professional judgment on behalf of, and in the name of, the principal. He may be given, within some limited area of expertise, complete independence to act as he deems best, binding his principal to all the beneficial or detrimental consequences. This is the role played by trustees, lawyers, and ghost-writers. This type of representation requires that the agent have great skill, but makes little or no demand upon the principal, who may leave everything to the judgment of his agent. Hence, there appears, at first, to be no reason why an animal cannot be a totally passive principal in this second kind of agency relationship.

There are still some important dissimilarities, however. In the typical instance of representation by an agent, even of the second, highly discretionary kind, the agent is hired by a principal who enters into an agreement or contract with him; the principal tells his agent that within certain carefully specified boundaries "You may speak for me," subject always to the principal's approval, his right to give new directions, or to cancel the whole arrangement. No dog or cat could possibly do any of those things. Moreover, if it is the assigned task of the agent to defend the principal's rights, the principal may often decide to release his claimee, or to waive his own rights, and instruct his agent accordingly. Again, no mute cow or horse can do that. But although the possibility of hiring, agreeing, contracting, approving, directing, canceling, releasing, waiving, and instructing is present in the typical (all-human) case of agency representation, there appears to be no reason of a logical or conceptual kind why that *must* be so, and indeed there are some special examples involving human principals where it is not in fact so. I have in mind legal rules, for example, that require that a defendant be represented at his trial by an attorney, and impose a state-appointed attorney upon reluctant defendants, or upon those tried *in absentia*, whether they like it or not. Moreover, small children and mentally deficient and deranged adults are commonly represented by trustees and attorneys, even though they are incapable of granting their own consent to the representation, or of entering into contracts, of giving directions, or waiving their rights. It may be that it is unwise to permit agents to represent principals without the latters' knowledge or consent. If so, then no one should ever be permitted to speak for an animal, at least in a legally binding way. But that is quite another thing than saying that such representation is logically incoherent or conceptually incongruous—the contention that is at issue.

H. J. McCloskey,[7] I believe, accepts the argument up to this point, but he presents a new and different reason for denying that animals can have legal rights. The ability to make claims, whether directly or through a representative, he implies, is essential to the possession of rights. Animals obviously cannot press their claims on their own, and so if they have rights, these rights must be assertable by agents. Animals, however, cannot be represented, McCloskey contends, and not for any of the reasons already discussed, but rather because representation, in the requisite sense, is always of interests, and animals (he says) are incapable of having interests.

Now, there is a very important insight expressed in the requirement that a being have interests if he is to be a logically proper subject of rights. This can be appreciated if we consider just why it is that mere things cannot have rights. Consider a very precious "mere thing"—a beautiful natural wilderness, or a complex and ornamental artifact, like the Taj Mahal. Such things ought to be cared for, because they would sink into decay if neglected, depriving some human beings, or perhaps even all human beings, of something of great value. Certain persons may even have as their own special job the care and protection of these valuable objects But we are not tempted in these cases to speak of "thing-rights" correlative to custodial duties, because, try as we might, we cannot think of mere things as possessing interests of their own. Some people may have a duty to preserve, maintain, or improve the Taj Mahal, but they can hardly have a duty to help or hurt it, benefit or aid it, succor or relieve it. Custodians may protect it for the sake of a nation's pride and art lovers' fancy; but they don't keep it in good repair for "its own sake," or for "its own true welfare," or "well-being." A mere thing, however valuable to others, has no good of its own. The explanation of that fact, I suspect, consists in the fact that mere things have no conative life: no conscious wishes, desires, and hopes; or urges and impulses; or unconscious drives, aims, and goals; or latent tendencies, direction of growth, and natural fulfillments. Interests must be compounded somehow

7. Ibid.

out of conations; hence mere things have no interests. *A fortiori*, they have no interests to be protected by legal or moral rules. Without interests a creature can have no "good" of its own, the achievement of which can be its due. Mere things are not loci of value in their own right, but rather their value consists entirely in their being objects of other beings' interests.

So far McCloskey is on solid ground, but one can quarrel with his denial that any animals but humans have interests. I should think that the trustee of funds willed to a dog or cat is more than a mere custodian of the animal he protects. Rather his job is to look out for the interests of the animal and make sure no one denies it its due. The animal itself is the beneficiary of his dutiful services. Many of the higher animals at least have appetites, conative urges, and rudimentary purposes, the integrated satisfaction of which constitutes their welfare or good. We can, of course, with consistency treat animals as mere pests and deny that they have any rights; for most animals, especially those of the lower orders, we have no choice but to do so. But it seems to me, nevertheless, that in general, animals *are* among the sorts of beings of whom rights can meaningfully be predicated and denied.

Now, if a person agrees with the conclusion of the argument thus far, that animals are the sorts of beings that *can* have rights, and further, if he accepts the moral judgment that we ought to be kind to animals, only one further premise is needed to yield the conclusion that some animals do in fact have rights. We must now ask ourselves for whose sake ought we to treat (some) animals with consideration and humaneness? If we conceive our duty to be one of obedience to authority, or to one's own conscience merely, or one of consideration for tender human sensibilities only, then we might still deny that animals have rights, even though we admit that they are the kinds of beings that *can* have rights. But if we hold not only that we ought to treat animals humanely but also that we should do so for the animals' own sake, that such treatment is something we owe animals as their due, something that can be claimed for them, something the withholding of which would be an injustice and a wrong, and not merely a harm, then it follows that we do ascribe rights to animals. I suspect that the moral judgments most of us make about animals do pass these phenomenological tests, so that most of us do believe that animals have rights, but are reluctant to say so because of the conceptual confusions about the notion of a right that I have attempted to dispel above.

Now we can extract from our discussion of animal rights a crucial principle for tentative use in the resolution of the other riddles about the applicability of the concept of a right, namely, that the sorts of beings who *can* have rights are precisely those who have (or can have) interests. I have come to this tentative conclusion for two reasons: (1) because a right holder must be capable of being represented and it is impossible to represent a being that has no interests, and (2) because a right holder must be capable of being a beneficiary in his own person, and a being without interests is a being that is incapable of being harmed or benefitted, having no good or "sake" of its own. Thus, a being without interests has no "behalf" to act in, and no "sake" to act for. My strategy now will be to apply the "interest principle," as we can call it, to the other puzzles about rights, while being prepared to modify it where necessary (but as little as possible), in the hope of separating in a consistent and intuitively satisfactory fashion the beings who can have rights from those which cannot.

VEGETABLES

It is clear that we ought not to mistreat certain plants, and indeed there are rules and regulations imposing duties on persons not to misbehave in respect to certain members of the vegetable kingdom. It is forbidden, for example, to pick wildflowers in the mountainous tundra areas of national parks, or to endanger trees by starting fires in dry forest areas. Members of Congress introduce bills designed, as they say, to "protect" rare redwood trees from commercial pillage. Given this background, it is surprising that no one[8] speaks of plants as having rights. Plants, after all, are not "mere things"; they are vital objects with inherited biological propensities determining their natural growth. Moreover, we do say that certain conditions are "good" or "bad" for plants, thereby suggesting that plants, unlike rocks, are capable of having a "good." (This is a case, however, where "what we say" should not be taken seriously: we also say that certain kinds of paint are good

8. Outside of Samuel Butler's *Erewhon*.

or bad for the internal walls of a house, and this does not commit us to a conception of walls as beings possessed of a good or welfare of their own.) Finally, we are capable of feeling a kind of affection for particular plants, though we rarely personalize them, as we do in the case of animals, by giving them proper names.

Still, all are agreed that plants are not the kinds of beings that can have rights. Plants are never plausibly understood to be the direct intended beneficiaries of rules designed to "protect" them. We wish to keep redwood groves in existence for the sake of human beings who can enjoy their serene beauty, and for the sake of generations of human beings yet unborn. Trees are not the sorts of beings who have their "own sakes," despite the fact that they have biological propensities. Having no conscious wants or goals of their own, trees cannot know satisfaction or frustration, pleasure or pain. Hence, there is no possibility of kind or cruel treatment of trees. In these morally crucial respects, trees differ from the higher species of animals.

Yet trees are not mere things like rocks. They grow and develop according to the laws of their own nature. Aristotle and Aquinas both took trees to have their own "natural ends." Why then do I deny them the status of beings with interests of their own? The reason is that an interest, however the concept is finally to be analyzed, presupposes at least rudimentary cognitive equipment. Interests are compounded out of *desires* and *aims*, both of which presuppose something like *belief*, or cognitive awareness. A desiring creature may want *X* because he seeks anything that is Ø, and *X* appears to be Ø to him; or he may be seeking *Y*, and he believes, or expects, or hopes that *X* will be a means to *Y*. If he desires *X* in order to get *Y*, this implies that he believes that *X* will bring *Y* about, or at least that he has some sort of brute expectation that is a primitive correlate of belief. But what of the desire for Ø (or for *Y*) itself? Perhaps a creature has such a "desire" as an ultimate set, as if he had come into existence all "wound up" to pursue Ø-ness or *Y*-ness, and his not to reason why. Such a propensity, I think, would not qualify as a desire. Mere brute longings unmediated by beliefs—longings for one knows not what—might perhaps be a primitive form of consciousness (I don't want to beg that question) but they are altogether different from the sort of thing we mean by "desire," especially when we speak of human beings.

If some such account as the above is correct, we can never have any grounds for attributing a desire or a want to a creature known to be incapable even of rudimentary beliefs; and if desires or wants are the materials interests are made of, mindless creatures have no interests of their own. The law, therefore, cannot have as its intention the protection of their interests, so that "protective legislation" has to be understood as legislation protecting the interests human beings may have in them.

Plant life might nevertheless be thought at first to constitute a hard case for the interest principle for two reasons. In the first place, plants no less than animals are said to have needs of their own. To be sure, we can speak even of mere things as having needs too, but such talk misleads no one into thinking of the need as belonging, in the final analysis, to the "mere thing" itself. If we were so deceived we would not be thinking of the mere thing as a "mere thing" after all. We say, for example, that John Doe's walls need painting, or that Richard Roe's car needs a washing, but we direct our attitudes of sympathy or reproach (as the case may be) to John and Richard, not to their possessions. It would be otherwise, if we observed that some child is in need of a good meal. Our sympathy and concern in that case would be directed at the child himself as the true possessor of the need in question.

The needs of plants might well seem closer to the needs of animals than to the pseudoneeds of mere things. An owner may need a plant (say, for its commercial value or as a potential meal), but the plant itself, it might appear, needs nutrition or cultivation. Our confusion about this matter may stem from language. It is a commonplace that the word *need* is ambiguous. To say that *A* needs *X* may be to say either: (1) *X* is necessary to the achievement of one of *A*'s goals, or to the performance of one of its functions, or (2) *X* is good for *A;* its lack would harm *A* or be injurious or detrimental to him (or it). The first sort of need-statement is value-neutral, implying no comment on the value of the goal or function in question; whereas the second kind of statement about needs commits its maker to a value judgment about what is good or bad for *A* in the long run, that is, about what is in *A*'s interests.

A being must have interests, therefore, to have needs in the second sense, but any kind of thing, vegetable or mineral, could have needs in the first sense. An automobile needs gas and oil to function, but it is no tragedy for it if it runs out—an empty tank does not hinder or retard its interests. Similarly, to say that a tree needs sunshine and water is to say that without them it cannot grow and survive; but unless the growth and survival of trees are matters of human concern, affecting human interests, practical or aesthetic, the needs of trees alone will not be the basis of any claim of what is "due" them in their own right. Plants may need things in order to discharge their functions, but their functions are assigned by human interests, not their own.

The second source of confusion derives from the fact that we commonly speak of plants as thriving and flourishing, or withering and languishing. One might be tempted to think of these states either as themselves consequences of the possession of interests so that even creatures without wants or beliefs can be said to have interests, or else as grounds independent of the possession of interests for the making of intelligible claims of rights. In either case, plants would be thought of as conceivable possessors of rights after all.

Consider what it means to speak of something as "flourishing." The verb *to flourish* apparently was applied originally and literally to plants only, and in its original sense it meant simply "to bear flowers: BLOSSOM"; but then by analogical extension of sense it came also to mean "to grow luxuriantly: increase, and enlarge," and then to "THRIVE" (generally), and finally, when extended to human beings, "to be prosperous," or to "increase in wealth, honor, comfort, happiness, or whatever is desirable."[9] Applied to human beings the term is, of course, a fixed metaphor. When a person flourishes, something happens to his interests analogous to what happens to a plant when it flowers, grows, and spreads. A person flourishes when his interests (whatever they may be) are progressing severally and collectively toward their harmonious fulfillment and spawning new interests along the way whose prospects are also good. To flourish is to glory in the advancement of one's interests, in short, to be happy.

Nothing is gained by twisting the botanical metaphor back

9. *Webster's Third New International Dictionary.*

from humans to plants. To speak of thriving human interests as if they were flowers is to speak naturally and well, and to mislead no one. But then to think of the flowers or plants as if they were interests (or the signs of interests) is to bring the metaphor back full circle for no good reason and in the teeth of our actual beliefs. Some of our talk about flourishing plants reveals quite clearly that the interests that thrive when plants flourish are human not "plant interests." For example, we sometimes make a flowering bush flourish by "frustrating" its own primary propensities. We pinch off dead flowers before seeds have formed, thus "encouraging" the plant to make new flowers in an effort to produce more seeds. It is not the plant's own natural propensity (to produce seeds) that is advanced, but rather the gardener's interest in the production of new flowers and the spectator's pleasure in aesthetic form, color, or scent. What we mean in such cases by saying that the plant flourishes is that our interest in the plant, not its own, is thriving. It is not always so clear that that is what we mean, for on other occasions there is a correspondence between our interests and the plant's natural propensities, a coinciding of what we want from nature and nature's own "intention." But the exceptions to this correspondence provide the clue to our real sense in speaking of a plant's good or welfare.[10] And even when there exists such a correspondence, it is often because we have actually remade the plant's nature so that our interests in it will flourish more "naturally" and effectively.

WHOLE SPECIES

The topic of whole species, whether of plants or animals, can be treated in much the same way as that of individual plants. A whole collection, as such, cannot have beliefs, expectations, wants, or desires, and can flourish or languish only in the human interest-

10. Sometimes, of course, the correspondence fails because what accords with the plant's natural propensities is not in our interests, rather than the other way round. I must concede that in cases of this kind we speak even of weeds flourishing, but I doubt that we mean to imply that a weed is a thing with a good of its own. Rather, this way of talking is a plain piece of irony, or else an animistic metaphor (thinking of the weeds in the way we think of prospering businessmen). In any case, when weeds thrive, usually no interests, human or otherwise, flourish.

related sense in which individual plants thrive and decay. Individual elephants can have interests, but the species elephant cannot. Even where individual elephants are not granted rights, human beings may have an interest—economic, scientific, or sentimental—in keeping the species from dying out, and *that* interest may be protected in various ways by law. But that is quite another matter from recognizing a right to survival belonging to the species itself. Still, the preservation of a whole species may quite properly seem to be a morally more important matter than the preservation of an individual animal. Individual animals can have rights but it is implausible to ascribe to them a right to life on the human model. Nor do we normally have duties to keep individual animals alive or even to abstain from killing them provided we do it humanely and nonwantonly in the promotion of legitimate human interests. On the other hand, we do have duties to protect threatened species, not duties to the species themselves as such, but rather duties to future human beings, duties derived from our housekeeping role as temporary inhabitants of this planet.

We commonly and very naturally speak of corporate entities, such as institutions, churches, and national states as having rights and duties, and an adequate analysis of the conditions for ownership of rights should account for that fact. A corporate entity, of course, is more than a mere collection of things that have some important traits in common. Unlike a biological species, an institution has a charter, or constitution, or bylaws, with rules defining offices and procedures, and it has human beings whose function it is to administer the rules and apply the procedures. When the institution has a duty to an outsider, there is always some determinant human being whose duty it is to do something for the outsider, and when the state, for example, has a right to collect taxes, there are always certain definite flesh and blood persons who have rights to demand tax money from other citizens. We have no reluctance to use the language of corporate rights and duties because we know that in the last analysis these are rights or duties of individual persons, acting in their "official capacities." And when individuals act in their official roles in accordance with valid empowering rules, their acts are imputable to the organization itself and become "acts of state." Thus, there is no need to posit any individual superperson named by the expression "the State" (or for that matter, "the company," "the club," or "the church.") Nor is there any reason to take the rights of corporate entities to be exceptions to the interest principle. The United States is not a superperson with wants and beliefs of its own, but it is a corporate entity with corporate interests that are, in turn, analyzable into the interests of its numerous flesh and blood members.

DEAD PERSONS

So far we have refined the interest principle but we have not had occasion to modify it. Applied to dead persons, however, it will have to be stretched to near the breaking point if it is to explain how our duty to honor commitments to the dead can be thought to be linked to the rights of the dead against us. The case against ascribing rights to dead men can be made very simply: a dead man is a mere corpse, a piece of decaying organic matter. Mere inanimate things can have no interests, and what is incapable of having interests is incapable of having rights. If, nevertheless, we grant dead men rights against us, we would seem to be treating the interests they had while alive as somehow surviving their deaths. There is the sound of paradox in this way of talking, but it may be the least paradoxical way of describing our moral relations to our predecessors. And if the idea of an interest's surviving its possessor's death is a kind of fiction, it is a fiction that most living men have a real interest in preserving.

Most persons while still alive have certain desires about what is to happen to their bodies, their property, or their reputations after they are dead. For that reason, our legal system has developed procedures to enable persons while still alive to determine whether their bodies will be used for purposes of medical research or organic transplantation, and to whom their wealth (after taxes) is to be transferred. Living men also take out life insurance policies guaranteeing that the accumulated benefits be conferred upon beneficiaries of their own choice. They also make private agreements, both contractual and informal, in which they receive promises that certain things will be done after their deaths in exchange for some present service or consideration. In all these cases promises are made to living persons that their wishes will be honored after they are dead. Like all other valid promises, they impose duties on the promisor and confer correlative rights on the promisee.

How does the situation change after the promisee has died? Surely the duties of the promisor do not suddenly become null and void. If that were the case, and known to be the case, there could be no confidence in promises regarding posthumous arrangements; no one would bother with wills or life insurance companies to pay benefits to survivors, which are, in a sense, only conditional duties before a man dies. They come into existence as categorical demands for immediate action only upon the promisee's death. So the view that death renders them null and void has the truth exactly upside down.

The survival of the promisor's duty after the promisee's death does not prove that the promisee retains a right even after death, for we might prefer to conclude that there is one class of cases where duties to keep promises are not logically correlated with a promisee's right, namely, cases where the promisee has died. Still, a morally sensitive promisor is likely to think of his promised performance not only as a duty (i.e., a morally required action) but also as something owed to the deceased promisee as his due. Honoring such promises is a way of keeping faith with the dead. To be sure, the promisor will not think of his duty as something to be done for the promisee's "good," since the promisee, being dead, has no "good" of his own. We can think of certain of the deceased's interests, however, (including especially those enshrined in wills and protected by contracts and promises) as surviving their owner's death, and constituting claims against us that persist beyond the life of the claimant. Such claims can be represented by proxies just like the claims of animals. This way of speaking, I believe, reflects more accurately than any other an important fact about the human condition: we have an interest while alive that other interests of ours will continue to be recognized and served after we are dead. The whole practice of honoring wills and testaments, and the like, is thus for the sake of the living, just as a particular instance of it may be thought to be for the sake of one who is dead.

Conceptual sense, then, can be made of talk about dead men's rights; but it is still a wide open moral question whether dead men in fact have rights, and if so, what those rights are. In particular, commentators have disagreed over whether a man's interest in his reputation deserves to be protected from defamation even after his death. With only a few prominent exceptions, legal systems punish a libel on a dead man "only when its publication is in truth an attack upon the interests of living persons."[11] A widow or a son may be wounded, or embarrassed, or even injured economically, by a defamatory attack on the memory of their dead husband or father. In Utah defamation of the dead is a misdemeanor, and in Sweden a cause of action in tort. The law rarely presumes, however, that a dead man himself has any interests, representable by proxy, that can be injured by defamation, apparently because of the maxim that what a dead man doesn't know can't hurt him.

This presupposes, however, that the whole point of guarding the reputations even of living men, is to protect them from hurt feelings, or to protect some other interests, for example, economic ones, that do not survive death. A moment's thought, I think, will show that our interests are more complicated than that. If someone spreads a libelous description of me, without my knowledge, among hundreds of persons in a remote part of the country, so that I am, still without my knowledge, an object of general scorn and mockery in that group, I have been injured, even though I never learn what has happened. That is because I have an interest, so I believe, in having a good reputation *simpliciter*, in addition to my interest in avoiding hurt feelings, embarrassment, and economic injury. In the example, I do not know what is being said and believed about me, so my feelings are not hurt; but clearly if I did know, I would be enormously distressed. The distress would be the natural consequence of my belief that an interest other than my interest in avoiding distress had been damaged. How else can I account for the distress? If I had no interest in a good reputation as such, I would respond to news of harm to my reputation with indifference.

While it is true that a dead man cannot have his feelings hurt, it does not follow, therefore, that his claim to be thought of no worse than he deserves cannot survive his death. Almost every living person, I should think, would wish to have this interest

11. William Salmond, *Jurisprudence,* 12th ed., ed. P. J. Fitzgerald (London: Sweet and Maxwell, 1966), p. 304.

protected after his death, at least during the lifetimes of those persons who were his contemporaries. We can hardly expect the law to protect Julius Caesar from defamation in the history books. This might hamper historical research and restrict socially valuable forms of expression. Even interests that survive their owner's death are not immortal. Anyone should be permitted to say anything he wishes about George Washington or Abraham Lincoln, though perhaps not everything is morally permissible. Everyone ought to refrain from malicious lies even about Nero or King Tut, though not so much for those ancients' own sakes as for the sake of those who would now know the truth about the past. We owe it to the brothers Kennedy, however, as their due, not to tell damaging lies about them to those who were once their contemporaries. If the reader would deny that judgment, I can only urge him to ask himself whether he now wishes his own interest in reputation to be respected, along with his interest in determining the distribution of his wealth, after his death.

HUMAN VEGETABLES

Mentally deficient and deranged human beings are hardly ever so handicapped intellectually that they do not compare favorably with even the highest of the lower animals, though they are commonly so incompetent that they cannot be assigned duties or be held responsible for what they do. Since animals can have rights, then, it follows that human idiots and madmen can too. It would make good sense, for example, to ascribe to them a right to be cured whenever effective therapy is available at reasonable cost, and even those incurables who have been consigned to a sanatorium for permanent "warehousing" can claim (through a proxy) their right to decent treatment.

Human beings suffering extreme cases of mental illness, however, may be so utterly disoriented or insensitive as to compare quite unfavorably with the brightest cats and dogs. Those suffering from catatonic schizophrenia may be barely distinguishable in respect to those traits presupposed by the possession of interests from the lowliest vegetables. So long as we regard these patients as potentially curable, we may think of them as human beings with interests in their own restoration and treat them as possessors of rights. We may think of the patient as a genuine human person inside the vegetable casing struggling to get out, just as in the old fairy tales a pumpkin could be thought of as a beautiful maiden under a magic spell waiting only the proper words to be restored to her true self. Perhaps it is reasonable never to lose hope that a patient can be cured, and therefore to regard him always as a person "under a spell" with a permanent interest in his own recovery that is entitled to recognition and protection.

What if, nevertheless, we think of the catatonic schizophrenic and the vegetating patient with irreversible brain damage as absolutely incurable? Can we think of them at the same time as possessed of interests and rights too, or is this combination of traits a conceptual impossibility? Shocking as it may at first seem, I am driven unavoidably to the latter view. If redwood trees and rosebushes cannot have rights, neither can incorrigible human vegetables.[12] The trustees who are designated to administer funds for the care of these unfortunates are better understood as mere custodians than as representatives of their interests since these patients no longer have interests. It does not follow that they should not be kept alive as long as possible: that is an open moral question not foreclosed by conceptual analysis. Even if we have duties to keep human vegetables alive, however, they cannot be duties *to* them. We may be obliged to keep them alive to protect the sensibilities of others, or to foster humanitarian tendencies in ourselves, but we cannot keep them alive for their own good, for they are no longer capable of having a "good" of their own. Without awareness, expectation, belief, desire, aim, and purpose, a being can have no interests; without interests, he cannot be benefited; without the capacity to be a beneficiary, he can have no rights. But there may nevertheless be a dozen other reasons to treat him as if he did.

12. Unless, of course, the person in question, before he became a "vegetable," left testamentary directions about what was to be done with his body just in case he should ever become an incurable vegetable. He may have directed either that he be preserved alive as long as possible, or else that he be destroyed, whichever he preferred. There may, of course, be sound reasons of public policy why we should not honor such directions, but if we did promise to give legal effect to such wishes, we would have an example of a man's earlier interest in what is to happen to his body surviving his very competence as a person, in quite the same manner as that in which the express interest of a man now dead may continue to exert a claim on us.

FETUSES

If the interest principle is to permit us to ascribe rights to infants, fetuses, and generations yet unborn, it can only be on the grounds that interests can exert a claim upon us even before their possessors actually come into being, just the reverse of the situation respecting dead men where interests are respected even after their possessors have ceased to be. Newly born infants are surely noisier than mere vegetables, but they are just barely brighter. They come into existence, as Aristotle said, with the capacity to acquire concepts and dispositions, but in the beginning we suppose that their consciousness of the world is a "blooming, buzzing confusion." They do have a capacity, no doubt from the very beginning, to feel pain, and this alone may be sufficient ground for ascribing both an interest and a right to them. Apart from that, however, during the first few hours of their lives, at least, they may well lack even the rudimentary intellectual equipment necessary to the possession of interests. Of course, this induces no moral reservations whatever in adults. Children grow and mature almost visibly in the first few months so that those future interests that are so rapidly emerging from the unformed chaos of their earliest days seem unquestionably to be the basis of their present rights. Thus, we say of a newborn infant that he has a right now to live and grow into his adulthood, even though he lacks the conceptual equipment at this very moment to have this or any other desire. A new infant, in short, lacks the traits necessary for the possession of interests, but he has the capacity to acquire those traits, and his inherited potentialities are moving quickly toward actualization even as we watch him. Those proxies who make claims in behalf of infants, then, are more than mere custodians: they are (or can be) genuine representatives of the child's emerging interests, which may need protection even now if they are to be allowed to come into existence at all.

The same principle may be extended to "unborn persons." After all, the situation of fetuses one day before birth is not strikingly different from that a few hours after birth. The rights our law confers on the unborn child, both proprietary and personal, are for the most part, placeholders or reservations for the rights he shall inherit when he becomes a full-fledged interested being. The law protects a potential interest in these cases before it has even grown into actuality, as a garden fence protects newly seeded flower beds long before blooming flowers have emerged from them. The unborn child's present right to property, for example, is a legal protection offered now to his future interest, contingent upon his birth, and instantly voidable if he dies before birth. As Coke put it: "The law in many cases hath consideration of him in respect of the apparent expectation of his birth";[13] but this is quite another thing than recognizing a right actually to be born. Assuming that the child will be born, the law seems to say, various interests that he will come to have after birth must be protected from damage that they can incur even before birth. Thus prenatal injuries of a negligently inflicted kind can give the newly born child a right to sue for damages which he can exercise through a proxy-attorney and in his own name any time *after* he is born.

There are numerous other places, however, where our law seems to imply an unconditional right to be born, and surprisingly no one seems ever to have found that idea conceptually absurd. One interesting example comes from an article given the following headline by the *New York Times:* "Unborn Child's Right Upheld Over Religion."[14] A hospital patient in her eighth month of pregnancy refused to take a blood transfusion even though warned by her physician that "she might die at any minute and take the life of her child as well." The ground of her refusal was that blood transfusions are repugnant to the principles of her religion (Jehovah's Witnesses). The Supreme Court of New Jersey expressed uncertainty over the constitutional question of whether a non-pregnant adult might refuse on religious grounds a blood transfusion pronounced necessary to her own survival, but the court

13. As quoted by Salmond, *Jurisprudence*, p. 303. Simply as a matter of policy the potentiality of some future interests may be so remote as to make them seem unworthy of present support. A testator may leave property to his unborn child, for example, but not to his unborn grandchildren. To say of the potential person presently in his mother's womb that he owns property now is to say that certain property must be held for him until he is "real" or "mature" enough to possess it. "Yet the law is careful lest property should be too long withdrawn in this way from the uses of living men in favor of generations yet to come; and various restrictive rules have been established to this end. No testator could now direct his fortune to be accumulated for a hundred years and then distributed among his descendants"—Salmond, ibid.

14. *New York Times*, 17 June 1966, p. 1.

nevertheless ordered the patient in the present case to receive the transfusion on the grounds that "the unborn child is entitled to the law's protection."

It is important to reemphasize here that the questions of whether fetuses do or ought to have rights are substantive questions of law and morals open to argument and decision. The prior question of whether fetuses are the kind of beings that can have rights, however, is a conceptual, not a moral, question, amenable only to what is called "logical analysis," and irrelevant to moral judgment. The correct answer to the conceptual question, I believe, is that unborn children are among the sorts of beings of whom possession of rights can meaningfully be predicated, even though they are (temporarily) incapable of having interests, because their future interests can be protected now, and it does make sense to protect a potential interest even before it has grown into actuality. The interest principle, however, makes perplexing, at best, talk of a noncontingent fetal right to be born; for fetuses, lacking actual wants and beliefs, have no actual interest in being born, and it is difficult to think of any other reason for ascribing any rights to them other than on the assumption that they will in fact be born.[15]

FUTURE GENERATIONS

We have it in our power now to make the world a much less pleasant place for our descendants than the world we inherited from our ancestors. We can continue to proliferate in ever greater numbers, using up fertile soil at an even greater rate, dumping our wastes into rivers, lakes, and oceans, cutting down our forests, and polluting the atmosphere with noxious gases. All thoughtful people agree that we ought not to do these things. Most would say that we have a duty not to do these things, meaning not merely that conservation is morally required (as opposed to merely desirable) but also that it is something due our descendants, something to be done for their sakes. Surely we owe it to future genera-

15. In an essay entitled "Is There a Right to be Born?" I defend a negative answer to the question posed, but I allow that under certain very special conditions, there can be a "right *not* to be born." See *Abortion*, ed. J. Feinberg (Belmont, Calif.: Wadsworth, 1973).

tions to pass on a world that is not a used up garbage heap. Our remote descendants are not yet present to claim a livable world as their right, but there are plenty of proxies to speak now in their behalf. These spokesmen, far from being mere custodians, are genuine representatives of future interests.

Why then deny that the human beings of the future have rights which can be claimed against us now in their behalf? Some are inclined to deny them present rights out of a fear of falling into obscure metaphysics, by granting rights to remote and unidentifiable beings who are not yet even in existence. Our unborn great-great-grandchildren are in some sense "potential" persons, but they are far more remotely potential, it may seem, than fetuses. This, however, is not the real difficulty. Unborn generations are more remotely potential than fetuses in one sense, but not in another. A much greater period of time with a far greater number of causally necessary and important events must pass before their potentiality can be actualized, it is true; but our collective posterity is just as certain to come into existence "in the normal course of events" as is any given fetus now in its mother's womb. In that sense the existence of the distant human future is no more remotely potential than that of a particular child already on its way.

The real difficulty is not that we doubt whether our descendants will ever be actual, but rather that we don't know who they will be. It is not their temporal remoteness that troubles us so much as their indeterminacy—their present facelessness and namelessness. Five centuries from now men and women will be living where we live now. Any given one of them will have an interest in living space, fertile soil, fresh air, and the like, but that arbitrarily selected one has no other qualities we can presently envision very clearly. We don't even know who his parents, grandparents, or great-grandparents are, or even whether he is related to us. Still, whoever these human beings may turn out to be, and whatever they might reasonably be expected to be like, they will have interests that we can affect, for better or worse, right now. That much we can and do know about them. The identity of the owners of these interests is now necessarily obscure, but the fact of their interest-ownership is crystal clear, and that is all that is necessary to certify the coherence of present talk about their rights. We can tell, sometimes, that shadowy forms in the spatial distance belong to human beings, though we know not who or how many they are; and this imposes a duty on us not to throw bombs, for example, in their direction. In like manner, the vagueness of the human future does not weaken its claim on us in light of the nearly certain knowledge that it will, after all, be human.

Doubts about the existence of a right to be born transfer neatly to the question of a similar right to come into existence ascribed to future generations. The rights that future generations certainly have against us are contingent rights: the interests they are sure to have when they come into being (assuming of course that they will come into being) cry out for protection from invasions that can take place now. Yet there are no actual interests, presently existent, that future generations, presently nonexistent, have now. Hence, there is no actual interest that they have in simply coming into being, and I am at a loss to think of any other reason for claiming that they have a right to come into existence (though there may well be such a reason). Suppose then that all human beings at a given time voluntarily form a compact never again to produce children, thus leading within a few decades to the end of our species. This of course is a wildly improbable hypothetical example but a rather crucial one for the position I have been tentatively considering. And we can imagine, say, that the whole world is converted to a strange ascetic religion which absolutely requires sexual abstinence for everyone. Would this arrangement violate the rights of anyone? No one can complain on behalf of presently nonexistent future generations that their future interests which give them a contingent right of protection have been violated since they will never come into existence to be wronged. My inclination then is to conclude that the suicide of our species would be deplorable, lamentable, and a deeply moving tragedy, but that it would violate no one's rights. Indeed if, contrary to fact, all human beings could ever agree to such a thing, that very agreement would be a symptom of our species' biological unsuitability for survival anyway.

CONCLUSION

For several centuries now human beings have run roughshod over the lands of our planet, just as if the animals who do live there and the generations of humans who will live there had no claims on them whatever. Philosophers have not helped matters by arguing that animals and future generations are not the kinds of beings who can have rights now, that they don't presently qualify for membership, even "auxiliary membership," in our moral community. I have tried in this essay to dispel the conceptual confusions that make such conclusions possible. To acknowledge their rights is the very least we can do for members of endangered species (including our own). But that is something.

APPENDIX

The Paradoxes of Potentiality

Having conceded that rights can belong to beings in virtue of their merely potential interests, we find ourselves on a slippery slope; for it may seem at first sight that anything at all can have potential interests, or much more generally, that anything at all can be potentially almost anything else at all! Dehydrated orange powder is potentially orange juice, since if we add water to it, it will be orange juice. More remotely, however, it is also potentially lemonade, since it will become lemonade if we add a large quantity of lemon juice, sugar, and water. It is also a potentially poisonous brew (add water and arsenic), a potential orange cake (add flour, etc., and bake), a potential orange-colored building block (add cement and harden), and so on, *ad infinitum*. Similarly a two-celled embryo, too small to be seen by the unaided eye, is a potential human being; and so is an unfertilized ovum; and so is even an "uncapacitated" spermatozoan. Add the proper nutrition to an implanted embryo (under certain other necessary conditions) and it becomes a fetus and then a child. Looked at another way, however, the implanted embryo has been combined (under the same conditions) with the nutritive elements, which themselves are converted into a growing fetus and child. Is it then just as proper to say that food is a "potential child" as that an embryo is a potential child? If so, then what isn't a "potential child?" (Organic elements in the air and soil are "potentially food," and hence potentially people!)

Clearly, some sort of line will have to be drawn between direct or proximate potentialities and indirect or remote ones; and however we draw this line, there will be borderline cases whose classification will seem uncertain or even arbitrary. Even though any *X* can become a *Y* provided only that it is combined with the necessary additional elements, *a*, *b*, *c*, *d*, and so forth, we cannot say of any given *X* that it is a "potential *Y*" unless certain further—rather strict—conditions are met. (Otherwise the concept of potentiality, being universally and promiscuously applicable, will have no utility.) A number of possible criteria of proximate potentiality suggest themselves. The first is the criterion of causal importance. Orange powder is not properly called a potential building block because of those elements needed to transform it into a building block, the cement (as opposed to any of the qualities of the orange powder) is the causally crucial one. Similarly, any pauper might (misleadingly) be called a "potential millionaire" in the sense that all that need be added to any man to transform him into a millionaire is a great amount of money. The absolutely crucial element in the change, of course, is no quality of the man himself but rather the million dollars "added" to him.

What is causally "important" depends upon our purposes and interests and is therefore to some degree a relativistic matter. If we seek a standard, in turn, of "importance," we may posit such a criterion, for example, as that of the ease or difficulty (to some persons or other) of providing those missing elements which, when combined with the thing at hand, convert it into something else. It does seem quite natural, for example, to say that the orange powder is potentially orange juice, and that is because the missing element is merely common tap water, a substance conveniently near at hand to everyone; whereas it is less plausible to characterize the powder as potential cake since a variety of further elements, and not just one, are required, and some of these are not conveniently near at hand to many. Moreover, the process of combining the missing elements into a cake is rather more complicated than mere "addition." It is less plausible still to call orange powder a potential curbstone for the same kind of reason. The criterion of ease or difficulty of the acquisition and combination of additional elements explains all these variations.

Still another criterion of proximate potentiality closely related to the others is that of degree of deviation required from "the normal course of events." Given the intentions of its producers, distributors, sellers, and consumers, dehydrated orange juice will, in the normal course of events, become orange juice. Similarly, a human embryo securely imbedded in the wall of its mother's uterus will in the normal course of events become a human child. That is to say that if no one deliberately intervenes to prevent it happening, it will, in the vast majority of cases, happen. On the other hand, an unfertilized ovum will not become an embryo unless someone intervenes deliberately to make it happen. Without such intervention in the "normal" course of events, an ovum is a mere bit of protoplasm of very brief life expectancy. If we lived in a world in which virtually every biologically capable human female became pregnant once a year throughout her entire fertile period of life, then we would regard fertilization as something that happens to every ovum in "the natural course of events." Perhaps we would regard every unfertilized ovum, in such a world, as a potential person even possessed of rights corresponding to its future interests. It would perhaps make conceptual if not moral sense in such a world to regard deliberate nonfertilization as a kind of homicide.

It is important to notice, in summary, that words like *important*, *easy*, and *normal* have sense only in relation to human experiences, purposes, and techniques. As the latter change, so will our notions of what is important, difficult, and usual, and so will the concept of potentiality, or our application of it. If our purposes, understanding, and techniques continue to change in indicated directions, we may even one day come to think of inanimate things as possessed of "potential interests." In any case, we can expect the concept of a right to shift its logical boundaries with changes in our practical experience.

POTENTIALITY IN THE ABORTION DISCUSSION

FRANCIS C. WADE

THE STRENGTH of the anti-abortion argument consists in the contention that the fetus is treated as a human being because of its potentiality to become an adult rational human. Thus the proper place to attack this argument is on the issue of potentiality. H. Tristram Engelhardt, Jr., has recently done so. He argued that potentiality is no more than a promise, not an actuality, and that consequently we should make a clear distinction between the actual "human being" (animal) and actual personal being (rational) in the development from conception to death.[1] I shall try to show, first that there is another understanding of potentiality that is equally as reasonable as his; and, second, that his argument by no means supplies "a rational solution to the question of the status of the fetus."[2]

I

Engelhardt is correct in thinking that potentiality implies continuity. The central purpose of the Aristotelian notion of potency is to explain continuity, both in becoming (one being acquires a new characteristic) and in generation-corruption (where one being is turned into another kind of being). If one denies continuity in change, he will have little use for potentiality, at least little use for the Aristotelian types. And there are types that should not be conflated: one to account for continuity in becoming and generation, another to account for continuity of a being going from not acting to acting. The first type, where something happens to a being, is called passive potency; the second type, where a being itself actively does something, is predictably called active potency.

Our interest does not hit directly on passive potency, though some important things about it need to be mentioned. Take the ex-

---

[1] "The Ontology of Abortion," *Ethics* 84, April 1974, pp. 217–234.
[2] *Op. cit.*, p. 218.

ample of a pale-skinned man becoming sun-tanned. Since the man does not cause his own tan but the sunlight does, this is a case of passive potency[3] to become tanned. Two things are significant here. One, that it is the man who was not tanned that becomes tanned. We are tempted to say that it is the same man who was not and now is tan, but then we would seem to be denying that he became at all, since if he is the same, how did he become what he was not? Now passive potency, the ability to *receive* a modification, makes it possible to talk sensibly about a thing becoming. Since the pale-skinned man has the passive potency to become tanned (by the sun), it is precisely this potency that is actuated by the sun. Then we can say that the man who was potentially tanned became actually tanned. That is, we say what the facts require, that the tanned man is both the same (man) and different (in quality) from the pale-skinned man. It was *his* potency that was actualized—the sameness factor; also it is the *actualization* of his potency—the difference factor.

The second point to notice is that one cannot say of passive potency that the subject possesses the quality it can receive. Potentially tanned skin is actually pale and is not tanned. In order to be potentially tanned the man must in fact be not-tanned. And to say that a man is potentially tanned is to say that *now* he is not tanned, though he can be. He can be, of course, provided some active outsider (sun rays, lamp rays, tanning substance) makes him go from what he was not to what he will be. Consequently we can think and say that the pale man is potentially tanned, but there is no reason to think and say that the tan is *present* in the pale man. What is present is passive potency and this supposes that "being tanned" is not present. And any one who would argue that a fetus has passive potency to become personal would have no argument, on this score, against abortion.

The second type of potentiality is active. Here the issue is not about what a being (patient) can receive but about what a being (agent) can do. The problem here is not located in the fact of action, for this is actuality. The problem arises in agents that go from not acting to acting. Here there must be some continuity between two

[3] Since passive potency gets its meaning and intelligibility from what actualizes it, there is the temptation to say that it is nothing. It *is* nothing of actuality; yet it can be located in the data. Water has no passive potency for sun-tanning; man's skin has. That in the data is what is meant by passive potency: what the man's skin has and the water does not have.

states of the agent, that prior to action and that during action. Otherwise there is little sense in saying that the action is the agent's; yet if the action is not the agent's, then it is another's and the same problem will arise with this other, and with any other, to infinity.

For our present consideration, I shall call action what any agent does, whether it is a human being, an animal, or the non-living (acid eroding). Contemporary discussions of action tend to limit the notion to actions of man and even to intended human actions.[4] I propose to consider action at the more general level as what a being does when it does something. And since "what a being does" can apply both to the results of the agent's doing ("He wrote a letter") and to his doing something ("He wrote"), my present interest hits on the doing of the agent.

In the Aristotelian tradition, this doing was called the action of the agent.[5] Richard Taylor calls action "agency," to distinguish it from causality, though he limits "agency" to self-determined actions.[6] I prefer to call action, with Gerard Smith, "the causing of the cause,"[7] and apply it to any agent that produces any change in itself or another.

The agents—I am tempted to say all agents—of our experience go from not acting to acting. One might want to counter this statement by saying that living beings are always living and this is a kind of doing. This is true, however, only because living is a state composed of many actions, each of which is a case of going from not acting to acting, though at least some of these actions must be going on as long as the being is alive. If there were a being that was always in action in the *same* act, we would conclude that that being was eternal, at least looking forward to the future, because acting is

---

[4] See Myles Brand (ed.), *The Nature of Human Action* (New York: Scott, Foresman, and Company, 1970), especially Richard Taylor, "Thought and Purpose," pp. 267–278.

[5] See Aristotle, *Physics* III, 3, 202a12–22. St. Thomas, *In XI Metaphysicam*, lect. 9, n. 2312 and *Summa Theologiae*, II, II, 90, a.3. For a contemporary source, see Marianne T. Miller, "The Problem of Action in the Commentary of St. Thomas Aquinas on the *Physics* of Aristotle," *The Modern Schoolman* XXIII, March 1946, pp. 135–167 and May, 1946, pp. 200–226.

[6] *Metaphysics* (New York: Prentice-Hall, 1963), pp. 50–52.

[7] Gerard Smith-Lottie Kendzierski, *The Philosophy of Being* (New York: The Macmillan Company, 1961), pp. 91–95. I owe much to Smith's discussion of potentiality.

one thing that beings do and the constant same action would require constancy in being. We experience no such beings and, if our past experience is a norm of sorts, we do not expect to meet such on earth. In other words, the action we are considering is that of a being that goes from not acting to acting.

Any account of such action must fulfill two conditions. First, the action that is going to be will have to be the agent's action. Second, the agent cannot be acting before it is acting. Thus action must be preceded by what is not yet action if the second condition is to be fulfilled. Moreover, this not-yet-action must be in the line of action in order to be truly *its* preceder. At the same time, this preceder must properly belong to the agent in order to fulfill the first condition, i.e., that the act will be the agent's. Now the one notion that fits these two conditions is that of tendency. It is the agent's, for only agents have tendencies. It is in the line of action but is not itself action; it is only the thrust or drive towards action. A plant will grow if its environment permits this. Even before its growing is actuated the plant is prepared to grow. In a way, then, the plant "grows" before it grows, in the sense that it "tends" to grow. "Tendency, then, is the prefixation of an agent upon operation even before the agent actually operates."[8]

Note the dynamic character of tendency. "Tendency" does not describe the sort of action that will be done; it only describes the thrust that prescribes an action. The sort of action will be described by the name of the agent. That a fish egg does the fishy kind of growing is owing to the kind or sort (fish egg) of being it is. That it gets off dead-center into its growing is what "tendency" highlights. Or take the example of the genotype. This can be called the pattern or blueprint of what a being will become by its action. But calling it a blueprint leaves out its critical active factor. Blue-prints do not *do* anything. Genotypes both control what will be done and *get their action going*. Thus their dynamic aspect is the presence of tendency to get action going and keep it going. Without that they would not be what they are: the guarantee (as far as they are concerned) of the future of the being.

---

[8] G. Smith-L. Kendzierski, *op. cit.*, p. 104. The term "operation" is used in place of "action" to include both transient action (where agent and patient are distinct beings) and immanent action or operation (where there strictly is no patient, as in knowing).

On this showing, the agent's actions have two determinants: 1) the prefixation of the agent's nature or constitution which describes the *sort* of action it will do; 2) the prefixation of the agent by tendency which prescribes acting rather than not. These two factors constitute active potentiality. One without the other would never put any unity into our experience that agents go from not acting to acting. Without the agent's constitution, there would be no reason why the growing fish egg should result in a fish rather than a park bench or a pink elephant. Our experience is that agents act according to their constitution. Or without tendency, there is no reason why the agent should act rather than not, being equally indifferent to either alternative. In our experience beings do act and, when they do, their indifference has been replaced by something (tendency) in themselves.

The core of the notion of active potentiality is the tendency of the agent. Now if there are different types of tendencies, there are different types of active potentiality. Some tendencies are so firmly set in the constitution of a being that its action takes place in a completely determined way. Max Scheler[9] describes the "vital drive" of the plant world and the "instinctual behavior" of the animals as the result of tendencies more ordered to the good of the species than to that of the individuals. By comparison, he describes "habitual behavior" and "practical intelligence" as actions specified by the individuals' knowledge and experience. For our purposes we can call Scheler's first type the actions of an active *natural* potentiality and the second type, actions of an active *specifiable* potentiality. The basis of our distinction is the relation of the potentiality to its action. In the natural type, beyond its given constitution nothing else from the side of the agent is needed for action. In the specifiable type some action beyond its constitution is needed from the side of the agent for it to act. For example, the nutritive action of a plant is from a natural potentiality; that of an animal eating food is from a specifiable potentiality since the food open to its eating is what its senses discover.

There is no question here of the relative importance to a being of the two kinds of potentialities. I should think it obvious that the

[9] *Man's Place in Nature*, trans. Hans Meyerhoff, (New York: The Noonday Press, 1961), pp. 11–20.

more unspecified a being's potentiality, the more free it is to specify them. The only issue I have looked to is the question of action, which is what active potentialities are for. And in this light, natural potentialities are more active because they are more tied to their actions. The most that can be said for specifiable potentialities is that they may or may not issue in action. All they offer is a promise, as Engelhardt notes,[10] and promises that may never be redeemed. A child has a specifiable potentiality for learning geometry; no one could say that for this reason he is now a geometrician. Between the child now and his being a geometrician there are a series of acts of learning, which he may choose or refuse to perform, and which specify the quality of being a geometrician. If he does not perform these learning acts, he will never be a geometrician. Here "potential geometrician" means that he is not a geometrician—though he is not "not-one" in the same sense that a brick would be.

The situation is different, however, when there is question of an active natural potentiality. Here there is not a matter of promise only but of guarantee insofar as the agent is concerned. Agents may not control their environment and, where they cannot, their actions may be restricted and even rendered ineffective by surrounding circumstances. But they are made to act and will act to their full capacity *insofar* as they can. Between natural potentialities and their action there is nothing needed except usable matter and this latter is from the side of the patient, not the agent. The agent's constitution is ready and prepared to act when conditions permit. This will of itself, supposing usable matter, develop all that is needed to become what it will be. A plant develops its roots and leaves and branches in its process of living, just as the animal fetus develops senses to be used later. However one accounts for this process, no one would say that the plants and animals in fact do not do their own self-developing from resources in their constitution.

Now how are we to talk about the leaves and branches of a seedling? Are they present or not? As full grown and even small branches they are not present. As that which will certainly become branches, if certain conditions obtain, they are already present. They are present in their active natural potentialities. What does this mean? Clearly a seedling does not *look* as if it has branches.

[10] *Op. cit.*, p. 224.

Were a potentiality to look like its action or the result of its action, it would not be a potentiality but an accomplished fact. So to apply the criterion of looks here is a kind of category mistake. An author, for example, has a plan of a book in his head long before he gets it to the stage where it can be looked at. The only issue here is whether the future is set and fixed in the active potentiality. Where the future is prescribed, then it is present in that prescription. The genotype is actually in the present its potential future because its constitutional prescription in the present will control and guarantee the future.

What has been said so far may be summarized in this way. The potentiality of the fetus to become an adult is not a passive potency, which is neutral to the future; nor a specifiable active potentiality, which is a very "iffy" promise; but is an active natural potentiality or tendency, which is a guarantee of the future as far as the agent is concerned. We are ready now to turn to Engelhardt's argument.

II

The thrust of Engelhardt's defense of abortion is to distinguish "human being" from "personal being." Then he can, in the first sentence of his article, say: "Abortion as an ethical issue involves the sense in which the fetus is a person to whom we owe obligations."[11] His phrase "fetus as a person" is an arbitrary addition. It is a human being that has a title to life, and this sets up an obligation on the part of other men. That is why all sorts of humans, good or bad, black or white, sane or insane, asleep or awake, conscious or unconscious have been accorded the title to life that an animal does not have. Engelhardt does not agree with this position, and consequently he tries to reduce "human being" to "animal (biological) being." This move is most unsatisfactory. In the tradition of the West "human" has always been distinguished from "animal." For the biologist, the human fetus is precisely not an animal fetus. But since Engelhardt wants to distinguish the fetus from the personal, he in effect sets up a new, and I think unjustified, category: the animal, the *animal-human*, and the personal.

[11] *Ibid.*, p. 217.

He begins his argument by referring to the way we speak of the fetus: we call the fetus an "it," not a "he" or "she," we do not credit it with sexual or personal roles. "At most, the fetus is an animal with a great promise of becoming more than an animal. . . . Yet descriptions of the fetus in frankly personal fashion would have to be appropriate if the fetus were considered a person."[12] For the moment I shall put off the discussion of the notion of person and how it is predicated of the fetus in order to see if our language does not at times deal with a "great promise" as if it were in the present. Take the case of high-yield corn.[13] The seed the farmer buys is just kernels of corn. These kernels, however, have the active potentiality to produce more corn per acre than ordinary strains of corn. And we, therefore, name this corn by its potentiality and farmers buy it as if it possessed its own future in the present. Were its future not guaranteed, the farmer would have a case for saying that he was swindled and could demand his money back. His point would be that the corn did not at the moment he bought it have the future it was said to have. This example seems to show that we do apply future predicates to present things when there is question of active natural potentialities.

---

[12] *Ibid.*, p. 220. It is interesting to note that Engelhardt in this part of his paper requires a fetus to show personal and sexual actions yet in the latter part of his article (p. 230) he is willing to let social roles (requiring no personal action of the infant) be the norm for presence of the person in the new-born baby. That is, he shifts away from what he calls a "stringent definition" of the human person to keep from advocating infanticide. I would do the same were I in his shoes, but I would also begin to suspect I had the wrong shoes on. Paul Ramsey ("Reference Points in Deciding About Abortion," in J. T. Noonan, ed., *The Morality of Abortion* (Cambridge: Harvard University Press, 1970), pp. 40–100) has argued that any satisfactory argument for abortion would have to exclude infanticide in the same sort of cases (p. 86). Though Engelhardt makes no reference to Ramsey's position, he is trying to meet this objection. He has no sympathy with Michael Tooley's position ("Abortion and Infanticide," *Philosophy and Public Affairs* 2, Fall 1972, pp. 37–65) that infanticide should be in the same category as abortion, since a baby is not strictly a person and has no right to life, as Tooley understands right to life (p. 46).

[13] I do not think that a kernel of corn is like the genotype. To make a legitimate comparison one would have to take the kernel at the moment it sprouts toward a corn stalk. John Finnis ("The Rights and Wrongs of Abortion," *Philosophy and Public Affairs* 2, Winter 1973, p. 144) makes a similar point regarding an acorn in comparison to a fetus, when criticizing the argument of Judith Jarvis Thomson ("A Defense of Abortion," *Philosophy and Public Affairs* 1, Fall 1971, pp. 47–66).

But we need to go beyond the fact of our usage of language to get at the data that justify such usage. The situation is not this: tendency has a value proper to it; action or operation has a further and different value proper to it. The *only* value a natural tendency has is its character as guaranteeing action. Try to conceive a tendency to nothing. What would it be? It certainly would not be a tendency, for there would be no action for it to issue in. Thus tendency has no value (or intelligibility) independent of its action-orientation. By the same token, operation has no value of its own independent of tendency because it has no being other than tendency expressing itself. That is all operation is: the completion or fulfillment of tendency. What value is "new" in operation is the flowering of tendency which completes itself by achieving its term. The novelty here is that of a being perfecting itself, not that of a plain Jane whose "beauty" comes from a cosmetic jar.

No doubt, as Engelhardt points out, the notion of potentiality, whether passive or active, does imply some doctrine about substance. All admit that the meaning of substance is a highly argued and complex doctrine; however, this fact does mean at least that one can find respectable philosophical company on either side of the question. Yet I fail to see how Engelhardt, who wants to deny one substance throughout man's growth, thinks he finds confirmation of his position from either Locke or Kant. Though Locke had no idea of what *substance in general* is, he was quite clear about affirming there are substances. In his correspondence with Bishop Skillingfleet he says: "To which I beg leave to say, that I ground not the being, but the idea of substance, on our accustoming ourselves to suppose some substratum; for it is of the idea alone that I speak there, and not on the being of substance: I cannot be supposed to question or doubt of the being of the substance, till I can question my own being."[14] As for Kant, substance is indeed a mental category, but one nevertheless that is required for the unity of experience. I take this to mean that in any case we must think with substance, if we are

[14] *The Works of Locke*, New Corrected Edition, X vols., (London: Thomas Hegg, 1823) Vol. IV, p. 18. Locke even holds that there are "thinking" substances: "If by spiritual substance your lordship means a thinking substance, I must dissent from your lordship, and say, that we can have certainty, upon my principles, that there is a spiritual substance in us" (p. 37).

going to think. And Engelhardt is concerned with thinking about abortion. Were he to rely on the Kantian doctrine of substance, would it make any difference in this *thought* whether there was a substance in nature or not?

But his central point is that we should distinguish two distinct stages in the development of man: the first stage, that of "human being," is the achieving of biological qualities; the second stage, that of personal being, is the actuality of one who can participate in social roles. He contends, as being more consonant with the facts, that "it is easier to construe the situation as a development from biological properties to personal properties with a consequent essential and substantial change in the significance of the bearer of the properties."[15] He finds a hint for his position in Aristotle and St. Thomas,[16] both of whom for biological reasons thought the embryo had a three-stage development, from vegetative life to sentient life to rational life. They thought that each of the three stages was the result of substantial change in which the former being was corrupted and the subsequent generated. For biological reasons Engelhardt wants to drop the first stage (vegetative) and keep the crucial distinction between animal and personal life. What he wants to question is: "Whether there is substantial continuity from conception to death."[17] Owing to Engelhardt's understanding of substance—his reference to Locke inclines me to say that for him substance is simply the properties together—either of two ontological situations could obtain in human ontogeny. First, the actual biological properties are distinct from the actual personal properties and therefore the bearers are different kinds of beings. Second, the same facts can be put into a developmental framework, so that the being would develop to one stage of actualization (animal being) and then at some point go beyond this first actualization to another (personal being) differing in kind and significance. The latter position is, as far as I can see, what Engelhardt holds.[18] Clearly his is a

[15] *Op. cit.*, p. 225. I shall have occasion to quote this text again (in footnote 18) with emphasis added.

[16] St. Thomas, *Summa Theologiae* I, 118, a.2, and Aristotle, *De Generatione Animalium* 2, 3, 736a.

[17] *Op. cit.*, p. 223.

[18] He says: ". . . that human ontogeny begins with the body as a 'what' or, at most a 'who' in the sense that an animal is a who, which then *because of development* of new properties, becomes a who in the personal

position that any one holding continuity of potentiality must face. The question, as I see it, is: Can active potentialities develop so that they become distinctly different potentialities?

One might introduce the notion of abstract as opposed to concrete potentialities, as Engelhardt does. He argues that the presence of an intact, normally developed brain is a concrete potentiality for conscious thought. By comparison, a fetus would have only an abstract and unaccomplished potentiality.[19] I would prefer to speak of these facts as remote and proximate potentialities, because I do not think that any active potentiality can be abstract. My reason is that active potentialities as tendencies are toward action and action cannot be abstract, since it produces existents. Aside, however, from the names used, there is a recognizable difference between remote and proximate potentialities. A fetus has no proximate potentiality to see when it has no eyes and no light to see by. It has at most a remote potentiality to vision. But do not read this "at most" as being a matter of lacking something. It has all it needs to build up in the dark eyes to see with in the light. Thus its remote potentiality is precisely the source of acquiring the proximate potentiality (functioning eyes) to see with. This relationship of proximate to remote can be stated in terms of specification of the remote by the proximate. But this in a sense leaves out the dynamic factors in potentiality. Taking this dynamism into consideration, it is more proper to say that the proximate potentiality is already set in the remote tendency. This way of speaking more accurately states why the fetus does in fact build up light-using eyes in the dark and why the neonate has a brain to develop conscious life. The remote tendency is the source of the drive and the determiner of any of its specifications; and a proximate potentiality is only a modification of the ever-present and active remote, fundamental potentiality.[20]

---

sense" (*Ibid.*, p. 223 italics mine). Also, the text quoted above: ". . . it is easier to construe the situation as development *from* biological properties *to* personal properties with a consequent essential and substantial change in the significance of the bearer of the properties" (p. 225, italics mine).

[19] *Ibid.*, p. 222.

[20] In this discussion it is important to recall that we are now talking of active potentialities (tendencies) and not about passive potencies. In the case of passive potencies the remote is less significant than the proximate. Ore can be made into a car, but as long as it is ore in the ground, it cannot be made into cars. With active potentialities, however, the remote is the more significant, since it controls what the being will become.

The distinction used above, between natural and specifiable tendencies, is not the same as remote and proximate, both of which can be natural tendencies, as in the fetus developing and using eyes. Both sets of tendencies, however, are related as the developing and the developed. Specifiable tendencies have, of course, to specify something. What they specify is a natural tendency. In the example used above, that of the animal's tendency to eat being specified by his sense of knowledge to eat this or that food, the specifiable tendency is not something extraneous to the being's constitution, i.e., to the natural tendency of the dog; rather it is a "free" completion of what the constitution is constructed to do.[21]

The central question is: Can a being have a new set of active potentialities—not proximate or specifiable ones—that it did not have before? Since such potentialities are part of the constitution of a being, this means that there would have to be a new being present. Thus Engelhardt maintains that the personal being is a new being, one not continuous with the "human" being that the fetus is. I find this position most unlikely. Three sets of facts militate against it.

First of all, there is no source for this new being. I presume that the creative act of God is not being called in here; certainly there is no evidence to warrant its introduction. Nor can the fetus be the source, since Engelhardt posits discontinuity between the fetus and the personal being. He suggests briefly[22] that the recognizably personal being may be a case of a qualitative change arising from progressive quantitative changes. How this could be *together with* discontinuity between fetus and person is a serious problem, seeing that new qualities come to what already is. Even worse, he will have to say that person is only a quality, an opinion that P. F. Strawson seems to have refuted.[23] The only source is other men. In fact, Engelhardt demands social roles—active as an adult and participative as an infant—in order for there to be an actual personal being.[24] Im-

[21] There is some development of active potentialities. They can, for instance, develop proficiency in acting by repeated actions. This in the Aristotelian tradition is called "habit," the steady, ready capability of acting well. This kind of development is not what Engelhardt had in mind.

[22] *Op. cit.*, p. 228.

[23] *Individuals* (London: Methuen and Co., 1959), pp. 99–102. Strawson appeals to usage: we say that "I" (person) *have* states of consciousness, just as we say that "I" (person) *have* corporeal characteristics. Qualities have nothing; they are had.

[24] *Op. cit.*, pp. 230–232.

portant as socialization may be to growth as person, I presume he is not saying that socialization *produces* or is the source of the person. My reason for the presumption: socialization cannot cause persons because it presupposes persons are already present. Where there is no person, the imposition of "social" relationships can produce only domestication, as with animals.[25] Consequently I find no adequate cause for this new type of being, his "personal being."

The second set of facts concerns the obvious biological continuity between the genotype and the adult man. It solves nothing to say: "Purely biological facts, as such, have no implications concerning psychological or personal reality."[26] The only truth this statement has depends on its being taken in the restrictive sense where it applies only to knowledge and not to things. When applied to things that biological statements deal with, it does not hold up. Engelhardt himself argues that developed brains (a biological fact) are necessary (imply concrete potentiality) for conscious life.[27] Moreover, the difference between a kitten and an infant I take to be a biological difference, yet this fact determines (implicates) the morality of my dealings with the two beings: drowning a kitten is not morally the same as drowning an infant.

The third set of facts that seem to exclude discontinuity in being is the role which the body, prepared basically in the fetal stage, plays in conscious life. Maurice Merleau-Ponty has shown that the "body is our medium for having a world."[28] The body provides

---

[25] Michael Landmann applies this same notion to man as a historical being. "As a cultural being he is a historical being too. And this also in a double sense: he both has power over and is dependent on history, he determines history and is determined by it" (*Philosophical Anthropology*, trans. by David J. Parent, (Philadelphia: Westminster Press, 1974) p. 221). Notice that man must *first* determine history before it can determine him. The same is true of social relationships. It is *because* the infant is what it is that the parents can act as they do in socializing him.

[26] *Op. cit.*, p. 226. He returns to this point on page 230, note 56: "I.e., purely biological observations, in that they prescind from any other notes of signification, cannot imply anything of nonbiological significance such as ethical obligations." Michael Tooley ("Abortion and Infanticide," *Philosophy and Public Affairs* 2, Fall 1972) uses a similar argument: "Difference in species is not per se a morally relevant difference" (p. 51). It is not the *difference* in species that sets up distinct moral relations but it is membership in Homo Sapiens that makes a being a man and his being a member of this species *is* morally relevant.

[27] *Ibid.*, p. 221.

[28] *Phenomenology of Perception*, trans. by Colin Smith, (London: Routledge and Kegan Paul, 1962), p. 146.

a space that is prior to conscious knowledge of space. "I am not in space and time, nor do I conceive space and time; I belong to them, my body combines with them and includes them."[29] Subtending conscious life, the body supplies "an 'intentional arc' which projects round about us our past, our future, our human setting, our physical, ideological and moral situation, or rather which results in our being situated in all these respects. It is this intentional arc which brings about the unity of the senses, of intelligence, of sensibility and motility."[30] J. P. Sartre also gives the body a major role in conscious life: "Being-for-itself must be wholly body and it must be wholly consciousness; it cannot be *united* with a body."[31] And, speaking from an entirely different philosophical tradition, John N. Findlay notes a similar dependence of our conscious life on bodily functions: "But our subservience to our cellular and molecular henchmen and the mechanical chains in which they are ordered arguably go much further. They not only present us with a doctored and slanted picture of the environment, and not only carry out our executive decisions, but, like an intrusive bureaucracy, take part in the proceedings of the council chamber and throughout channel its deliberations and decisions."[32] Such interaction and dependence of the conscious (personal) and bodily (animal) seems to argue for a continuity of being between the fetus which prepares a body of this special sort and the adult who lives his conscious life through this body prepared by the fetus.

As a confirming argument for his position that the man-animal is distinct from the man-rational, Engelhardt finds a similar distinction at the other end of life, that between death of the person (brain-death) and biological life which continues some time after brain-death.[33] Clearly for him we can and should distinguish between the personal being and the biological being at the beginning of life just as we do at the end. His confirming reason is no stronger than his supposition: that death is an event. Death could just as well be a process—or better the winding down of a process. And

[29] *Op. cit.*, p. 140.

[30] *Op. cit.*, p. 136.

[31] *Being and Nothingness*, trans. by Hazel E. Barnes, (New York: Philosophical Library, 1956), p. 305, italics his.

[32] *Psyche and Cerebrum* (Milwaukee: Marquette University Press, 1972), p. 21.

[33] *Op. cit.*, p. 222.

where, *within* a process, can one say with certainty that up to this point you have X and not Y and beyond this point you have Y that is other than X?

The same difficulty militates against his main argument. His notion of person requires that to be a person means to take personal predicates (having self-conscious actions) and before that point there is no person. But there are good reasons for thinking that a person is a term that applies to the upper reaches of a process, as Louis Dupré argues. "If personhood consists of self-determination, it comprehends at once an actual achievement and the nature which provides the potential for this achievement. In an essentially dynamic entity, the potential forms a single reality with the actual. At the same time, since a dynamic entity can only gradually be realized, the degree of actuality enters into the very definition of personhood."[34] Dupré agrees that fetuses are not persons because this term applies only to an advanced stage of actuality, that of having self-determining actions. But he excludes the conclusion that personhood demands a new being, since for him actuality is the perfection of a potentiality which is present in its actualization. In other words, personhood is an important difference but it does not require a different being; rather it requires the same being more actualized.

There is always a problem in defining things by their functions. When such things are not functioning, how should we speak of them? The older definition of man as rational animal was not taken functionally. You would have to leave out all of the early stages of man, much of the final stages, and lots of the middle stages when functioning reason is not noticeable. The same trouble arises with person if you define it functionally, as Engelhardt sees, when he must, against his own argument, call babies persons, not because of any action of their own—as his definition of person demands—but owing to the social roles given them by society.[35] Insisting on functions in the name of clarity may lose more than it gains.

---

[34] "Philosophical Considerations," *Beginning of Personhood*, a Symposium edited by Donald G. McCarthy (Houston: The Institute of Religion and Human Development, 1973), p. 23. See also his "New Approach to the Abortion Problem," *Theological Studies*, Vol. 34, September 1973, pp. 484–485.

[35] *Op. cit.*, pp. 230–231.

Since the issue, as Engelhardt sees it, does hit on the being of the fetus and/or the person, it would make sense to go beyond functions to the being in question. Boethius (480–524 A.D.), one of the founders of medieval thought, used this ontological definition of a person: "the individual supposit of a rational nature."[36] Read "supposit" to mean "substance." Then he is saying that person is the subject of existence (that is, substance) of the kind proper to a rational being. Now if we read "rational" to be a kind of thinking that is achieved rather than given, i.e., thinking that goes from not thinking to thinking, then we mean that a person does not begin with thinking; a person begins with not thinking and then thinks. A person needs, therefore, some contact with being, some *thing* to think about. Since human persons exist in this material world, this world will have to supply the things that persons must begin with. This means that in order to think a person must have contact points (senses and brain) with the material world. But a brain and senses are only structured by vegetative powers that build them up and keep them in repair. Hence a person's need for a body. On this view a rational person is a being that builds up a body and brain and senses in order to carry on acts of self-conscious knowing and self-determination, i.e., the person's own fully intellectual life. Rather than saying that such a being is an animal with reason added, it would be better to say that a human person is a "hairy spirit."[37]

What we have just said may be stated in terms of natural active potentialities. Earlier we said that the only way two sets of natural tendencies could constitute one being was that one could be further specified by another. In the former discussion and in the example used—a dog's tendency to eat being specified by using his senses—the obvious implication was that the biological tendencies were later specified by the conscious tendencies. Now, I would like to suggest an opposite view, namely, that the natural tendency to think and to choose is basic to the being of the fetus, and the biological tendencies (the ones most clearly active in the genotype) are only specifications of the radical tendency to become a thinking being. Only by the specification of a body and a brain can this fetus ever become the actually thinking being its nature tends to. Consequently, it

[36] *De Persona et Natura*, Ch. 3, PL. 64; 1345.

[37] This phrase was the last line of a Goliardic poem written by G. Smith. In Latin it goes: "*Spiritus pilosus*."

is not metaphorical to say that the fetus is in this sense personal: its whole natural thrust is to become a functioning person. And this is true of all the stages of its existence and continues even after it has partially attained personhood (as is the case with me and you), constantly striving to become more fully a person. Aristotle stated it this way: "All men by nature desire to know."[38]

The view of man that I have just stated, not argued, is not original with me. It is, I think, the view of man that St. Thomas developed. Anton C. Pegis attributes it to St. Thomas: "Such briefly and in outline, is the last line of defense that St. Thomas would adopt. The answer to the unity of man's nature lies in the soul, in the soul it lies in the intellect, and in the intellect it lies in the fact that, by itself, the human intellect is not the complete intellectual power of the intellectual substance that the soul is. Hence arises the notion of an intellect incarnated in the senses in order to be adequately an intellect; hence also the notion of soul and body as forming together an intellectual substance, wholly intellectual, but of diminished intellectuality."[39]

By way of conclusion it should be noted that no positions have been advanced that would, of themselves, either justify or exclude abortion, since moral solutions include a balancing of rights. The sole issue was that of potentiality of the fetus. One conclusion seems justified: there is a solid alternative to Engelhardt's view on potentiality. A second conclusion, following from the first, is: Engelhardt has not produced "rational grounds for deciding the status of the fetus and for thus allowing a positive stance with regard to the reform of the abortion laws."[40] B. A. Brody had argued that legal questions "rapidly turn into a discussion of the status of the fetus and of whether destroying the fetus constitutes the taking of human life. Since these latter questions seem difficult, if not impossible, to resolve upon rational grounds, frustration results."[41] Engelhardt proposed to supply rational grounds for deciding the status of the fetus and indirectly to solve the legal question. As far as I can see, he has not done so.

Marquette University

[38] *Metaphysics* I, 1, 908a 23.

[39] "St. Thomas and the Unity of Man," in J. A. McWilliams (ed.), *Progress in Philosophy* (Milwaukee: Bruce Publishing Company, 1955), p. 171.

[40] *Op. cit.*, pp. 218–219.

[41] "Abortion and the Law," *The Journal of Philosophy* LXVII, June 17, 1971, p. 357.

Children's Rights: A Test-Case for Theories of Right

BY NEIL MACCORMICK, EDINBURGH

I am not confident that I could give, far less justify, a comprehensive list of the rights which children have, but I feel no unease in saying that they do have rights. I don't have a theory of children's rights, but I do at least have a theory of rights which can make sense of saying that children have them. Just because the concept of 'children's rights' is difficult to square with some theories of what it is for anyone to have a right, children's rights are a good test case for theories of rights in general. First things first. Let us be clear that it makes sense to ascribe rights to children at all before we go on to work out substantive theories as to the rights they should be accorded. The former is what will be made clear in this paper.

In broad and general terms there are two competing theories as to the nature of rights[1]: the theory which says that having a right of some kind is to do with the legal or moral recognition of some individual's choice as being preeminent over the will of others as to a given subject matter in a given relationship; and the other theory which says that having a right is having one's interests protected in certain ways by the imposition of (legal or moral) normative constraints on the acts and activities of other people with respect to the object of one's interests. Between various manifestations of the will theory and the interest theory there has been a long running, but inconclusive, series of test matches. Today we have a test case, in the light of which I shall show, to my own entire satisfaction, the untenability of all forms of will theory, in place of which I shall suggest as an alternative a theory more along the lines of traditional interest theories.

Let me start from what seems to me a simple and barely contestable assertion: at least from birth, every child has a right to be nurtured, cared for, and, if possible, loved, until such time as he or she is capable of caring for himself or herself. When I say that, I intend to speak in the first instance of a moral right. I should regard it as a plain case of moral blindness if anyone failed to recognise that every child has that right. Certainly, it has not been a universally recognised legal right

[1] See, e.g., G. W. Paton, *A Text-book of Jurisprudence*, 4th ed., Oxford 1972, ed. by G. W. Paton and D. P. Derham, at pp. 285–290, for a review of this opposition of theories.

20 ARSP (Archiv für Rechts- und Sozialphilosophie), Bd. LXII/3 (1976)

– think of the law of Republican Rome – but to my way of thinking that only means that some or perhaps many legal systems have been morally deficient, which is scarcely a startling observation. (As it happens, our legal systems do at present grant the right in question, so for us, now, it is a legal as well as a moral right.)

There are, however, morally acute and clear-sighted people who would deny not the substantive moral tenet involved in ascribing that right to all children, but the appropriateness of expressing the moral tenet through the linguistic device of the noun 'a right'. 'Say, if you will, that morality demands, or the law demands, that all children be nurtured, cared for, and, if possible, loved, but do not say they have a right to such treatment, for so to use the term right is to obfuscate.'

That objection is grounded in the will theory of rights. It could be expanded, along lines laid down by H. L. A. HART[2], in some such terms as follow: Rights (understand 'claim-rights', 'rights of recipience')[3] presuppose duties as their correlative. Duties exist when there exist legal or social rules of a particular kind, in virtue of which individuals in certain circumstances are required to act or abstain from acting in certain ways. For any individual whose circumstances are those specified in such a rule, it is true to say that he has a duty to act or abstain from acting as specified.

Of the rules which impose duties, some provide that the performance by a duty bearer of the required act (or abstention) is to be conditional on some other person's choice, either in the sense that it is to be performed only if and when he so requests, or in the sense that that other person can waive the requirement, and, if he does, the act (or abstention) need not be performed. When A's being required to do his duty is

[2] See H. L. A. Hart, "Definition and Theory in Jurisprudence", *L.Q.R.* 70 (1954), p. 37, esp. at p. 49; "Are there Any Natural Rights", repr. in *Political Philosophy*, ed. A. M. Quinton, Oxford 1968, esp. at p. 58, where it is said that to ascribe rights to babies or animals is perhaps to "make an idle use of the expression 'a right'"; "Bentham on Legal Rights", in *Oxford Essays in Jurisprudence (2nd series)*, ed. A. W. B. Simpson, Oxford 1973. For another recent example of an essentially similar argument, see W. J. Kamba, "Legal Theory and Hohfeld's Analysis of a Legal Right", *Juridical Review*, 1974, pp. 249–262.

[3] On terminology, see W. N. Hohfeld, *Fundamental Legal Conceptions*, New Haven 1919, third reprint 1964; for the expression "rights of recipience" see D. D. Raphael, *Problems of Political Philosophy*, London 1970, pp. 68–71.

in either sense left in B's discretion, B may properly be said to have a right against A, a right that A act or abstain in the manner contemplated in the rule. On this view, a legal or moral right is equivalent to a legal or moral power of waiver or enforcement of duties; at any rate, rights exist only when people have such normative power over duties of others. (Although this analysis applies only to 'claim-rights' in the HOHFELD scheme, the theory suggests that what is common to all types of right is that they make the choice, or the will, of the right holder paramount in a given relationship.)

If that view is accepted as yielding a satisfactory recommendation as to the usage of the noun 'a right', then it must indeed be inept to ascribe to children the right to care, nurture and love. A baby cannot in fact, cannot in morals, and cannot in law relieve his or her parents[4] of their duty towards him or her in those matters.

But adherents of the 'will theory' have a standard tactic for avoiding the awkward example of children. They say that it is sufficient if either B or some other person C acting on B's behalf has the relevant powers over A's duty in respect of B.

For the case we are considering, the tactic is unemployable. Standardly, in the case of children, the party who can in legal (or indeed in social) matters act on a child's behalf is his or her parent or guardian. But it is at least possible to imagine a legal system in which a parent's duty to care for and nurture his or her own child is neither subject to the parent's issuing a self-directed request on the child's behalf nor indeed to any possibility of waiver by the parent as the child's representative. That is so whether or not the law accords to the parent powers of waiver or enforcement over duties owed to the child by third parties. What is more, speaking morally, there seems to be no reason whatever to suppose that the child or anyone acting on the child's behalf should be permitted or empowered to waive the parental duty or in any sense to acquiesce in its non-performance.

It might be said that the contemporary British legal systems do give just that power to certain public officials, in that procedures exist where-

[4] Here, and elsewhere, I assume for the sake of simplicity, that the duty towards children is a duty primarily owed by the 'natural parents'. But, as is pointed out later, the opinion that children have the right in question does not necessarily entail the opinion that it is the *parents* who bear the correlative duty. Throughout, for the sake of simplicity, I ignore questions of adoption, legitimacy, etc.

by in appropriate circumstances children may be removed from their parents' care and transferred to the care of other persons in pursuance of a judicial order. Short of that, too, welfare officers acting in the interests of children have power in various ways to 'keep up to the mark' parents whose performance of their parental duties is in some degree deficient.

One who rejects the 'will theory', as I do, can say, as I say, that such legal provisions are desirable because they protect and further the rights of children. To regard such powers as constitutive of rights (as the will theory does), is to foreclose the possibility of justifying them on the ground that they do protect rights which might otherwise be insecure, and thus in my submission to confuse the substantive right with ancillary remedial provisions. It is unduly anglo-centric to erect the brocard *ubi remedium ibi ius* into an analytic truth.

In any event, that example of those legal provisions would not serve to save the theory that powers of waiver or enforcement of duties are essentially constitutive of 'rights', even if it were proferred in its defence. When a child is taken by law out of the tutelage of its parents and put into the care of some other person, the measure is not conceived as being a waiver of the parent's duty – the parent may indeed be penalised for the acts of neglect which justify the order. The point is that in the interests of the child, fulfilment of the functions of care and nurture especially in infancy is so fundamentally important that someone else is appointed to undertake their fulfilment as a duty on the ground that the parent is temporarily or permanently unable or unwilling to do so. It is a case of substituted performance of a duty which is so important in the child's interest that penal or compensatory remedies for its breach are inadequate. Substituted performance is no waiver. The function is not one of 'letting off' the parent, rather it is one of protecting the child. In consequence, the transfer of care is not deemed to release the parent from the duty in the sense of exempting him or her from the possibility of penalties for its breach.

As for enforcement provisions which fall short of transferring care of the child, these lack the discretionary character essential to the 'will theory'; it is not the case that the child or someone deemed to be acting on the child's behalf has an option of enforcing the duty of care and nurture, which option may or may not be exercised according to arbitrary choice. If the child needs greater care than is being provided, there is not discretion to be exercised; that greater care must be provided.

Of course, there is discretion in judging any question of 'need', but it is discretion of a kind not contemplated by the will theory.

We are put, as lawyers say, to our election. Either we abstain from ascribing to children a right to care and nurture, or we abandon the will theory. For my part, I have no inhibitions about abandoning the latter. It causes me no conceptual shock or mental cramp to say that children have that right. What is more, I will aver that it is *because* children have that right that it is good that legal provisions should be made in the first instance to encourage and assist parents to fulfil their duty to care and nurture, and secondarily to provide for its performance by alternative foster parents when natural parents are disqualified by death, incapacity, or wilful and persistent neglect. *Ubi ius, ibi remedium.* So far from its being the case that the remedial provision is constitutive of the right, the fact is rather that recognition of the right justifies the imposition of the remedial provision.

Is this merely a trivial issue of linguistic preferences? Only in part, and that a small part. I think that it is morally important that we should recognise the moral importance and the significance of moral rights, and legally useful to have a clear conception of legal right which recognises the straightforwardly analogical relationship between legal and moral rights. (That they are analogical in form does not, of course, mean that they are identical in content.) In so saying, I do of course court BENTHAM's posthumous condemnation, if not, in his case, subhumous rotation. In his view, the locution 'a moral right' was either a devious way of talking about what ought to be done, an obscure way of asserting that the law ought to confer certain rights, or just plain nonsense[5].

I counter-claim that there is a significant difference between asserting that every child ought to be cared for, nurtured and, if possible, loved, and asserting that every child has a right to care, nurture and love. One way of showing the difference is to show that there are statements which could intelligibly be advanced as justifications of the former proposition but which could not be intelligibly be advanced in justification of the latter. For example, along the lines of SWIFT's *Modest Proposal*, one could suggest as a reason why children ought to be cared for, nurtured, and loved, that that would be the best way of getting them

[5] See, e.g., *Bentham's Works*, ed. Bowring, 1843, vol. II, pp. 501 f., vol. III, pp. 221 f.

to grow into plump and contented creatures fit to enhance the national diet. Or again, one could argue that a healthy society requires healthy and well nurtured children who will grow into contented and well adjusted adults who will contribute to the G.N.P. and not be a charge on the welfare facilities or the prison service. (KEITH JOSEPH has recently adumbrated the latter argument, if I understood him rightly.)

Of course only one of these is a moral, or indeed a serious, argument. But neither is an argument which could be used directly to justify the proposition that children have a right to care, nurture and love. Why not? Because both advance reasons for giving children care, nurture and affection solely on the ground that their well-being is a fit means to an ulterior end. I do not say that there can be no moral argument that certain beings ought to be treated in a certain way in order to achieve some end other than their well being. I do say that such arguments are necessarily inept in justifying the ascription to them of a right to that treatment. Consider the oddity of saying that turkeys have a right to be well fed in order to be fat for the Christmas table, or of saying that children have a right to care and nurture lest they become a charge on the taxpayer. It may not have escaped notice that the same oddity would attach to saying that children have a right to be cared for because that is a way of maximising general utility. So it may be no wonder that BENTHAM was so dismissive of the notion of moral rights. But it would be a wonder if he were believed.

To argue, on the other hand, that each and every child is a being whose needs and capacities command our respect, so that denial to any child of the wherewithal to meet his or her needs and to develop his or her capacities would be wrong in itself (at least in so far as it is physically possible to provide the wherewithal), and would be wrong regardless of the ulterior disadvantages or advantages to anyone else — so to argue, would be to put a case which is intelligible as a justification of the opinion that children have such rights. To generalise: the ascription of a right to some class of beings seems to require the following presuppositions: for the class in question (in our case, children) there is some act or omission (in our case, the acts and omissions involved in care, nurture and love) performance of which in the case of each and every member of the class will satisfy, protect, or advance some need, interest or desire of each such individual; and secondly: satisfaction of that need, interest or desire is of such importance that it would be wrong to deny it to any such individual regardless of ulterior advantages in so doing. Of course, the second of these conditions is intrinsically contentious, and argument might rage inconclusively over the question whether denial of some form of treatment to every member of a given class would be wrong. But to observe that is to observe only what is obvious, that in relation to their substance, rights belong to the class of essentially contested concepts.

Even that generalised formulation is perhaps too specific, just because it unnecessarily begs substantive moral questions in tying an elucidation of the notion of 'having rights' solely to 'want-regarding' categories such as needs, interests and desires. This is the characteristic failing of the 'interest theory'. It is uncontroversial that satisfaction of needs, interests and desires is a part of 'the good' for individuals, but it is controversial whether it is exhaustive of and constitutive of the good. A formal account of rights can and should be neutral on that substantive moral question. So I shall generalise further and say this: to ascribe to all members of a class C a right to treatment T is to presuppose that T is, in all normal circumstances, a good for every member of C, and that T is a good of such importance that it would be wrong to deny it to or withhold it from any member of C. That as for moral rights: as for legal rights I should say this: when a right to T is conferred by law on all members of C, the law is envisaged as advancing the interests of each and every member of C on the supposition that T is a good for every member of C, and the law has the effect of making it legally wrongful to withhold T from any member of C.

What has been said may suggest that one cannot believe in the category 'moral rights' unless one accepts in some form the principle that sentient beings ought to be respected as ends in themselves. If that is so, I do not regret it. I am inclined to the view that a belief in respect for persons is indeed an essential precondition of a belief in moral rights. And I am also inclined to the view that respect for persons is both a fundamental and an ultimate moral principle[6].

Be that as it may, the above reflections have, I hope, indicated why the proposition that all children ought to be cared for, nurtured and loved is far from identical with the proposition that every child has a

[6] As it stands, this passage is open to the charge of begging at least one question; but I put it forward very tentatively, and would call in aid David Raphael's very persuasive Presidential Address to the Aristotelian Society (D. D. Raphael, "The Standard of Morals", *Proceedings of the Aristotelian Society*, vol. XCVI (1974–75), p. 1).

right to be treated so. It is indeed possible, and now possible to see why it is possible, to advance the latter proposition as a specific kind of justification for the former, but not (without more) *vice versa*. It is also trivially true that children's having that moral right can be advanced as a reason why they ought to be accorded the parallel legal right. That the one proposition can genuinely be adduced as a reason for adhering to the other, however, in itself indicates that BENTHAM was wrong in thinking them identical (or, rather, in thinking that the former was reducible to the latter so far as it made sense at all).

What I have said so far seems to entail at least the possibility that rights are or could be logically prior to duties. That may seem very shocking, but it is true. AUSTIN and HOHFELD might be scandalised, but I can appeal to law to mitigate the scandal, by showing that the law sometimes confers rights which are logically prior to duties. An interesting instance of such a right statutorily conferred upon children is to be found in section 2(1)(a) of the Succession (Scotland) Act 1964: "Subject to the following provisions of this Part of this Act, (*a*) where an intestate is survived by children, they shall have right to the whole of the intestate estate."

By virtue of that, whenever any person domiciled in Scotland dies having left no valid will, there automatically vests in his children (if any) a right to the whole of that part of his estate statutorily denominated 'the intestate estate'. At the moment of its vesting, the right is not a 'real right' involving ownership of the estate or any part of it. It is a right to receive, in due course, a proportionate share in the assets remaining in the executor's hands after satisfaction of prior claims. But note that at the moment at which the right vests there is as yet no executor to bear the correlative duty. The executor must be judicially confirmed or appointed in due course, and what is more, if the estate is solvent those who have beneficial rights in it are normally preferred to other parties in the appointment of an executor dative. So any child who is of sufficient age may, in virtue of the right conferred by the Act, have a resultant if defeasible right to be appointed as executor. His appointment as such will in turn result in his acquiring the duties of executor, including the duty of distributing the intestate estate to those (including himself) who have the right thereto in virtue of section 2.

The intelligibility of that statutory provision indicates that the vesting of rights may be both temporally and logically prior to the vesting of duties correlative thereto. Since that is intelligible, it cannot be an objection to the argument herein advanced that it contemplates the possibility of rights being logically prior to duties. On the other hand, it may be noted that the statute could not be intelligible if the will theory were correct.

It certainly does not seem to me in any way objectionable to say that it is *because* children have a right to care and nurture that parents have the duty to care for them. There might be other and different grounds (e.g. saving taxpayers' money) for imposing such a duty on parents or on whomsoever it may be imposed; but recognition of children's rights is one distinctive reason for doing so. I find it a much more peculiar view to suppose that parents' having the duty is a logical prerequisite of children's having the right; *a fortiori* if it is added that someone has to have discretion over its performance.

Surely there is much more sense in the opinion that it is because children have the right, and because their parents stand in a particular natural relationship to their own children, that it is the parents upon whom in the first instance the duty of care and nurture is incumbent. But only in the first instance; in default of parents (death, incapacity, fecklessness), the children's right remains and other means must be sought to fulfil it. That in modern societies the responsibility is deemed a state responsibility indicates only one possible solution to the problem.

There may be other cases in which we are much more certain that children have a right to something than we are certain about what is the right, or the best way of giving effect to it. That every child has a right to be educated to the limits of his or her abilities seems to me clear. But whose is the duty and the rightful power to provide it and to rule as to what constitutes a satisfactory education seems to me much less clear. The parents? The local authority? The central government? A church? The child? There can be heated dispute over the rival claims of all these, and more besides, even among those who are in no doubt about every child's right to have a proper education, indeed especially among those.

In the foregoing pages I have suggested that children's rights provide a test-case for rival theories about rights in general, and that the 'will theory' fails the test. What I have offered in the alternative is, in effect, a variant of the 'interest theory' advanced in various forms by such writers as IHERING[7], AUSTIN[8] and BENTHAM[9] (whose rejection of the concept 'a moral right' should not blind us to the value or the generalisability of his theory of legal rights). As I have said, to ascribe to all members of a class C a right to treatment T is to presuppose that T is in all normal circumstances a good for every member of C, and that T is a good which it would be wrong to withhold from any member of C. Certainly recognition of a right involves the imposition of duties on other persons than the right-holder, but what duties, and upon whom, is a matter which in any case needs careful definition in order best to secure the right. When the legislature confers a right *eo nomine*, as in the Succession (Scotland) Act discussed above, it is in effect left to the courts to effect a structure of duties and remedies sufficient to secure the right in question.

Although it appears, for the reasons stated here, that the will theory cannot be accepted as yielding a satisfactory analysis of legal or moral rights, the central point which the theory stresses is one which should not be denied. It is certainly true that apart from such cases as those of children or the mentally incapacitated, the holder of a legal right is normally permitted and empowered in law to choose whether or not on any given occasion he should avail himself of his right by insisting on performance by another party of the relevant duty. What is more, in the case of 'private rights', breach of a correlative duty ordinarily gives rise to a 'remedial' right which in turn the right holder has an option to exercise or not as he sees fit. The remedial right is enforced by exercising as against the wrongdoer the power of initiating legal proceedings. For quite obvious reasons, out of the whole class of legal rights, it is this subclass of private rights supported by private remedial rights and private powers of initiating proceedings which is of central concern in the practice of the law.

But while conceding the truth, and the practical importance, of these points, I would strongly contend that powers of waiver or enforcement are essentially ancillary to, not constitutive of, rights (whether primary rights or remedial rights). That contention, when coupled with that

[7] See R. von Ihering, *Geist des römischen Rechts*, III, p. 332.

[8] See J. Austin, *Lectures on Jurisprudence*, c. XVII.

[9] See H. L. A. Hart, "Bentham on Legal Rights", *op. cit.* supra n. 2., and references therein. For a contemporary defence of a version of 'interest theory' see also G. Marshall, "Rights, Options, and Entitlements", in: Simpson (ed.), *op. cit.* supra n. 2, pp. 228–241.

concession, is acceptable only if good reason can be shown, in terms of the theory here advanced, why it should be normal that rights (as here explained) carry with them the power of waiver or enforcement, and a free option as to its exercise.

To recur to my earlier elucidation of a legal right, and to improve a little on it, let this be said: a law which is conceived as conferring on members of Class C a right to treatment T, is envisaged as advancing the interests of each and every member of C on the supposition that T is (normally) a good for each and every member of C. (Save in the case of legislation expressly conferring 'rights' *eo nomine*, it may be disputable whether a law is so conceived and should be so construed.) On that footing, there would be good reason to leave it to any right holder to choose whether other parties need or need not on any given occasion respect his primary right, and whether to enforce or not to enforce remedial rights in the case of breach of the primary right, only if there is some good reason to leave it to the choice of individuals whether to have or not have what is, or is from the legislator's point of view believed to be, good for them.

Is there then any good reason why individuals should be permitted to choose whether or not to have what they, or others, think is good for them? From a certain standpoint in political philosophy, that of liberalism as classically expressed, for example, by John Stuart Mill in his *Essay on Liberty*, the answer is 'Yes'. To be a liberal is indeed to believe *inter alia* that nobody should ever be forced to pursue his own good, however that may be defined; but exceptions are allowed for, notably children and the mentally incapacitated. One ground which can be asserted as supporting both the principle and the exception is that people can be presumed to be the best judges of what is for their own good or in their own interest, but that presumption does not hold in certain defined cases, for example young children and mentally incapacitated people. To put it another way: save in such exceptional cases, freedom of action is a good which ought to be accorded to every person except in the case of actions harmful to others. (Notice that on the present theory, that would lead on to saying that people have a right to freedom; a right which would be barely intelligible if we accepted a *definition* of 'right' in terms of the will theory.)

It is now obvious that if anyone accepts the theory advanced in this paper as to the nature of rights, and also accepts (as I do) the liberal principle just adumbrated, he must further accept that in all normal cases rights ought to carry with them powers of waiver or enforcement. That the legal system does in fact normally confer just that power of waiver or enforcement on right holders should accordingly be taken as implying no more than the unsurprising truth that the liberal principle is deeply embedded in our law, if less so now than in the later nineteenth century. It would be equally unsurprising that questions about private rights should be regarded as being of practical importance only in legal systems imbued to some extent with liberal principles. I conclude that the theory here advanced can fully accomodate the valid insights of the will theory in the context of a liberal legal system.

On the other hand, the will theory fails as an explanation of rights because it cannot account for such important rights as the children's rights discussed in this essay. The presumption that people are the best judges of what is good for them and of whether to have it or not is not and should not be extended to children, certainly not to young children. Neither in law nor in what I take to be sound morality can children's rights be regarded as carrying the option of waiver or enforcement by themselves or on their behalf. Children are not always or even usually the best judges of what is good for them, so much so that even the rights which are most important to their long-term well being, such as the right to discipline or to a safe environment, they regularly perceive as being the reverse of rights or advantages. It does not follow that adults act well if they permit their children to waive those rights, or if they enforce them only at their children's insistence.

I am at once glad and regretful to discover that it is possible for me to acknowledge that my children have rights, without being thereby committed to the outrageous permissiveness to which my natural indolence inclines me[10].

[10] Subject to all proper disclaimers of their responsibility for my obstinacy in error, I have warmly to thank several colleagues for criticism of, and advice on, drafts of this paper: D. D. Raphael, E. M. Clive, E. Colvin, and Z. K. Bankowski.

ANIMAL RIGHTS

By R. G. Frey

I

THE question of whether animals possess rights[1] is once again topical, largely as a result of the recent surge of interest in animal welfare and in the moral *pros* and *cons* of eating animals and using them in scientific research.[2] If animals do have rights, then the case for eating and experimenting upon them, especially when other alternatives are available, is going to have to be that much stronger; and those who engage in and support these practices are going to be increasingly beleaguered. Animal rights may not give vegetarians and animal liberationists all that they want, but the existence of such rights would unquestionably strengthen the cases of both camps. Arguments to show that animals do have rights, therefore, are at a premium. In what follows, I want to suggest that the most important such argument fails.

II

The argument in question consists in using the cases of babies and the severely mentally-enfeebled to force the inclusion of animals within the class of right-holders. Those who use the argument proceed this way: they first cite the many and various criteria by which philosophers and others have tried to show why human beings possess rights but animals do not, and then claim of each and every one of these criteria that it would exclude babies and the severely mentally-enfeebled as right-holders; since we all agree that babies and the severely mentally-enfeebled do have rights, each and every one of the criteria must be rejected as a criterion for the possession of rights. The form of the argument, then, is as follows:

(1) Each and every criterion for the possession of rights that excludes animals from the class of right-holders also excludes babies and the severely mentally-enfeebled from the class of right-holders;

(2) Babies and the severely mentally-enfeebled, however, do have rights and so fall within the class of right-holders;

[1] I refer here and throughout this paper, and in this I align myself with all the current writing on the subject of animal rights, to moral rights.

[2] See, for example, J. Feinberg, 'The Rights of Animals and Future Generations', in W. Blackstone (ed.), *Philosophy and Environmental Crisis* (Athens, Georgia, 1974); S. & R. Godlovitch, J. Harris (eds.), *Animals, Men and Morals* (London, 1971); A. Linzey, *Animal Rights* (London, 1976); T. Regan, 'The Moral Basis of Vegetarianism', *Canadian Journal of Philosophy*, vol. V, 1975, pp. 181–214; T. Regan, P. Singer (eds.), *Animal Rights and Human Obligations* (Englewood Cliffs, New Jersey, 1976); P. Singer, 'Animal Liberation', *The New York Review of Books*, vol. XX, no. 5, April 5, 1973, pp. 17–21; P. Singer, *Animal Liberation* (London, 1976).

(3) Therefore, each and every one of these animal-excluding criteria must be rejected as a criterion for the possession of rights.

Obviously, this argument is essentially negative and indirect, in that it does not aim so much to establish directly the positive thesis that animals have rights as to establish the negative thesis that animal-excluding criteria for the possession of rights will not do, since they exclude as well babies and the severely mentally-enfeebled. (Of course, the implication of the negative thesis is that, if we go on to adopt a criterion for the possession of rights that *includes* babies and the severely mentally-enfeebled within the class of right-holders, then it will include animals within the class of right-holders.) Thus, for example, rationality as a criterion must be discarded, for otherwise we obtain a singularly objectionable result:

> If we accord moral rights on the basis of rationality, what of the status of newly born children, "low grade" mental patients, "intellectual cabbages" and so on? Logically, accepting this criterion, they must have no, or diminished, moral rights.[1]

Instances of this argument abound, and by means of it possession of rationality or of a language, the recognition and discharge of moral obligations, the possession of a culture, the acceptance of and participation within societal and communal relationships, the possession of interests (where this connotes that something *S* is in one's interest, that one cares or exhibits concern about *S*, and perhaps that one is prepared to do something about and even to think that one ought to do something about *S*), etc., are all rejected as criteria for the possession of rights.

I want to suggest that the present argument does not work. It hinges upon premiss (2), that is, upon treating the cases of babies and the severely mentally-enfeebled as open and shut so far as the possession of rights is concerned. Premiss (2), however, is not obvious and requires defence; but the best defences of it, *if they stand at all*, specifically exclude animals from the class of right-holders. Therefore, either premiss (2) cannot be defended or else premiss (1)—that every animal-excluding criterion for the possession of rights also excludes babies and the severely mentally-enfeebled—is false; either way, this important argument for animal rights fails.

III

Is it so very clear that babies and the severely mentally-enfeebled do have rights—do have rights, that is, without the addition of *further arguments* which themselves exclude animals as right-holders?

For example, consider again the rationality requirement:

[1] A. Linzey, *Animal Rights* (London, 1976), p. 24.

Only beings which are rational possess rights.

Given a suitably restrictive analysis of rationality, babies and the severely mentally-enfeebled will be excluded from the class of rational beings and so from the class of right-holders; on this requirement, they simply have no rights. Since, upon the same analysis of rationality, animals also are not rational, it follows that they have no rights either.

Now there are three arguments by which one might try to include babies and the severely mentally-enfeebled within the class of right-holders and so to defend premiss (2); each in turn, however, specifically excludes Fido from this class.

(1) One might try to include the baby by means of the *potentiality argument*: the baby is potentially rational. Of course, the baby is not at present rational, and if actual rationality is insisted upon, then the baby has no rights. On the other hand, the potentiality argument does separate the case of the baby from that of Fido, who is not conceded even potential rationality.

(2) One might try to include the severely mentally-enfeebled by means of the *similarity argument*: in all other respects except rationality and perhaps certain mental accomplishments, the severely mentally-enfeebled betray strong similarities to other members of our species, and it would and does offend our species horribly to deprive such similar creatures of rights. If this argument is rejected, on the ground that rationality is the requirement for possessing rights and other similarities are beside the point, then the severely mentally-enfeebled do not have rights. On the other hand, the similarity argument does separate the severely mentally-enfeebled from Fido, who does not bear anything like (even) sufficient physical similarities to ourselves to warrant similar inclusion.

Animal liberationists, of course, will also object to the similarity argument on the ground that it smacks strongly of speciesism. For it does enshrine, if not advocate, active discrimination against other species in favour of our own.

(3) One might try to include both babies and the severely mentally-enfeebled by means of the *religious argument*: babies and the severely mentally-enfeebled possess immortal souls. If this argument is rejected, on the ground that, even if they possess immortal souls, beings must also possess rationality in order to have rights, or on the ground that there is no good evidence for the existence of such souls, then neither babies nor the severely mentally-enfeebled possess rights. On the other hand, the religious argument does separate both from Fido, who is not conceded an immortal soul by the argument's proponents.

The upshot is this. Unless one of these three arguments is accepted, we have no basis upon which to differentiate the cases of babies and the severely mentally-enfeebled from that of animals; and if all three of the arguments *are rejected*, and there are serious objections to each, then it follows on the requirement under consideration that babies, the severely mentally-enfeebled and animals are alike in not being right-holders. In other words, the best defences of premiss (2) collapse, with the result that the premiss cannot sustain the weight put upon it. If, however, one of these three arguments *is accepted*, so that babies and the severely mentally-enfeebled are held to fall within the class of right-holders, then we find that that argument itself specifically *excludes* animals from the class of right-holders. In other words, premiss (1) is false, since not every animal-excluding criterion for the possession of rights excludes babies and the severely mentally-enfeebled.

For these reasons, then, I conclude that either premiss (2) cannot be defended or else premiss (1) is simply false, so that, in either case, this most important argument in behalf of animal rights fails.[1]

University of Liverpool

[1] I am grateful to the editor and to my colleagues H. M. Robinson and P. Helm for comments and suggestions.

RIGHTS AND BORDERLINE CASES

Jeffrie G. Murphy*

Introduction

Two competing theories of justice are currently dominating discussion within contemporary Anglo-American moral, social, political, and legal philosophy. The Welfare-State Liberal theory of John Rawls, developed most fully in his book *A Theory of Justice*,[1] contains a sustained defense of the partial redistribution of wealth within society in order to improve the position of the most unfortunate members of society. The Libertarian theory of Robert Nozick, presented in his book *Anarchy, State, and Utopia*,[2] is based on the claims that justice is the respecting of people's *rights*, that people's rights are respected when they are allowed to keep and control that to which they are *entitled*, and that people are entitled to any holding which they have legitimately acquired—that is, without using force, theft, or fraud (activities which would violate the rights of others). Since the kind of redistribution called for by Rawls' theory of justice would necessarily involve taking from some people (primarily through taxation) holdings to which they have a right, Nozick argues that an application of Rawls' theory will have unjust consequences: it will fail to show the proper respect for people's rights upon which any correct theory of justice must be based.

The present Article is an exploration of the concept of *a right*—a concept which is, as Nozick claims, central to the concept of justice.

---

* Professor of Philosophy, University of Arizona. B.A. 1962, Johns Hopkins University; Ph.D. 1966, University of Rochester. An earlier version of this essay was originally delivered as a lecture at the "Conference on the Rights of the Unborn, Children and Retarded Persons," University of Rochester Medical Center, Nov. 19, 1976. It was also presented at the Mountain-Plains Philosophy Conference on "Human Rights," University of Wyoming, Apr. 1, 1977. I am very grateful for the valuable discussions the Article received at both of these conferences, for these discussions forced me to see important changes that had to be made in the Article.

1. J. Rawls, A Theory of Justice (1971).
2. R. Nozick, Anarchy, State, and Utopia (1974).

The Article is based on the assumption that one way to develop an understanding of this important moral concept is to examine cases—called "borderline" here—where the ascription of rights seems doubtful or problematic. If we can understand what goes wrong in the doubtful cases, then perhaps we can develop a more satisfactory account of the clear cases. Although not written with such a purpose in mind, the Article may also be viewed as a tentative start toward showing that a generally Rawlsian theory of justice or rights can make an important place for those moral claims which Nozick calls entitlements.

THE PROBLEM

The nature and importance of the problem to be discussed in this Article has been well stated by Joel Feinberg:

> In the familiar cases of rights, the claimant is a competent adult human being, and the claimee is an officeholder in an institution or else a private individual, in either case, another competent adult human being. Normal adult human beings, then, are obviously the sorts of beings of whom rights can meaningfully be predicated. Everyone would agree to that . . . . On the other hand, it is absurd to say that rocks can have rights, not because rocks are morally inferior things unworthy of rights (that statement makes no sense either), but because rocks belong to a category of entities of whom rights cannot be meaningfully predicated. That is not to say that there are no circumstances in which we ought to treat rocks carefully, but only that the rocks themselves cannot validly claim good treatment from us. In between the clear cases of rocks and normal human beings, however, is a spectrum of less obvious cases, including some bewildering borderline ones. Is it meaningful or conceptually possible to ascribe rights to our dead ancestors? to individual animals? to whole species of animals? to plants? to idiots and madmen? to fetuses? to generations yet unborn? Until we know how to settle these puzzling cases, we cannot claim fully to grasp the concept of a right, or to know the shape of its logical boundaries.[3]

Feinberg's point can be summarized in this manner: We all recognize clear cases of individuals (competent adult human beings) to whom the ascription of rights, both moral and legal, is nonproblematic—indeed, it is obviously justified. We also recognize clear cases (such as rocks) of entities which not only do not have rights but *could not*

3. Feinberg, *The Rights of Animals and Unborn Generations*, in PHILOSOPHY AND ENVIRONMENTAL CRISIS 44 (W. Blackstone ed. 1974).

have rights, such ascription being conceptually ludicrous. In addition to these clear cases, we also are confronted with a large class of borderline cases—individuals who have *some* of the features normally found in individuals who are clearly rights-bearers, but who do not seem to have *quite enough* of such features to make us confident in ascribing rights to them. They are of such a nature (for example, severely retarded) that they lack certain features (such as the power of rational choice) normally found in rights-bearers. Indeed they may even be of such a nature (for instance, irreversibly comatose) that they seem disturbingly similar in relevant respects to those entities (such as rocks) which clearly cannot be rights-bearers. All these considerations tempt us to say that they are *not* rights-bearers at all.

But there are temptations in the other direction as well. We are inclined to say that even the severely retarded, for example, may not be treated just *any* way we feel like—that a certain kind of decent treatment is *owed* to them, just as a certain kind of decent treatment is *owed* to animals and the insane. I use the term "owed" at this point merely to indicate that we feel that the decent treatment is done at least in part *for the sake of these creatures* and not simply for our own sakes —to protect our sensitive feelings with respect to the hardships of other creatures—and that the decent treatment is *obligatory* on us and is not optional or supererogatory in the way that certain acts of kindness or beneficence are. For example, the feeling that we owe the severely retarded something and that any decent treatment we give them is not just a matter of charity is behind the temptation to say that even creatures such as these borderline ones *do* have rights. Perhaps they do not have as many rights as properly ascribable to competent adult humans, but they have some rights nevertheless. It is my hope in what follows to make a start toward sorting out our conflicting temptations here and to suggest a way, both conceptually clear and morally adequate, in which both sides can be satisfied—at least partially.

The Nature and Importance of Rights

I shall argue that we use the language of rights to do at least *two different* (though related) moral jobs, and that a failure to keep clear the distinction between these two jobs is behind a substantial amount of the fruitless philosophical controversy surrounding the question of whether borderline cases do or do not have rights.

One important function of the language of rights, stressed by such philosophers as John Locke and especially Immanuel Kant, has been to mark out the special kind of treatment (called "respect" by Kant) which is particularly fitting or appropriate to *autonomous, rational persons.*[4] There does seem to be something special about such persons (Kant calls it their "dignity") in that their destinies, at least in large measure, can be rationally controlled by their own choices or decisions. They are, to use another Kantian phrase, self-legislating members of a kingdom of ends (a community of other self-legislators).

In the spirit of Kant, Robert Nozick uses the phrase "rational creature" as "short for beings having those properties in virtue of which a being has those full rights that human beings now have."[5] This special feature of persons seems to provide a ground for a special set of moral claims (natural or human rights) which are appropriate only for such creatures and not for any other animals. These basic natural or human rights are articulated by Locke as follows: "No one ought to harm another in his life, health, liberty or possessions."[6] This list is *negative* (it prohibits certain kinds of *interferences*) because only in this way can the special status of persons be protected and respected —their status as creatures who must be left their own "moral space" to work out their own destinies according to their own choices and decisions. Positive interference with them, even if benevolently or paternalistically motivated, would be an affront to their dignity or status as persons. Persons, Kant argued, are ends and not means only; they are not to be sacrificed or used as instruments or resources for the achieving of others' ends without their consent. They are inviolable. Stressing this inviolable nature of persons has been the central focus of many who have written on rights, and—for what I hope are obvious reasons—I shall label their accounts of rights as accounts of *Autonomy Rights.*

Those like Kant who have stressed Autonomy Rights have not regarded such rights claims as being the only important part of morality, but they have certainly regarded them as the *most important* part. Kant argues that those duties resting on rights are absolute and decisive (he calls them "perfect") when in conflict with any other moral considerations—for example, when in conflict with such "imperfect" duties as beneficence (helping others in need). These imperfect duties do not rest on rights (I do not violate another's rights simply by refusing to help him), admit of "latitude in time and manner of their fulfillment" (I must simply do *something* for *some* people *some* of the time) and

4. *See generally* I. KANT, FOUNDATIONS OF THE METAPHYSICS OF MORALS (L. Beck ed. 1959) (originally published in 1785); I. KANT, METAPHYSICAL ELEMENTS OF JUSTICE (J. Ladd ed. 1965); J. LOCKE, TWO TREATISES OF GOVERNMENT (P. Laslett ed. 1965) (Second Treatise).

5. R. NOZICK, *supra* note 2, at 299.

6. J. LOCKE, *supra* note 4, § 6, at 311.

never take precedence over claims of genuine rights. *Rights claims are morally basic because the value of autonomy which they capture is evaluatively basic.* This, in very general and oversimplified terms, is the view of such writers as Kant and Nozick.

Another quite different tradition in moral and social philosophy, best represented by John Stuart Mill and our contemporary John Rawls, involves the view that rights claims are *not* morally basic. Rather, they are *derivative* from more general moral principles. "To have a right," Mill suggests, "is to have something which society ought to defend me in the possession of."[7] The central idea here is that rights claims function, not to mark some specially fine feature of persons, but rather to mark out which of all moral claims *ought to be enforced by the state*; in other words, which ones *ought to be law.* On this view, a creature may be said to have a right to *X* if and only if it is morally reasonable, all things considered, to *guarantee X* to that creature as a matter of law.

Mill's own version of rights theory meets shipwreck in the answer he gives to the question: "How do we decide what is morally reasonable?" Mill, alas, is a utilitarian—one who claims that the basic or most important moral requirement is to maximize human happiness. This theory is so obviously morally bankrupt[8] that very few contemporary moral philosophers take it at all seriously. I will not take time here to reiterate all the things wrong with the theory. Suffice it to say, as a summary objection, that utilitarianism fails to pay attention to those important *autonomy* values discussed above and thus fails to articulate a satisfactory conception of *justice* or *respect for persons.* It does not, as any correct theory of justice would, rule out the sacrifice of persons for the general good.[9]

Just because Mill's ultimate moral theory is defective, however, it does not follow that his analysis of rights as claims that society ought to enforce is defective. Though John Rawls (a contemporary anti-utilitarian) says very little about rights, his analysis appears similar

---

7. J. MILL, UTILITARIANISM 66 (Piest ed. 1957). According to Mill, society's mechanisms of defense are the *law* and the social pressure of *opinion.* *See id.* at 35-37. In order to simplify matters, I shall concern myself only with the former.

8. As John Rawls has shown, this theory could be used to justify such morally heinous practices as slavery. *See* J. RAWLS, *supra* note 2, at 158-59.

9. Even if a utilitarian does rule out such sacrifice, he will do so for the *wrong reason.* As Rawls has noted, slavery cannot be wrong because the benefits derived by the slaveholder can never outweigh the burdens imposed on the slaves. *See id.* This kind of argument fails to appreciate that any benefits derived by the slaveholder are *immoral to count* because they are benefits which are unjustly acquired by the exploitation of human beings and to which he thus has no *right.* Analogously, we do not wait before morally condemning a rape in order to make sure that the pleasure derived by the rapist did not outweigh the pain experienced by the victim.

to that of Mill.[10] However, he does not give a utilitarian answer to the question of what is morally reasonable for society to enforce. Rather, he says we should ask ourselves this question: "If a group of ideally rational beings came together in order to pick rules to govern their mutual relations, which rules would they be compelled (by the power of their rationality) to pick?" This decision-theoretical interpretation of classical social contract theory is basic in Rawls' outlook.

Since I believe that, in spite of certain very serious problems,[11] Rawls' theory is very helpful in illuminating certain moral issues, I should like to discuss it in a bit more detail. As already indicated, Rawls suggests that we use the idea of a social contract as a model of rational decision in morality. That is, we shall regard as rationally justified any moral principle (or any social practice) if that principle (or practice) would be unanimously agreed to, adopted, or contracted for by a group of rational agents coming together, in what Rawls calls the "original position," in order to pick principles and then practices to govern their relations with each other as members of a common community. The "original position" is simply a hypothetical situation of priority to moral rules and social practices. Unanimous consent is required because it captures our intuitive notion of what is *fair* as an agreement (because this precludes anyone's being coerced), and this intuitive notion of fairness is prior to developed moral rules or prin-

---

10. What follows is not an attempt to give an accurate depiction of the exact details and structure of Rawls' argument in *A Theory of Justice.* As any student of Rawls will immediately realize, I am collapsing together certain elements in his theory (for instance, the distinction between the stage of the "original position" and the stage of the "constitutional convention") and am skimming over details (such as the distinction between "self-interested" and "mutually disinterested" motivation) which Rawls regards as theoretically important. I am also ignoring some serious problems faced by the theory. While such matters are of theoretical interest, a careful exploration of them is, in my judgment, simply not necessary for present purposes. It would be, indeed, merely a distraction in the present context. Thus the reader should perhaps view the following simply as a set of variations on a Rawlsian theme. The notion of a *minimum floor* which I shall employ is drawn from R.M. Hare's discussion of "insurance strategies" in Part II of his review of *A Theory of Justice.* Hare, Book Review (pt. II), 23 PHILOSOPHICAL Q. 241-52 (1973).

One important point of detail, however, should perhaps be stressed. In suggesting that Rawls' theory can be used to provide a derivative analysis of at least certain rights as guarantees that society should enforce, no suggestion is being made that autonomy is unimportant in his theory. On the contrary, the contractors in Rawls' social contract theory are thought of as autonomous in something like Kant's sense; and what these contractors agree to protect or legally guarantee first is a set of certain basic liberties.

11. *See* READING RAWLS (N. Daniels ed. 1976). This is an anthology of critical essays on *A Theory of Justice* and contains a bibliography of other critical essays on Rawls' theory. Two book length attacks on Rawls' theory are B. BARRY, THE LIBERAL THEORY OF JUSTICE (1973) and R. WOLFF, UNDERSTANDING RAWLS (1977). Though serious and fundamental problems have been located in Rawls' theory, no one has yet, in my judgment, done to Rawls' theory what Rawls has done to the theory of utilitarianism—Rawls has not simply shown its weak points, but also *replaced it* with a theory that is clearly superior. Rawls' theory is certainly not the only game in town. but it still seems to me the best.

ciples. Indeed, according to the theory, such rules or principles will grow out of this intuitively acceptable setting. This is why Rawls speaks of justice *as* fairness. In an attempt to avoid begging any moral questions (for example, by smuggling certain controversial moral values into the very conception of rationality), Rawls stipulates that rational agents in the original position are primarily *self-interested*—primarily concerned to promote their own welfare (which includes promoting the welfare of those about whom they care deeply, such as members of their families). An important and controversial restriction on Rawls' model of a rational being is that such a being is said to operate under a "veil of ignorance"[12]—he is said to know what in general can happen to persons in various positions in society but not to know what *his* own actual position is likely to be. According to Rawls, this prevents the rational contractors from making choices on the basis of *morally irrelevant* considerations such as skin color. For example, in trying to decide whether or not to adopt a practice of slavery, each agent would know in general what it is like to be a slave, but none of the agents would know the probability of *his* being a slave.[13] Finally, Rawls suggests that each rational agent will value a set of primary goods (liberty, security, self-respect) and will always choose to minimize, as far as possible, threats to these goods. Rawls defines primary goods as "things that every rational man is presumed to want. These goods normally have a use whatever a person's rational plan of life."[14]

Given this brief sketch of an elaborate intellectual machinery, we are now in a position to see how Rawls attempts to show that rational persons would *not* choose utilitarianism as a basic moral principle. Since utilitarianism allows for the sacrifice of the few if this results in substantial benefit to the majority, it would never be unanimously agreed to in the original position. Rational agents, caring most about protecting such primary goods as liberty ("minimaxing," in the economists' language), and having no guarantee (because of the veil of ignorance) that they will not be members of the sacrificed class, will choose a principle which does not allow such sacrifice. To return to the slavery example: Since no rational agent would be willing to run the risk of being a slave, rational agents would not unanimously agree to a principle which allowed slavery. As one can easily see, Rawls views rational people as *cautious* people—people who plan their lives on the least favorable set of assumptions about how things will turn out.

12. *See* J. RAWLS, *supra* note 1, at 12, 19.
13. For Rawls, basic social choice is choice under nearly total uncertainty.
14. J. RAWLS, *supra* note 1, at 62.

Though they perhaps miss out on the bliss and exaltation of the gambler, they also (and this matters much more to them) miss out on the irrevocable disasters to which gamblers are prone.

What does all this have to do with rights? I will suggest the following as a Rawlsian-inspired analysis: An individual should be understood as having a right to *X* if and only if a law guaranteeing *X* to the individual would be chosen by rational agents in the original position. This concept of a right I shall call a *Social Contract Right*.

We have, then, *Autonomy Rights*, concerned to respect the choices and decisions of persons, and *Social Contract Rights*, concerned to provide morally justified legal guarantees. These are related, but a few moments of reflection should persuade us that they are not identical. If you promise that you will meet me for dinner and then simply stand me up without good reason, you have shown insufficient respect for my humanity, treated me with contempt, and violated an autonomy right of mine. For surely it is part of the meaning of "I promise," sincerely uttered in the proper circumstances, that it gives a right to the person to whom the promise is made. But should all such rights be enforced by law? Surely not. Any state which sets for itself the goal of enforcing every promise, no matter how trivial, would be financially bankrupt and morally intrusive. This is why only certain promises (regarded as important enough to be made into *contracts*) are enforced by the state.

Consider another example: Suppose I am poor, unable to afford decent food and medical care. Does this mean that any of my autonomy rights have been violated? Not necessarily. Others may simply have exercised their right to leave me alone. They have neglected me but not interfered with me, and autonomy rights require only noninterference. And yet, many would want to say, the poor have a *right* to a decent standard of living, education, and health care. But why, if no considerations of autonomy are involved?[15] A Rawlsian answer here strikes me as plausible: Rational persons, in the original position, would want to protect themselves against certain major losses and harms. Thus they would probably agree to a *minimum floor* of security below which no member of society would be allowed to fall. Even selfish people, caring about their own welfare, would want to guard against the kind of destruction of primary goods that would result if they became severely disadvantaged, as people often do, through no

15. In real, as opposed to hypothetical cases, it is going to be difficult to claim that autonomy is not involved at all. One's status as a rational agent, a maker of free choice and decisions, is going to be impaired by severe hardships.

fault of their own, but simply through their "bad luck on the social and natural lottery."[16]

In summary, most Autonomy Rights are going to be adopted as Social Contract Rights (though not all, as my promise example shows), because rational agents in the original position will surely want to protect themselves against interference with their ability to determine their own future by their own choices. Social Contract Rights are going to be broader in scope than Autonomy Rights, however, because rational agents in the original position—in addition to caring about the protection of their autonomy against interference—are going to want to protect themselves against certain major hardships and sufferings. They know that they are sentient as well as sapient. They are thus likely to adopt minimum floors of security (income, health care, and the like) and speak of these as *rights*. There will be neither confusion nor immorality here so long as they remain clear about the status of these rights—that they are Social Contract Rights and not Autonomy Rights. The main point in calling them rights is to emphasize that they are *guaranteed*—nonoptional.

What if autonomy as a value seems to compete with minimum floors as a value? Which will take precedence? In the original position, decisions will be made—not just about what rights to recognize—but about the priority of these rights claims. This is a difficult problem, but not, in my judgment, obviously insoluble.[17] At this point, I shall

---

16. J. Rawls, *supra* note 1, at 74.

17. Whatever the rational solution will be, it will *not* be the highly counterintuitive one sometimes suggested by Kant—namely, that all autonomy rights (grounding perfect duties) will, no matter how trivial, take precedence over any other moral consideration (perhaps grounding an imperfect duty), no matter how serious. To borrow an example from Joshua Rabinowitz: No morally decent society is going to forbid that I simply take Jones' rope to throw to a drowning person if Jones, who (let us grant) has a Nozickian entitlement to the rope, refuses to let me have it or says I may have it only if I pay him several thousand dollars for it. It is a Kantian perfect duty that I do not take Jones' rope and "only" an imperfect duty that I attempt to save the drowning person. What response can we make to this point except "so what?"

There is insight in Kant's attempted ordering, however, and I think it is this: That the *most important* of the perfect duty requirements resting on the *most important* rights (those which protect autonomy in a serious sense) can be said to take precedence over even the most important of the imperfect duty requirements. Killing Jones, spoiling his health, or taking his liberty away for a substantial amount of time, for example, do not seem acceptable steps to take even to save a drowning person. Taking his rope, however, does not seem to be in the same ballpark with these intrusions. Unless Jones is really weird, the temporary loss of his rope will not interfere with his autonomy in any serious way—it will not keep him from leading one of those meaningful lives which are, according to Nozick, bound up with the concept of rights. *See* R. Nozick, *supra* note 2, at 50-51. Some of these Kantian insights are captured in Rawls' notion of the priority of liberty, and his claim that his principle of "most extensive liberty compatible with like liberty for others" is lexically ordered prior to all other moral principles. In saying all this, I am admittedly making some assumptions I cannot presently defend: (1) that autonomy rights claims can be ordered on a scale of moral importance and; (2) that interferences with life, health, and liberty are typically more serious rebukes to autonomy than are threats to money and possessions. I think this resist the strong temptation to consider in even greater detail the fascinating abstract issues raised by the Rawlsian outlook on rights, and return to the more practical issues with which I began.

Borderline Cases Again

I shall not attempt to consider all of the borderline cases noted by Feinberg, but shall confine myself to a discussion of the extent to which, if at all, *children* have rights, and the extent to which, if at all, *retarded individuals* have rights. I shall further confine my discussion to *very young* children and individuals who are *more than minimally* retarded. If we consider 17 year-old "children," or "retarded persons" with IQs of 85, it would seem unduly severe to treat them as any less than autonomous persons with the rights appropriate to that status. The actual location of the dividing line between, for example, child and adult, is bound to be somewhat arbitrary and the cases barely on either side somewhat arbitrarily classified. Thus, it is useful, at least at the start of a discussion of these issues, to consider individuals noncontroversially within the class in question.[18]

Children

Young children certainly are not fully rational and autonomous (to the degree of normal competent adults) and thus clearly cannot be held to enjoy the basic Autonomy Right of having their destinies determined by their own choices and decisions. However, there is one very good reason for often *treating* them *as if* they had such a right. Treating children as though they are autonomous aids them in *developing* into genuinely autonomous persons; treating them as responsible persons aids them in *becoming* responsible persons. Such "fictions" have a way of becoming self-fulfilling prophecies. We shall, of course, want to place limits on such treatment in the interest of the child and pick our instances of fictional autonomy ascription wisely. For example, if a

ordering will have something to do with what I want to call the "internal" relation that one's very self (the person that one is, the meaning in one's life) stands in to one's life, liberty, and bodily integrity, as contrasted with the "external" relation that one stands in with respect to money and tangible things. These are themes I hope to be able to develop at some length in a future paper: to try to make sense of the "internal-external" metaphor (now admittedly just a vague intuition), establish its moral significance, and put it to use. For example, I will attempt to show where philosophers like Nozick go wrong in identifying taxation with forced labor.

18. A full treatment of these issues would obviously require finer distinctions—with rights graded accordingly—than can be captured by the vague terms "very young" and "more than minimally retarded." Here I am simply concerned to give a general idea of how, in my judgment, discussion of these issues should proceed. For a more detailed treatment, see Murphy, *Incompetence and Paternalism*, 60 *Archiv für Rechts- uund Sozialphilosophie* 465-86 (1974).

small child decides that he does not want to take the penicillin prescribed for a streptococcus infection in his throat, this would be a bad case in which to let his decision prevail in the interest of developing future autonomy.

Of course, as a normal child grows older, he will acquire greater and greater autonomy. Rights to self-determination can be correspondingly extended, paternalism being phased out gradually. But do not children sometimes, particularly when very young, have a *right* to paternalism—action in their interest either to prevent certain kinds of harms (such as child abuse, subjection to parental superstition with respect to proper medical care) or to provide them with certain benefits (such as a proper education) necessary for having or developing a satisfying life? Here I would answer *yes*—children do have such rights to paternalistic intervention on their behalf. However, the younger and less autonomous they are, the greater the need for intervention—it is *paternalism* after all. What this shows is that the rights here cannot be Autonomy Rights but must be understood as Social Contract Rights. Rational agents in the original position, knowing that they could be born into the class of children and knowing that—even as adults—they will care deeply about any children they may have, will surely want to establish certain minimum floors for children—certain levels of security and education below which no child will be allowed to fall. Thus, paradoxical as it may initially seem, I should argue that there are rights to be treated paternalistically. The paradox disappears, of course, if we remember that we are speaking of rights—not as ways of respecting autonomy—but as legal guarantees society should provide, perhaps as ways of allowing autonomy to develop in those cases where it is not yet present.

Retarded Persons

Autonomy considerations are even less relevant here than they were with respect to children. Retarded persons normally have little chance of ever becoming autonomous, and so the "fictional" argument given for sometimes treating nonautonomous children as if they were autonomous will not apply here—at least not nearly to the same extent. Here we are dealing with a class of persons who will never be in a position where it could reasonably be claimed that their destinies ought to be determined by their own choices and decisions, so if there are rights here, they will for the most part be rights to a certain kind of paternalistic protection.

Are there such rights? Again I should be inclined to answer *yes*, and again the answer is based on social contract grounds. Anyone could become mentally defective or have a mentally defective child (about whom one might care very deeply), and thus rational persons presumably would want to provide a certain minimum floor below which such people should not be allowed to fall. Here what will be relevant is to guarantee a certain level of security and a certain level, not of education, but of training. At the very least (if we have any sense of the good)[19] we shall want to protect them against suffering, including any kind of mental suffering of which they may be capable. The right to be protected against such suffering is like the right to security and training in that it is clearly a Social Contract Right and not an Autonomy Right. In other words, it is simply that which any decent society would guarantee by law to its disadvantaged members.[20]

---

19. I believe that rational agents, as parties in the original position, can have a less selfish conception of the good than that which seems to be stipulated by Rawls. The primary good which Rawls allows them to value is good *to themselves* or *their immediate families*—it is *their* liberty, security, and self-respect which they value and want to secure. The motive for this restriction seems to be the laudable one of wanting to avoid begging any substantive questions in the theory by smuggling in controversial moral claims into the model of rational choice. But are there not noncontroversial moral views, views which constitute the "facts" on which morality is based or which are the presuppositions for its very intelligibility? Surely, for example, it is noncontroversial that *suffering is bad* and, within moral limits, is to be opposed. Another way of stating this is that the *interests* of any creature have a prima facie claim to satisfaction—something which rational agents, who understand what morality is, can surely accept. *See* Feinberg, *supra* note 3, at 49. This expanded notion of primary good will have two interesting results. With respect to borderline cases it will, unlike a theory totally grounded in self-interest, make it possible to see the social contract rights extended in these cases as at least in part extended for *their* sakes, and not merely our own. The alternative, as Feinberg notes, is highly counterintuitive. Second, even animals may gain entry into the world of rights given an expanded conception of the good. Rawls himself might want to agree with much of this, for his conception of the good might not be as selfish or as individualistic as I have suggested, though it is extremely common for his critics to interpret him in this way. *See* Rawls, *Fairness to Goodness*, 84 PHILOSOPHICAL REV. 536 (1975).

20. Parties in the original position may know that people frequently value objects, such as works of art, and thus may want legal protections for these objects. Does this mean that a stone (if made into a sculpture) may have rights after all? In answering this question *no*, I should want to make three points: First, the Rawlsian apparatus requires our imagining certain misfortunes that might befall us and attempting to protect ourselves against them. It could befall me that I might become mentally disabled, but it seems to make no sense at all to suggest that it might befall me that I could become a stone. I cannot imagine myself as an occupant of *that* position. Animals pose interesting problems in this regard. *See* Nagel, *What is it Like to be a Bat?*, 83 PHILOSOPHICAL REV. 435 (1974). Second, given the expanded conception of the good noted above, see discussion note 19 *supra*, parties in the original position will sometimes act for the sake of sentient creatures in order to protect the interests of those creatures. But a stone (even if a great work of art) does not have either a sake nor does it have any interests. Third, my entire discussion is to be understood as accepting Feinberg's conceptual restrictions on the meaningful use of the concept of a right, and I agree with him that ascription of rights to stones is unintelligible. This is why I used phrases such as "creatures have a right to *X* if and only if" and "individuals have a right to *X* if and only if" and *never* the phrase "objects have a right to *X*." The upshot of this is the following: Laws protecting works of art or any other objects do not confer rights on these objects. If any rights are recognized here, it is simply *our* rights as human beings (or the rights of future generations) to enjoy these objects. Here we are acting for our own sakes. *See* Hubin, *Justice and Future Generations*, 6 PHILOSOPHY & PUB. AFF. 70-83 (1976).

CONCLUSION

At this point, it would be useful to have a tidy *list* of exactly those rights which will be possessed by children and the retarded. I will plead my philosophical vocation as an excuse for not providing such a list, however, since it could be compiled only if we leave the world of abstract thought and begin to gather actual empirical information (which I do not possess) on the exact characteristics of children and retarded persons—what they are in fact capable of at various stages. I have been concerned simply to provide a moral framework in which discussions of their rights can be clarified; and I hope that others, if they accept the framework, will be able to fill in the practical and factual information necessary for its actual employment. At this point the philosopher must give way to the lawyer, the behaviorial scientist, and the physician.[21]

I would, however, close with one caution to those who may be inclined to draw up lists of rights for children, the retarded, or any other disadvantaged people. The caution is simply this: Do not give into the romantic and knee-jerk liberal temptation to multiply rights beyond necessity. Autonomy Rights may seem restrictive, but Social Contract Rights are restrictive also—they are, remember, concerned with *minimum floors.* The more one attempts to go above the minimum to assert something more substantial as a matter of right, the more one runs the risk of developing a list of "rights" which are either so economically expensive to support or so morally intrusive to enforce that no sane society will in fact support or enforce them.[22] They will be paid at most a kind of lip service in manifestos—something which cheapens the concept of a right, makes people cynical about rights, and deprives them of their moral force. Social Contract Rights require, not simply noninterference, but *positive* steps to aid. The positive step taken in most complex modern societies, of course, is taxation. If, for example, we are going to have programs to benefit the retarded, someone is going to have to *pay* for such programs. If they are minimum floor programs resting on Social Contract Rights, then taxation may be the appropriate mechanism for funding. If they go beyond this, how-

---

21. After reading the present essay, Professor David Wexler of the University of Arizona College of Law called my attention to the monograph A. STONE, MENTAL HEALTH AND THE LAW: A SYSTEM IN TRANSITION (National Institute of Mental Health, 1975). Its author, Alan A. Stone, is a Professor of Law and Psychiatry at Harvard University. His discussion, *see* especially *id.* at 15-19, overlaps mine to a certain extent and explores some of the interesting constitutional issues arising in this area.

22. A reasonable minimum floor will, of course, be in part a function of what any particular society, or the entire world, is economically and technologically capable of at a given time in history.

ever, private funding seems in order. When we are under the spell of some good cause, and when we see that the chances of private funding of such a cause are unlikely, we are tempted to manufacture even more "rights" so that we can make our cause eligible for public funding through taxation. But the money available in society is not manna from heaven, to use Robert Nozick's metaphor, falling on the ground to be used for whatever good purpose we see fit. It is *earned* by people and is something over which they may plausibly claim to have a right.[23] Rational persons in the original position would want to protect themselves and their families against certain disasters, and this is why they would agree to minimum floors. Such persons also, however, would surely want to control at least a substantial portion of their earnings to spend as they see fit, and this is why they would be reluctant to agree to anything above minimum floors. Thus, crusades to go above minimum floors as a matter of *right* tend to themselves run the risk of inviting violations of other important rights. If such violations are also economically expensive, they will be opposed for both practical and moral grounds. The final victim of this sort of tension will simply be the important concept of a right itself.

23. Granted the insight of this Nozickian claim, a qualification (perhaps overly cynical) must be added: Many people with substantial wealth in society have done nothing remotely resembling *working for* or *earning* that wealth as we normally understand these terms. Nozick sometimes seems to attempt to marshal our Puritan sympathies for the work ethic (and even our Marxist sympathies for the labor theory of value) on behalf of people who, though very wealthy, neither work nor "mix their labor" with anything: "Consider . . . how they grow; they toil not, neither do they spin."

Inquiry, 22, 23–54

Moral Rights and Animals

H. J. McCloskey
La Trobe University

In Section I, the purely conceptual issue as to whether animals other than human beings, all or some, may possess rights is examined. This is approached via a consideration of the concept of a moral right, and by way of examining the claims of sentience, consciousness, capacities for pleasure and pain, having desires, possessing interests, self-consciousness, rationality in various senses. It is argued that only beings possessed actually or potentially of the capacity to be morally self-determining can be possessors of rights. In Section II, normative questions concerning the rights animals might possess if they were to be capable of possessing rights are discussed. The approach followed is that of considering the kinds of argument advanced in support of human rights, and whether these arguments, and the rights they are claimed to establish, are transferable to animals, and whether there are or might be specifically animal rights. In Section III the question of what is or could be the goal of one who recognizes and seeks to respect all rights, animal and human, is raised. In particular, the issue as to whether a goal of maximizing the satisfaction of rights could remain a coherent one if animal rights are acknowledged, is explored.

Importance of this Inquiry: The issue of what constitutes morally proper treatment of and concern for animals and animal welfare *vis-à-vis* human beings and their well-beings, is obviously of the greatest practical as well as of considerable theoretical importance. To be mistaken here, to advocate and to encourage others as well as one's self to act on the basis of mistaken views, be they views which favour animals wrongly at the expense of humans or humans wrongly at the expense of animals, is to be, and to foster conduct which morally may be, gravely wrong. The kind of view to be arrived at here must affect moral priorities in a very basic way. Error therefore is to be avoided. Yet there are few areas in ethics which present greater, more difficult, conceptual and normative problems. Certainty is impossible; at best we can hope for rationally based belief.[1]

The issue of whether or not non-human animals, all or only some, may and do possess rights relates in an important way to the question of the morally proper treatment of and concern for animals and their well-being *vis-à-vis* human beings and their well-beings. The nature of the duties human persons have in respect of animals will be significantly influenced by the nature of the rights, if any, that animals possess. There are good reasons for believing that it is via the claim that animals possess rights that the strongest kind of case, both for improved treatment and for greater concern at a higher level, is to be made out. This is partly because rights are seen prima facie at least as giving rise to duties in others, to important, comprehensive duties of active assistance to, protection of, the possessor of the right, partly because rights are seen to be constraints, if not absolute constraints, constraints of a very stringent character on what it is permissible to do and refrain from doing in respect of the possessor of the right. The possession of moral rights by animals would both impose important duties and seriously limit the moral freedom of human persons.

However, the moral considerations in favour of better treatment of and concern for animals based on the contention that they possess moral rights are not alternative to, but rather they are such that they may be reinforced and supplemented by other ethical considerations which in no way rest on the view that animals possess rights. Typically, the claim that animals possess rights is seen as adding to and strengthening other important considerations. Thus, even if it could be shown that animals do not possess rights and are incapable of possessing rights, many other kinds of considerations would need to be explored to determine what constitutes morally proper treatment of animals. Thus, whether or not they accept the principle of hedonistic utilitarianism, most people today recognize that animal pain and suffering, even if not animal pleasure and happiness, are factors of which account is to be taken in our moral deliberations, and which, if fully and adequately noted, would lead to different, improved treatment of many animals. Acceptance of the principle of hedonistic utilitarianism, with its insistence on the duty to promote pleasure equally with that of eliminating pain, would lead to an even more drastic rethinking of how morally we ought to treat animals, if it were to be applied on the basis of a proper understanding of the relevant facts. P. Singer's discussion in *Animal Liberation* is illuminating in this connection, and this even though there is scope for interpretation concerning the details of the utilitarian calculus.[2] Acceptance of the hedonistic principle as simply one among a number of principles in an ethical pluralism of the kind developed by Richard Price, W. D. Ross and others, would also lead to considerable modification of conventional moral theory and practice. Another possible approach towards a rethinking of the proper moral treatment of animals is via a more careful thinking out of ideal utilitarianism in terms of the kinds of things G. E. Moore and other ideal utilitarians have acknowledged to be intrinsic goods. Implications in respect of the treatment of animals seem there not to have been worked out in full. Again, it may be possible to argue for a rethinking of conventional morality as it bears on the treatment of animals by way of a more basic, radical rethinking of ideal utilitarianism, by attributing intrinsic value to life, animal life, sentient life, conscious life, self-conscious life. P. Singer and others seem currently to be exploring this kind of radical rethinking of ideal utilitarianism.[3] Clearly, whether or not animals possess rights, ethically important conclusions concerning how they ought to be treated would follow if claims that life, sentient life, conscious life, self-conscious life, possessed intrinsic value, could be sustained. Utilitarianism does not provide the only possible avenue to a rethinking of morality in this area, although it is true that it is via utilitarianism that such rethinking is so commonly approached. Other approaches are possible, although they seem as yet not seriously to have been explored. Thus just as it might be argued that it is intrinsically wrong to take innocent human life (whether or not it possesses intrinsic value), so it may be argued that it is intrinsically wrong to take innocent animal life. (Conservationists and preservationists seem often implicitly although not explicitly to adopt such a position in respect of exterminating species; and there is an increasing movement towards acceptance of such a principle, at least as a prima facie one in the condemnation as immoral of the vandalism called hunting and of the arbitrary killing of unwanted pets at holiday seasons, and the like.) If such a principle could be shown to be a sound one, it would bear very importantly on how we ought to treat animals.

Thus, to show that animals do not possess rights and cannot be bearers of rights, is still to leave open a good many questions concerning what are our moral obligations in respect of animals. Nonetheless, to establish that animals, some or all, can and do possess rights, is to establish something positive and important, although, as will be argued in Section III, it is to establish something much less important and the implications of which are far less clear, than advocates of the view that animals possess rights have suggested is the case.

I. Conceptual Issues: The Concept of a Moral Right: Possible Bearers of Moral Rights

Often those who claim that animals possess rights do not mean what they claim – they simply misuse the language of rights to express their belief that we have important, stringent, commonly neglected duties in respect of animals.[4] Others who appear to wish to maintain that animals possess moral rights, seem on closer scrutiny really to wish simply to argue that animals ought to be accorded legal rights, legal rights to life, freedom from avoidable suffering, and the like. This discussion is not concerned to examine views such as these. Rather it is directed at examining the claim that in the strict, literal sense of the term 'moral rights', animals can be and are possessors of moral rights. To assess this claim the concept of a moral right needs first to be elucidated.

1. *The Concept of a Moral Right*

Moral rights are distinct from privileges, legitimate claims on others, duties owed by others to us, powers, liberties, or the like, that we ought to possess, or which ought to be accorded us. Rights are entitlements to do, enjoy, have, have done, such that where there are no other relevant moral factors to be taken into account, when we do, enjoy, have, demand that to which we have a right, morally we need offer no further justification to others, other than that we possess a right, the ground of which can be indicated. Moral rights thus have two aspects. They are entitlements which confer moral liberties on their possessors to do, demand, enjoy, etc.; and they are entitlements which impose moral constraints on others, to abstain from interference, to do, to assist, etc.

Moral rights are distinguished from legal rights, rights as members of voluntary associations, churches, clubs, trade and professional associations, and from rights as participants in games. We may lack the moral right to do that which we have a legal or other institutional right to do. The moral rights are the important rights in that they override other rights. Lack of a moral right to do what we have legal or other rights to do renders them morally null and void. The characterization of a right as a moral right is therefore an important, positive characterization. It is to mark out that the right is based on moral considerations or grounds, and that morally it is an entitlement that is to be respected, both by its possessor and by others. It morally opens avenues for its possessor, and closes avenues for others, commonly imposing on them duties of abstaining from interference, and of protecting and aiding the possessor of the right in his enjoyment of his right. To claim that a right is a moral right is to claim something about the entitlements of the possessor, not simply concerning the duties of others. It is to say that morally he is acting as he is entitled when he acts, takes, enjoys, demands what he has a moral right to do, take, etc. The first-person question, 'Have I the right to . . . ?' is important with all kinds of rights. With moral rights, it is central and basic. We can have no moral right unless we are at least prima facie entitled to do, demand, etc., that to which we have a right.

Basic moral rights are possessed by their possessors independently of other beings. My moral right to moral autonomy and integrity springs from my nature and being; it depends on no one else, and is conferred by no one else. However, certain moral rights may be conferred on us by others who possess the moral right to do so. I may confer on another the right to the use of my property. Some would argue that parents may confer not simply the legal but also the moral right on their children who are minors, to marry. What is important in respect of accorded rights, and what limits the kinds and numbers of moral rights that may be accorded, by contrast with the basic, intrinsic rights, is the fact that for a right to be accorded there must be a person possessed of the moral right and power to accord the right. Once the right is accorded it comes to be possessed by the being to whom it is accorded, as long as it is accorded. By contrast, all institutional rights, legal and other, are accorded; none is intrinsic to the possessor.

It is commonplace to speak of rights as being possessed. Yet, when one reflects on what it is that is being expressed by talk of moral rights as being possessed, it is less clear what we mean than our ready use of such language might suggest. One use of the word 'possess' is to refer to attributes that people have or possess – blue eyes, blonde hair. People have rights; yet they are not attributes nor are they a kind of capacity, power or ability. A right is an entitlement that is ours, that we own, that belongs to us. To deny us the enjoyment of our rights is to deny us what is ours. Legally, to own something is to have legal rights in respect of it. Morally to own something is morally to have rights in respect of it, rights of control, use, or the like. The ownership of a moral right cannot be that, a moral right to a moral right, *ad infinitum*. This suggests that rights must be owned, possessed in a distinct sense again. The elucidation of that sense, however, presents problems.

Rights and duties, whilst obviously connected, are clearly distinct. There is no simple correlativity of rights and duties. Duties in respect of *X* need imply no rights in *X* – e.g. duties of charity in respect of *X*. Rights possessed by *X* need not imply any duties in others, for example rights to moral autonomy and integrity of the terrorist. One may have a moral right to follow one's erroneous conscience, yet others may have no duty, prima facie or other, to refrain from preventing one from so acting. The lack of correlativity of duties and rights is of obvious importance in the context of discussion of the rights of animals. To show that animals possess moral rights, moral rights against persons, it is not sufficient to establish that persons have duties in respect of animals.

Perhaps the most important feature of talk about moral rights, and that which most distinguishes such talk from talk about duties, is the reference to exercising, claiming, forgoing, yielding up one's rights. Whilst there may be rights which morally we may not be able to give up, which we continue to possess irrespective of whether we consent to forgo them, and which morally we must exercise, the concept of a moral right is such that there is no logical incompatibility between possessing a moral right and being able to waive it, yield it up, surrender it, or hold it but to choose, temporarily or for life, not to exercise it. The notion of exercising, acting on the basis of our rights, is central to rights. If the possessor of the right cannot himself exercise it, really to be a right it must admit in principle of being claimed and exercised on his behalf by some other person or persons.

These various features of the concept of a moral right are relevant to who or what can be a bearer of a moral right.

2. *Possible Bearers of Rights*

The problem as to the kind of being to which it is possible meaningfully to ascribe rights has no parallel with other moral concepts. There are no serious problems in respect of such moral concepts as ought, duty, right, and good.

(a) Considerations based on the concept of a right: The concepts most nearly related to that of a right would seem to be those of duty and obligation. These concepts relate to action, and to those capable of action. The agent who has a duty, who is under a moral obligation, must be capable of doing what he is obliged to do; he must be capable of acting. By contrast, this, at first sight at least, would seem not necessarily to be the case in respect of rights. To possess a right, it would seem not to be necessary actually to be able to act in ways relevant to the right. We seem meaningfully to ascribe rights to those who have suffered strokes and are in comas. First appearances may, however, be misleading here. Thus whilst it is true that, besides the rights which are entitlements which we may ourselves exercise by doing, demanding, requiring, there are also entitlements simply to enjoy, receive, have done, nevertheless the notion of accepting, not exercising, waiving the latter kind of right has meaning and import. Further, where the right relates to action, and where the possessor of the right is incapable of action, whilst the ascription of the right then typically has as its major import implications about how others ought to act, these obligations are not the essence of the right, but things that follow from it. Thus, possession of a right by *X* who is incapable of action of any kind, may create duties and rights in others to goods, services, liberties, removal of obstacles and impediments, and the like; yet there remains that essential core of the right, by virtue of which it can be exercised, not exercised, waived, forgone. These relate to actions by or on behalf of the possessor of the right.

That the duties are distinct and follow from the right is evident from the fact that were there no other beings capable of duties, and even where the possessor of the right himself had no specific duties, the ascription of a right such as a right to take his own life, would be meaningful and important. Indeed, the ascription of a right to a person at that time subject to no duties, temporarily incapable of action, where there are no other free agents with duties in respect of him, is meaningful. However, it is meaningful only on the basis of the possibility of action at some future time.

This suggests that the reason there seems to be a kinship between the concepts of duty and obligation on the one hand, and of a right on the other, lies not in there being some sort of correlativity of rights and duties, but in both deriving meaning and content from the possibility of action – in the case of duty, in the person subject to the duty, in the case of rights, in the possessor of the right or in someone who, by virtue of the right, has duties to act or refrain from acting in certain ways in respect of the possessor of the right, where his duties are coloured by how the possessor of the right would will to exercise or not exercise his right, in so far as this can be determined or inferred. In brief: The basic thought in the ascription of moral rights is that there be the possibility or potentiality of action. This suggests that the paradigm possessor of a right is an actor or potential actor, one who can act by doing what he is entitled to do, or act by demanding, claiming, requiring, what he is entitled to demand, claim, require. Where there is no possibility of action, potentially or actually, in the being towards whom duties are held, and where the being is not a member of a kind which is normally capable of action, we withhold talk of rights, and confine ourselves to talk of duties. Relevant here is the fact that the core use of talk about rights is first-person rights talk, talk in terms of possession, exercise, demanding recognition of them. Whilst for pragmatic, political reasons, including reasons of justice, it is often important to appeal to the rights of other people, the primary issue with rights as with duties, is the first-person one, 'To what do I have a moral right?', 'How shall I exercise my right?', 'Shall I insist on my rights, or shall I forgo them in the interests of the common good, charity, harmony or the like?' Where the possessor of the right is himself incapable of exercising, claiming, demanding his right, the ascription of the right is fully meaningful only on the basis of an hypothesis that it can be exercised, claimed, demanded, in a real and meaningful way, on his behalf, as he would exercise, claim, demand, or waive it, were he to be capable of such action. More will be said later in explanation and justification of this contention.

(b) Considerations arising from paradigm possible possessors of rights: Philosophers have commonly ascribed rights to God (implicitly rather than explicitly) and to free rational, morally autonomous agents. There seems to be nothing paradoxical in so ascribing rights. Thus Locke sought to derive the rights he attributed to men from rights possessed by God.[5] This is most evident in his discussion of the right to life. Other philosophers have simply argued from the assumption that normal adult human beings can possess rights, since they have the relevant capacities in respect of exercising, claiming, yielding rights, and in respect of the content of the rights claimed, rights such as those to life, liberty, private property, moral autonomy and integrity. The puzzle cases have been and are human 'monsters', human 'vegetables', and infants. These are seen to be puzzle cases because, when we think of God and normal adult human beings as paradigm cases of possible possessors of rights, we are thinking of them as capable of being morally entitled to act, to make demands for goods, benefits, services, and to receive or decline such. It is because they are actors, and more, moral actors, capable of acting according to what they are entitled to do, and capable of refraining from doing what they are not entitled to do, that we believe that we can meaningfully ascribe them rights. It is true that in ascribing some rights we seem to be asserting entitlements to goods and services independently of any capacity for action by the possessor of the right; yet even there there is the implication in respect of action, that the right could have been waived, not exercised, had its possessor been capable of this. Further, if the only rights this kind of being could ever possess were rights of this kind, where he could exercise no judgment in respect to them, we should be reluctant to speak of such beings as possessing rights and as being capable of possessing rights. It is *qua* moral agent, possessed of a capacity to be morally self-determining, that we attribute the basic rights, the ascription of which gives some meaning and import to the ascription of these other kinds of rights in the puzzle cases.

That it is the capacity for moral autonomy, for moral self-direction and self-determination, that is basic to the possibility of possessing a right is confirmed by the fact that if we imagine the existence of any other kind of being, be it an angel, a purely spiritual being, a Martian, a whale, a dolphin, or the like, whether or not it be thought to possess sentience, capacity for feeling, for pain and pleasure, or the like, we should meaningfully ascribe rights to them if we believed them to be possessed of a capacity for moral self-determination, for moral autonomy. What is commonly overlooked in this connection by those who argue that other factors such as sentience, capacity for pleasure and pain, and the like, are basic to the possession of rights, is the fact that a being may be lacking in various of these capacities, and yet be a paradigm case of a possessor of rights. Thus it is commonly denied that God is capable of experiencing pain (and pleasure), yet this seems irrelevant to whether or not He has the capacity to possess rights, for example the right to inflict pointless suffering. Some human beings lack the capacity to experience pain. That too is irrelevant to whether they can be possessors of rights. Those that lack the capacity to experience pain commonly possess a capacity for pleasure, but were that not so, it too would be irrelevant. This is because it is capacity for action, moral action, that is basic to the ascription of rights.

There are problems in respect of potential persons, the very young, on the one hand, and on the other hand ex-persons, the brain-damaged, the extremely senile, the non-persons, those born with damaged or undeveloped brains and who have no potentiality to become persons. When speaking uncritically, unreflectively, we ascribe the possibility of possession of rights, and even the possession of rights to all such human beings. When we so ascribe rights, I suggest we are doing something akin to what we are doing when we describe a cat as a quadruped, knowing that some cats are born with more and others with fewer than four legs. *Qua* cat, an animal, even this animal born with only three legs, is naturally a quadruped. *Qua* human being, where human beings naturally and normally become persons, human beings are possessors of rights. However, if we are to speak with strict accuracy, we must deny rights and the possibility of possession of rights to ex-persons, non-persons who have no potentiality to become persons. Potential persons, infants who will come to be persons, possessed of rational, moral wills, such that they will be able to exercise their rights, are differently placed. Here everything turns on the importance that is to be attached to potentiality and the grounds for attaching this importance. Whatever criteria are indicated as the relevant criteria for the capacity to possess rights, this problem will arise, although it will be more acute, less easy to resolve in terms of some criteria than of others. Considerations to be outlined in (c) below bring out how reference to the capacity for rational, moral self-determination, moral autonomy, makes the ascribing of rights to potential persons more reasonable than ascribing them to those who potentially possess other attributes claimed to be the basis for being a bearer of rights.

(c) Attributes which have been claimed to be relevant to the capacity to be a bearer of a right: Few if any would wish to deny that mere things, inanimate objects, stones, mountains, paintings, buildings, and the like, cannot be possessors of rights. Yet we may have very comparable duties in respect of things to those we have towards some of those persons who possess rights of recipience. Thus we may have duties to protect, care for, preserve, a valued, valuable inanimate object, just as we may have a duty to protect the life of a possessor of a right to life. The duties may be exactly parallel, yet we resist the move to speak of the inanimate object of the duties as a possessor of rights. Here it may be argued that this is because the duties are not duties to the inanimate object, they are not duties accepted *for the sake of* that object, but rather that ultimately they are duties to possessors of rights, to human persons. Against this, whilst it is true that such duties are often explained in terms of the rights of and duties to human beings, this is not necessary, either normatively or conceptually, for the ascription of such duties to be meaningful. An ideal utilitarian may argue for the duty to preserve a beautiful painting, mountain, or the like, without any reference to their appreciation by human beings. We could meaningfully accept that we have the duty to make serious financial sacrifices to preserve a work of art, a desert region, or other inanimate object, for its own sake and not for the sake of future human beings. Yet, when so explained, the duty is clearly distinct from a right in the inanimate object. This is because for us to accept the object of the duties as being a possessor of a right, the duty must be seen to derive from the right. Mere things may be the objects of duties; they may even give rise to duties, as ideal utilitarians have claimed. However, they cannot be bearers of rights which give rise to duties. This is because they cannot exercise rights, nor have them exercised for them.

The distinction between inanimate and animate things is an important one for many purposes. In the sphere of rights, it seems to be of little importance. Certainly, few, even among those who wish to argue that animals, some or all, may be bearers of rights, wish to argue that mere capacity for life is all that is necessary for something to be a bearer of rights. Again, the reason for this seems to be that mere life does not necessarily carry with it any suggestion of a capacity for action. It is nonetheless important to note what is being claimed and conceded when it is acknowledged that plants cannot be bearers of rights. We can have duties in respect of plants, to care for and protect them as ends in themselves, to refrain from pointless mutilation of them. We can ascribe them value for their own sakes, and act to benefit them for their own sakes, at the expense of human goods. In an extended sense of 'interests' we can speak of the interests of a plant, such that a command, 'In my absence so act as to protect the interests of this tree', would be an intelligible one. Pruning is seen to be contrary to the interests of certain kinds of plants, the application of certain fertilizers to be in their interests, and so on. Plants respond to stimuli, to light, heat, etc. Animal-eating plants do so in a more obvious way than do some other plants, so much so that some may wish to speak of them as being stimulated to 'act', in some very extended analogous sense of 'act'. The distinction between plants and animals is not a sharp one, but is such that any one who sought to argue that all animals possessed or could possess rights, would encounter problems in justifying not extending the claim to encompass plants as well. The reason for the reluctance to ascribe rights to plants lies in the fact that they are seen to be things, incapable of action, lacking selves, wills, identities as beings.

This brings us to a consideration of animals and the features of animals which have been claimed to be relevant and adequate grounds for the ascription of rights. Features which are said to mark off animals, or animals that can be bearers of rights, from plants and mere things, include sentience, consciousness, capacity for pleasure and pain, capacity to have desires, capacity to have interests, self-consciousness, rationality in some fuller sense or senses, such as a capacity to conceptualize, construct a language, communicate with others, engage in acts of creativity, be able to make moral judgments and act on the basis of them.

Sentience: *The Concise Oxford Dictionary* explains that sentient means 'having the power of sense-perception'. More commonly, sentience is interpreted as the capacity for feeling. Perception and capacity to experience feelings are clearly distinct. A being may perceive that *X* is red, but be incapable of any feeling reaction of any kind. A being may experience feelings but be devoid of the capacity to perceive, the feelings resulting entirely from internal causes. We therefore need to consider separately the claims of sentience as sense perception and as the capacity for feelings.

Sense-perception covers a whole range of things from a capacity to respond to a stimulus, as with such plants as animal-eating ones, to sense-perception as we know it in man, where it involves not simply a response to outside stimuli but a cognitive apprehension of an outside reality as such. Mere capacity to respond to stimuli seems irrelevant to the question of capacity to be a bearer of rights. So too with the capacity to experience sensations as of redness, heat, hardness. In so far as these involve consciousness – it is not clear that they must do so – they may best be considered when considering the claims of consciousness. Perception in the sense of a full cognitive awareness of an outside reality as such would seem to involve not simply consciousness but self-consciousness, awareness of an awareness of sensation as providing knowledge of a non-self to the self. It may best be discussed when considering the claims of self-consciousness.

Sentience understood as the capacity for feeling, including feelings such as those of pleasure and pain, heat and cold (where not necessarily related to perception of external reality), and the like, seems again to have little relevance to the capacity to be a bearer of rights. This is evident if we consider a being that is sentient only in this sense of sentience, having no capacity for sense-perception. There might well be duties concerning it, arising out of its capacity to feel, but they would be independent of whether or not the being possessed rights. Such a being might be said to have interests by virtue of its capacity to experience feelings, depending on how the concept of interests is construed. If desires are essential for interests, then, since the capacity for experiencing feelings is distinct from the capacity to desire, they would lack interests. If the feelings had no relation to pleasure and pain, it is unlikely that we should wish to attribute interests to such sentient beings, other than in the extended sense of 'interests' in which plants might be said to have interests.

The capacity to experience pleasure and pain seems to have greater moral significance than the mere capacity to experience feelings of other kinds. However, again, apart from the fact that this capacity might be a ground for ascribing interests, and interests be a ground for ascribing a capacity for possessing rights, the moral significance of the capacity to experience pleasure and pain seems to relate only to duties, not to the capacity to be a bearer of rights. Again, all that need be considered here is the animal which possesses this one capacity.

Importance has been attributed to consciousness, both as a source of value, and as relating to the capacity to be a bearer of rights. Yet it is hard to see its relevance to either. Consciousness may be consciousness of sensation, feeling, perception, mere thoughts. A being may be conscious of another being's existence, without being capable of any feelings in the sense of pleasure or pain, and without any awareness of itself as a self. It is hard to see how mere consciousness of this kind, a consciousness of shape, colour, size, and the like, can be of relevance here. So too with mere consciousness of feelings. At best only certain kinds of conscious beings can possess value, be bearers of rights. This brings us to a consideration of special capacities attributed to certain beings possessed of consciousness.

The capacity to have desires has been advanced by some as a candidate for a criterion which marks off those who may be possible bearers of rights. A number of issues need to be distinguished here. One relates to what is involved in the capacity to have a desire. R. G. Frey has argued, with some cogency, that to desire, as distinct from having a need, is to have a belief that one lacks that which is desired, and hence, that to be capable of desiring, a being must be capable of belief.[6] This in turn suggests that for a being to have a capacity to desire, it must have a large number of rational capacities, and, in a real sense, be a rational animal. It must be able to conceptualize, hold beliefs, be self-conscious and not simply conscious, conscious of itself as believing that it lacks that which is desired. When we speak of animals as having desires, we commonly do not use the word 'desire' in this strict sense which marks off needs and desires. Indeed, we are rarely if ever in a position to know that these conditions of desiring are met in the cases of animals. A second point of importance is that the mere capacity to desire as such, rather than as an aspect of rationality, seems to have little to do with being a bearer of rights. It is *qua* rational activity that desiring seems to have serious claims to consideration as a relevant criterion. This is confirmed by the fact that it is desire as an intellectual activity that is relevant, not as some sort of animal drive or appetite. A purely intellectual being such as God, a Kantian being with a holy will, or the like, is capable of desiring in the intellectual sense; it is incapable of appetitive desires. If capacity to desire is seen to be a necessary and sufficient condition for being a bearer of rights, it must be construed intellectually, otherwise such paradigm cases of possessors of rights would be excluded as not meeting the criterion. A third issue raised by desires and the capacity to desire, if this account of desire is correct, is that of whether rationality, in the respects that desiring involves rationality, is a relevant ground for possession of rights. Much here will depend on how the details are to be filled out. If there is no capacity for alternative action other than along the lines directed by the desire, and if there is no way of marking off belief and desire from what occurs in computers which are programmed to develop 'beliefs' as means to achieving goals, the rational capacities seem to have little moral significance. It is because the notions of belief and desire carry with them the suggestion of self-activity and self-determination that they appear to be morally relevant. Yet they do not necessarily involve either self-activity or self-determination.

Quite a number of philosophers including myself have argued that the capacity to have interests, or the having of interests, is all that is necessary for a being to be capable of being a bearer of rights.[7] The thought here has been that rights which cannot be claimed directly by their possessor, involve the possibility of representation by a proxy; that were it not in principle possible for either the possessor of the rights or a proxy to claim the rights, it is not meaningful to ascribe either rights or the possibility of possessing rights. From this kind of basis, attempts have been made to argue that beings capable of sense-perception, feelings, feelings of pleasure and pain, of desires, are capable of possessing interests, and indeed, do possess interests. Much of the debate has turned on whether only human beings, or even only some human beings, may possess interests.

I now believe my arguments here to have been mistaken, misconceived, and misdirected in quite a number of ways. First, I wish to concede that the concept of interests is a much looser one than I previously suggested. The original usage of the expression 'interests' may well have been, and its present paradigm use may still be, such as to relate interests to persons, where a person's interests relate to his good as that person as a physical and spiritual being. His good, and hence his interests, are distinct from his well-being, and are determined by many factors including his physical and mental well-being, the roles he has adopted and identified with himself, and his rational aspirations and ideals. We may distinguish what is in a man's interests from what is dictated by his welfare, from what he desires, what he desires most, from what will give him most pleasure and least pain, and so on. Thus, with human persons there is no equation of feelings, maximizing certain feelings, satisfying desires, or the like, with the realization of their interests. Whatever its original range of application, the concept of interests is no longer restricted to human interests. We also speak of interests in the strict sense of interests in respect of corporate bodies, states, churches, business corporations, voluntary associations such as sporting clubs, where various of these contrasts do not arise, and where the interests of the organization relate to its good which may be distinct from the good of all the present members of the organization. It could well be in the interests of a state or a multinational corporation that it thwart the interests of all its present members. Some organizations see and act on this kind of basis, withholding funds as reserves which could well be paid as dividends, to secure future growth, where the interests of the organization are seen to lie in expansion and longevity. We seem now to be prepared to extend the range of application of the expression 'interests' even further, and to speak of the interests of a thing where it is a living thing possessed of a good which can be affected by its actions or by human actions. Certainly, if it is legitimate to speak of the interests of ICI, where these are distinct from those of its share-holders and employees, it is hard to see why we should resist the extension of talk about interests to animals and plants. They possess goods which can be affected by what they 'do' or what is done to them. Further, provided we are clear as to what we are speaking of when we speak of interests, no philosophical point of substance would seem to turn on the range of application of the concept of interests. If I am right in this, then the questions of whether desires, capacity to feel pleasure or pain, are essential or sufficient for the having of interests, are non-questions. Relevant here is the fact that the attempt to restrict the range of application of the concept of interests, and to write more and more into the concept, simply obscures the solution to our problem concerning the necessary conditions for being a bearer of rights. This is evident from J. Feinberg's account of why plants cannot have interests, and of all that must be written into that concept to establish this. Feinberg writes:

> Yet trees are not mere things like rocks. They grow and develop according to the laws of their own nature. Aristotle and Aquinas both took trees to have their own 'natural ends'. Why then do I deny them the status of beings with interests of their own? The reason is that an interest, however the concept is finally to be analyzed, presupposes at least rudimentary cognitive equipment. Interests are compounded out of *desires* and *aims*, both of which presuppose something like *belief*, or cognitive awareness.[8]

A second respect in which I believe my earlier position to have been mistaken is in linking interests and the having of interests, with the having of the capacity to be a bearer of rights. I know of no convincing argument to this effect. L. Nelson who, in his *System of Ethics*, from a very different standpoint had developed the same view, seems to offer only the flimsiest of arguments, definitional fiats rather than genuine arguments.[9] Thus he writes:

> According to the principle of personal dignity, every being that has interests, in other words, every person, has a claim to respect for his interests. This claim is the person's right. Thus every person is a subject of rights; for he is, by definition, a subject of interests.[10]
>
> To subsume a being under the concept of person, it is sufficient that this being be capable of experiencing pleasure and pain: for pleasure and pain designate those interests of which we are conscious independently of any judgment, and which do not necessarily operate as impulses of the will. Any being that can feel pleasure or pain is therefore a subject of rights, and has dignity in the sense defined above.[11]

J. Feinberg seeks to offer a serious argument by reference to his analysis of the concept of interests as one involving conative and cognitive life (see the passage quoted above concerning why plants cannot be possessors of interests), and in terms of animals, some at least, as possessors of interests and those attributes on which the possession of interests rest, and hence being the kinds of things that can be recipients of goods for *their* – not our – sakes. Here Feinberg writes:

> Now . . . a crucial principle . . . namely, that the sorts of beings who *can* have rights are precisely those who have (or can have) interests. I have come to this tentative conclusion for two reasons: (1) because a right holder must be capable of being represented and it is impossible to represent a being that has no interests, and (2) because a right holder must be capable of being a beneficiary in his own person, and a being without interests is a being that is incapable of being harmed or benefitted, having no good or 'sake' of its own. Thus, a being without interests has no 'behalf' to act in, and no 'sake' to act for.[12]

A number of objections may be urged to such an argument. The claim made in (2) has already been contested and rejected in the discussion of things and plants. The claim in (1) will be argued against in the next paragraph on the grounds that representation of rights is something very different from representation of interests. More generally, this general argument simply transfers the problem that Feinberg and others pose in terms of interests, to that of determining whether animals have desires, aims, beliefs, and the other relevant capacities necessary for them to be bearers of rights. And of course, argument will still be needed for accepting the possession of such capacities as a ground for attributing rights.

A third respect in which I wish to modify my view about rights and interests relates to the consideration that interests can be represented. I argued, and I believe, rightly, that it is possible to represent a being in respect of its interests, although the practical difficulties in the way of doing so are very considerable. However, in principle, we can seek to make informed judgments about what constitute the interests of a being, whether it be a person, a child, an animal, or a plant. This fact alone, that the interests of plants can be judged, protected, fostered, by a representative itself suggests that nothing of importance concerning rights follows from the possibility of there being representatives of the interests of non-humans. However, there is a more basic, positive objection to any attempt to argue that those who are capable of possessing interests are capable of possessing rights. The important objection lies in the fact that rights and interests are completely distinct things. A possessor of rights may wish to exercise his rights contrary to his interests. It may be in a person's interests to deprive him of the opportunity to exercise his moral rights. A person may, on moral grounds, wish to exercise his rights contrary to his interests. He may lack the moral right to pursue his interests – this is so when his interests involve evil actions and ends, as with the racist leader, the professional criminal, and the like. It is the paternalist who seeks to protect the individual's interests, where he deems the individual not to be the best judge or guardian of his own interests. The *laissez-faire* liberal opposes paternalism in favour of securing the individual in the enjoyment of his rights, albeit at the expense of his enjoyment of his interests. The criteria as to success in representing a person in the exercising of his rights are very different from those relating to interests. Indeed, there are moral as well as practical problems in determining what is the morally proper way to represent one who cannot communicate his wishes in respect of the exercise of his rights. Thus, that interests may be represented tells us nothing about whether or not rights can be represented. There are very considerable problems involved in representing a person in respect of their interests – the mistakes of well-meaning paternalists are only too well known. With rights, what has to be determined and represented by the representative is something much more difficult to determine. It is how the possessor of the rights who cannot express his wishes – who may not even be conscious or have wishes – would wish to exercise his rights, indeed, whether or not he would wish to claim his rights. This involves reading his mind, his moral mind, not simply determining what is for his good. Where there is no mind or will, actually or potentially, to be read, there can be no representation of rights nor of the exercising or waiving of moral rights.

Rights are moral rights. How they are to be exercised involves moral issues. A person representing another who cannot communicate his wishes must make moral judgments on that person's behalf about how to exercise his rights. By contrast, a judgment about what action or actions are dictated by a person's interests typically raises no moral question although in special cases it may do so. Pursuit of interests may involve doing what is gravely immoral, what one lacks the right to do. The view that has been canvassed by R. M. Hare, P. Singer, and others that interests *qua* interests ought to be respected, and respected equally, rests on a completely uncritical appraisal of what is involved in interests and their pursuit.

A final point concerning rights and interests that is worth noting here is that we are fully aware that organizations may have interests *qua* organizations, but deny that the organizations *qua* organizations can have moral rights. It is officials of the organization who have or lack moral rights to act on behalf of the organizations. The organization itself cannot have moral rights; this is because, as an organization, it is incapable of moral judgment, moral decision, moral action. What holds of organizations seems equally to hold of plants, all lower animals, and indeed of all animals which are incapable of moral judgment which allows them morally to determine whether to exercise their rights and how, or whether to waive them.

Consciousness and self-consciousness have each been claimed to be a sufficient condition for the ascription of rights. What has already been said makes it clear enough that mere consciousness establishes nothing. Only certain kinds of consciousness have any sort of claims to serious consideration. That their claims are unsound becomes evident if one considers what might be expected to be the stronger case of self-consciousness.

Here again, if we consider self-consciousness as such and not special kinds of self-consciousness, there seems to be little to suggest that self-consciousness has special claims. Consider self-consciousness which consists simply in the capacity to be aware of one's self as thinking or sensing, perceiving red objects, imagining them, but without the capacity to feel pleasure or pain, and without the capacity to act, choose, decide, make valuations, moral decisions, and the like. Mere self-awareness seems to be of little importance. It is the *kind* of being that is self-aware that is of importance. This leads on to a consideration of the claims of rationality, and of what is involved in rationality, and of the kind or kinds of rationality that are relevant to the possession of rights.

Consciousness and self-consciousness are aspects of rationality. Ability to conceptualize is another capacity relating to reason. Capacity to choose, decide, to act on the basis of conscious decisions, are other rational activities. The capacities morally to evaluate and to act on the basis of these moral evaluations are two further rational capacities.

There are problems in ascribing rights to beings possessed of rational capacities, even of highly developed, higher rational capacities, capacities to conceptualize, communicate, and the like, if this falls short of a capacity to act and to decide to act on the basis of a moral evaluation of the alternative possible actions. This is evident from a consideration of the paradigm cases of possessors of rights, free moral agents. In accepting and exercising their rights, they must call upon their moral capacities, make moral judgments and act within the limits of their moral entitlements. What is true and important about the argument from representation and interests, where the possessor of rights is one who cannot speak for himself and who can only exercise rights via a representative or proxy, is that possession of rights, involves the possibility of representation, moral representation, not representation of interests. Mere rationality without the rational capacity for moral judgments is not enough, since it is the moral will that must be represented. It is not what is in a rational being's interests, nor what a rational being wills, but what he wills within the limits of his moral rights, that the representative must seek to represent. The capacity for moral deliberation and decision is a crucial factor. Just as one may lack a right to what is in one's interests, so one may lack a right to that which one rationally wills. Thus there are two things involved in representing a possessor of rights in respect of his rights. The one relates to the area bounded by the rights possessed. The other relates to what is willed as being within these moral boundaries. Just as a legal representative representing a person in the exercise of his legal rights must first determine what are that person's legal rights, what their bounds are, and then and only then what he wills to do within these boundaries, so too in respect of moral rights. Supporting this argument is the fact that where representation is in principle impossible in respect of either legal or moral rights, the ascription of rights to one who can in no way himself claim his rights, is meaningless. Consider here the conferring of property rights by the state on someone who is permanently, irreversibly in a coma, where the conferring of the property rights is linked with a denial of all legal rights to others legally to represent that person or otherwise act to protect, secure the property rights on his behalf. We should say that the conferring of such property rights was a sham, a mockery, and not a reality. So too in respect of moral rights where no significant meaning can be given to moral representation of the so-called possessor of the right, the human being in an irreversible coma, the being without a moral will, potentially or actually, the being which lacks the capacity to formulate moral concepts and hence to make moral judgments, potentially or actually.

This leaves us with seeming problems in respect of infants, the permanently insane, the psychopath, and the irreversibly brain damaged. I suggest that there is no problem in respect of the latter. They lack the capacity to be bearers of rights. With most who are declared to be insane, there is limited sanity and a real moral capacity, such that they may be real possessors of rights. Further, it is seldom that we can say with confidence that there is not potentiality for sanity and moral autonomy. The psychopath constitutes a worrying case. If it could be known with certainty that there is no potentiality for moral autonomy, then the logic of the above argument would dictate the conclusion pressed on other grounds by A. I. Melden.[13] With infants the problem is that of potentiality. It is one which arises in respect of most candidates for acceptable criteria for being a bearer of rights. I suggest that it is meaningful to ascribe rights here on the basis of what would be/will be the moral will of the being who is now an infant.

As regards animals, the position is clear. If an animal has the relevant moral capacities, actually or potentially, then it can be a possessor of rights. The evidence available to date about the rational capacities of animals is far from complete, but to date it appears to be decidedly unfavourable to the view that any animals possess the relevant moral capacities. Thus, whilst research on chimpanzees, monkeys, and many other animals, reveals a significant degree of rationality which provides an important ground for justified moral demands that they be better treated than they now are, the degree and kind of rationality fall far short of that necessary for moral judgment and moral self-determination. Although there is limited evidence in respect of certain animals of a capacity for seeming 'self-sacrificing', 'disinterested', 'benevolent' actions in limited, somewhat arbitrary areas, there is no real evidence of a capacity to make moral judgments, morally to discriminate when self-sacrifice, gratitude, loyalty, benevolence is morally appropriate, and more relevantly, to assess their moral rights and to exercise them within their moral limits. However, further research on animals such as whales and dolphins, although seemingly not in respect of monkeys, apes, chimpanzees, may yet reveal that man is not the only animal capable of being a bearer of rights. It may for this reason be morally appropriate for us meanwhile to act towards the former animals *as if* they are possessors of rights.

II. Normative Questions: The Rights Animals Might Possess if they Could Possess Rights

If animals were to be capable of possessing rights, what rights would they possess? For all the concern by animal rightists about the rights of animals, relatively little has been written concerning this normative question; what has been written is not impressive. Thus, rather than follow the unsatisfactory discussions in this area where so often it is assumed that successfully to show that animals, some or all, can possess rights, is to show that they do possess the rights to life and to freedom from suffering, or that, because some unsatisfactory arguments for certain human rights seem to admit of restatement in respect of animals, that animals and humans are on all fours in respect of these rights – I shall proceed in a more positive way by looking at how arguments concerning human rights proceed, first examining their general patterns, and then briefly noting particular arguments for particular rights. This discussion will reveal that the establishing of the existence of moral rights is a subtle, complex matter, that the arguments available in respect of human rights do not establish either that all humans possess the same rights, or that where they do possess the same rights, they possess them equally. Further it will be evident that most of the important arguments relating to human rights, rights such as those to life, liberty, self-development, private property, privacy, and the like, are not transferable to animals.

1. *The Kinds of Considerations Urged in Support of Human Rights*

If the considerations urged in support of human rights are examined, it will be found that the more important are:

(a) A persistent claim more common in the eighteenth century than today, has been that certain rights are self-evidently so. It is an appeal which I suggest is appropriate in respect of certain basic rights, if 'self-evident' is understood correctly, as by W. D. Ross in the context of his discussion of our knowledge of the principles of prima facie obligation. Rights such as the rights to life as persons, to moral autonomy and integrity, to respect as persons, appear to be rights which are self-evident, and in respect of which, argument other than that directed at clarification of what is involved in acknowledging the moral right is neither necessary nor possible. No animal right appears to be a self-evident right. The facts which make the right to life of persons a self-evident right do not hold of animals.

(b) Theistic arguments that seek to derive human rights from God's right – for example, Locke's argument for man's right to life – have figured prominently in discussions of human rights. Such arguments are equally possible in respect of animal rights but seem not to have been forthcoming. On the contrary, orthodox Christianity denies that God confers rights on animals, whilst those Eastern religions which prescribe respect for animals seem not to do so simply *qua* animals. In any case, there are problems in the way of theistic arguments for rights, making as they do, the existence of human moral rights depend on the existence of God, and explaining them as accorded and not as intrinsic rights. Few moral philosophers today would be happy to accept the view that there can be no rational grounds for belief in the existence of human moral rights if God does not exist, or cannot be known to exist.

(c) Many arguments that have been urged in support of specific human rights, for example J. S. Mill's arguments for the right to liberty in *Liberty*, proceed by reference to the claim that certain things, knowledge, rationality, rational belief, self-development, right living, moral responsibility, pleasure and happiness (interests), are intrinsically good. The precise details of such arguments are hard to fill in, and seem to vary from writer to writer. Some writers, including Mill on one possible interpretation, seem to assume that we have a right to what is intrinsically good, or at least, a right to access to what is intrinsically good. A more likely interpretation of Mill's argument is that unless rights to access to these goods are accorded to civilized adult human beings, these persons will be unable to enjoy these goods, that these goods will be lost to mankind, and hence, that moral and legal rights must be accorded to civilized adults.

These are important arguments. The first version either rests on a claim that we have as a self-evident right, a right to these goods, or to access to them, or it is incomplete and requires filling out by reference to an argument in support of this more basic right. It is significant that the argument is seen to establish not that all human beings possess rights such as the right to liberty, equally, but only that some humans, mature, civilized adults possess that right, and then not always, that is, not equally. If the basic right to goods or to access to them could be shown also to hold of animals, this argument would have a limited application in respect of them. It would be limited in two ways. Most, but not all of the goods upon which it rests, are goods not available to animals. Secondly, the considerations which tell against ascribing various rights on this basis to children, the insane, the weak, and the gullible, would in a large measure also hold in respect of animals. Their exercise of such rights would more often lead to evils than to goods. However, this would not always be so, for example, in respect of pleasure and freedom from pain. Where captivity leads to pointless suffering, or where an animal such as a chimpanzee is harmlessly and with pleasure collecting and eating bananas and other food, to interfere with its liberty would be to deprive it of pleasure, even to cause it pain. Relevant here is J. Rachels's discussion.[14] However, as is evident from the Millian argument, only very limited rights, rights of only some few animals, could be argued for along these lines.

The second version of the argument, that which Mill probably intended to urge, would seem to be a telling argument for according legal rights, and for social rights, if meaning can be given to the latter concept. It is less evidently sound as an argument for moral rights. Typically moral rights are possessed intrinsically rather than accorded by someone else, other than in the case of property rights where moral rights may be transferred. Nonetheless, it is true that a moral authority, God or the state in so far as it is or may be a moral authority, could accord moral rights, but the circumstances in which this could occur must be very special ones. The same limitations hold in respect of the kinds of goods on which the argument rests, and concerning those with the capacity and judgment successfully to seek and realize these goods if accorded the relevant rights.

As noted earlier, those who claim that animals possess rights often mean simply that animals ought to be accorded legal and/or social rights. If this is what they mean, they would do well to state their position more accurately. They would then see that this Millian argument might well provide qualified – very qualified – support for their position.

The real worry about these arguments, whether they be arguments for human or animal rights, is that the version which seeks to establish what would be genuinely moral rights rests on a claim that we have a basic moral right to goods or to access to goods, when it is far from clear that we possess such a right, whilst the other version avoids this very questionable assumption by arguing only for accorded rights, where the only plausible meaning that can be given to the accorded rights is as legal or social, but not as moral rights.

(d) Many arguments for rights proceed by deriving rights from duties, from duties in others, or duties in the being claimed to possess the right.

Rights as based in duties in others: Certain rights and duties – most evidently, contractual rights and duties between specific persons – are correlative in the sense that the duty of *X* to *Y*, confers a right in *Y* against *X*, and vice versa. Indeed, the promise or contract which creates the right and duty, may well be said to create both in the one act such that it is the promise which is the source of both, rather than the duty the source of the right, or the right, the duty. Such rights as contractual rights are obviously one kind of special case. Duties of justice are also of this kind. Consider here rights and duties which derive from merit, desert, possession of a relevant attribute. Here rights and duties may also be correlative, although they need not always be such since the duties need not be to determinate persons but to groups of persons, etc. There are other cases in which duties to determinate persons, for example, duties of parents to their children, are commonly thought to create correlative rights in the children. However, again, as with the case of promising, I suggest a closer examination of the case reveals that a strong case for the children being said to have a correlative right can be developed only by establishing that the duty and right spring from the same source. Otherwise we can simply, although usefully, speak *as if* the children have rights against their parents by virtue of their parents' duties, but strictly this will not be the case. This is confirmed by cases of duties of charity to specific persons. No matter how specific these duties are, the person who is the object of the duty of charity has no real right against the person subject to the duty to help him. A case to the contrary can be made out only if the right and the duty are to be derived from some common base.

What then of more general duties towards others – towards other human beings in general, or towards conscious beings, sentient beings, or the like? I suggest that rights do not follow from such duties. At best we can talk as if rights are conferred by the duties, but often this will be seriously misleading. Further it would involve a very drastic revision of our ordinary conception of a right. This is important in the context of animal rights, as it would be along these lines that the most plausible avenue of argument for animal rights could otherwise have been developed. Clearly we have a duty not to inflict pointless suffering on sentient beings, non-human and human. We have a duty not to destroy beautiful objects and beings. And so on. The former duty would confer certain rights to freedom from suffering on all animals capable of suffering and the latter duty would confer certain rights to life and freedom from mutilation on some members of the animal kingdom, many carnivores, birds, etc., although in the case of the former, possibly at the expense of a right to freedom, if there were the correlativity of duties and rights that is being denied here. Vexed questions would of course have arisen on this view concerning beauty and which animals possessed rights on this count. Similarly, were there such a correlativity, and had men the duty not to exterminate or let die endangered species, the members of such species would have possessed the right to life on that count.

Since not all duties create correlative rights, the most relevant arguments here when considering animal rights might seem to be those that relate to the duties which do involve correlative rights. Yet here too there appear to be problems. The rights which rest on promises and contracts and the duties created by them cannot arise in respect of animals. Animals cannot make promises, and we cannot make promises to animals. The duties of justice are the other important kinds of duties that carry with them correlative rights. Here it is commonly assumed that the duties of justice relate only to humans, and that therefore the relevant correlative rights can hold only of humans. However, if one considers the accounts that have been given of justice, the rendering to each what is due, treating equals equally, unequals unequally in the relevant respects, discriminating only on the basis of a relevant difference, there seems no reason in the nature of justice itself why its principles could not be extended, if there were no other grounds for rejecting such an extension. I suggest that the reason the principles are not so applied is because the notion of a right held by the object of the duty of justice is so basic and intrinsic to the whole concept of justice, that where the object of the duty is apprehended as one who is incapable of rights, it is seen therefore to be incapable of being an object of a duty of justice. Since here we are proceeding on the hypothesis that animals could possess rights, it would follow that they could be the objects of duties of justice, and hence possess the rights that are correlative with these duties. The substantial question would then become that of determining what duties of justice could hold in respect of animals.

The key to justice is the treating of equals equally, discriminating only on the basis of a relevant difference. Some, such as P. Singer and others, who see animals as coming under the orbit of justice, see as the basic duty of justice that of respecting all interests, whatever their nature and content, equally, the relevant equality being equality in being possessors of interests. There are obvious objections to treating interests as a relevant basis for treatment – some interests are evil, and ought to be overridden, thwarted, morally ignored. It is what makes up the content of interests that is relevant to justice. This varies from person to person, being to being. I suggest that a serious approach to animal rights via justice would involve examining why, when, and in what ways, considerations such as desert, merit, well-being, levels of well-being, needs properly understood, wishes, desires, are relevant considerations in respect of justice in the treatment of human beings, and then considering whether these considerations apply as dictates of justice in respect of animals. Much is made in discussions of justice of the claims based on needs. If the concept of need is used as a normative concept, its use prejudges the normative question, and the relevant task would be that of determining what ought to be called needs. If the concept is used as a non-normative one, then it will be evident that the needs of humans – and seemingly the same sort of thing will hold of other beings – should be taken into account not because they are needs, but because they are needs of a certain kind of being, human beings; and where the neglect to satisfy them leads to certain kinds of evil results.[15] Justice does not dictate that all needs of all human beings be satisfied. Needs *qua* needs carry no moral weight – otherwise plant needs, the needs of lower animals, and the like, morally would have to be taken into account. Similarly in respect of well-being and levels of well-being. The kind and quality of well-being are of importance, not well-being in the abstract. Thus the unravelling of what justice would dictate in respect of animals is a very subtle, complex, difficult enterprise. However, whilst many considerations of justice, merit, desert, and the like, will not apply to animals, some relevant considerations will apply such that some rights of justice may be derived from the relevant duties, if the other basic difficulty about the possibility of possessing rights could be overcome.

Rights as based on duties of the possessor of the right: Many arguments for human rights proceed from the fact that human beings are moral agents with moral duties. Thus, whilst the Thomistic theory of natural law derives both rights and duties from man's natural (and supernatural) end, many exponents of natural rights theories seem to argue for specific natural rights from the duty man has to attain his natural (and supernatural) end, and from his right to carry out that duty. Such arguments are among the more straightforward, important arguments for human moral rights. They obviously are not available in respect of animals.

(e) It is also argued that rights spring from man's capacity to be a moral agent, a moral person. A basic, self-evident right, and one which carries with it many far-reaching, derivative rights, is the right to be a moral being.

This right does not spring from any duty such as a duty to be a moral being; the mere capacity to be a moral agent self-evidently confers the right to be such. From this right flow many other rights, including the rights to life, to moral liberty, self-development, to care for one's offspring and generally to carry out the duties one has as a person and as a unique person. This is one of the most powerful arguments for human rights. It is not available in respect of animals.

As is evident from the discussion in (c) many arguments for rights which are commonly seen as being basic rights are in fact arguments from some more basic right such as the right to access to intrinsic goods, the right to be a moral being, the right to be self-developing, the right to life. In so far as these basic rights can appertain only to free agents, to persons, to that extent the arguments from them can hold only of free agents.

It is important to note that the above considerations upon which claims about human rights are based do not seek to establish that all human beings possess the same rights, nor that, where they do possess the same rights, they possess them equally. They imply that different people may have different rights, and that men may have different rights to different degrees or under different conditions, and that not all the rights possessed by men need be possessed by them all their lives. The same kinds of qualifications would carry over in respect of any rights animals may be shown to possess in terms of such considerations.

2. *Human Rights and their Possible Relevance to Animals and Animal Rights*

Rights commonly claimed in respect of human beings include the rights to life and health; the rights to moral and physical integrity; the right to happiness and to freedom from suffering; the right to liberty; the right to self-development; the right to private property; marriage and family rights; rights to knowledge, true and rational belief; the right to education; the right to privacy.

Various of these rights cannot apply to animals. This is so in respect of the rights to moral integrity, self-development, knowledge, true and rational belief, and to education as it is understood by those who stress that right, because of the lack of the relevant capacities. There are some problems on this count in respect of the rights to private property, to marry, to have and care for one's offspring. However, important aspects of these rights, for example, with private property rights, rights of use if not of control and disposal, are possible for animals. Various of the arguments urged in support of these rights in respect of humans – from the right to life, etc., if such rights hold of animals – appear to be transferable, although notwithstanding Rachels's ingenious although utterly unconvincing discussion, not Locke's very unsatisfactory labour argument for private property.[16] (That whole argument depends on the concept of the person, of the labour as labour of a rational, planning being, which knows what it is doing. We think of human activity as capable of creating rights because and in so far as it is rationally directed towards planned goals. Mere human activity seems not even prima facie to create rights. Even less that of animals, parasites, predators, and the like. Further, the argument assumes the absence of prior ownership. It assumes a right of the first labourer unrestrictedly to appropriate that on which he labours, albeit that his labour is only a small element of what he appropriates. These assumptions have never been satisfactorily dealt with. They become even more difficult to handle if the animal kingdom is to be included in the group of labourers. Is anything in the world free of pre-ownership? Can any meaningful application be given to the labour theory in the contemporary world given existing ownership and pre-ownership by humans and animals?)

Our earlier discussion brought out the limited nature of the arguments available in support of an animal right to liberty. Animals are incapable of positive liberty. The Kantian arguments for a right to liberty from respect for autonomy, especially moral autonomy do not apply to animals. And, as already noted, the utilitarian arguments apply only with great qualifications in respect of human beings, and with vastly more qualifications in respect of animals, and then only in respect of a right to negative liberty, a right to limited freedom from interference for certain animals. The same utilitarian considerations may give other animals a right to be confined and protected. Even greater qualifications would seem to hold in respect of the right to privacy. The arguments relevant to the human right – which I myself deny to be a basic human right – most likely to be transferable to animals are those from there being a need, from happiness via the need, and those from the enjoyment of privacy as essential for security from evils and harm. Obviously, as bird-watchers and animal-watchers generally so commonly claim, few if any animals are harmed by unobtrusive, secret invasions of their privacy.

The human rights of most obvious relevance to those concerned with animals and animal rights are the rights to life and to freedom from suffering. These are the least discussed and least argued of all human rights. The right to freedom from suffering is implicitly covered by the utilitarian arguments discussed in (c) above. The same sorts of qualifications which hold in respect of humans would hold of animals, but more so. And the basic difficulties encountered by the kinds of arguments for rights noted there remain. The less unsatisfactory arguments for the right to life of humans proceed by reference not to life in the abstract, but to the kind and quality of life of which human beings are capable. They point to features of human life and existence that are not shared with animals. Different arguments are necessary in respect of animals. If it could be shown that animal life – some or all – has intrinsic value, an attempt to establish animal rights to life could be made in terms of the utilitarian arguments. However, as is evident from P. Singer's thoughtful, careful discussion, there are difficulties in the way of plausibly attributing intrinsic value to animal life.[17]

3. *Specifically Animal Rights*

Would there be specifically animal rights, tiger rights, pelican rights, tape-worm rights, if animals were to be capable of possessing rights? I suggest that any specifically animal rights are likely only to arise from special needs of the different animals, where these are needs that ought to be respected. Thus carnivores, needing to kill other animals in order to live, might be claimed to have the right to kill these other animals, whereas their vegetarian victims may lack the right to kill other animals except in self-defence, but have the right to eat grass, leaves, or the like, provided they leave enough for other animals. Problems which arise from pursuing this line of thought may best be discussed in Section III.

III. Respecting Rights, Animal and Human

The arguments and considerations on which rights are grounded are such as to imply two things about rights, whether they be animal or human. The one is that no right is always an absolute right – some are prima facie rights, always rights but not always absolute rights, some are conditional rights, only rights under certain conditions, and even then possibly only prima facie and not necessarily absolute rights. The other implication is that rights are not possessed by all members of a species *qua* member of a species, but *qua* possessor of relevant attributes. This means that different beings may possess different rights, and the rights they possess they may possess to different degrees. It is evident from the discussion in Section II that if animals were to be capable of possessing rights, rights to life, freedom from suffering, liberty, and the like, they would possess rights to different degrees, from one another, and with respect to human possessors of rights.

Further, rights clash with one another. We are familiar with this in the human situation, and seek to resolve these clashes by weighing up the conflicting rights in terms of their various stringencies, when it is impossible to find some way of avoiding the conflict. There are conflicts within particular rights, between the claims of the right to life of different individuals, and between the claims of different rights, to life, liberty, property, moral integrity. It is impossible to set out priority rules for resolving such conflicts. They are to be resolved only by reference to the relative stringencies of the rights involved; and this is to be determined by reference to the ground of the right, and the basis on which the individuals concerned come to possess the rights. In many cases, the conflicts seem rationally to be irresoluble. Consider here the right to life as a right of recipience, and the clashes over conflicting needs for help. The problems posed by clashes of human rights then are immense. However, we are clear about our goal. Our goal is that of the maximum satisfaction of or respect for rights, taking into account the relative stringencies of rights.

If it were to be shown that animals possess moral rights, the problems posed by clashes of rights would become vastly more difficult. Besides the clashes within human rights, and between human and animal rights, we should be faced with clashes between animal rights. Since animals are incapable of engaging in the relevant moral deliberations and acting to resolve the conflicts, it would be left to man to act to resolve them. Can he satisfactorily do this? Indeed, are there possible moral solutions of such conflicts? Consider here the rights to life, health, freedom from suffering. Today, because of the reasons discussed earlier in this paper, it would generally be agreed that these rights are rights of recipience. The considerations bearing on this would seem to hold, if rights apply at all, in respect of the rights of at least certain animals. The human person faced with the conflict between the rights of carnivores and predators, of disease-causing, debilitating parasites, and like animals, on the one hand, and their victims on the other, would have to weigh the rights to life, health, freedom from suffering of the aggressors, against the rights to life, health, freedom from suffering of the victims. Is this possible? Is a meaningful solution possible? Indeed, is it possible meaningfully to speak of the rights to life of the victims – rights which normally are seen to carry with them a right to self-defence and to be defended by others in whose care they are – and at the same time speak of the aggressor's right to kill? Surely the human guardian of animal rights would be faced with logically incompatible demands, a demand that he protect the threatened animal to safeguard its right to life as a right of recipience, and, at the same time, to prevent interferences with the aggressor's right to kill – and to life – where it too is a right of recipience. It is not simply that there can be no priority rules, nor that the weighing up of the conflicting rights is extremely difficult, but that there is a logical incompatibility in the claims made by the rights. The possessor of a right to life has a right not to be let die, and not simply not to be killed. Yet this involves killing or allowing to be killed another possessor of an equally stringent right to life. So too with the rights to health and to freedom from suffering. This problem would not be a remote, rare one. If our domestic pets, cats and dogs, cannot lead healthy, happy lives on vegetarian diets, we should be confronted with this problem immediately it were established that they possess these rights. I suggest therefore that there would not simply be vastly difficult practical problems and calculations to be faced in determining what constituted the maximum morally right satisfaction of rights. There would also be the theoretical problem of whether acceptance of the kinds of rights that are likely to be ascribed to animals is compatible with the maximum satisfaction of rights' remaining a meaningful, logically coherent goal.

NOTES

1 I am much indebted to Dr. Jan Srzednicki of the University of Melbourne for reading a draft of this paper, and making a number of important critical and constructive comments concerning it.

2 *Animal Liberation*, Random House, New York 1975.

3 See P. Singer, 'Animals and the Value of Life', in Tom Regan (Ed.), *Matters of Life and Death*, Random House, New York 1979.

4 The UNESCO proposed charter of animal rights would seem to be no more than this, a very misleading way of drawing attention of duties in respect of animals; it may also be a demand that legal rights be accorded to animals.

5 J. Locke, *Second Treatise of Civil Government*, Ch. II, esp. Sect. 7.

6 R. G. Frey, 'Russell and the Essence of Desire', forthcoming in *Philosophy*.

7 See my 'Rights', *Philosophical Quarterly*, Vol. 15 (1965). Also relevant are: T. Regan, 'McCloskey on Why Animals Cannot Have Rights', *Philosophical Quarterly*, Vol. 26 (1976), R. G. Frey, 'Interests and Animal Rights', *Philosophical Quarterly*, Vol. 27

(1977), and J. Feinberg, 'The Rights of Animals and Unborn Generations', in W. Blackstone (Ed.), *Philosophy and Environmental Crisis,* University of Georgia Press, Athens, Georgia 1974.

8 Op. cit., p. 52.

9 L. Nelson, *System of Ethics,* trans. by N. Guterman, Yale University Press, New Haven 1956.

10 Ibid., p. 99.

11 Ibid., p. 100.

12 Op. cit., p. 51.

13 A. I. Melden, *Rights and Persons,* Blackwell, Oxford 1977, esp. Ch. VI.

14 See J. Rachels, 'Do Animals Have a Right to Liberty?' in T. Regan and P. Singer (Eds.), *Animals and Human Obligations,* Prentice-Hall, Englewood Cliffs 1976.

15 See my 'Human Needs, Rights and Political Values', *American Philosophical Quarterly,* Vol. 13 (1976).

16 Op. cit., p. 208.

17 'Animals and the Value of Life'.

Annette Baier

The Rights of Past and Future Persons

No one doubts that future generations, once they are present and actual, will have rights, if any of us have rights.[1] What difference is made if we say, not that they *will* have, but that they *do* have rights—*now?* I see two main points of difference—first, that those rights will then give rise to obligations on our part, as well as on their contemporaries' part; and, second, that what they have a right *to* will be different. In addition to whatever political and civil rights they have or will have, they will also each have a right to a fair share of what is then left of the earth's scarce resources. If they *now* have rights, they have rights to a share of what is *now* left of those scarce resources. To believe that they have rights is to believe that *we* must safeguard those rights and that, where the right is to a share, that we must share with them, and that the size of our share is affected by their right to share.

Should we believe that future persons not merely *will* have rights, but that they presently *do* have rights? To decide this I shall first consider whether any conceptual incoherence would result. Having eliminated that threat, I shall turn to the question of what rational or moral grounds there might be for the belief. I shall argue that some of the reasons for recognizing obligations to future persons are closely connected with reasons for recognizing the rights of past persons and that these reasons are good ones. In addition there are the obligations that arise from our responsibility for the very existence of those future persons, through our support of social policies that affect the size and nature of the human population in the future. I shall argue that we have good reason to recognize these obligations to future persons, whether or not we see them as arising out of their rights.

I turn first to the question of what we are committed to in asserting that a person has a certain right. I take it that this is to assert:

This is a revision of a paper originally read in a symposium at the Eastern Meeting of the American Philosophical Association, December 28, 1973. It has not been previously published.

(*a*). That at least one other person has an obligation to the right-holder. This obligation may be to refrain from interfering with some activity of the right-holder or to take some positive steps to secure for the right-holder what he or she has a right to. These steps may be ones that benefit the right-holder or some third party, as would be the case if I have promised a friend to feed his cat. He thereby has a right to my services that are intended to benefit the cat. Following Feinberg's[2] terminology, I shall say that the obligation is *to* the right-holder and *toward* whomever is the intended beneficiary.

(*b*). There is, or there should and could in practice be, socially recognized means for the right-holder, or his or her proxy, to take appropriate action should the obligations referred to in (*a*) be neglected. This action will range from securing belated discharge of the obligation, to securing compensation for its neglect, to the initiation of punitive measures against the delinquent obligated person.

I think that this account covers both legally recognized rights and also moral rights that are more than mere "manifesto" rights,[3] since clause (*b*) requires that effective recognition could be given to such rights. Such effective recognition can of course be given only to a set of nonconflicting rights, and so I assume that to claim anything as a right is to claim that its effective recognition is compatible with the effective recognition of the other rights one claims to exist.[4] To claim a moral right to something not effectively recognized as a right is to claim that it could without contradiction to other justifiably recognized rights *be* given recognition, that only inertia, ignorance, greed or ill-will prevents its recognition.

This account of what it is to have a right differs in another sense from the account that is more commonly given. The point of difference lies in the extension of power to claim the right from the right-holder to his spokesman, vicar, or proxy. This extension is required to make sense of the concept of rights of past or future generations. I think we already accept such an extension in empowering executors to claim the rights of the deceased whose wills they execute. The role of executor is distinct from that of trustee for the heirs. We recognize obligations both *to* and *toward* the legal heirs, and *to* the person who made the will. Where the legal heirs are specified only as the "issue" of certain persons known to the will-maker, we already accept the concept of an obligation, owed by the trustees, to look after the interests of such not-yet-determinate persons.

Can those who protect the rights of future persons be properly regarded as their spokesmen, claimants of their rights in the present, when they, unlike executors of wills, cannot be appointed by the original right-holder? The rights of past persons, claimed by their recognized spokesmen, are person-specific rights to have their legally valid powers exercised, while the rights in the present claimed for future persons will be general human rights. No one needs to be privy to the individual wills of future persons to claim their right to clean air. Already recognized spokesmen for known past persons, claiming their particular rights, need knowledge of them, their deeds, and their wishes, and so are sensibly required to have a special tie to the original right-holder, initiated by him. Spokesmen for future persons, claiming general rights, need no such tie.

If future generations have rights, then we, or some of us in some capacity, have obligations to and presumably also toward them, and their spokesman should be empowered to take action to see to it that we discharge those obligations. I see no conceptual incorrectness in attributing such rights. Admittedly we do not now recognize any person as the proper spokesman, guardian, and rights-claimant for future generations. But we could, and perhaps we should.

The fact that future generations are not *now* living persons is irrelevant to the issue, if, as I have argued, we are willing to speak of the rights of those who are no longer living persons. The fact that we do not and cannot have knowledge of the special characteristics and wishes of future generations is, I have claimed, also irrelevant to the recognition of their rights to basic nonspecial human requirements, such as uncontaminated air. Our dependence on fossil fuels may be, compared with the needs of past generations, quite special, and there may be good reason not to extrapolate that need into the distant future. But there is no reason to think that the need for air will be lessened by technological progress or regress in the future. Our ignorance of precisely *who* future generations will be, and uncertainty of how numerous they will be, may be relevant to the priority of our obligations to them, compared with obligations to the living, should conflicts arise; but it is not relevant to the reality of obligations to future persons, nor to the moral priority of such obligations over our tastes for conspicuous consumption or our demands for luxury and for the freedom to waste or destroy resources.

As lawful heirs of specific past persons, some of us may have a right to what those persons intended us to possess, should there be sufficient moral reason to recognize the disputed right to pass on private property and to inherit it. By contrast, we all inherit a social order, a cultural tradition, air and water, not as private heirs of private will-makers but as members of a continuous community. We benefit from the wise planning, or perhaps the thoughtless but fortunate conservation, of past generations. In so far as such inherited public goods as constitutions, civil liberties, universities, parks, and uncontaminated water come to us by the deliberate intention of past generations, we inherit them not as sole beneficiaries but as persons able to share and pass on such goods to an indefinite run of future generations. It was, presumably, not for this generation in particular that public spirited persons in past generations saved or sacrificed.

Rights and obligations are possessed by persons not in virtue of their unique individuality but in virtue of roles they fill, roles that relate to others. For example, children, *qua* children, have obligations to and rights against parents *qua* parents. My obligations as a teacher are owed to my students, whoever they may be. When I discharge obligations to them, such as ordering textbooks, I do not and need not know who those students will be. As long as I believe that determinate actual persons will fill the role of students, will occupy a position involving a moral tie to me, my obligations are real and not lessened by my ignorance of irrelevant details concerning those role-fillers. As long as we believe there will be persons related to us as we are related to past generations, then any obligations and rights this relation engenders will be real. Whether there will be such persons is something about which we can have well-based beliefs, especially as it is to some degree up to us whether to allow such roles to be filled.

The ontological precariousness of future generations that some see as a reason for not recognizing any rights of theirs is not significantly greater than that of the future states of present persons. In neither case does ignorance of details about the future, or the possible nonexistence in that future of those who would benefit from discharge of obligations in the present, affect the reality of our obligations. To make sacrifices *now* so that others may benefit in the future is always to risk wasting that sacrifice. The moral enterprise is intrinsically a matter of risky investment,[5] if we measure the return solely in terms of benefits reaped by those toward whom obligations are owed. Only if virtue is its own reward is morality ever a safe investment. The only special feature in a moral tie between us and future generations lies in the inferiority of our knowledge about them, not in the inferiority of their ontological status. They are not merely possible persons, they are whichever possible persons will in the future be actual.

So far I have found no conceptual reason for disallowing talk of the rights of future persons. Neither their nonpresence, nor our ignorance of *who* exactly they are, nor our uncertainty concerning how many of them there are, rules out the appropriateness of recognizing rights on their part. The fact that they cannot now claim their rights from us puts them in a position no different from that of past persons with rights in the present—namely, a position of dependency on some representative in this generation, someone empowered to speak for them. Rights typically are *claimed* by their possessors, so if we are to recognize rights of future persons we must empower some persons to make claims for them.

Another thing that can be done with a right is to waive it. Past persons who leave no will waive the right that they had to determine the heirs of their private property. Since nothing could count as a sign that future generations waive their rights against us, then this dimension of the concept of a right will get no purchase with future generations, unless we empower present persons not merely to claim but also to waive rights of future persons. Waiving rights and alienating them by gift or exchange are both voluntary renunciations of what a right puts in the right-holder's secure possession. However, waiving rights, unlike alienating them, does not involve a transfer of the right. Since the rights that are transferred are always special rights, and the rights of future persons that we are considering are general ones, there can be no question of transferring such rights. But might a proxy waive them? Guardians of present persons (children, incompetents) do have the power to waive some rights on behalf of their wards, but the justification for this practice, and any exercise of it, depends upon the availability of special knowledge of what will and will not benefit the right-holder. It is barely conceivable that we or any official we appointed could have such knowledge of the special needs of some future generations. If we were facing the prospect of a nuclear war and foresaw that any immediate successor generations would live in the ruins of civilization as we have known it, we might judge that there was no point in trying to preserve, say, the Bill of Rights for one's successors, although they had a *prima facie* right to inherit it. One might on their behalf waive that right, in extreme conditions, and bury the Constitution, rather than prolong our agony to fight for it. But such scenarios are bizarre, since it is barely conceivable that those who would bequeath to future generations the effects of a nuclear war would care about the rest of their bequest, about the fragments that might be shored against our ruin. The benefits that might be gained for future generations by empowering any of their ancestors to waive some of their rights seem minimal. Still, this is a question not of the conceptual absurdity of waiving a recognized right of future generations but of the practical wisdom of giving another this power.

I conclude that no conceptual error is involved in speaking of the rights of future generations. The concept of a right includes that of the justified power of the right-holder or his spokesman to press for discharge of obligations affecting his particular interests, or to renounce this power. The concept has already shown itself capable of extension to cover the rights of past persons and could as easily accommodate the rights of future generations if we saw good reason thus to extend it.

What might give us such a reason? I have already spoken of our position in relation to past generations whose actions have benefited us, either by planning or by good luck. The conservative way to decide the *moral* question is to ask whether we ourselves claim anything as a matter of right against past generations. Do we feel we had a *right* to be left the relatively uncontaminated water we found available to us, as a generation? Do we feel that the Romans, whose cutting down of forests left barren, eroded hillsides, violated a right of later generations? I think that we do not usually attribute to past generations the obligation to save for us, we do not accept their savings as only our just due, we do not usually condemn past generations where their actions have had bad effects in the present. But the reason for this may be that we are reluctant to attribute obligations where we are uncertain of the ability to meet them. Past generations, unlike ours, were rarely in a position to foresee the long-term effects of their actions, so are rightly not blamed by us for any harm they caused. Where what they did had good consequences for us, we accept these not as our due but as our good fortune. Where past generations deliberately saved or conserved for us, we accept their savings not as something they owed us, even when they may have believed they did owe it, but as something they chose to give us, where the "us" in question includes future generations.

It is possible that we stand to future generations in a relation in which no previous generation has stood to us; so that, although we have no rights against past generations, future generations do have rights against us. This is a possible position one might defend. Our knowledge and our power are significantly different even from that of our grandparents' generation, and might be thought to give rise to new moral relationships and new obligations. Before turning to consider how we might determine what those new obligations are, and how to find for them a common ground with old obligations, I want to look more closely at our relations to past generations and to ask if there is anything they might have done that would have given us a reason to blame them for failing in their obligations to us.

I take as an example of a benefit made possible by the actions of earlier generations my own education at the University of Otago in New Zealand. This university was founded extraordinarily early in the establishment of the colony because of the high priority the Scottish colonists gave to education and to its free availability. The existence of a distinguished university, and of the institutions supporting and financing it, was due to the efforts of people in my great grandparents' generation. Had they not made that effort, or had they or later generations established a university that only the wealthy could attend, I would have had no ground for complaint against them. They did not owe me a university education. But had an intervening generation allowed the university and its supporting institutions to founder, and done so from unwillingness to spend on its upkeep the resources that could be used for personal profit, I and my generation *would* blame those who failed to pass on the public benefits they themselves inherited. One obligation that every generation has toward subsequent generations is to leave "as much and as good" of the public goods previous generations have bequeathed them. This obligation arises as much from a right of past persons to have their good intentions respected as it does from any right of future persons, but I think there *is* a right to have passed on to one those public goods that, but for ill will or irresponsibility, would have been passed on. If I had been deprived of an education because a previous generation had destroyed an already founded university for the sake of its own greater luxury, I would feel that *my* rights, as well as those of the university's founders, had been overridden. It is interesting to note that the rights of past benefactors and their future beneficiaries give rise to one and the same obligation. Indeed, if we consider the motivation of the university's founders, who were heirs to a Scottish tradition of investment in public education, we find that they saw themselves as much as *preservers* as creators, as passing on, in new and difficult conditions, a heritage they had themselves received. As one of their hymns put it:

> They reap not where they laboured,
> We reap where they have sown.
> Our harvest will be garnered
> By ages yet unknown.

The metaphor of seed and harvest is the appropriate one where what is passed on, sown, is the same good as was received or harvested from the earlier sowing by others. The obligation that each generation has, which is owed equally to past and future generations, is the obligation to preserve the seed crop, the obligation to regenerate what they did not themselves generate.

That this obligation can be seen as due, indifferently, to past or future persons shows something of considerable importance about obligations in general and about the moral community. Earlier I said that rights are possessed not in virtue of any unique individuality but in virtue of roles we fill. The crucial role we fill, as moral beings, is as members of a cross-generational community, a community of beings who look before and after, who interpret the past in the light of the present, who see the future as growing out of the past, who see themselves as members of enduring families, nations, cultures, traditions. Perhaps we could even use Kant's language and say that it is because persons are *noumenal* beings that obligations to past persons and to future persons reinforce one another, that every obligation is owed by, to, and toward persons as participants in a continuing process of the generation and regeneration of shared values.

To stress the temporal continuity of the moral community is not to deny that accumulating knowledge and increasing power make a difference to the obligations one has. Earlier I said that the reason we do not morally condemn earlier generations for those actions of theirs whose consequences are bad for us is the reasonable doubt we feel about the extent to which they knew what they were doing. If the overgrazing that turned grasslands into deserts were thought by us to have been a *calculated* policy to increase a past generation's nonrenewed wealth, at our expense, we would condemn them for it. Any obligations we have to generations future to us that find no exact analogue in obligations past persons owed us arise, I believe, both from special features of our known control over the existence and the conditions of life of future generations and from our awareness of what we owe to past generations. We are especially self-conscious members of the cross-generational community, aware both of how much, and how much more than previous generations, we benefit from the investment of earlier generations and of the extent to which we may determine the fate of future generations. Such self-consciousness has its costs in added obligations.

Another sort of obligation we may have to future generations arises out of our failure to discharge other obligations to them. We, unlike earlier generations, are in a position to control population growth and to attempt to gear it to the expected supply of essential resources. Where we are failing to use this ability responsibly, we incur obligations to compensate our victims in a future overcrowded world for the harm we have thereby done them. Special efforts to increase, not merely to conserve, needed food and water resources are the appropriate accompaniment to our neglect of the obligation not to overbreed.

Our special position, relative to previous generations, in the procession of human possessors of knowledge and power, gives us the ability to end the sequence of human generations as well as to be self-conscious and deliberate in our procreative or regenerative activities. It is a consequence of my version of the cross-generational moral community that this power to end the human community's existence could justifiably be exercised only in conditions so extreme that one could sincerely believe that past generations would concur in the judgment that it all should end. I do not think that anyone, past, present, or future, has a right to exist, and certainly no merely possible person has such a right. But we do not need the rights of possible persons to restrain us from bringing about the end of human life, the rights of past persons and the very nature of membership in a moral community rule that out in all except the very direst circumstances. Just as we have no *right* to use up all scarce resources in our generation for our own luxury or whim but, rather, an obligation to renew what we use, to pass on what we received, so we have no right to decree the ending of an enterprise in which we are latecomers. To end it all would not be the communal equivalent of suicide, since it would end not only our endeavors but those invested endeavors of all our predecessors. Only if they could be seen as concurring in the decision not to renew human life, or not to allow it to be renewed, could such a decision be likened to suicide.

I have said almost nothing about the theoretical basis for the obligations and rights I have claimed exist. Indeed, I am not sure that theories are the right sort of thing on which to ground assertions about obligations. In any case I shall not here go into the question of which moral theory would best systematize the sorts of reasons there are for recognizing the rights and obligations I have invoked. Kant's moral theory, if it could be stripped of its overintellectualism, Burke's account of a cross-generational community, if it could be stripped of its contractarian overtones, Hume's account of the virtues recognized by us humans who see ourselves as "plac'd in a kind of middle station betwixt the past and the future" who "imagine our ancestors to be, in a manner, mounted above us, and our posterity to lie below us,"[6] Rawls's idea of social union, of a continuing community in which "the powers of human individuals living at any one time takes the cooperation of many generations (or even societies) over a long period of time,"[7] if this could be used, as he does not use it, to give an account of the right as well as the good, all these give us assistance in articulating the reasons that we should recognize obligations of piety to past persons and responsibility to future ones. I do not think that either utilitarian theories or contractarian theories, or any version of any moral theory I am familiar with, captures the right reasons for the right attitudes to past and future persons. Perhaps we need a new theory, but the "intuitions" it will ground are, I believe, very old ones. I have relied, rather dogmatically, on those intuitions that I think are fairly widely shared, but before attempting to summarize in broad outline the factors relevant to our obligations to future generations I need to make clear a few points about the community in which such obligations arise.

First, it is not a community to which one *chooses* to belong, but one in which one finds oneself. By the time any moral reflections arise, one is already heir to a language and a way of life, and one has already received benefits from those particular older persons who cared for one in one's initial extreme dependency and who initiated one into a way of life. This way of life typically includes conventions to enable one voluntarily to take on obligations as well as to renounce and transfer some rights; but not all obligations are self-imposed, and those that are arise from institutions, like that of promising, which depend for their preservation on other obligations that are not self-imposed. As Hume said: "We are surely not bound to keep our word because we have given our word to keep it."[8] We may, and usually do, "agree," as Hume put it, or go along with the customs we find in force, including the custom of promising and demanding that promises be kept, since we see the benefits of having such a practice; but any obligations there may be to support existent practices depend not on the prior consent of the obligated but on the value of the practice to all concerned and on their reliance on it.

Reliance creates dependency, and the second point I wish to make is that the relations that form a moral community, and which, once recognized, give rise to obligations, all concern dependency and interdependency. Some of these dependency relations are self-initiated, but the most fundamental ones are not. The dependency of child on parent, for example, is a natural and inevitable one, and the particular form it takes is socially determined but certainly not chosen by the child. Socially contrived dependencies shape, supplement, and balance natural and unavoidable dependencies. Rights and duties attach to roles in a network of interdependent roles, which if it is wisely designed will conserve and increase the common store of goods, and if it is fairly designed will distribute them equitably. Some morally significant and interrelated roles are ones we all occupy in sequence—the dependent child becomes the adult with children in his care, those who care for the dependent elderly themselves become old and in need of care. Similar to these roles in their reference to earlier and later persons, but unlike them in that we do not occupy them in temporal succession, are the roles of inheritor from past generations, executor and determiner of the inheritance of future generations. In filling these roles one both receives and transfers goods, but the transfer involved is of necessity nonreciprocal, only a *virtual* exchange, and the taking begins to occur too early to be by choice.

The third point is that the cross-temporal moral community in which one finds oneself is not restricted to those who share one's own way of life, but extends to all those with whom one stands, directly or indirectly, in dependency or interdependency relations. Although a seventeenth-century Scotsman may have had no ties, social or economic, with Maoris in New Zealand, or even any knowledge of them, he has indirect ties if his descendants have economic and social and political relations with them. Interdependency is transitive, and so relates me to all those with whom either earlier or later participants in my particular way of life have stood in interdependent relationships.[9] Thus the tie linking "those who are living, those who are dead, and those who are yet to be born"[10] is a cross-cultural one and brings it about that (at least) no one human is alien to me.

What facts about our own dependency relations to past and future generations are relevant to deciding what rights and duties those relations should entail? As far as our own duties to past and future generations go, the relevant facts are these: first our relatively privileged material position, compared with that of most members of most previous generations; second, our dependency for this on past generations as well as our own generation's efforts; third, our power to affect the lot of future generations; fourth, our comparatively extensive knowledge of the long-term effects of our policies; and fifth, the fact that when past generations conserved or saved deliberately for the sake of future generations (in creating parks, writing and fighting for constitutions) there is no reason to think that it was for us in particular, but rather that it was done on the assumption that we would pass on the inheritance. To sum up, the chief facts are our indebtedness to the past and our dangerously great ability to affect the future. We, like most of our forebears, are the unconsulted beneficiaries of the sacrifice of past generations, sometimes seen by them as obligatory, often in fact nonobligatory. If we owe something in return, what is it, and what can we do for those who benefited us? The most obvious response is to continue the cooperative scheme they thought worth contributing to, adapting our contributions to our distinctive circumstances. What is distinctive is our increased ability to plan and foresee the future (and to recognize the dangers of overplanning). If we say that all generations have owed it to the moral community as a whole, and to past generations in particular, to try to leave things no worse than they found them, then we too have that obligation. In addition, in as far as past generations, by supererogatory effort, left things *better* than they found them, we owe it to them to pass on such inherited benefits. We must not poison the wells, even such wells as we have deepened.

We, unlike our ancestors, are better able to judge and control what will benefit and harm our descendants, so our obligations are correspondingly more determinate. Does our special position warrant speaking of the rights of future generations and not just of our obligations toward them? I have argued that past generations have rights against us, that we not wantonly waste or destroy what they made possible for us to have, not intending it for us only. It would therefore be appropriate to recognize spokesmen for their rights. Should spokesmen for future generations, as well as for past generations, be empowered to ensure that we discharge our obligations, take our "trusteeship" seriously, and should we see our obligations as arising out of the rights of future generations?

When we speak of obligations as arising out of rights, we do several morally pertinent things. First, we put a certain emphasis on determinate interests that these rights protect and individuate our obligations by reference to these individual interests of persons. Second, we give a certain guarantee of moral priority to the protection of these definite central interests over negotiable goods. Third, we give the person whose interest a right protects a certain power of individual initiative to claim or demand or waive the right.[11] In all three aspects the concept of a right goes along with that of a certain individualist version of respect for persons and involves seeing obligations as arising out of this respect.

I have argued for a convergence of important interests of past and future persons, so that obligations to future persons do not stem from consideration of their interests alone. But their interests are of undeniable importance and merit a high priority, so that the first two dimensions of rights apply here. The third ingredient, respect for the rightholder's initiative in claiming a right, could only be fictionally present in the case of future generations, if we recognized a spokesman for them. I see no reason in principle why we should not speak of rights of future generations as well as of our obligations to them, but on the other hand I see nothing very important to be gained by doing so. As long as we recognize our obligations to consider the good of the continuing human community, it matters little whether we speak of the rights of future persons. Whether an official agency to execute our collective obligations were seen as a guardian of the interests of future persons or as a spokesman for their rights would make little difference to the responsibility of such an agency. To speak of their rights would be to commit ourselves to the priority of whatever rights we recognized over our own lesser interests. Until we are clear exactly what priority we are willing to give to the interests of future persons, and to which of their interests we will give this priority, it would be less misleading not to use the language of rights. We should first recognize that we have obligations, then devote ourselves to clarifying the precise content of these. If when that is done we find that we do believe we should give priority to certain definite individuated rights of future persons, we can then recognize and itemize such rights.

I have not detailed the content of our obligations to future persons, but have addressed myself only to the general question of whether there are any. I shall end by repeating the features of our own relationship with future persons that I have claimed to be relevant to these obligations. Future persons stand to us in several morally pertinent roles that give rise to obligations on our part:

1. As those who, like us, depend upon naturally self-renewing resources like air, soil, and water, which none of us produced, they are owed the use of these resources in an unpoisoned state.
2. As intended heirs, with us, of the public goods past generations created, often at great cost and sacrifice, they are owed their share in these goods.
3. As those whose existence we could have prevented, but which we owe it to past generations not to prevent wantonly or for our own increased luxury, they have a right to a tolerable and so to a not-too-crowded existence. Our duty to the past is to ensure that, short of catastrophe, there be future persons. Our duty to those persons is to ensure that there not be too many of them.
4. As victims of our probable failure to meet the last mentioned obligation, they are owed some compensation from us. This means, for example, that we as a society should be working on methods to increase food supplies beyond those that would be needed should our justifiable population policies succeed.

I have claimed that there is no conceptual counter-reason, and that there is good moral reason, to recognize obligations to future generations, to recognize that either they, or past generations, or both, have a moral right to our discharge of such obligations. I agree with Golding that "if obligation to the past is a superstition, so is obligation to the future,"[12] and I have tried to suggest that, if both these are superstitions, then all obligation is superstition.

NOTES

1. I do not take it for granted that any of us do in any morally significant sense have rights. We do of course have legal rights, but to see them as backed by moral rights is to commit oneself to a particular version of the moral enterprise that may not be the best version. As Hegel and Marx pointed out, the language of rights commits us to questionable assumptions concerning the relation of the individual to the community, and, as Utilitarians have also pointed out, it also commits us more than may be realistic or wise to fixing the details of our moral priorities in advance of relevant knowledge that only history can provide.

2. J. Feinberg, "Duties, Rights and Claims," *American Philosophical Quarterly,* vol. 5, no. 2 (April 1966).

3. J. Feinberg, *Social Philosophy* (Englewood Cliffs, N.J.: Prentice-Hall, 1973), p. 67. The term 'manifesto rights' is from Joel Feinberg, who writes, "[I am] willing to speak of a special 'manifesto sense' of 'right,' in which a right need not be correlated with another's duty. Natural needs are real claims, if only upon hypothetical future beings not yet in existence. I accept the moral principle that to have an unfulfilled need is to have a kind of claim against the world, even if against no one in particular. . . . Such claims, based on need alone, are 'permanent possibilities of rights,' the natural seed from which rights grow." (p. 67)

4. I assume that while it makes sense to speak of *prima facie* and possibly conflicting obligations, statements about rights gave final moral decisions, so there are no *prima facie* or conflicting rights.

5. I have discussed this in "Secular Faith," *Canadian Journal of Philosophy* (March 1979).

6. David Hume, *Treatise of Human Nature,* ed., Selby Bigge (Oxford University Press, 1968) p. 437.

7. John Rawls, *A Theory of Justice,* p. 525. Rawls uses this idea of a cross-temporal social union to explicate the concept of the good, but in his account of justice he restricts the relevant moral community, those who make an agreement with one another, to contemporaries who do not know their common temporal position.

8. David Hume, *Enquiry Concerning the Principles of Morals,* ed., Selby Bigge (Oxford: Clarendon Press, 1935), p. 306.

9. This transitivity of dependency and interdependency does not imply any strong cultural continuity; but I do assume that, where the dependency is recognized and so is obligation-engendering, there is sufficient common culture for some sort of understanding of intentions to be possible. Even if, as those like Michael Foucault believe, there is radical discontinuity in human culture, so that we are deluded if we think we can understand what Plato or Hume meant, it is nevertheless a significant fact that we try to understand them and that we get insight from those attempts. Indeed, part of the

intention of any writer, artist, or producer of other meaningful human works, may be to provide something that can be reinterpreted. We do not need to see the heritage of the past to be fixed in form in order to value it, nor see future persons as strict constructionists, finding only our intentions in our works, in order to work for them.

10. Edmund Burke, *Reflections on the Revolution in France* (London: Macmillan, 1910), pp. 93-94.

11. H. L. A. Hart stresses this element in the concept of a right in "Are There Any Natural Rights?", *Philosophical Review,* vol. 64 (1955), and in "Bentham on Legal Powers" in *Oxford Essays in Jurisprudence.* Second Series, ed., A. W. B. Simpson (Oxford: Clarendon Press, 1973).

12. M. P. Golding, "Obligations to Future Generations," *Monist* (January 1972), p. 91. [Reprinted in this anthology, pp. 61-72.]

7

Justice and Equality

One condition of the ideal moral judgment (see 4.2) is impartiality, understood as compliance with the formal principle of justice. That principle requires that all individuals be given their due, something we fail to do if similar individuals are treated dissimilarly. The principle is said to be a formal principle because by itself it does not specify what individuals *are* due. The principle implies only that, whatever this is, justice will not be done if, without being able to cite a morally relevant difference, individuals are treated differently.

Justice, understood as a formal principle, obviously is not enough. Unless we have some reasonable basis for determining what individuals are due, we will lack principled grounds for deciding when two or more individuals are *morally relevantly* similar or dissimilar, and, lacking this, we will also lack a principled basis for deciding what each is due as a matter of strict justice. Thus arises the need to give a normative interpretation of justice.[1]

Not surprisingly, there is no single interpretation or theory of justice. Such is the nature of competing theories in any discipline; it is not peculiar to moral philosophy. The disagreements that exist should not encourage us to believe that there is no rational way to separate the wheat from the chaff. Indeed, the overarching objective of the present chapter is to do just that. I shall proceed as follows. Three interpretations of justice will be explained and critically assessed (7.1–7.2). Two of the three (perfectionism and utilitarianism) will be rejected and the third (the equality of individuals) will be defended. This latter interpretation rests on postulating that certain individuals have a distinctive kind of value (inherent value), and both the nature of this value and the criteria for its attribution will be explained (7.2–7.5). These considerations will provide the basis for acceptance of the respect principle (7.6), a principle that stipulates a direct duty of justice owed to all those individuals who have inherent value. That principle, it will be argued, applies to our dealings with moral agents *and* moral patients, and applies equally, since, for reasons offered in the sequel, moral agents and patients must be viewed as possessing equal inherent value. Attempts to dispense with the respect principle and the postulate of inherent value on which it rests, in particular the option offered by rule utilitarianism, will be considered and refuted (7.7). The respect principle will be defended as a valid moral principle (7.8), and the connection between that principle and the harm principle will be explained (7.9).

7.1 UTILITARIAN AND PERFECTIONIST THEORIES OF JUSTICE

Though they were not called by this name, the previous chapter brought us in touch with alternative utilitarian interpretations of formal justice. Recall the importance utilitarians place on counting each for one, no one for more than one. That seems eminently just in spirit and intent, eminently *egalitarian*: no one individual is viewed as being more or less entitled to the same consideration accorded other relevantly similar individuals. Now, it is fundamentally important to emphasize that equal consideration, for utilitarians, is a *predistributive* requirement. For hedonistic utilitarians, for example, individuals are treated equally, are treated as justice requires, if their pleasures and pains are considered and counted as equal in importance to the like pleasures and pains of any other(s). That is what every individual is due, as a matter of justice, and those who are denied equal consideration and weighting of their equal pleasures, given hedonistic utilitarianism, may validly claim, or have claimed on their behalf, that they have been treated unjustly. I shall have a good deal more to say about utilitarian interpretations of justice in the present chapter (see, especially, 7.7).

Utilitarianism is not the only normative interpretation of justice, and not all theories are as egalitarian as utilitarianism aspires to be. The ancient Greek philosopher Aristotle and the nineteenth-century German philosopher Friedrich Nietzsche, for example, advance *perfectionist theories of justice*, according to which what individuals are due, as a matter of justice, depends on the degree to which they possess a certain cluster of virtues or excellences, including intellectual and artistic talents and a character that expresses itself in the performance of heroic or magnificent deeds. Those who possess such virtues abundantly are due more, as a matter of justice, than those who possess them to a limited degree or not at all. It is, therefore, a short step from accepting a perfectionist theory of justice to allowing highly differential treatment of individuals who differ in the extent to which they possess the virtues favored by such a theory; and it should come as no surprise that, enamored as he was by such a conception of justice, Aristotle, for example, thinks that some human beings are slaves by nature—are, as it were, born to be slaves, so bereft are they of even the minimum capacity for artistic, intellectual, and other virtues. *Their* function is to serve the higher, more deserving interests of the virtuous—for example, by carrying out such tasks as growing food and collecting refuse, tasks for which they are naturally suited by their intellectual and aesthetic poverty, work that relieves the virtuous of the need to spend their time in such low-level pursuits and thus provides them with the leisure necessary to develop their artistic and intellectual virtues optimally. Nor can those consigned to serve their natural masters complain of a lack of justice. They get exactly what is their due. Since a just society calls for arrangements that further the perfection of the virtuous, those lacking the preferred virtues cannot complain of any injustice in being required to serve the needs of the artistic and intellectual elite.

Perfectionist theories of justice are morally pernicious, providing, as they do, the foundation of the most objectionable forms of social, political, and legal discrimination—chattel slavery, rigid caste systems, and gross disparities in the quality of life available to citizens in the same state, for example. But perfectionist theories are objectionable at a deeper level. Whether individuals have the talent necessary to acquire the favored virtues (e.g., ability to do higher mathematics) is beyond their control. What natural talents individuals have, to hearken back to a helpful phrase of Rawls's, is the result of "the natural lottery." Those who are born with intellectual or artistic gifts have not themselves done anything to deserve preferred treatment, any more than those who are born lacking these gifts have done anything to deserve being denied those benefits essential to their welfare. No theory of justice can be adequate that builds justice on so fortuitous a foundation, one that could sanction forwarding the "higher" interests of some over the vital interests of others, even to the point where the latter could be enslaved by the former, thereby having their liberty and other benefits acutely diminished, *in the name of justice*. Though consensus is a rare thing in the cloakrooms of philosophy, few, if any, philosophers today would defend a perfectionist theory of justice, for the reasons given (though not only for these). We shall have occasion to remind ourselves of the perils of perfectionism and the need to avoid them in the argument that follows. But it will also be suggested, in a different context, that considerations about the number and variety of one's abilities are morally relevant considerations in some unusual cases (see 8.13).

Viewed against the backdrop of perfectionist theories of justice, Bentham's declaration about each counting for one, no one for more than one must be perceived as a breath of fresh egalitarian air, and it is small wonder that this aspect of utilitarian philosophy was highly instrumental in bringing about many of the most important political, legal, and economic changes in the direction of a more egalitarian society, especially during the nineteenth century, especially in England. Though the actual consequences of the utilitarian push for equality are today viewed as commendable, the status of the equality principle in utilitarian theory is quite another matter, as was explained in the preceding chapter (6.3). Those arguments will not be aired here, though they will concern us later (7.7). Here I shall embark on offering an alternative interpretation of formal justice, one that is distinctly nonperfectionist and, though egalitarian, nonutilitarian. The ways in which the interpretation of justice favored here differs both from perfectionist and utilitarian theories of justice will be explained as we proceed. A defense of that interpretation must await its clear statement (see 7.8).

7.2 INDIVIDUALS AS EQUAL IN VALUE

The interpretation of formal justice favored here, which will be referred to as *equality of individuals*, involves viewing certain individuals as having value in themselves. I shall refer to this kind of value as *inherent value* and begin the discussion of it by first concentrating on the inherent value attributed to moral agents.

The inherent value of individual moral agents is to be understood as being conceptually distinct from the intrinsic value that attaches to the experiences they have (e.g., their pleasures or preference satisfactions), as not being reducible to values of this latter kind, and as being incommensurate with these values. To say that inherent value is not reducible to the intrinsic values of an individual's experiences means that we cannot determine the inherent value of individual moral agents by totaling the intrinsic values of their experiences. Those who have a more pleasant or happier life do not therefore have greater inherent value than those whose lives are less pleasant or happy. Nor do those who have more "cultivated" preferences (say, for arts and letters) therefore have greater inherent value. To say that the inherent value of individual moral agents is incommensurate with the intrinsic value of their (or anyone else's) experiences means that the two kinds of value are not comparable and cannot be exchanged one for the other. Like proverbial apples and oranges, the two kinds of value do not fall within the same scale of comparison. One cannot ask, How much intrinsic value is the inherent value of this individual worth—how much is it equal to? The inherent value of any given moral agent isn't equal to any sum of intrinsic values, neither the intrinsic value of that individual's experiences nor the total of the intrinsic value of the experiences of all other moral agents. To view moral agents as having inherent value is thus to view them as something different from, and something more than, mere receptacles of what has intrinsic value. They have value in their own right, a value that is distinct from, not reducible to, and incommensurate with the values of those experiences which, as receptacles, they have or undergo.

The difference between the utilitarian-receptacle view of value regarding moral agents and the postulate of inherent value might be made clearer by recalling the cup analogy (see 6.2). On the receptacle view of value, it is *what goes into the cup* (the pleasures or preference-satisfactions, for example) that has value; what does not have value is the cup itself (i.e., the individual himself or herself). The postulate of inherent value offers an alternative. The cup (that is, the individual) has value *and* a kind that is not reducible to, and is incommensurate with, what goes into the cup (e.g., pleasure). The cup (the individual) does "contain" (experience) things that are valuable (e.g., pleasures), but the value of the cup (individual) is not the same as any one or any sum of the valuable things the cup contains. *Individual moral agents themselves have a distinctive kind of value,* according to the postulate of inherent value, but not according to the receptacle view to which utilitarians are committed. It's the cup, not just what goes into it, that is valuable.

Two options present themselves concerning the possession by moral agents of inherent value. First, moral agents might be viewed as having this value to varying degrees, so that some may have more of it than others. Second, moral agents might be viewed as having this value equally. The latter view is rationally preferable. If moral agents are viewed as having inherent value to varying degrees, then there would have to be some basis for determining how much inherent value any given moral agent has. Theoretically, the basis could be claimed to be anything—such as wealth or belonging to the "right" race or sex. More likely, the basis might be claimed to be possession of certain virtues or excellences, such as those favored by Aristotle. On this latter (perfectionist) account of inherent value, those who have abundant intellectual or artistic skills would have more inherent value than those who have some, and these latter individuals would have more than those who lack these virtues completely. To accept this view of the inherent value of moral agents is to pave the way for a perfectionist theory of justice: those with less inherent value could *justly* be required to serve the needs and interests of those with more, even if it is not in the interests of those who serve to do so. And the subjugated could have no grounds to complain of the injustice of the treatment they receive. Because they have less inherent value, *they* would get what they deserve. Such an interpretation of justice is unacceptable. Equally unacceptable, therefore, is any view of the inherent value of moral agents that could serve as the basis of such a theory. We must reject the view that moral agents have inherent value in varying degrees. All moral agents are equal in inherent value, if moral agents have inherent value.

Three corollaries of the conclusion just reached are worth noting. First, the inherent value of moral agents cannot be viewed as something they can earn by dint of their efforts or as something they can lose by what they do or fail to do. A criminal is no less inherently valuable than a saint, if both are moral agents and if moral agents have inherent value. Second, the inherent value of moral agents cannot wax or wane depending upon the degree to which they have utility with respect to the interests of others. The most beneficent philanthropist is neither more nor less inherently valuable than, say, an unscrupulous used-car salesman. Third, the inherent value of moral agents is independent of their being the object of anyone else's interests. When it comes to inherent value, it matters not whether one is liked, admired, respected, or in other ways valued by others. The lonely, forsaken, unwanted, and unloved are no more nor less inherently valuable than those who enjoy a more hospitable relationship with others. To view all moral agents as equal in inherent value is thus decidedly egalitarian and nonperfectionist.

"But why," it might be asked, "should we prefer the view that all moral agents have equal inherent value over the egalitarianism associated with utilitarianism? Since both are equally egalitarian, why choose *the postulate of inherent value*, to give a name to the view being championed here, in preference to utilitarianism?" This question concedes more to utilitarianism than is its due, since, for reasons advanced in the previous chapter (6.3), it is unclear how, if at all, utilitarian theory *can* find room within itself to account for its version of equality. But there is a further difference between the implications of utilitarian theory and the postulate of inherent value, one that strengthens the latter as it weakens the former. Recall the unsavory moral implications of act utilitarianism, including in particular the utilitarian justification of secret killings of moral agents. For the act utilitarian, we are guilty of no injustice if we kill a moral agent in order to bring about the best aggregate balance of good over evil for all concerned, assuming that everyone's interests were counted and weighted equitably. This approach to ethical judgment assumes that the only kind of value that falls within the scope of a concern for justice is the kind that, so to speak, "goes into" receptacles (e.g., pleasant experiences). Given the postulate of inherent value, however, concern for justice must look to a different kind of value. If moral agents have inherent value, we cannot ignore that value when attempting to determine what treatment is just or unjust. In particular, since this kind of value is not the same as, is not reducible to, and is incommensurate with the kind of value that "goes into" receptacles, we cannot be treating a moral agent as justice requires if the justification is claimed to reside merely in the instrumentality of the act in bringing about the best aggregate balance of, say, pleasures over pains for all those affected by the outcome. No killing of a moral agent, then, whether done in secrecy or not, can be just if its justification assumes that moral agents are mere receptacles. This does not mean that it must always be wrong to kill a moral agent. What it means is that killing a moral agent cannot be in keeping with the requirements of justice, *if* moral agents have inherent value and *if* the defense is an act utilitarian defense. A defense of that kind assumes that moral agents are mere receptacles, which, given the postulate of inherent value, they are not. That this postulate enables us to avoid the counterintuitive implications of act utilitarianism in the case of secret killings of moral agents must surely count as a point in favor of, rather than a point against, viewing moral agents as inherently valuable.

Similar remarks apply to the possible justification of other harms done to moral agents by moral agents. To cause moral agents to suffer or to deprive them of their liberty, for example, cannot be defended merely by appealing to the better balance of, say, pleasure over pain for all concerned. To suppose otherwise is again to assume that moral agents are *merely* receptacles of valuable experiences and so may be treated in ways that optimize these values without the victims being treated unjustly. All that is required to insure just treatment, on utilitarian grounds, is that the preferences (pleasures, etc.) of all affected by the outcome be considered and that equal preferences (pleasures, etc.) be counted equally. But if moral agents have a value that is *not* reducible to or commensurate with the value of their own or everyone else's valuable experiences, then how moral agents are to be treated, if they are to be treated justly, cannot be determined *merely* by considering the desires, and the like, of all involved, weighting them equitably, and then favoring that option that will bring about the optimal balance of goods over evils for all involved. To suppose otherwise is to assume that questions of just treatment can be answered by ignoring the value of the individual moral agent, which, if moral agents are viewed as equal in inherent value, simply is not true. Moreover, because all moral agents are viewed as equal in inherent value, if any have such value, what applies to how some may be justly treated applies to all, whatever their race, say, or sex. Given the postulate of inherent value, no harm done to *any* moral agent can possibly be justified merely on the grounds of its producing the best consequences for all affected by the outcome. Thus are we able to avoid the counterintuitive implications of act utilitarianism if we deny the receptacle view of moral agents and postulate their equal inherent value.

7.3 "ALL ANIMALS ARE EQUAL"

To this point I have restricted my comments on inherent value to the inherent value of moral agents. It might be thought—and it is thought by some, most notably Kant, for reasons explained in an earlier chapter (5.5)—that the notion of inherent value or some related idea (e.g., conceiving of moral agents as "ends in themselves") applies to all moral agents and only to moral agents. But the attempt to restrict inherent value to moral agents is arbitrary. As we saw in the previous discussion of indirect duty views (5.6), any position that denies that we have direct duties to those moral patients with whom we have been and will continue to be concerned (normal mammalian animals, aged one or more, and those human moral patients like these animals in the relevant respects) is rationally defective. Some of our duties regarding animals are duties we owe directly to them. Moreover, as was argued above (5.6), some of the harms done to these moral patients are harms of the same kind as harms done to moral agents. We cannot consistently hold, therefore, that moral agents and patients can never be harmed in relevantly similar ways. They can. Thus, if we view all moral agents as having equal inherent value, if we rely on this account of the value of these individuals to avoid the counterintuitive implications of act utilitarianism, denying that the harm done to some moral agents can be justified merely on the grounds that harming them brings about optimal consequences for all concerned, if some of these harms done to moral agents are harms of the same kind as harms done to moral patients, and if the duties not to harm either moral agents or moral patients in these ways are prima facie duties owed directly to each, then it would be arbitrary to regard moral patients as lacking inherent value or to suppose that they have the status of mere receptacles. If, in short, we postulate inherent value in the case of moral agents, then we cannot nonarbitrarily deny it of moral patients.

Some might concede that moral patients must be viewed as having *some* inherent value, if we postulate inherent value in the case of moral agents, but deny that the inherent value of moral patients is equal to that possessed by moral agents. But the grounds on which this could be argued will inevitably confuse the inherent value of individuals with (a) the comparative value of their experiences, (b) their possession of certain favored virtues (e.g., intellectual or artistic excellences), (c) their utility relative to the interests of others, or (d) their being the object of another's interests. And this confusion will prove fatal to any attempt to defend the view that moral patients have less inherent value than moral agents. Since the inherent value of moral agents does not wax or wane depending on *their* comparative happiness or *their* total of pleasures-over-pains; it would be arbitrary to maintain that moral patients have less inherent value than moral agents because *they* (i.e., moral patients) have less happy lives or because *their* total of pleasures-over-pains is less than that of moral agents—even if this were true, which it may not be in some cases. Moreover, since one cannot suppose that moral agents have varying degrees of inherent value depending on the extent to which they possess some favored virtues or have varying utility with respect to the interests of others, without paving the way for the unjust treatment of those who have less by those who have more—treatment that would be allowed by discredited perfectionist theories of justice—one cannot *nonarbitrarily* maintain that how much inherent value moral patients have depends on the degrees to which they possess the virtues in question or on how much utility for others they have. Morality will not tolerate the use of double standards when cases are relevantly similar. If we postulate inherent value in the case of moral agents and recognize the need to view *their* possession of it as being equal, then we will be rationally obliged to do the same in the case of moral patients. *All* who have inherent value thus have it equally, whether they be moral agents or moral patients. All animals *are* equal, when the notions of 'animal' and 'equality' are properly understood, 'animal' referring to all (terrestrial, at least) moral agents and patients, and 'equality' referring to their equal possession of inherent value.[2] Inherent value is thus a *categorical* concept. One either has it, or one does not. There are no in-betweens. Moreover, all those who have it, have it equally. It does not come in degrees.[3]

7.4 INHERENT VALUE AND REVERENCE FOR LIFE

Those who, like Kant, restrict inherent value to moral agents limit this value to those individuals who have those abilities essential for moral agency, in particular the ability to bring impartial reasons to bear on one's decision making. The conception of inherent value involved in the postulate of inherent value is more catholic, applying to individuals (e.g., human moral patients) who lack the abilities necessary for moral agency. If moral agents and moral patients, despite their differences, are viewed as having equal inherent value, then it is not unreasonable to demand that we cite some relevant similarity between them that makes attributing inherent value to them intelligible and nonarbitrary. In the nature of the case this similarity cannot be something that varies from individual to individual, since that would allow their inherent value to vary accordingly. Thus, no physical characteristic (e.g., having two eyes or five fingers) can mark the relevant similarity; nor will species membership suffice (e.g., belonging to the species *Canus lupus* or *Homo sapiens*); nor will still more general biological classifications do (e.g., being an animal). One characteristic shared by all moral agents and those moral patients with whom we are concerned is that they are *alive*, and some thinkers evidently believe that it is the possession of this characteristic that marks off the class of individuals who have inherent value from those who do not. Albert Schweitzer is perhaps the most famous thinker whose position invites this interpretation, and his famous ethic of "reverence for life" enjoys wide currency in many public discussions of how we ought to live, not only regarding how we ought to treat one another, in our reciprocal relationships as moral agents, but also regarding how we ought to treat other living things, including moral patients. But there are problems concerning both the scope and precision of Schweitzer's principle, some of which Schweitzer himself, perhaps unwittingly, exposes without resolving in the following passage:

> True philosophy must commence with the most immediate and comprehensive facts of consciousness. And this may be formulated as follows: "I am life which wills to live, and I exist in the midst of life which wills to live". . . . Just as in my own will-to-live there is a yearning for more life, and for that mysterious exaltation of the will which is called pleasure, and terror in face of annihilation and that injury to the will-to-live which is

> called pain; so the same obtains in all the will-to-live around me, equally whether it can express itself to my comprehension of whether it remains unvoiced.
>
> Ethics thus consists in this, that I experience the necessity of practising the same reverence for life toward all will-to-live, as toward my own. Therein I have already the needed fundamental principle of morality. It is *good* to maintain and cherish life; it is *evil* to destroy and to check life. . . . A man is really ethical only when he obeys the constraint laid on him to help all life which he is able to succour, and when he goes out of his way to avoid injuring anything living. He does not ask how far this or that life deserves sympathy as valuable in itself, nor how far it is capable of feeling. To him life as such is sacred. He shatters no ice crystal that sparkles in the sun, tears no leaf from its tree, breaks off no flower, and is careful not to crush any insect as he walks. If he works by lamplight on a summer evening he prefers to keep the window shut and to breathe stifling air, rather than to see insect after insect fall on his table with singed and sinking wings.[4]

Among the many things that are unclear in this passage is why those who are enjoined to have reverence for all *life* should take care not to shatter an ice crystal, since there is no clear sense in which ice crystals are "alive" or exhibit "will to live." That ice crystals may be beautiful, and that conscientious sojourners would not needlessly destroy their beauty or the beauty of nonliving nature generally, is arguable—though not easily! But *if* we are enjoined not to destroy the beauty of the natural order, even when the object of beauty is not alive, then we are in need of a more general principle than that of "reverence for (all) life." More importantly, reliance on a more general principle will imply that *being-alive* is not a necessary condition of something's having inherent value, with the result that "the ethic of reverence for life" will not be the *sole* fundamental principle its champions imply that it is.

In reply to these difficulties it might be suggested that *being-alive* is a *sufficient* condition of an individual's having inherent value. This position would avoid the problems indigenous to the view that being-alive is a necessary condition, but it stands in need of quite considerable analysis and argument if it is to win the day. It is not clear why we have, or how we reasonably could be said to have, direct duties to, say, individual blades of grass, potatoes, or cancer cells. Yet all are alive, and so all should be owed direct duties if all have inherent value. Nor is it clear why we have, or how we reasonably could be said to have, direct duties to collections of such individuals—to lawns, potato fields, or cancerous tumors. If, in reply to these difficulties, we are told that we have direct duties only to some, but not to all, living things, and that it is this subclass of living things whose members have inherent value, then not only will we stand in need of a way to distinguish those living things that have this value from those that do not but more importantly for present purposes, the view that being-alive is a sufficient condition of having such value will have to be abandoned. Because of the difficulties endemic both to the view that being-alive is a necessary condition of having inherent value and to the view that this is a sufficient condition, and granting that moral agents and moral patients share the important characteristic of being alive, it is extremely doubtful that the case could be made for viewing this similarity as the relevant similarity they share, by virtue of which all moral agents and patients have equal inherent value.

7.5 INHERENT VALUE AND THE SUBJECT-OF-A LIFE CRITERION

An alternative to viewing being-alive as the relevant similarity is what will be termed *the subject-of-a-life criterion*. To be the subject-of-a-life, in the sense in which this expression will be used, involves more than merely being alive and more than merely being conscious. To be the subject-of-a-life is to be an individual whose life is characterized by those features explored in the opening chapters of the present work: that is, individuals are subjects-of-a-life if they have beliefs and desires; perception, memory, and a sense of the future, including their own future; an emotional life together with feelings of pleasure and pain; preference- and welfare-interests; the ability to initiate action in pursuit of their desires and goals; a psychophysical identity over time; and an individual welfare in the sense that their experiential life fares well or ill for them, logically independently of their utility for others and logically independently of their being the object of anyone else's interests. Those who satisfy the subject-of-a-life criterion themselves have a distinctive kind of value—inherent value—and are not to be viewed or treated as mere receptacles.

The claim that the value of those individuals who satisfy this criterion is *logically* independent of their utility for, and the interests of, others must be kept distinct from, and not confused with, the obvious fact that the welfare of those who satisfy this criterion is *causally* related to their perceived utility and the interests of others. Actively to harm either a moral agent or patient (e.g., to cause either gratuitous suffering) is to do something that causally detracts from their individual welfare, just as actively to benefit either (e.g., by providing either with the opportunity to pursue their desires, when it is in their interests to do so) is prima facie to contribute to their welfare. Especially in the case of human moral patients, individuals who, because of a variety of conditions, are incapable to varying degrees of taking care of themselves, how they fare in life is to a very considerable degree causally dependent on what we do to them or for them. For example, young children and the mentally enfeebled of all ages lack the requisite knowledge and sometimes even the requisite physical abilities to satisfy even their most basic needs and correlative desires. If we do not act on their behalf, they will fare ill. But even in the case of these individuals, their having a welfare, their being the experiencing subject of a life that fares well or ill *for them*, logically independently of their utility for us or of our taking an interest in them—this fact about them is not causally dependent on what we do to or for them. Indeed, the very possibility of our doing anything that affects their experiential welfare, for good or ill, *presupposes* that they are the experiencing subjects of such a life, on their own, as it were. And the same is true both of those moral patients (e.g., animals in the wild) who can take care of themselves without the need of human intervention and of those humans who are moral agents. Though what we, as moral agents, do to each other causally affects how we fare during the course of our individual lives, that we are the subjects of such a life is not similarly causally dependent on what others do to or for us. We have this status in the world, as do moral patients, whether human or animal, on our own; having this status is *logically* part of what it is for us or them *to be* in the world.

The subject-of-a-life criterion identifies a similarity that holds between moral agents and patients. Is this similarity a relevant similarity, one that makes viewing them as inherently valuable intelligible and nonarbitrary? The grounds for replying affirmatively are as follows: (1) A relevant similarity among all those who are postulated to have equal inherent value must mark a characteristic shared by all those moral agents and patients who are here viewed as having such value. The subject-of-a-life criterion satisfies this requirement. *All* moral agents and *all* those moral patients with whom we are concerned *are* subjects of a life that is better or worse for them, in the sense explained, logically independently of the utility they have for others and logically independently of their being the object of the interests of others. (2) Since inherent value is conceived to be a categorical value, admitting of no degrees, any supposed relevant similarity must itself be categorical. The subject-of-a-life criterion satisfies this requirement. This criterion does not assert or imply that those who meet it have the status of subject of a life to a greater or lesser degree, depending on the degree to which they have or lack some favored ability or virtue (e.g., the ability for higher mathematics or those virtues associated with artistic excellence). One either *is* a subject of a life, in the sense explained, or one *is not*. All those who are, are so equally. The subject-of-a-life criterion thus demarcates a categorical status shared by all moral agents and those moral patients with whom we are concerned. (3) A relevant similarity between moral agents and patients must go some way toward illuminating why we have direct duties to both and why we have less reason to believe that we have direct duties to individuals who are neither moral agents nor patients, even including those who, like moral agents and those patients we have in mind, are alive. This requirement also is satisfied by the subject-of-a-life criterion. Not all living things are subjects of a life, in the sense explained; thus not all living things are to be viewed as having the same moral status, given this criterion, and the differences concerning our confidence about having direct duties to some (those who are subjects) and our not having direct duties to others (those who are not subjects) can be at least partially illuminated because the former meet, while the latter fail to meet, the subject-of-a-life criterion. For these reasons, the subject-of-a-life criterion can be defended as citing a relevant similarity between moral agents and patients, one that makes the attribution of equal inherent value to them both intelligible and nonarbitrary.

Three further points require our attention before turning to the task of articulating and defending the principle of justice grounded in the notion of inherent value. First, though satisfying the subject-of-a-life criterion marks a relevant similarity, one that makes the attribution of inherent value to moral agents and patients both intelligible and nonarbitrary, the claim has not been made, nor does anything said in the above imply, that satisfying this criterion is a *necessary* condition of having inherent value. It *may* be that there are individuals, or possibly collections of individuals, that, though they are not subjects of a life in the sense explained, nevertheless have inherent value—have, that is, a kind of value that is conceptually distinct from, is not reducible to, and is incommensurate with such values as pleasure or preference satisfaction. The issues here are extremely complicated. As I have argued elsewhere, the very possibility of developing a genuine ethic *of* the environment, as distinct from an ethic *for its use*, turns on the possibility of making the case that natural objects, though they do not meet the subject-of-a-life criterion, can nonetheless have inherent value.[5] Attempts to show that this is conceptually absurd are inconclusive at best, while attempts to show that postulating inherent value in natural objects or collections of such objects, though intelligible, is unnecessary, suffer from a similar fate. Nevertheless, it is extraordinarily difficult to give an intelligible account of inherent value in this connection. For example, though criteria can be given regarding when, say, an oak tree is good of its kind (i.e., good as an oak tree), and though these criteria are not dependent on a good oak tree's having utility for others or being the object of anybody's interests,[6] an oak tree's being good of its kind by itself has no more moral significance than, say, a cancer cell's or a murderer's being good of their kind.[7] And the same applies to collections of oak trees (or cancer cells, or murderers). Those who would work out a genuine ethic of the environment in terms of the inherent value of natural objects (trees, rivers, rocks, etc.) or of collections of such objects are not logically debarred from undertaking the task by anything said or implied in these pages, since the subject-of-a-life criterion is set forth as a sufficient, not as a necessary, condition of making the attribution of inherent value intelligible and nonarbitrary. While no one is denied the possibility of working out such an ethic, however, those who aspire to do it certainly have their work cut out for them. (For further remarks on environmental ethics, see 9.3.)

Second, and relatedly, the argument of the present section does not logically preclude the possibility that those humans and animals who fail to meet the subject-of-a-life criterion nonetheless have inherent value. Since the claim is made only that meeting this criterion is a sufficient condition of making the attribution of inherent value intelligible and nonarbitrary, it remains possible that animals that are conscious but not capable of acting intentionally, or, say, permanently comatose human beings might nonetheless be viewed as having inherent value. As in the case of nonconscious natural objects or collections of such objects, however, it must be said that it is radically unclear how the attribution of inherent value to these individuals can be made intelligible and nonarbitrary. The difficulties alluded to in the earlier discussion of viewing being-alive as either a necessary or sufficient condition of having such value may be taken as illustrative of the kind of difficulty one is likely to encounter in this quarter (see 7.5). It may be that animals, for example—which, though conscious and sentient (i.e., capable of experiencing pleasure and pain), lack the ability to remember, to act purposively, or to have desires or form beliefs—can only properly be viewed as receptacles of what has intrinsic value, lacking any value in their own right. One should avoid being doctrinaire on this point. In any event, the attempt to resolve these issues is well beyond the scope of the present work and so, as in the case of exploring the foundations of an environmental ethic, marks a point at which it is incomplete. (For further observations on this matter, see 9.3.) This incompleteness does not infect the adequacy of the subject-of-a-life criterion, however, when this is understood as a sufficient condition in the sense explained, nor does it undermine the claim that normal mammalian animals, aged one or more, as well as humans like these animals in the relevant respects, can intelligibly and nonarbitrarily be viewed as having inherent value.

Third, it is important to emphasize that the preceding argument in support of the subject-of-a-life criterion does not commit "the naturalistic fallacy"—the view, *very* roughly speaking, that it is a fallacy to infer values from facts. The position argued for in the above cannot fairly be reduced to the following:

Premise (1)	Some individuals are the subjects of a life that fares well or ill for them, logically independently of their utility for others or of their being the object of another's interests (a fact).
Conclusion (2)	Therefore, these individuals have inherent value (a value).

The present work is not the proper occasion to address the question, Is the naturalistic fallacy a fallacy? Whether it is or not, the argument of the preceding pages is considerably more complicated than the movement from premise (1) to conclusion (2) would suggest. To view certain individuals (e.g., moral agents) as having equal inherent value is a *postulate*—that is, a theoretical assumption. As befits any theoretical assumption, however, it is not one made without reason. On the contrary, it is an assumption that vies with alternative theories about the value of moral agents, in particular the views that they lack value in their own right and are only receptacles of experiences that are valuable in themselves (the utilitarian view) or that they have value in their own right but a kind of value that varies from individual to individual, depending upon the possession of favored virtues (the perfectionist view). And there *are* reasons for accepting this postulate. To postulate that moral agents have equal inherent value provides a theoretical basis for avoiding the wildly inegalitarian implications of perfectionist theories, on the one hand, and, on the other, the counterintuitive implications of all forms of act utilitarianism (e.g., that secret killings that optimize the aggregate consequences for all affected by the outcome are justified). The role of the subject-of-a-life criterion must be viewed, if it is to be viewed fairly, against this larger background. The reasons we have for postulating equal inherent value for all moral agents and patients are logically distinct from that criterion. That criterion is introduced *after* we have indicated the reasons for postulating that moral agents and patients have equal inherent value, not before; thus, its role is not to "derive" the equal inherent value of moral agents *or* of moral patients; rather, its role is to specify a relevant similarity among all those individuals who, by force of argument, are to be viewed as having equal inherent value, if we postulate it in the case of all moral agents, a similarity that makes the attribution of inherent value to them intelligible and nonarbitrary. Reasons have been advanced in the preceding for regarding the subject-of-a-life criterion as equal to this task. To characterize the argument of the previous pages as amounting to the inference from premise (1) to conclusion (2), therefore, is not to characterize that argument. It is to caricature it.

7.6 JUSTICE: THE PRINCIPLE OF RESPECT FOR INDIVIDUALS

The view that moral agents and moral patients have equal inherent value is not itself a moral principle since it does not itself enjoin us to treat these individuals in one way or another. In particular, the postulate of inherent value does not itself provide us with an interpretation of the formal principle of justice, the principle, it will be recalled, that requires that we give each individual his or her due. Still, that postulate does provide us with a basis for offering such an interpretation. If individuals have equal inherent value, then any principle that declares what treatment is due them as a matter of justice must take their equal value into account. The following principle (*the respect principle*) does this: *We are to treat those individuals who have inherent value in ways that respect their inherent value.* Now, the respect principle sets forth an egalitarian, nonperfectionist interpretation of formal justice. The principle does not apply only to how we are to treat some individuals having inherent value (e.g., those with artistic or intellectual virtues). It enjoins us to treat *all* those individuals having inherent value in ways that respect their value, and thus it requires respectful treatment of all who satisfy the subject-of-a-life criterion. Whether they are moral agents or patients, we must treat them in ways that respect their equal inherent value. In its present form, however, the respect principle lacks the precision it is reasonable to require of a moral principle. It does not specify *what* respect for such value requires. Some general comments in this regard may now be offered.

To put matters in their most general negative form first, we may say that we fail to treat individuals who have inherent value with the respect they are due, as a matter of strict justice, whenever we treat them *as if they lacked* inherent value, and we treat them in this way whenever we treat them *as if they were mere receptacles* of valuable experiences (e.g., pleasure or preference satisfaction) or *as if their value depended upon their utility* relative to the interests of others. In particular, therefore, we fail to display proper respect for those who have inherent value whenever we harm them so that we may bring about the best aggregate consequences for everyone affected by the outcome of such treatment. The grounds for claiming that such treatment is disrespectful and unjust should be apparent. It can hardly be just or respectful to harm individuals who have inherent value merely in order to secure the best aggregate consequences for everyone affected by the outcome. This cannot be respectful of inherent value because it is to view the individual who is harmed *merely* as a receptacle of what has value (e.g., pleasure), so that the losses of such value credited to the harmed individual can be made up for, or more than compensated, by the sum of the gains in such values by others, *without any wrong having been done to the loser*. Individuals who have inherent value, however, have a kind of value that is distinct from, is not reducible to, and is incommensurate with such values as pleasure or preference satisfaction, either their own or those of others. To harm such individuals *merely* in order to produce the best consequences for all involved *is* to do what is wrong—*is* to treat them unjustly—because it fails to respect their inherent value. To borrow part of a phrase from Kant, individuals who have inherent value must never be treated *merely as means* to securing the best aggregate consequences.

The respect principle, as a principle of justice, requires more than that we not harm some so that optimific results may be produced for all affected by the outcome; it also imposes the prima facie duty to assist those who are the victims of injustice at the hands of others. This is not peculiar to the present interpretation of formal justice. All initially plausible ethical theories recognize both the duty not to act unjustly oneself as well as the duty to assist those who are the victims of injustice at the hands of others. Justice, that is, not only imposes duties of nonharm; it also imposes duties of assistance, understood as the duty to aid those who suffer from injustice. All individuals who have inherent value are to be given their due, and sometimes what they are due is our assistance. I shall return to this topic in the sequel (9.1).

Like utilitarian interpretations of formal justice, the interpretation provided by the respect principle is not a principle of distributive justice; neither it nor they lay down conditions that must be met if the distribution of benefits (goods) and harms (evils) arising as the result of a given act or rule are just distributions. In opposition to utilitarian interpretations, however, the interpretation of justice in terms of respect for individuals having inherent value *rules out, in advance, the permissibility of arriving at any distribution in certain ways*. No individual who has inherent value may justly be treated as a mere receptacle in order to secure optimal consequences for all affected by the outcome. How the benefits are distributed among the beneficiaries is irrelevant to assessing the injustice involved in securing them. Thus, while both utilitarian interpretations of equality and the respect principle are predistributive principles, the two differ fundamentally in what they can allow, something that will become increasingly clear as we proceed (see, especially, 8.12).

7.7 RULE UTILITARIANISM AND JUSTICE

The objections raised against utilitarianism in the previous chapter and the contrast drawn between utilitarianism and the interpretation of formal justice favored in the present one have focused on act utilitarianism. As was mentioned in the initial survey of utilitarian theory (4.4), not all utilitarians are act utilitarians; some are rule utilitarians. The latter hold that the rightness or wrongness of a given act is to be determined by its conforming or failing to conform to a valid moral rule, and rules are said to be valid, according to rule utilitarianism, if (roughly speaking) general observance of them promotes the overreaching utilitarian goal of bringing about the best aggregate consequences for all affected by the outcome. The same kind of dispute about what counts as "the best consequences" that divide act utilitarians plays a similarly divisive role among rule utilitarians, so that there are rule utilitarians who are hedonists, some who are preference utilitarians, and so forth. As important as this dispute is, the differences that separate rule utilitarians from one another go beyond what does or does not have intrinsic value. Some rule utilitarians argue for 'ideal rule utilitarianism,' a position that regards rules as valid *if* everybody's following them *would* yield the best consequences, even though there is little chance that many people will. Others argue for nonideal utilitarian visions of morality, contenting themselves with asking what rules it is reasonable to believe that most people will (normally) follow or at least will (normally) think should be followed. And still others offer yet different interpretations of the rules that, as utilitarians, they seek to validate. For reasons too apparent to need reciting, it will not be possible to assess all varieties of rule utilitarianism. It must be sufficient for now to indicate why rule utilitarianism, of whatever form, has seemed to some utilitarians to be preferable to act utilitarianism, how a rule utilitarian might respond to the objections I have raised against act utilitarianism, and how a rule utilitarian could dispute the necessity of postulating inherent value and of formulating a principle of justice that relies on this postulate. Then I shall indicate why, despite the apparent strengths of rule utilitarianism, its claims to adequacy are more shadow than substance.

Consider the case of killings done in secret. The act utilitarian, it has been argued, is committed to permitting such killings if they bring about a better total balance of intrinsic good over evil for those affected by the outcome. That the victim loses a lot—indeed, loses everything!—is no cause for moral alarm, nor can it be the occasion for cries of injustice, *if* his interests (pleasures, etc.) were considered and counted equally with the like interests (pleasures, etc.) of others. The rule utilitarian will protest. The rule against killing ("Thou shalt not kill" or "It is wrong to kill") is a valid moral rule, and its validity does not mysteriously vanish when killings are done in secrecy or when the killers reap a harvest of intrinsic values for themselves, goods that more than compensate for the loss on the victim's part. Since this rule is valid, and since killing in secrecy, even if it brings about the best consequences for all those affected by the outcome, is not a valid exception to it (killing in self-defense, for example, might be), those who kill in such circumstances do what is wrong, the rule utilitarian will aver, and the wrongness of their act can be accounted for by utilitarianism after all—by rule utilitarianism, that is.

Now, the grounds for denying the permissibility of such acts, the rule utilitarian can contend, do not require that we either postulate that certain individuals have 'inherent value' or offer interpretations of justice in terms of giving those who have such value the 'respect' they are due. The immorality of harming any moral agent, for example, whether by killing her or by making her suffer, merely to optimize the best aggregate consequences, is nicely accommodated for by appeal to valid moral rules against harming anyone in these ways, the validity of these rules resting on the utility of having them. Rule utilitarianism, therefore, is a simpler theory than any theory that postulates that certain individuals have inherent value, its advocates will claim, since it can account for what its competitor accounts for without making the additional, unnecessary assumption that some individuals have inherent value. And since, other things being equal, the simpler theory should be chosen (see 5.6), utilitarianism wins the day.

There are familiar objections to rule utilitarianism—for example, whether, in its nonideal forms, it is at bottom indistinguishable from act utilitarianism and so heir to all the objections that confront that version, and whether, in its ideal forms, it really is a form of utilitarianism at all. We will bypass these objections on the present occasion.[8] There are other, less familiar but no less damaging, criticisms of rule utilitarianism that will concern us.

The view that we have *direct* duties to moral patients has been defended in an earlier chapter (5.6). If a moral theory is to be adequate, it must provide a credible account of these duties. Rule utilitarianism fails in this regard. Granted, if we concede the equality principle to rule utilitarians—a large assumption, it should be noted—they will be in a position to hold that the interests (pleasures, etc.) of moral patients must be considered and counted equally with the like interests (pleasures, etc.) of any other individual, including moral agents. But this, as we have seen, is a *pre*distributive requirement that *by itself* in no way guarantees that we will have any of the same direct duties to moral patients that we have to moral agents, over and above considering their respective interests and counting them equally. Whether we are obliged on rule utilitarian grounds not to harm moral patients—as we are on that view, let us grant, not to harm moral agents—must depend on whether there are distinctively utilitarian grounds for recognizing a rule setting forth a direct duty against harming the former. The rule utilitarian fails to show that we have such duties to moral patients. In the case of the rule against harming moral *agents*, what the rule utilitarian can argue is the following: If we were to accept rules that allowed that some moral agents could be harmed in certain ways while other moral agents would be protected in this respect, then those persons who belonged to the victimized group would naturally feel resentful and envious, feelings that, Hare remarks, are "disagreeable state(s) of mind (which) lead people to do disagreeable things."[9] To allow rules that foster and encourage envy and resentment and the "disagreeable things" these feelings give rise to, is hardly conducive to promoting the best consequences for all involved, and it is arguable (though not easily!) that a rule utilitarian could object to the adoption of rules that permit harming some moral agents but not others because of the consequences for, and brought into being by, those moral agents not covered by the rule.

This kind of argument (let us call this *the argument from envy*) simply is not available to the rule utilitarian, when the individuals at issue are moral patients, whether animals or human moral patients like these animals in the relevant respects. To feel envy over how some are treated or resentment about one's own situation, because moral rules sanction preferred treatment for others, presupposes that one is able to take stock of how the parties involved are treated, recognize the differences in the treatment they receive as a result of the rules, and, as a consequence of this realization, feel envious or resentful. Moral agents can do this. Moral patients cannot. The latter simply lack the intellectual sophistication to do so. They may be *treated* wrongly as a result of certain rules, but no one will claim that they can or will *recognize* their treatment as wrong because of these rules. Neither, then, is it plausible to maintain that they will feel the envy or resentment attending this recognition in the case of moral agents.

Similarly deficient are appeals to so-called diminishing marginal utility. "Almost always," Hare writes, "if money or goods are taken away from someone who has a lot of them already, and given to someone who has little, total utility is increased, other things being equal."[10] In the case of the distribution of money to moral patients, what Hare claims is, strictly speaking, false. If we give money or other comparable goods to moral patients, there is no reason to believe that total utility will be increased and very good reason to believe that just the reverse will transpire. Lacking as these individuals are in those capacities that would enable them to appreciate the use they can make of money, relative to their own interests, there is no reason to believe that they would, and good reason to believe that they would not, make use of their financial windfall in ways that increase their own interests and thereby increase total utility. To put money and other comparable goods in the hands of a chimpanzee or a young child won't serve the cause of maximizing utility.

In response it can be said that of course we are not to give money and other comparable goods *directly* to moral patients; rather, we are to distribute these goods to other, competent humans in whose care moral patients are entrusted. It is in this way, we may be asked to believe, that we can optimize total utility and thereby provide the needed basis for a rule against harming moral patients. The money used to provide them with the opportunities to satisfy their desires or fulfill their purposes is of greater utility than the comparable sums we might spend in pursuit of other desires or purposes.

This response begs all the important empirical questions that, in the nature of the case, rule utilitarians must answer. What would be the consequences, all considered, if money and other comparable goods were distributed in this way, and how would these consequences fare in comparison with the total consequences that would result if we decided against such a distribution? Unless we know this, it is arbitrary to assume that a rule against harming moral patients, many of whom permanently lack the ability to promote utility by what they do (what contribution to "the general welfare" can the senile make?), can be defended by appeal to declining marginal utility. For it might be that the harms done to these individuals, if we decided not to recognize a rule against harming all or some of them, would be more than offset by the benefits others could thereby obtain. For example, might not the consequences be better, all considered, if we allowed scientific research on morons? In order to take a principled position on this matter, when one's position turns on considerations about the comparative total consequences of our recognizing or not recognizing such a rule, one needs the relevant empirical questions answered, and answered in detail. As is "almost always" the case (recall the earlier criticism of Singer on a similar point, 6.4), the utilitarian does not have the necessary details at hand. And this serves his position ill. Appeals to declining marginal utility can only be as forceful as knowledge of the facts allows. Where knowledge gives way to speculation, these appeals lose their force. Even allowing that appeals to declining marginal utility may carry the day for the utilitarian in some contexts, they are weak and ineffective in the present one.

How, then, can the rule utilitarian account for our having a direct prima facie duty not to harm moral patients? One reply that, as it were, has always been in the wings might now be thrust to center stage: though moral patients cannot feel envy or resentment as a result of discriminatory rules, which makes the argument from envy inapplicable in their case, *other* individuals, it might be argued, *will most certainly* be angered and outraged were we not to recognize a rule against harming moral patients. The parents, relatives, and friends of human moral patients, for example, will certainly feel this way, and those who labor for the better treatment of animals will have comparable feelings in response to those speciesist practices the absence of this rule would allow. Now, these feelings, like those of envy and resentment, are disagreeable, and are likely to lead these people to do disagreeable things, things that, were they to become common—as they would (let us assume) if we failed to recognize the rule in question—would most certainly be detrimental to optimizing overall aggregate utility. In this way, then, it might be argued, the necessary utilitarian backing for recognizing a rule against harming moral patients is provided and is supported by as much empirical certainty as it is reasonable to require on the part of the utilitarian. Moral agents *will* behave badly, because they *will* be angered and outraged if we fail to protect moral patients by having a rule against harming them. We know this. It is not mere speculation.

This response, however plausible it may seem, simply will not do. It has the effect of transforming our *direct* prima facie duty not to harm moral patients into an *indirect* duty. We are to recognize a rule against harming moral patients, according to this reply, not because of the harm done directly to them, nor because of the harm they will do to others as a result, but because of the adverse consequences that would obtain for, and as a result of the actions of, *others* (parents, friends, etc.) if we did not recognize such a rule. For reasons advanced at length in the critical discussion of indirect duty views in chapter 5, *the duty not to harm moral patients is a direct duty we have to them*, and the adequacy of any theory stands or falls depending on whether and, if so, how well it can account for this direct duty. The rule utilitarian's having recourse to the last reply is symptomatic of that theory's failure to meet this requirement.

The critical discussion of rule utilitarianism to this point can be summed up by posing the following dilemma: (1) If rule utilitarians affirm that there is a moral rule against harming moral patients, a rule that generates a direct duty not to harm them, then they fail to ground this rule *either* by appealing to the argument from envy (moral patients cannot feel envious or resentful because of rules that discriminate against them and favor others) *or* by appealing to declining marginal utility (an appeal that will beg all the essential empirical questions). Nor can they ground this rule merely by appealing to the harms moral patients endure (e.g., suffering), since the very question at issue is whether we ought to recognize a direct duty not to harm these individuals, *judged on rule utilitarian grounds*, and it is an open question, so far as rule utilitarianism is concerned, whether having such a rule would or would not serve to bring about gains on the part of others that more than compensate for the losses on the part of the moral patients who are harmed. What *other* fact, then, *about moral patients themselves*, if not their envy and the disagreeable deeds this would give rise to on their part, *could* provide a utilitarian reason for recognizing a direct duty against harming them? None comes readily to mind, and though the preceding discussion does not conclusively prove that no such fact can be found, the onus of proof is certainly on the rule utilitarian to find one. Unless or until he does—and it is fair to say that it is most unlikely that he will—the attempt to ground a rule against harming moral patients on the disutility that results from what *they* will feel or what *they* will do, as a result of being harmed, seems certain to prove inefficacious.

That is the first horn of the rule utilitarian's dilemma. The second one is this: (2) If, in the face of the grave difficulties just summarized, rule utilitarians have recourse to the "disagreeable" mental states that would be produced in the minds of *others* (e.g., parents) if we were not to recognize a rule that generated a duty not to harm moral patients (e.g., children), then the rule utilitarian would have *a* utilitarian reason for having such a rule, but the duty that the rule generated could no longer be regarded as a *direct* duty owed to moral patients. Now, since the case has been made that we have direct duties to moral patients, the rule utilitarian must avoid (2) at all costs. Accordingly, the adequacy of rule utilitarianism stands or falls on how well it can account for our having a *direct* prima facie duty not to harm moral patients. In view of the reasons offered in (1), we have very strong reasons indeed for denying that it can pass this test. Rule utilitarianism lacks the wherewithal to ground direct duties owed to moral patients.

Rule utilitarians might reply to this dilemma by contesting our earlier arguments against indirect duty views, especially those parts of that argument that involve appeals to our intuitions. What one wants, these utilitarians might say, echoing Singer's words, is a "sound theory" against which to test our intuitions, not a proliferation of appeals to our intuitions as a way to test the soundness of a theory. This *sounds* very well and good, but the burden of proof, it will be recalled, is on those who proclaim it to show that what they want done, can be done. *Can* we get a "sound theory" without appealing to our reflective intuitions? This brings us to a final set of objections to rule utilitarianism, when that theory is assumed to stand on its own, as it were, immune to criticisms of it based on appeals to reflective intuitions.

Recall the difficulties posed for utilitarians in the previous chapter (6.3), when they are asked to explain the status of the equality principle. Depending on the theory of value advanced by any given utilitarian, the equality principle will require that intrinsic goods (e.g., preference satisfactions, or pleasures) be considered, no matter whose they are, and that equal weighting be observed (i.e., equal pleasures, or preferences, are to be counted equally). But what can be the *status* of the equality principle within any version of *rule* utilitarianism? It cannot be a fundamental moral principle, since the principle of utility, and that principle alone, is supposed to have this status. Nor can it be a derivative moral principle, a "valid rule," since the equality or inequality of pleasures, preferences, interests, etc. cannot depend on the utility of weighing them as equal or unequal. The equality principle, in short, cannot have the status of a *moral* principle (or rule) within rule utilitarian theory. Neither can it have the status of a *formal* principle, a principle that must be met if any putative moral principle is to qualify as a genuine moral principle. The respect principle has the status of a moral principle, and yet it does not enjoin us to count equal preferences, pleasures, and so forth, equally. At the very most the equality principle, as understood by rule utilitarians, can have the status of a *conditional formal principle*, one that we must accept if, starting with our own individual interests, pleasures, and so on, we then take the moral point of view.

As was noted in the earlier discussion (6.3), however, this argument could at most establish that those who begin to do their ethical thinking from the point of view of their own self-interest would commit themselves to *a* consequentialist principle; the validity of utilitarianism—the view that the principle of utility is the *sole* moral basis of morality—does not follow. Rule utilitarians, therefore, cannot rely on our (assumed) acceptance of the conditional equality principle, as they understand it, to secure our commitment to utilitarianism. Moreover—and for present purposes more fundamentally—some *reason* must be given as to why we should begin thinking about what is moral or immoral from the vantage point of our individual self-interest. *Why* begin there, after all? Certainly a compelling reason would be at hand if it could be shown that, starting from this point, we reach a sound moral theory. But, for reasons just adduced for a second time, if one starts from one's own self-interest, one does not reach (i.e., one is not committed to) the principle of utility as *the one and only* valid moral principle. So the burden of showing why we should, not simply that we might, begin to do our ethical thinking by starting with our own self-interest must be shouldered by those who advocate this as the place to begin. That burden has not been adequately borne by those who would have us start there, not by Narvesonian rational egoists, not by Rawlsian original contractors, and not by preference or other utilitarians. Just as in our earlier discussion of the equality principle and act utilitarianism, therefore, my present finding is that rule utilitarians cannot extract a commitment from us to accept utilitarianism even were we to accept the conditional equality principle (more on this point in a moment). To claim that, when compared with any theory that involves postulating inherent value, rule utilitarianism is simpler and therefore preferable, is to assume the greater part of what rule utilitarians must show—namely, that their theory is at least equal to its theoretical competitors in illuminating why we have those duties we have (rule utilitarianism is not equal to this task since, among other reasons, it cannot adequately account for our direct duty not to harm moral patients) *or* that, apart from testing the theory against our intuitions about such duties, there are *independent* grounds for recognizing the theory as sound (rule utilitarians fail to show this since, among many reasons, they fail to show that acceptance of conditional equality commits one to the theory of utilitarianism). Rule utilitarians, in short, have yet to provide compelling reasons to accept their theory, and we have good reasons to reject it. That theory may be simpler than a theory that involves postulating inherent value, but simplicity isn't everything. (As to why we should not accept the conditional equality principle, see below, 8.13.)

7.8 DEFENDING THE RESPECT PRINCIPLE

In the earlier chapter on ethical theory a procedure was sketched for testing the validity of alternative ethical principles. We begin with our unexamined moral beliefs (our prereflective intuitions) and initiate the process of critical assessment by making a conscientious effort to make an ideal judgment in their case. We strive to be impartial, "cool," rational, conceptually clear, and as informed as we can be. Those beliefs that withstand this process of critical evaluation cannot be fairly described as beliefs we "just happen" to have or summarily dismissed as prejudices. They are considered beliefs, or intuitions in the reflective sense, beliefs that may then be used as a basis for identifying general moral principles that systematize these intuitions and as a touchstone against which competing ethical principles can be tested, subject, it will be recalled, to the proviso that some of these beliefs may themselves stand in need of revision or abandonment if they cannot be accounted for by principles shown to be valid in other respects. If we engage in this process of critical reflection, the case can be made for rational acceptance of the respect principle.

Among our prereflective intuitions are those that concern when it is wrong to harm a moral agent. It is, we believe (unless we have already pledged our allegiance to utilitarianism), wrong to kill a moral agent just so that an optimal balance of intrinsic goods over evils may be secured by all those affected by the outcome. And it is similarly wrong to harm a moral agent in other ways for similar reasons—for example, to cause a moral agent gross suffering or to deny her the satisfaction of her basic needs or the opportunities to acquire essential skills on the grounds that this will optimize the balance of good over evil for all affected by the outcome. These are beliefs we hold, not only before, but after we have begun to reflect critically on them, not because of excessive emotional involvement, *or* because we arbitrarily favor some moral agents (say, women or Americans) over others, *or* because we are fuzzy-minded about the concepts of 'moral agency' or 'harm,' *or* because we are ill informed about the relevant facts; nor can it be claimed that the beliefs are irrational because they lead to inconsistent consequences. These beliefs qualify as *considered* beliefs, and they should therefore play a legitimate role in the reflective formulation and assessment of alternative ethical principles.

Now, the respect principle illuminates and unifies, by identifying relevant grounds for, these beliefs. That principle requires that we not treat moral agents as if they were mere receptacles of value, lacking any value in their own right. This is what we would be doing if we supposed that the harms done to one moral agent could be justified merely by appealing to the optimal aggregate balance of intrinsic good over intrinsic evil secured by all those affected by the outcome. The respect principle will not allow this. Those who have inherent value have a kind of value that is distinct from, is not reducible to, and is incommensurate with intrinsic values, either their own intrinsically valuable experiences or those of others. We must treat such individuals with the respect due them, as possessors of such value, and this we will manifestly fail to do if we treat them in ways that could only be justified if moral agents were viewed as something that, given the postulate of inherent value, they are not—namely, as mere receptacles of value, lacking any value in themselves. The respect principle thus both matches and goes some way toward the goal of systematizing our considered beliefs about the wrongness of harming moral agents.

One wants more from a moral principle than this, however. There are other relevant criteria, set forth and defended in the earlier chapter on ethical theory, that a valid ethical principle must meet. The respect principle meets them. That principle is *consistent* certainly. It does not assert or imply that we can treat some moral agents (e.g., Jews) as if they were mere receptacles while denying that we can do this in the case of others (e.g., white Anglo-Saxon Protestants). It lays down a requirement concerning how any and all moral agents must be treated, as a matter of strict justice. Every moral agent is to be given his or her due, and what each is due, as a matter of strict justice, is the same respectful treatment due any other. The respect principle, therefore, is eminently egalitarian, providing an alternative interpretation of Bentham's declaration that each is to count for one, no one for more than one. Moreover, because this principle applies to our treatment of all moral agents, it has *adequate scope*. There are literally billions of cases where it daily applies. It does not become operative only, say, when bridge is being played or at high table. As for *precision*, the respect principle makes clear, intelligible requirements: We are *not* to treat any moral agent in ways whose possible justification consists *merely* in appealing to the optimal aggregate consequences that result for all those affected by the outcome. In its present form, it is true, the respect principle provides negative direction only and, by itself, it fails to provide the needed guidance concerning when, and if so why, it is justifiable to harm a moral agent. These are matters that will concern us in the following chapter (see 8.7ff.). Even in its present form, however, the respect principle meets the relevant criteria for evaluating a moral principle: it is consistent, has adequate scope and precision, and matches a broad range of our reflective intuitions. What its logical status is (that is, whether it is a fundamental or derivative moral principle) remains an open question at this point (on this question, see 8.12). What is not open to serious question is whether, having identified this principle, having explained how it unifies and illuminates our considered beliefs about when it is wrong to harm moral agents in a broad range of cases, having satisfied the legitimate requirements of scope, precision, and consistency, and having done all this in an unemotional, disciplined fashion, in deference to the requirements of impartiality, rationality, and the other conditions that give content to the ideal moral judgment—what is not open to serious question is whether, having done all this, we have failed to take any steps in the direction of justifying acceptance of the respect principle. If the foregoing considerations do not provide good reasons to accept that principle, one can only ask what *could* provide good reasons for accepting any principle.

Respect For Moral Patients

The interplay between our pretheoretical beliefs and principles, such as the respect principle, is a two-way street, and we must, therefore, consider the implications of accepting this principle. This requires asking how other unconsidered beliefs we may happen to have match this principle. In particular, it requires asking whether the scope of the respect principle can be nonarbitrarily limited only to how moral agents may be treated. The arguments of the past three chapters provide the grounds for claiming that any and all attempts to limit the scope of the respect principle to moral agents must be deficient. Against indirect duty views, it was argued that we have a direct prima facie duty not to harm moral patients; thus, we cannot maintain that the respect principle applies only to our dealings with moral agents on the grounds that (a) this principle applies only to how we may treat those individuals to whom we have direct duties and that (b) we have no direct duties to moral patients. Nor can we avoid recognizing that moral patients fall within the principle's scope on the grounds that they have no inherent value or less inherent value than moral agents; this will not do because attempts to disenfranchise moral patients in this way will lay the groundwork for a perfectionist theory of justice, a theory that will either sanction unjust treatment of some moral *agents* or avoid this—but only at the price of arbitrariness. To accept the respect principle, in short, commits us to recognizing that it applies also to our dealings with moral patients. *They* are not to be treated as if they are mere receptacles. We cannot justify harming *them* merely on the grounds that this will produce an optimal aggregate balance of intrinsic goods over intrinsic evils for all concerned. *We owe them* respectful treatment, not out of kindness, nor because of the "sentimental interests" of others, but because justice requires it. If our prereflective intuitions about how all or some moral patients may be treated happen to differ from how they must be treated, if the respect principle is accepted, then these beliefs will have to be changed. Not to change them, given the arguments most recently advanced, and assuming the respect principle is accepted, is to expose oneself to the charge of being prejudiced, and rightly so.

These implications of the respect principle—that moral patients generally, and animals in particular, are to be treated with respect *and* that respectful treatment is their due, as a matter of strict justice—may strike some people as so bizarre that they will want to avoid accepting the respect principle and the postulate of inherent value on which it rests. The cumulative force of the arguments presented in the last three chapters is that there is no rational, nonarbitrary way to avoid this principle and this postulate so long as it is reasonable to believe (and reasons have been given to support believing) that it is prima facie wrong to harm moral agents *and* that harming them cannot be justified merely on the grounds that this is necessary to bring about optimal aggregate consequences for all concerned. If just this much is accepted, there is no rational, nonarbitrary way to avoid viewing harm done to moral patients in the same way. And once this has been shown, it can then be shown (and has been shown) that the leading attempts to account for this duty without postulating inherent value and without relying on the respect principle must be inadequate either because they will fail adequately to account for this duty in the case of moral agents (a cardinal failure of act utilitarianism and rational egoism) or because they will fail adequately to account for this duty in the case of moral patients (a singular failure of rule utilitarianism and Rawls's and Kant's positions). And if, finally, we are told to abandon the attempt to validate ethical principles or test ethical theories by having recourse to our reflective intuitions because they are prejudices or because we can construct a sound ethical theory without relying on them, our reply should be that the former claim simply is untrue and the latter demonstrably unsubstantiated. For these reasons, then—all of them taken in concert, no one of them taken in isolation from the rest—we have good reason to accept the respect principle, the postulate of inherent value on which it is based, and the full range of implications that flow from their acceptance.

7.9 THE DERIVATION OF THE HARM PRINCIPLE

Although its logical status remains an open question at this point, the respect principle clearly is more fundamental than the harm principle since this latter principle can be derived from the former (on the logical status of the respect principle, see 8.12). The derivation proceeds as follows: The respect principle rests on the postulate of inherent value, and the case has been made for intelligibly and nonarbitrarily viewing all those who satisfy the subject-of-a-life criterion as having value of this kind. Now, those who satisfy this criterion are the subjects of a life that is experientially better or worse for them, logically independently of their utility for others and their being the object of another's interests. Those who satisfy this condition, in short, are individuals *who have an experiential welfare*—whose experiential life fares well or ill, depending on what happens to, or is done to or for, them. The notions of benefit and harm thus apply to our thought and talk about these individuals, benefits consisting of opportunities for the satisfaction of desires and the fulfillment of purposes that are in the interests of these individuals, and harms being what detract from their individual welfare. Because those who have a welfare, in the sense explained, have inherent value, and because those who have inherent value are owed treatment respectful of this value, those who have a welfare are owed treatment respectful of their distinctive kind of value. Prima facie, therefore, we fail to treat such individuals in ways that respect their value if we treat them in ways that detract from their welfare—that is, in ways that harm them. We have, in short, a prima facie direct duty not to harm those individuals who have an experiential welfare, which is precisely what the harm principle declares. The respect principle, then, not only succeeds in matching our considered beliefs about when it is wrong to harm moral agents but also provides the basis from which a second moral principle (the harm principle)—a principle of direct duty whose validity was defended in an earlier context (5.6)—can be derived. And that must surely count as an additional point in favor of rational acceptance of the respect principle.

To show that the harm principle is derivable from the respect principle is not to show that no matter what the circumstances, it is always wrong to harm another, either a moral agent or a moral patient. This issue will be explored at length in the following chapter (8.7ff). Even at this juncture, however, the following should be clear. Those cases, if any, in which individuals may justifiably be harmed must not contravene the requirement of just treatment set forth by the respect principle. For example, the justification of the harm done cannot rest on the assumption that the harmed individual is a mere receptacle of value, lacking any value in his own right. That would be to treat the harmed individual unjustly because disrespectfully, and no harm done to a moral agent or patient can be justified if it is unjust.

7.10 SUMMARY AND CONCLUSION

The formal principle of justice stipulates that each individual is to be given his or her due. This much is uncontroversial. The controversy begins when we ask what individuals *are* due. Answers to this question offer normative interpretations or theories of justice. Three such interpretations were considered: (1) perfectionism, which holds that what individuals are due depends on the degree to which they possess certain virtues (e.g., intellectual skills); (2) utilitarianism, which holds that what individuals are due is equal consideration of their interests (or pleasures, etc.); and (3) the equality of individuals view, which holds that what individuals are due is equal respect for their equal inherent value. Perfectionism was rejected (7.1) because it would justify the unjust exploitation of the less virtuous (e.g., the less intelligent) by the more virtuous; and utilitarian interpretations were rejected because they either fail to account for the full range of the wrongful acts that may be done to moral agents (a central defect urged against act utilitarianism in an earlier chapter, 6.2) or because (7.7) they fail to account for the full range of our direct duties to moral patients (a central defect of rule utilitarianism). The equality of individuals interpretation overcomes these defects, first, because all those individuals who have inherent value have it equally (thus the unsavory implications of perfectionism are avoided) and because, second, we would fail to show respect for the inherent value individuals possess if we were to treat them in the ways that act utilitarianism and rule utilitarianism would sanction or require.

The notion of inherent value was explained (7.2). Those who have value of this kind are more than receptacles of the value that attaches to their experiences, the view of individuals and their value (or lack of value) common to all forms of utilitarianism. Inherent value is distinct from, not reducible to, and incommensurate with intrinsic values (e.g., pleasure). The postulate of inherent value must be defended on theoretical grounds, and the attempt was made to offer such a justification. If we do not make this postulate, it was argued, we will be unable to account for our considered beliefs (our reflective intuitions) about when it is wrong to harm either moral agents or moral patients. Though this postulate will oblige us to construct a less simple theory than some (e.g., utilitarianism), that is a price we must be willing to pay if we are to have the most adequate theory, all considered.

To deny that moral patients have inherent value, or to affirm that they have less inherent value than moral agents, it was argued (7.3), is arbitrary. "All animals are equal" is true, when understood in context. The question of the relevant similarity shared by all those who have equal inherent value was addressed. This similarity cannot be, say, some physical characteristic or some biological fact (e.g., species membership). The view that it is being-alive was considered and rejected (7.4), and the subject-of-a-life criterion was clarified and defended (7.5). Individuals are subjects of a life if they are able to perceive and remember; if they have beliefs, desires, and preferences; if they are able to act intentionally in pursuit of their desires or goals; if they are sentient and have an emotional life; if they have a sense of the future, including a sense of their own future; if they have a psychophysical identity over time; and if they have an individual experiential welfare that is logically independent of their utility for, and the interests of, others. This criterion is a sufficient condition for making attributions of inherent value intelligible and nonarbitrary. Whether it is a necessary condition was left an open question.

As a matter of strict justice, then (7.6), we are required to give equal respect to those individuals who have equal inherent value, whether they be moral agents or moral patients, and, if the latter, whether they be humans or animals. That is something each is due (7.8). Injustice arises when we treat those who have such value in ways that fail to display proper respect (for example, by treating them as if their value was reducible to their utility for others).

The harm principle, a principle that sets forth a prima facie direct duty not to harm either moral agents or patients, is derivable from the respect principle (7.9), when we note that (1) those individuals who satisfy the subject-of-a-life criterion are individuals who are intelligibly and nonarbitrarily viewed as meriting respect because they are intelligibly and nonarbitrarily viewed as possessing inherent value, and that (2) as subjects-of-a-life, all have an experiential welfare. Prima facie, therefore, we fail to show respect for these individuals when we do anything that harms them. Whether and, if so, how the duty not to harm these individuals may be justifiably overridden are issues that remain to be examined, but no harm done to moral agents or patients can be justified if it is unjust. No harm can be justified, accordingly, if it contravenes the respect principle, treating the harmed individuals as mere receptacles of value or as things whose value is reducible to their utility relative to the interests of others.

The Growth of Children's Rights

BY CARL WELLMAN, SAINT LOUIS

A right, as I conceive it, is a system of autonomy. A legal right is a structure of legal liberties, claims, powers and immunities; a moral right is a complex consisting of ethical liberties, claims, powers and immunities. Each right has one or more core elements that define its essential content but it also contains a number of associated elements that give its possessor freedom and control with respect to that core. Thus, the essential function of a right is to allocate autonomy within some defined sphere to one party vis-à-vis second parties in the event of any conflict of wills or confrontation between these parties.

Assuming, then, that every right necessarily contains at least one liberty and at least one power, it follows that only beings capable of acting, acting in the morally relevant sense of intentionally carrying out rational choices, are capable of possessing a right. A legal or ethical liberty is a liberty of acting in some specific manner; a legal or ethical power is a power of performing some action with legal or ethical consequences. Hence, it makes no sense to ascribe liberties or powers to any being incapable of action. Since liberties and powers are essential ingredients in rights, it makes just as little sense to ascribe rights to any being incapable of action. Accordingly, infants, who obviously lack any capacity to act rationally, can possess no rights at all. Normally adults, who are mature moral agents, have many legal and moral rights. Presumably children acquire their rights as they develop into moral agents.

Although children might acquire all their rights full-blown on the day when they finally achieve full maturity, I doubt that this is so. My hypothesis is that children's rights gradually grow as children gradually develop the various capacities of a moral agent. It is not merely that the child may acquire one right before another, although this is true. Since rights are complex structures of normative elements, the child may acquire one part of a right before it acquires the other parts of the same right. In fact, a single normative element, such as an ethical liberty or power, may change as the child grows into an adult. Let me test my hypothesis by examining two rights of the child in some detail.

1. The Right to Freedom of Movement

The United Nations *Universal Declaration of Human Rights* asserts that "Everyone has the right to freedom of movement and residence within the borders of each state". Although this is primarily a right of adults, it presumably belongs to children also, for the first article reads in part "All human beings are born free and equal in dignity and rights". No explicit definition of this human right is given here or in the *International Covenant on Civil and Political Rights*. I interpret it to be the most primitive part of the human right to liberty, liberty in the basic sense of being unconfined or unbound, of being free to go anywhere within a given area. Children clearly do not enjoy unrestricted freedom of movement. Parents often strap an infant into an easybaby, confine a baby to a play pen or refuse to let a small child play outside during inclement weather. Schools typically have high fences around their playgrounds and forbid their pupils to leave the premises during school hours. The state usually forbids juveniles to enter bars and sometimes imposes a curfew upon the young. Where and when does the right to freedom of movement enter the picture?

The core of the human right to freedom of movement is a bilateral ethical liberty, the ethical liberty of moving about within the borders of one's state paired with the ethical liberty of refraining from such movement. The child exercises this liberty when he goes to his room and brings back a toy to show a guest, when she walks over to a friend's house to play, when he refrains from going to a high school dance, or when she takes a bus downtown to shop. No doubt there are boundaries to one's ethical liberty of movement other than the borders of one's state; even an adult has a duty not to trespass on the property of another. But let us leave the content of this core liberty undefined for the moment and consider first its necessary conditions.

It makes no sense to say that someone possesses an ethical liberty of movement until that person is capable of movement. More than the random motions of the infant or the reflex knee jerk of an adult are required. Purposive or intentional movement is necessary because the exercise of an ethical liberty is an action, and an action in the ethical sense is essentially voluntary. Clearly the newborn infant is incapable of movement in this ethical sense; he or she has to learn even to roll over in the crib or to reach for a rattle. Nor does the child acquire the capacity to move all at once. After learning to roll over and reach, it gradually learns to crawl, walk, run, ride a bike, find his or her way about the neighborhood, take a bus about town, travel to distant cities, and so on. Thus, the scope or range of ethical liberties of movement it makes sense to ascribe to a child grows as the child grows and develops his or her capacities of movement.

The core of the moral right to freedom of movement is a bilateral liberty, a liberty of moving *or* not moving about within the borders of one's state. One exercises a bilateral liberty by opting for or against some possible movement, by choosing whether or not to move and then acting on one's choice. I do not presuppose any very complex or rich concept of choice here; one can choose without deliberation and with very partial awareness of available options. But some awareness of the possibility of moving or refraining from moving in some manner and an opting for one rather than the other is essential to the exercise of any bilateral liberty. Once more, the mere infant lacks the ability to conceive of alternative actions and, therefore, lacks the capacity to choose to move or not to move in any way. Only after the child has acquired the ability to entertain possible movements and to opt for or against one of them does it make sense to ascribe any bilateral liberty of movement to the child. As the child learns more and more about itself and its world, the child becomes capable of entertaining conceptions of more and more kinds of movement. Thus, the content of the bilateral liberty it makes sense to ascribe to the child grows richer and richer.

A third precondition of the meaningful ascription of a bilateral liberty to the child may seem paradoxical at first. The child is not capable of possessing a liberty until the child is capable of having contrary duties. The reason for this is that to assert that someone has an ethical liberty to do something is to assert that that person does not have any duty to refrain from doing that act. One might, I suppose, insist that stones have no duty to refrain from tripping hikers and that guns have no duty to refrain from killing innocent children; for stones and guns, not being moral agents, cannot be said to have moral obligations at all. But to ascribe ethical liberties to stones or guns on these grounds is surely to empty the concept of an ethical liberty of its intended meaning, the ascription of a liberty of action. Similarly, it is pointless to ascribe ethical liberties to children before they become capable of having duties or moral obligations. I suggest that to be a moral agent in this sense one must be capable of understanding practical reasons and controlling one's acts by moral constraints. This is because the bindingness of moral obligation consist in the reasons why one ought or ought not to perform some action. Thus, it is only after the child has developed some capacity for practical reasoning that he or she can intelligibly be said to possess any ethical liberties. And as the child's capacities of understanding and acting on more and more complex reasons grows, the child can meaningfully be said to have more and more complex liberties of movement.

Clearly, the child cannot meaningfully be said to possess any human right to freedom of movement until he or she can be said to possess the bilateral ethical liberty of movement or refraining from movement that is its defining core. The child is incapable of possessing this core element until he or she has developed his or her capacity to move intentionally, to choose between moving and not moving in some manner, and to control his or her action by moral reasons. When the child has these three capacities to some degree, it makes sense to ascribe to him or her a bilateral ethical liberty of movement. The content of this bilateral liberty one could meaningfully ascribe continues to grow as the child continues to develop these presupposed capacities.

To say that the child is capable of possessing a bilateral liberty of movement is not, of course, to say the child actually possesses it. For a child capable of possessing a liberty of movement is equally capable of possessing a duty not to move in that manner. Is a child's ethical liberty of movement as great as that of the normal adult? Probably not, for the child is subject to special moral constraints that impose on him or her duties not to move about in various ways. A child old enough to grasp the moral import of a parental command probably has a duty not to play in the street or leave the immediate neighborhood if these movements have been forbidden by mother or father. The slightly older child's inability to cope with wild animals or to find his or her way about in the forest impose upon that child a moral obligation not to wander off alone during a wilderness camping trip. Assuming that one has at least a prima facie moral obligation to obey the law, a juvenile has an obligation not to enter bars or other legally forbidden places where adults are at liberty to go. Moral constraints such as these appear to be more numerous and restrictive for very young children and to allow more freedom for older children. If this appearance is not misleading, then the content of the child's bilateral ethical liberty of movement expands as the child grows older. Thus, not only does the child's capacity to possess ethical liberties grow as the child matures, but the liberties actually possessed grow also. As the child's duties to refrain from various movements wane, the child's ethical liberty of movement waxes commensurately.

The bilateral ethical liberty at the core of the human right to freedom of movement is normally protected by a perimeter of moral duties, the most important of which is the moral duty of the parent regarding the child not to interfere with the child's freedom of movement. From birth the parent, upon whom falls the primary duties of caring for the child, has a duty to allow the infant some freedom of movement in its crib in order that he or she can develop his or her motor abilities and begin to explore its tiny world. Later the parent has a duty to permit, and even help, the growing child to roam the house, go outside to play, walk to the homes of playmates, go to and from school, go on shopping excursions and to sports events, etc. This parental duty of noninterference with, and perhaps facilitation of, the movements of the child is grounded in the child's need to develop its capacities, to broaden its horizons and learn to cope with an increasingly complex world, to associate freely with other persons of all ages, and to achieve increasing independence. The parent has this duty regarding the child long before the child becomes capable of possessing any ethical liberties whatsoever. But after the child has acquired some bilateral liberty of movement, this parental duty remains to serve as a moral protection for its free exercise.

This is not to say that it is always morally wrong for a parent to restrict the child's freedom of movement. Since the parental duty of noninterference is merely a prima facie duty, it is often overridden by contrary moral obligations of a more stringent sort, such as the duty to protect the child from serious harm, the duty to prevent the child from harming others, and even the duty to promote the effective functioning of the family. It is morally permissible, for example, for a parent to keep the sides of the crib up so that the baby will not fall or climb out, to forbid the small child to climb a neighbor's tree, or to require that an older child remain within calling distance just before mealtime. One need not fear that the parental duty of noninterference will be overridden so often and so completely as to be rendered nugatory. Although it is permissible for a parent to confine a baby to a crib for extended periods of time, it would be wrong to tie it down so that it could not even wriggle about or roll over; although a parent may forbid a young child to play in the busy street, it would be wrong to forbid the youngster to play outside at all.

What begins as a parental duty of noninterference *regarding* the child later becomes a parental duty *to* the child. Relative duties, or duties to some second party, are a very special class of duties; many duties are not owed to anyone at all. The difference between a duty regarding and a duty to appears most striking in the case of a duty regarding some inanimate object. My son has contracted to shovel the neighbor's walk whenever it snows. This is a duty regarding my neighbor's sidwalk, but it is surely not a duty owed to that strip of lifeless concrete. It is a duty to our neighbor because it is the neighbor who has the ethical power to claim performance or remedy in the event of threatened or actual nonperformances of that duty. Thus, a duty of x to y is a duty of x together with a power of y. The bearer of a relative duty is the party upon whom the obligation of performance lies, and the party to whom the duty is owed is the party with the power of claiming performance or remedy. A very young child surely lacks such an ethical power of claiming, for it lacks the language skills to say "I demand that you stop confining me to the house because you are responsible for developing my abilities and my knowledge of the world". It is not just a matter of learning to make the correct noises in the appropriate circumstances. The child must come to understand what it is for the parent to have a duty of noninterference regarding the child and that the child has a special moral standing with respect to that duty that enables the child to claim performance of that duty. I am not suggesting, of course, that the child must come to a theoretical knowledge of all this and be prepared to give an adequate philosophical formulation of it. But I am insisting that ethical claiming is an intentional action and that some comprehension of what one is doing in making an ethical claim is required before anyone can meaningfully be said to possess the ethical power of claiming. Only when the child has developed at least a rudimentary understanding of moral duties and personal relations does the parental duty regarding the child become a parental duty of noninterference to the child.

The moral right to freedom of movement contains several other associated elements, but let me mention only one – the state's moral duty to enforce the parental duty of noninterference with the child's freedom of movement. Although this duty is very limited in scope, it can be of crucial importance in extreme cases. Imagine that a parent keeps a young child restrained in a crib so much of the time that the child has no opportunity to learn to walk or that a single parent locks a child in its room all day while he or she goes out to work. Under such circumstances, the state would have a moral obligation to intervene in the family and force the parent to cease and desist from such grossly unjustified interference with the freedom of movement of the child. Although this moral duty of the state begins as merely a duty regarding the child, in due course it grows into a moral duty to the child when the child becomes capable of claiming state intervention vis-à-vis the parent.

2. The Right to Special Protection

In addition to the human rights children share with adults, they also possess certain special rights of their own. The United Nations *Declaration of the Rights of the Child* asserts that "The child shall enjoy special protection". The context makes it clear that this right of the child is grounded in two special needs of the child. The child is more vulnerable than the adult to certain sorts of injury or harm, such as "all forms of neglect, cruelty and exploitation". In addition, the child more than the adult needs "opportunities. . . to develop physically, mentally, morally, spiritually and socially in a healthy and normal manner"

While the right to freedom of movement is a primitive form of a liberty-right, the right to special protection is a basic claim-right. When complete, its core consists of a set of ethical claims of the child against its parents, other individuals and the state to those special protections it needs to prevent the serious harms to which it is peculiarly liable and to promote the full development of its human capacities. Accordingly, the parent ought to protect the child from malnutrition, exposure to the elements, physical injury, disease, exploitation by older children, growing up uneducated, etc. An adult bystander has a moral obligation to rescue a small child playing on its own near a pond from a brutal bully, a roughly affectionate Saint Bernard, or deep water. The state has a duty to protect a child from parental neglect or abuse. Since the most important of these core claims is the child's ethical claim against its parents, let us concentrate on that.

In part, this ethical claim of the child against its parents consists of the parental moral duty regarding the child to provide those forms of special protection that are necessary to prevent serious harms or promote human development. Examples come readily to mind. The parents have a duty regarding the child to put up the sides of the crib while the baby is there, to keep poisons out of reach of the young child, to keep the child away from the open fire and the edge of a cliff, to see that the child is vaccinated against measles and polio, and to prevent the child from acting on terribly harmful choices such as dropping out of school at a very early age. These parental duties regarding the child begin at least when the child is born and continue at least until the child has achieved sufficient independence to leave home and set out on its own.

But the ethical claim of the child against the parents consists in more than the moral duty of the parents regarding the child; it also contains the child's ethical power of claiming performance of this duty or remedy for nonperformance from the parents. The newborn infant does not and could not possess this ethical power. Since the exercise of the power of claiming is a linguistic action, the child does not acquire any such power until it has become capable of purposive action and learned the language of claiming. Moreover, making an ethical claim is a very special sort of action presupposing some recognition of the parental duty being claimed and some understanding of the parent-child relation by virtue of which the child has the ethical standing required to claim this special protection. Surely only after the child has had some experience of moral obligations and personal relations can the child be meaningfully said to possess any ethical power of claiming from the parents their moral duty to provide special protection. But when the child has acquired this degree of moral maturity, the parental duty of special protection *regarding* the child becomes a duty *to* the child and the child may then be said to possess a corresponding ethical claim against the parents. From this time on, this core claim can function as the center of a claim-right of the child.

The content or scope of the child's ethical claim against its parents to special protection continues to grow, or at least change, for the range of protections needed by the child to prevent serious harm and promote human development changes through time. As the child's world grows from the crib to the home to the neighborhood to the school to the community and so on, the dangers to which the child is exposed increase in number, variety, and perhaps in potential destructiveness. Accordingly, the range of protections the parent ought morally to provide for the child grows also. Fortunately, this is only half the story. As the child's ability to cope with the world increases, its needs for special protection, protection unnecessary for the normally functioning adult, also disappear. Thus, while a parent ought to strap an infant into an easy-baby placed on the kitchen table, the kindergartener has no need to be strapped into its chair at the dinner table. Although a parent ought to leave a babysitter with a young child when going out for the evening, the parent normally has no such duty to the teenage son or daughter. Very roughly it can be said that the child's claim-right to special protection grows as the child's world grows, diminishes as the child's abilities grow, and eventually fades away entirely. When the child has grown into the adult, the child no longer has any right to *special* protection.

Ethical claims, like legal claims, can typically be waived by their possessors. Associated with the child's full claim-right to special protection is the child's ethical power of waiving its ethical claim againts its parents to provide special protection. But at what point does the child become capable of thus extinguishing the parental duty to provide protection? Imagine a child going off to kindergarten, its first expedition to the neighborhood school. Although the school is within walking distance, the walk will take the child outside the block or two within which it has learned to wander freely and across a couple of busy streets. Quite likely the child will need some special protection until it has learned the best route to and from school and until it is more used to crossing main streets. Typically the parent will escort the child to and from school for a few days. But before long the child can waive its claim to this form of protection by saying to the parent "You don't need to come with me anymore". What conditions must be satisfied in order for this speech act to constitute a genuine exercise of the power of waiving the child's ethical claim against the parent to special protection? (1) The child must possess an ethical claim against the parent for such protection. This means that the child cannot acquire the power to waive any ethical claim until after the child has acquired the ethical power to claim performance of or remedy for nonperformance of the correlative duty. (2) The child must be free not to waive the claim if it so desires. Although this aspect refers primarily to the absence of external constraints upon the action of the child, it does also presuppose that the child has acquired the capacity of rational choice and purposive action. (3) In order for the act of waiving the ethical claim to be fully voluntary, the child must also understand what it is doing in exercising its power of waiving that claim in this instance. Even in a rudimentary case like this one, this understanding is fairly complex. The child must understand that the parent has a duty to it to provide special protection because of their child-parent relation. The child must understand that this relative duty confers on the child the special standing of claimant with the ethical powers of claiming or waiving performance of this duty. The child must understand that by waiving its ethical claim against the parent it would be releasing the parent from any duty to the child to provide this sort of protection. Thus it must have some reasonable grasp of the sorts of risks to which it would be exposing itself were it to waive its ethical claim. All this sounds complicated, and it is. But I believe that under normal circumstances a kindergartener will have this sort of understanding.

Consider another example, that of a child who has been badly beaten up by the neighborhood bully one or two times. Even quite a young child would probably possess the ethical power of claiming performance of the parental duty of providing special protection against his danger. (I am assuming that it is a genuine danger because the bully is strong and brutal, not just frightening in manner.) Young children quickly learn that their parents owe them protection and almost as soon learn how to claim the protection owed to them. There is some reason to believe that children acquire the ethical power to waive any claim somewhat later than they acquire the claim itself. This is because one typically claims performance or remedy for nonperformance in the immediate or near future, but one waives performance into a somewhat more distant future. It requires a greater moral maturity to appreciate the relevance of more distant actions and events in order to understand what one is doing in waiving a claim than in understanding what one is doing in making a claim concerning a more immediate future. Again, the presumption that the linguistic act expresses the real will of the child is greater when only short-term desires are involved than when longer-range interests are at stake.

The act of waiving an ethical claim of the child against the parent extinguishes the parent's duty *to* the child, but it may leave in existence a slightly diminished but still considerable duty *regarding* the child. In this respect, duties arising from the parent-child relation differ from duties arising from the promisor-promisee relation. The latter is a personal relationship voluntarily and mutually assumed by the parties to it. Therefore, the promisee has the power to undo what he and the promisor have previously done. But the parent-child relation is much more complex than this. The child had no part in bringing this relation into existence; normally, at least, the parents conceived the child without his or her consent. Again, the relation between parent and child is not just one between two individuals agreeing among themselves; it involves two roles in the socially defined institution of the family. This is why the child's act of waiving performance of the parent's duty to the child cannot always completely remove the parent's duty regarding the child. This comes out fairly clearly in the case of baby-sitting. The responsible parent will not leave a young child alone, especially at night. Now that grandparents and aunts so seldom live in the family unit, the parents discharge their duty to their child by providing a baby sitter. At some point in his or her growing maturity, however, the child can waive his or her claim to be provided with a sitter. Imagine that the child does say to the parent, "You need not get a baby sitter tonight; I am old enough to take care of myself". If the child is old enough to possess an ethical claim of this sort against the parent, to be capable of waiving this claim freely, and to understand what it is doing in waiving its claim to be baby-sat, this act does release the parent from the duty *to* the child. But if the risk to the child is considerable, perhaps the parents are driving out of town for the evening and no close friends are nearby, the parent may still have a duty regarding the child to leave a sitter with the child. But given the additional condition of the child's reasonable ability to cope with the probable risks, the child's act of waiving does release the parents from all obligation to provide a baby sitter that evening.

Of the several additional associated elements that make up the child's full moral right to special protection, let me mention only one more, the child's ethical power of refusing special protection. Let us imagine that the parents continue to provide baby sitters for the child even after he or she has grown into a normal teenager. To be sure, a teenager may have some need for special protection; probably he or she is somewhat less capable than an adult in the event of a serious fire or a burglary carried out by armed and ruthless men. But at some point, special protection provided for the child is also imposed upon the child against its will. No longer will the child say merely "You need not get a baby sitter for me this evening"; the youth approaching adulthood will protest "I refuse to let you get a baby sitter for me". At this point the teenager may well be quite properly standing on his or her rights, and the parent who persists is guilty of overprotection. There are two kinds of overprotection. One is simply unnecessary; it is not genuine protection at all because it does not answer to any substantial risk. The other is excessive protection that invades the rights of the protected. When this sort is refused by the child, the child's act of refusal imposes upon the parent a moral duty to cease and desist from the sort of protection what has been rejected by the child.

But does the child really have the ethical power of refusing special protection, the power of imposing upon the parent a duty to refrain from providing some form of protection? That the child does have this ethical power, even in the case of needed protection, is most plausible in the case of medical protection. The parent has a moral duty regarding the very young child to see that it is vaccinated against such serious childhood diseases as measles, diptheria, tetanus and polio. When the child grows old enough to understand the dangers of these diseases and its dependence upon the parent for protection from them, this duty regarding the child becomes a duty to the child. At some point in the growing maturity of the child, however, the child's consent becomes morally necessary to render such medical treatments of the child morally permissible. This is because injecting vaccines into the child without the child's consent violates the child's moral rights to bodily integrity and personal security. Therefore, if the child refuses to consent to such medical treatment, the treatment is morally wrong. Since one has a duty to refrain from doing a morally wrong act, or even from being an accomplice in such wrongdoing, the child's refusal of such medical protections imposes upon the parent a duty to refrain from imposing them. Medical protection reveals most clearly the grounds of the child's ethical power to refuse special protection. In those cases where special protection would invade the rights of the child, the refusal of the child to waive those rights leaves the rights standing to make the medical treatment that invades them wrong.

Refusing to consent, as opposed to doing nothing, does more than leave those rights standing. To go ahead and invade the rights of the child in the face of an explicit refusal is an additional and greater moral wrong because it is a flagrant lack of respect for the child in a situation where there can be no pretence of presumed consent.

What conditions must be satisfied for the child to possess this ethical power to refuse consent to special protection from its parent? Like consent to medical treatment, the refusal of special protection is valid only when it is free and informed. This means that the child cannot possess the power to refuse any sort of special protection until the child has become capable of rational choice and purposive action, until the child understands what it is to waive or refuse to waive an ethical claim-right, and understands what would be at stake in this particular act of refusing consent – that is, what risks one would be incurring and what moral rights one would be refusing to waive. The last feature, of course, points to a new complexity. The child's refusal changes the moral situation only because it constitutes an act of refusing to consent to being treated in some manner that would, in the absence of consent, violate some moral rights of the child. Thus, the additional condition required for the child to acquire the ethical power to refuse special protection is that the child does acquire the rights to bodily integrity, personal security, privacy and all the others that might be violated by parental protections. But these matters must be postponed for another occasion.

A further complication appears in the case of another form of special protection. Suppose that a high school boy or girl gets a job waiting on table at a restaurant some distance from home. Although the child is expected to walk home after a daytime stint on duty, the parent may insist on escorting the child home when he or she gets off work late at night. (At least, I would provide this protection for my son or daughter living in a medium risk area in Saint Louis.) When the chiild has begun to feel confident and independent, he or she might say to the parent "I refuse to let you escort me home any more". Since the high school youth is almost an adult and may be as morally mature as many adults, the child presumably does have the moral rights to privacy and self-determination, rights that may be invaded by the parental action of providing a late-night escort from work to home. Accordingly, the youth's act of refusing this form of special protection does impose on the parent a prima facie duty to cease and desist. But this duty is only prima facie and may, upon occasion, be overridden by a stronger contrary prima facie duty of the parent regarding the child to provide continuing protection. Whether this is so will depend in considerable measure upon the gravity of the risks to which the unescorted youth would be exposed. Thus, it might be that a parent ought to continue to escort a high school girl home when there would no longer be any obligation to impose this special protection upon a high school boy, who is presumably much less exposed to the danger of rape. Another morally relevant factor is the severity of the burdens that would fall upon the parent, who still has a duty to care for the child, in the event that the untoward harm were to eventualize. If assaults are common in the area and the parent would be obligated to provide medical treatment for an assaulted child, then perhaps the refusal of the child to consent to special protection is less compelling from an ethical point of view.

In any event, it becomes clear that the child's moral right to special protection is rather complex and that it changes dramatically as the child grows up. What begins as ethical duties of the parent, other individuals and the state regarding the child to provide special protection change into moral duties to the child when the child acquires the power to claim their performance or remedy in the event of their nonperformance. The content or scope of these core ethical claims grows as the child's world grows and the variety of dangers to which it is exposed increases. Later the child acquires the additional power of waiving its ethical claims to special protection; still later it acquires the ethical power of refusing to consent to forms of special protection imposed upon the child by an overprotective parent. In the end, of course, the child grows into the adult, and the adult no longer has any moral right to *special* protection, to those forms of protection needed by the child but not by the adult.

3. Conclusion

In spite of the *United Nations Universal Declaration of Human Rights*, it is not true that "All human beings are born free and equal in dignity and rights". The infant has no human or moral rights at all because, lacking the capacity for any sort of voluntary action, it is not the sort of being who could meaningfully be said to possess either a liberty or a power, both essential ingredients in every right. The question then arises as to when and how the child acquires his or her rights. The child does not acquire a complete set of rights all at once, perhaps on that day when he or she becomes fully capable of rational choice and intentional action. Nor does the child acquire rights seriatim, one after the other but each one complete in itself. A right is a complex structure of liberties, claims, powers and immunities, and the child typically acquires some of these normative elements before others. Even one part of a right can expand or contract as the child grows more mature and the conditions of the child's life change. Hence, the growth of children's rights is piecemeal, fragmentary, overlapping and complicated.

Confusing as the moral terrain of childhood may be, it can be mapped provided one identifies the proper system of coordinates. The growth of rights takes place on two distinct levels. First, there is the growth in the child's capacity to possess each element of a specified right. Thus, the child cannot meaningfully be said to possess the ethical liberty of doing some action until the child possesses the ability to do that sort of action intentionally and, paradoxically, becomes capable of restraining an impulse to do that sort of action because of the practical reasons against that action. Since an ethical claim is quite different from an ethical liberty, its semantical presuppositions are also different. The child cannot be said to possess an ethical claim to something until the child has learned the language of claiming, understands what correlative duty he or she would be claiming, and has some grasp of the personal relation between the claimant and the duty-bearer by virtue of which the child has the ethical standing to make his or her claim.

The child's capacity to possess a specified right is one thing; its actual possession of that right another. The second level on which rights grow is that of the content of each normative element the child actually possesses. For example, the range of movements the child is ethically at liberty to engage in will change as the child's abilities to move about in the world develop and as the moral obligations of the child to refrain from certain sorts of movement change. Similarly, the content of the child's ethical claim against the parent to provide special protection will expand or contract as the child comes to need new sorts of protection or acquires the abilities required to cope with various dangers without parental intervention. What determines the content of any ethical element possessed by the child is, of course, the grounds of that sort of element. Since the grounds of a liberty of action are quite different from the grounds of a power of claiming, different sorts of elements will grow in different ways and even at different times.

I began by assuming my general theory of rights. Not everyone, I fear, will share my conception of a right. Let me close with a word or two to the friendly opposition. Does your conception of a right, like mine, entail ethical liberties, powers and claims? If it does, then our differences are largely irrelevant to the present purpose. You must confront head-on the same problems with which I have been struggling in this paper and, in the end, you will be driven to conclusions roughly like mine. On the other hand, if your conception of a right does not entail liberties, powers and claims, then our differences do matter. But I wonder why, as you conceive them, rights matter. What can be the practical significance of a children's right that implies no liberty of action of the child and no ethical claim of the child against the parent, other individuals or the state? And how will your conception of a right identify the coordinates on which one can draw a map applicable to the constantly changing terrain of childhood.

Résumé/Zusammenfassung

Le Développement des Droits des Enfants: Etant donné que les droits doivent contenir des libertés et des pouvoirs, il n'y a que des êtres capables d'exercer ces libertés et ces pouvoirs qui soient capables de posséder ces droits. Les petits enfants, donc, n'ont pas de droits légaux ou moraux. Les enfants acquérissent petit à petit ces droits, undroit après l'autre et chaque droit petit à petit au fur et à mesure que ces enfants développent leurs propres capacités psychologiques pour des choix rationnels et pour l'action. Cette étude va illustrer ce processus par examiner en détail le droit humain de liberté de mouvement et le droit de l'enfant de protection particulière.

Die Entwicklung von Kinderrechten: Subjektive Rechte enthalten notwendigerweise Freiheiten sowie Befugnisse; deswegen haben nur diejenigen Individuen subjektive Rechte, die Freiheiten genießen und Befugnisse ausüben. Daraus läßt sich ableiten, daß Neugeborene weder subjektive noch moralische Rechte haben. Kinder erlernen subjektive Rechte allmählich – zuerst das eine, später ein anderes, noch später auch weitere Teile des ersteren. Dieser Prozeß wird in der sich allmählich entwickelnden psychologischen Fähigkeit der Kinder zu rationaler Wahl und rationalem Handeln widergespiegelt. Der Aufsatz veranschaulicht detailliert diesen Prozeß, indem er das menschliche Recht auf Bewegungsfreiheit sowie das kindliche auf besonderen Schutz untersucht.

Anschrift des Autors:
Prof. Carl Wellman, Washington University, Dept. of Philosophy, Campus Box 1073, St. Louis, Missouri 63130, USA.

MORAL AUTONOMY, SELF-DETERMINATION AND ANIMAL RIGHTS

1. Introduction

Two perspectives dominate the general attempt to articulate the philosophical foundations of the animal liberation movement. On the one hand there is the utilitarian perspective typified by the work of Peter Singer. Here the morality of our treatment of nonhumans, and for that matter humans, is determined by an overarching concern to maximize a utility function. In Singer's case this utility function is in some way composite. Singer urges the maximization of objective preference satisfaction and the maximization of pleasure. The scope of these norms is not arbitrarily limited. In the case of the first, all creatures who have preferences or desires are covered. The second includes all those creatures with the capacity to experience pleasure. The maximization of the utility function does not take into account species membership except instrumentally. Moreover it is merely of instrumental concern that this or that individual is treated in this or that way. The treatment of individuals is determined solely by reference to the utility function.

On the other hand there is a Kantian perspective, perhaps best represented by Tom Regan. Within this tradition the attempt to work out a philosophical basis for animal liberation has been less programmatic. It has not involved the straightforward extension of an established tradition in ethics. It is typified by a concern to show that animals can be properly regarded as ends-in-themselves and that their lives have a kind of non-instrumental value. In its most radical form the Kantian perspective attributes equal value to human and nonhuman lives. Thus Regan asserts that "all who have inherent value have it equally, whether they be human animals or not."[1] To say that a life has inherent value is to say that it has value as an end-in-itself. And one way of representing the content of this claim is to say that there is a collection of core rights which attach to any life which has inherent value and which equally protect such lives from instrumental uses. Moreover the possession of these core rights by an individual should guarantee considerable moral protection: while not absolutely binding they should not be easily overridden. Some plausible candidates for these core rights are the right to life, the right to liberty, the right to flourish as a member of whatever kind one is, the right not to be used to further the ends of others. Possession of these core rights will, on Regan's view anyway, be guaranteed by the fact that an individual is a subject of a life, that an individual is in at least a minimal sense a psychological being.

It should be clear that the Kantian tradition more than the utilitarian tends towards the absolute proscription of certain ways of treating nonhumans. Thus it is the former rather than the latter which provides most resistance to the suggestion that nonhumans be used as subjects in experiments from which increasing amounts of good might plausibly flow. My intention is to defend the Kantian approach from two potential powerful attempts to undermine it. These attempts seek to demonstrate that there are properties possessed virtually exclusively by humans and which are necessary conditions for the coherent ascription of core rights. The two properties that I have in mind are the property of being self-determining and the property of being morally autonomous. These properties are especially interesting in this context because they are connected closely, on the Kantian view, to what is thought to be distinctively morally significant about human persons. What I intend to show is that there are many kinds of nonhumans to whom it is coherent to ascribe moral rights in exactly the way they are ascribed to humans.

The argument has two general and connected trends. First it is suggested that there is a suitably robust sense in which many kinds of nonhumans are autonomous and self-determining, which sense gives point to the ascription of rights to such nonhumans. Second it is suggested that understandings of autonomy and self-determination which exclude nonhumans are reflections of insufficiently examined human chauvinism which has no sound theoretical basis in moral theory. The argument is developed through a discussion of two recent arguments for the exclusionist view, one by Phillip Montague and one by H. J. McCloskey.[2] McCloskey believes that a necessary condition for being a possessor of rights is that one be morally autonomous. This requirement excludes virtually all nonhumans, and many humans as well, from the scope of rights. Montague thinks that only beings which are self-determining can possess rights in a sense not reducible to some other moral category such as obligation and that only (some) humans are self-determining. Their views are usefully considered conjointly. Their criteria for rights ascription are related and the routes by which they seek to establish their conclusions are similar. Moreover Montague highlights an important issue that McCloskey leaves underdeveloped, namely the issue of what it is to exercise a right. Conversely, McCloskey discusses issues that Montague does not discuss but which seem closely connected with Montague's position. And taken together the two views are appropriately thought of as representing the Kantian case against animal rights.[3]

2. *The Importance of Moral Rights for Nonhuman Animals*

A useful beginning is to review the degree to which Montague and McCloskey do think that nonhumans are morally considerable. Both accept that the animal liberation position is not completely eroded even if their own views about rights are correct. McCloskey thinks that there are duties of which nonhumans are the direct objects, for example the duty to render them assistance when their interests are threatened. He also allows that an ideal utilitarianism might attribute intrinsic value to animal lives. This, like the right to life possessed by humans, provides a strong reason for not taking animal lives and for ensuring that they are preserved. There will be differences in the policies that the two approaches generate. The ideal utilitarian will hold that, given certain empirical assumptions about causes and their consequences, nonhuman animal lives are replaceable, whereas the violation of a right to life cannot be put right by the creation of another entity whose right to life is respected. One could also imagine an ideal utilitarianism in which intrinsic value is attributed to the natural activities of animals in their natural states. This would be functionally somewhat similar to the right to liberty possessed by humans. It would provide a reason for not interfering in the lives of nonhumans, for not capturing them, caging them or compelling them to serve human interests. However, unlike the right to liberty this attribution of value only indirectly affords protection to the individuals that fall within its scope. These individuals are afforded protection in virtue of instantiating certain natural kinds. They are not afforded protection in virtue of being individuals which, *qua* individuals, have inherent worth. And of course the hedonistic act-utilitarian principle, which is included among the principles in the ethical pluralism McCloskey apparently favours, requires consideration of nonhumans. Similarly Montague's view provides some scope for the development of animal liberation objectives. He remarks that "Infanticide—as well as such things as cruelty to animals and non-therapeutic experimentation on the severely retarded—is immoral even if infants, animals, and the severely retarded have no exerciseable rights."[4]

Neither McCloskey's view nor Montague's view is totally human chauvinist. The former accepts that possibly some nonhumans (e.g., dolphins) can have rights and both are exclusionist with respect to large numbers of humans. Moreover both accord nonhuman animals quite a degree of moral considerability. Consequently it might be thought that apart from theoretical niceties nothing is to be gained for the animal liberation position by challenging the exclusiveness of moral rights. This is not so.

On both McCloskey's and Montague's views, and indeed generally, moral rights are powerful instruments for securing benefits for, and protecting the interests of, individuals which possess them. McCloskey observes that moral rights are "entitlements which confer moral liberties on their possessors to do, demand, enjoy, etc.: and they are entitlements which impose moral constraints on others to abstain from interference, to do, to assist, etc."[5] The extra moral significance of rights is considerable. The belief that a human being has a specific moral right would likely serve as a tie-breaker in cases where human and nonhuman interests conflict and are, in other respects, evenly matched. It may play an even more powerful role. Where the choice is between depriving a nonhuman of its liberty and thereby causing it to suffer considerably and depriving a human person of his or her liberty and thereby causing him or her to suffer a little, the violation of the human's right to liberty might be thought a reason for favouring him or her even where all other morally relevant considerations strongly favour the nonhuman.

Even where philosophers have been willing to grant that nonhumans have moral rights there is sometimes a reluctance to concede that they have them in quite the same way, or to the same degree, that humans have them. For example, Mary Anne Warren remarks that "animal liberationists must recognise that although animals do have significant moral rights, these rights are not precisely the same as those of human beings; and may sometimes be overriden . . . in situations where it would not be morally acceptable to override human rights for similar reasons."[6] The claim is not that there are some moral rights that human persons possess and which are not possessed by nonhumans; the claim is that the very same rights are somehow differently possessed by the two categories of beings. Warren's defence of her view has two components. First she says that this is what we are inclined to think. And of course this appeal to commonsense morality carries little weight unless some rational foundation can be found for it. This is what the second component, which emphasizes the rationality and moral autonomy of humans as against nonhumans, is supposed to provide. What seems to be at the bottom of Warren's modified exclusionist view are the notions of moral autonomy and self-determination more extensively developed by McCloskey and Montague.

Both the view that nonhumans cannot and do not have rights and the view that they have rights of a different order or to a different degree substantially erode the degree to which nonhumans are morally considerable. The Kantian approach to animal liberation requires the defeat of both views. It should be clear then that establishing that nonhumans can have rights in just the same way and to the same degee as humans involves more than theoretical niceties.

3. Non-Reducible Rights and the Argument from Self-Determination

Consider first Montague's arguments. He observes that "individuals attempting to establish the existence of certain obligations have increasingly tended to do so by arguing for the existence of rights which they take to underlie those obligations."[7] He instances James Rachels's defence of the view that we have an obligation not to confine nonhumans in terms of their having a right to liberty.[8] Montague suggests that the thought motivating Rachels's claim is "that obligations imply rights and that the rights implied are the grounds of the obligations which imply them."[9] He goes on to argue that the appeal to rights in this case, and most others, does not ground or explain the claim that we have the obligations in question. We are invited to consider the obligation not to lie. This may be taken to imply that there is a right not to be lied to but "one cannot justify the judgement that A is obligated not to lie to B by stating that B has a right not to be lied to, because the two claims are logically equivalent."[10] In this, and many other cases, talk of rights and obligations simply reflects two different points of view from which the same issue is morally evaluated. Both points of view reflect the claim that lies ought not to be told:

> . . . much talk about rights is really talk about obligations, and in many cases it would be better to frame these discussions in terms of references to obligations rather than references to rights. I see no advantage whatsoever, for example, in speaking of the right not to be killed rather than the obligation not to kill; and appealing to the former rather than the latter to argue against abortion, or the wanton destruction of animals, for example has a significant disadvantage in the way it raises questions about the sorts of individuals that are capable of possessing rights.[11]

Certainly talk in terms of rights is a way of translating moral issues into a discourse in common use. Presumably it is for this reason that Peter Singer, for instance, has talked in terms of animal rights despite being an act-utilitarian. Singer could respond to Montague's challenge by simply dropping talk of rights altogether. Any normative slack that this creates is immediately taken up by his *real* normative theory. Dropping the claim that animals have rights does not leave him with an embarrassing cluster of free-floating obligations since they are explicable in terms of his composite utility principle.[12]

What of animal liberationists who are not utilitarians, such as Regan and Rachels? Both condemn certain morally rotten ways of treating nonhuman animals and conclude that we have quite specific obligations concerning them. This requires that some general account be given of the basis of these obligations. Regan says that the obligations flow from rights.

This move couches the issue within a familiar rhetoric and it indicates how obligations to nonhumans might be integrated into conventional normative moral theory. Thus Regan, arguing from what he hopes is the firm premise that it is wrong to inflict gratuitous suffering on human morons, says:

> . . . I have not shown that human morons do have any rights. To do this I would have to show that what I believe is true, actually is true—namely that (1) it is *only* if they have rights that we can give a sufficiently firm theoretical basis for the conviction in question, (2) that this conviction is true, and (3) that the adequacy of theories depends on their ability to illuminate and account for such convictions.[13]

The question to ask is whether Regan's commitment to (1) plays the necessarily significant role that he thinks it does. Acting on Montague's suggestion, Regan could ground his judgements in obligations. Obligations feature in conventional morality and their point is readily enough understood. Moreover the obligations that Regan says we have in the case of animals would not be free-floating or theoretically unintegrated even if they did not have their real basis in rights. Regan gives an excellent account of why we have an obligation not to cause gratuitous suffering to animals. He links the situation to one in which human morons are caused to gratuitously suffer and shows that our reactions to the two cases can be seen to have a shared basis in our moral psychology.

It is worth considering at this point a reply that Rachels gives to an argument of Donald Van De Veer's:

> Van De Veer objects that in order for my argument to be successful it must be proved that "creatures with interests thereby have correlative rights." But I don't think so. All that is needed is to show that, for each plausible account of why humans have a right to liberty, a similar account may be provided in the case of other animals.[14]

The point of Rachels's strategy is to show that the moral reasons we have for not treating humans in particular ways can be parallelled in the case of nonhumans. This involves showing that there is no property possessed by humans and not possessed by nonhumans which unambiguously forms the basis for exclusionist practices of some kind. This procedure can be followed without bringing in rights at all. We first of all list features common to the two situations. We then suggest that these features provide the foundation for the moral judgement in the case of humans and then we urge that there are no reasons for thinking that these same features, or appropriate variants of them, do not play a similar function in supporting a moral evaluation in the case of nonhumans. A moral theory couched in terms of obligations, where the basis for these can be set down in the manner just alluded to, seems in no way theoretically inferior to one couched in terms of rights. What is important is the sorts of actions that are prescribed or proscribed. And of course the features of the obligation theory which generates the relevant evaluations will in many cases be functionally equivalent to features of a theory of rights.

Given this, Regan's remark that "we are driven to invoke the idea of rights for serious-minded, theoretical, non-rhetorical reasons . . . in the case of arguing well for the obligation to be vegetarian"[15] is not compelling, at least in one sense. The issue of whether nonhumans can have rights becomes important in those cases where attempts are made to support exclusionist practices by arguing that the functional equivalences suggested by Rachels do not obtain. The question of rights typically becomes significant here for two reasons. First, the alleged differential distribution of alleged morally relevant properties is typically articulated via the rhetoric of rights. Second, the range of permissible actions affecting an entity possessing the allegedly rights-supporting properties is typically restricted. (The most extreme cases of this are moral theories which treat rights as side-constraints on the pursuit of the good.) In effect, Montague's reason for saying that there are tactical reasons for eschewing rights-talk in the case of nonhumans is two-edged. The suggestion does provide a means for securing some animal liberation objectives, for example the abolition of LD50, Draize and feedlot farming. However, it does not secure the full-range of animal liberation objectives, including a prohibition on the subjugation of nonhuman interests to human interests, unless two conditions are satisfied: (i) Rights-talk is not retained within the human domain, (ii) No species-differentiated theory of morally relevant properties is retained. The two conditions are related: securing (ii) requires that (i) be secured. Montague's remarks about the merits of avoiding attributing rights to nonhumans is not premised on the satisfaction of these two conditions. Indeed he seeks to mark out a domain of moral considerability which is the exclusive preserve of (some) humans.

Montague thinks that "the distinction between rights which are the grounds of obligations arnd those which are not corresponds to the distinction between exerciseable rights and non-exerciseable rights."[16] This distinction is supposed to mirror D. D. Raphael's distinction between rights of action and rights of recipience. The latter are rights to be treated in certain ways, for example kindly rather than cruelly, or rights to receive something. The former are rights to act, to do, to pursue a project, to be self-determinng. Montague says:

> Exerciseable rights are related to liberties in that both are concerned with freedom of action, but having a right to act implies that freedom of action in some area is so important that others are obliged not to interfere with its exer-

> cise in that area. In this way exerciseable rights are the grounds of obligations and obligations not to interfere with freedom of action in areas specified by the rights . . . non-exerciseable rights are not distinct from the obligations to which they correspond, and hence cannot serve as the grounds of those obligations.[17]

The upshot of this view, if it is correct, is that only entities capable of exercising rights can possess non-reducible rights. This leaves the animal liberationist with two options. First he or she might argue that nonhuman animals are capable of exercising rights. Second he or she might argue that the allegedly non-reducible rights are in fact reducible. I shall do both.

What is it then to exercise a right? Montague does not say a great deal about this. He does say that he is "inclined to view the exercise of a right as an action in some fairly full-blooded sense."[18] Thus where the right to life is construed as the right not to be killed it is reducible. Where it is construed as a "collection of exerciseable rights concerned with matters of life and death . . . (including) . . . the right to defend oneself against aggressors and the right to obtain and use objects necessary to keep oneself alive"[19] it is non-reducible. It would seem that in Montague's view whether or not a right is non-reducible is determined by the content of that right. Moreover the content of such rights will exclude certain kinds of entities from the scope of the rights in question. The right to express one's political beliefs is arguably a right that human persons possess and which fish do not possess. However this concession still leaves open the possibility that nonhumans possess certain exerciseable rights, for example the right to self-defence. Moreover the exerciseable, and hence non-reducible, rights that nonhumans possess might overlap in areas of special significance with the rights possessed by humans and to an extent that guarantees nonhumans an inviolability such as that sought by Regan. There may be a set of core rights which human and nonhumans possess in common. Even if human persons have more and different rights than do nonhumans it does not follow that it is permissible that the interests of the latter be overridden when they conflict with the interests, even significant interests, of the former. If there is a conflict between meeting a human's right to X and to Y and meeting a nonhuman's right to X, then perhaps the additional right that is at stake in the human's case will swing the decision in the human's favour. However, even this does not automatically follow. Certainly in cases where the right to Y is not a core right and the right to X is, the decision does not obviously go the human's way.

I have said that the content of a right determines whether or not a right is exerciseable. The question then is whether nonhumans are the proper subjects of rights which are exerciseable. Now Montague claims that to exercise a right is to act in some full-blooded sense and, further, that acting in some full-blooded sense requires that the action is intentional under some description. Montague thinks that this requires that the putative right holder must possess language. Two ways of undermining Montague's exclusionist position clearly suggest themselves. First, one could attempt to show that exercising a right, in some suitably robust sense, does not require acting intentionally. Second, one could attempt to show that nonhumans, despite not possessing language, can act intentionally. I shall pursue the first option since, being neutral between competing views in philosophy of mind and language, it promises the most security for the animal liberationist position.

Consider Montague's right to life understood as an exerciseable right involving the right to defend oneself against aggressors and the right to obtain what is necessary to stay alive. And for the sake of simplicity let us ignore the problem of conflicting rights and, in particular, conflicting rights to life. Presumably the idea is that the right marks out a range of activities that its possessors are at liberty to do or are entitled to do. Moreover the idea seems to be that the entitlements flow from the fact that the possessors of the right have a capacity for acting and for doing within the circumstances marked out by the right. Acting or doing within these circumstances is to exercise the right to life. One exercises the right to defend oneself against aggressors when one fights off an aggressor or creates barriers that thwart aggression. Now it seems quite obvious that nonhumans behave in these kinds of ways. They act so as to protect themselves and they act so as to obtain what they require in order to stay alive; they gather food, they mark out territory, they build shelter.

Perhaps it might be argued that only creatures capable of representing their actions to themselves as the exercising of their rights can possess exerciseable rights. The cost of such an argument is high. By intellectualising the exercising of rights to this degree one risks excluding huge numbers of humans from the scope of non-reducible rights talk. If the criteria for possessing rights are loosened to include most humans it is highly likely that many nonhumans will be included as a consequence. Perhaps there are exclusionists who are willing enough to restrict the possession of non-reducible rights to entities who are at least minimally acquainted with political philosophy. Such a move may indeed make their position consistent but it does threaten significant deeply held convictions that we could reasonably expect to be preserved by an adequate normative theory. Worse, the differentiating property on which the exclusionist view is made to depend is insufficiently robust to support the view. This can be seen if we reflect for a moment on one common way in which humans exercise the right to life. They do not typically think of themselves as exercising the right in question. Rather they act, often unreflectively and instinctively, within the area of permissible action marked out by the right.

The advocate of animal rights is able to accept the idea, shared by both Montague and McCloskey, that non-reducible rights are conceptually bound up with the idea of freedoms or entitlements to act in various ways. The concept of a right gets its purchase where there is an entity with an active element, where such an element can be understood in terms of goals, desires, wants, inclinations, instincts, attitudes, preferences and the like. Certainly the concept is at home in situations where there are full-blooded actions but it would be perverse to deny that it is also at home in cases where action is not so cognitively mediated. In such cases it makes clear sense to draw the distinction between "freedom from" and "freedom to" which distinction is supposed to underpin Montague's distinction between reducible and non-reducible rights. Take the example of a migratory bird. Capturing the bird may cause it to suffer by preventing it from realising a natural propensity. But here the suffering is caused because it is prevented from positively doing something and not just through having something done to it. The range of actions open to it is restricted and an action which it would positively do if unrestrained is among those ruled out. To say that the bird is not having a freedom to do restricted is false and perverse.

I earlier said that questions might be asked about the soundness of Montague's claim that there are some non-reducible rights, viz., those underpinned by freedoms to. Why should these be viewed as not susceptible to reduction in the manner of other rights? Imagine that Montague has the alleged non-reducible right to life. One way of recasting this is to say that it is permissible for Montague to defend himself from aggression. One might go on to say that the permissibility of the action derives from the impermissibility of actions by others which constitute invasions of some domain defined in terms of certain of Montague's interests. One might then go on to say that others are obliged not to act in certain ways which affect Montague. The suggestion is that alleged non-reducible rights can be viewed as obligations on the part of others not to act in certain ways, as obligations not to interfere, to let alone, to let be or the like. In this way alleged irreducible rights can be reduced to obligations. At least talk in terms of obligations on the one hand and rights on the other are different ways of making the same moral point.

Montague has not shown that nonhumans cannot possess non-reducible rights and he has not established the superior moral significance of humans to nonhumans. The argument from self-determination fails.

4. *The Argument from Moral Autonomy*

McCloskey agrees with Montague that "the notion of exercising, acting on the basis of our rights, is central to rights"[20] and believes that if a being is to possess rights there must be some coherent sense in which its rights can be claimed, exercised, waived and forgone "by or on behalf of the possessor of rights."[21] He goes on to suggest that when this requirement is properly understood and amplified it is clear that only morally autonomous, self-determining agents can possess rights. Thus nonhumans cannot possess rights not because they cannot make claims, since these can be made through proxies, but because, lacking moral autonomy, they are not the kinds of creatures on whose behalf proxies can in any coherent sense act with respect to rights. If this argument can be successfully developed and defended it provides a powerful device for excluding nonhumans from the scope of rights.

Let us accept as a minimal requirement that an entity can only possess rights if it possesses a will. I mean this to be understood generously. What is required is that there be desires, preferences, inclinations, wants, attitudes or the like. Nonhumans meet these conditions and if McCloskey's attempt to narrow them is unsuccessful then we may presume that nonhumans can possess rights.

Consider first McCloskey's rejection of sentience as a sufficient condition for the possession of rights. The argument turns on the observation that "it is commonly denied that God is capable of experiencing pain (and pleasure), yet this seems irrelevant to whether or not He has the capacity to possess rights."[22] This does not straightforwardly show that sentience does not suffice to undergird the attribution of rights. To think that it does, as McCloskey seems to, is to confuse necessary with sufficient conditions. The case of God shows that sentience is not a necessary condition but it does not show that it is not sufficient. The argument must be more subtle. Perhaps the idea is that if we think about the God case we will see that what is fundamental to the attribution of rights is exemplified in that case. In other words the case is offered as a paradigm case of rights possession which reveals what essentially undergirds the attribution of rights.

Consider this suggestion in the context of another putative sufficient condition for rights ascription which McCloskey rejects, namely the capacity for desire. He says at one point: "it is desire as an intellectual activity that is relevant, not some sort of animal desire or appetite. A purely intellectual being such as God . . . is capable of desiring in the intellectual sense; it is incapable of desiring in the intellectual sense; it is incapable of appetitive desires."[23] The implication of these remarks is that appetitive desire is not sufficient for possession of rights.

How is this implication made good? The example does not straightforwardly establish that appetitive desire is not sufficient for possession of rights. It establishes only that it is not necessary. Again what must be being offered is the kind of paradigm case argument suggested earlier. However it is not remotely obvious that the example serves its desired purpose. Granted, it involves a paradigm possessor of rights, but it does not establish that it is desire as an intellectual activity that is essentially relevant. In fact it is plausible to think of it as suggesting a way of extending the scope of rights from that which it has in the context of cumulative speciesist practices. First we note that in the paradigm case possession of rights is associated with a capacity for intellectual desire and then we suggest that it is desire in a general sense, unrestricted by socially and intellectually embedded practices, that undergirds the attribution of rights. We might suggest that the sufficient condition for possession of rights is disjunctive, that in order to possess rights a being must possess either the capacity for intellectual desire or the capacity for appetitive desire. Moreover the two disjuncts are not bound together in an arbitrary way; they both involve kinds of desire. The disjuncts are connected through the idea of a being with a will. It is reasonable to claim then that nonhumans which lack the capacity for intellectual desire nevertheless can possess moral rights. They can possess them if they have the capacity for desire.

Perhaps McCloskey's argument might be strengthened if we turn to a consideration of moral autonomy. The argument is pursued via the suggestion that the concepts of *rights* and *interests* are completely distinct. Presumably McCloskey thinks that it is the attribution of interests to nonhumans that smoothes the way for attributing rights to them. He observes that "a possessor of rights may wish to exercise his rights contrary to his interests."[24] Specifically, a possessor of rights may exercise his or her rights contrary to his or her interests for moral reasons. Thus I might have a right to pursue my own projects instead, say, of helping someone else in theirs. However, I might think that the other person's project is more morally significant than mine and so decide not to do what I have a right to do. McCloskey apparently thinks that such considerations show that moral self-determination or autonomy is necessary for possession of rights. Clearly he thinks that nonhumans, apart from some cetaceans, are not morally self-determining. I accept this last point but dispute the necessity claim.

It is the possibility of giving up one's rights contrary to one's interests for moral reasons that is supposed to undermine the very possibility of representing nonhumans with respect to rights. Despite certain practical difficulties the interests of nonhumans can be represented but:

> With rights, what has to be determined and represented is something much more difficult to determine. It is how the possessor of rights who cannot express his wishes—who may not even be conscious or have wishes—would wish to exercise his rights, indeed, whether or not he would wish to claim his rights. This involves reading his mind, his moral mind, not simply determining what is for his good.[24]

There are several lines of reply to this. First, it needs to be pointed out that nonhuman behaviour can be expressive of the wish, will, desire not to take advantage of certain freedoms or opportunities. A nonhuman that defends its young to the point of severe injury or death when it could easily escape is expressing a desire, will or inclination to act contrary to its interests. Of course it will be replied that the nonhuman's choice is a manifestation of an instinct rather than the expression of its will. There are two weaknesses in this reply. It seeks to co-opt the idea of a will to the process of rationally willing; it construes the idea of a will in an overly intellectualised way. It also downplays the role that instinctive responses play in the moral psychology of human persons.[25]

Second, it is not clear why attributing moral rights to nonhumans requires that we be able to determine when they might waive those rights or choose not to act within the entitlements the rights provide. Grant McCloskey's point that rights are essentially the kinds of things that can be waived. It does not follow from this that whenever an entity possesses some right that right can be waived. This only follows from the much stronger, and anything but obvious, premise that rights are essentially the kinds of things that can be waived in all instances. Certainly it would be a mistake to require that wherever rights are properly attributed the same things be true of them. What McCloskey must establish is that the possibility of waiving rights is a necessary feature of every attribution of them. The argument given for this is slender to say the least. He notes that in the paradigm instances of possession of rights the beings concerned are capable of refraining from what they are, by right, entitled to do. It follows from this that rights can be waived but it does not follow that they always can be. It is also pertinent to note that paradigm instances of rights possession are likely to contain considerable human chauvinist assumptions.

There is a third line of reply to McCloskey. Consider the morally despicable case of a laboratory animal imprisoned with the latest shampoo dripping into its eyes. It is too easy to imagine how things are for the animal in this situation and it is easy to understand what the animal would prefer. In every sense that is important it does seem possible to read its will. And given that the misery to which it is condemned is so gross and that the reasons for it are so trivial and mercenary, it makes little sense to suppose that it would, if it could, waive its right to liberty or its right not to be made to suffer. It is difficult to imagine a rational human person waiving his or her right in such circumstances. The offer to do so would constitute evidence of irrationality or utterly perverse altruism or absurd supererogation. It is plausible to presume that a nonhuman would not, even if it could, waive its right to X in those cases where it would be irrational, perverse or absurd for a human to waive his or her right to X. Just as we think it irrational, perverse or absurd for a human to offer himself or herself up for the gastronomic delectation of his or her conspecifics we should presume that nonhumans would not, even if they could, waive their rights to continued life in those circumstances in which nonhumans are typically devoured by humans.

McCloskey attempts to connect the capacity to exercise moral rights with the capacity for moral evaluation. He says, somewhat opaquely, that "in accepting and exercising their rights [possessors of rights] must call upon their moral entitlements."[26] However it is less than obvious that exercising one's rights, understood as acting within one's entitlements, necessitates calling on moral capacities. The evaluations that determine whether or not an individual has the right to act in some way or other can be made by another individual. To exercise a right I do not have to know, or even believe, that I am exercising a right. I might never have thought about rights let alone have beliefs about them. Presumably this does not mean that I cannot have them. One can imagine an intelligent, rational being devoid of all moral sense to whom it is nevertheless coherent to attribute rights. Such a person may desire to perform many harmless actions and it does not stretch our moral notions too far to suggest that with respect to these the agent has a right to liberty.

5. Conclusion

Enough has been said to defeat the exclusionist claims of Montague and McCloskey and to provide the conceptual space for the Kantian defence of animal liberation. The discussion has also indicated that nonhumans are autonomous in a substantial sense provided that the notion of autonomy is not, as it should not be, overly intellectualised.

Robert Elliot

Brisbane College of Advanced Education
Australia

NOTES

1. Tom Regan, "Animals and Rights" in Peter Singer (ed.) *In Defence of Animals* (Oxford: Basil Blackwell, 1985) p. 44.

2. H. J. McCloskey, "Moral Rights and Animals," *Inquiry*, 22 1 (1979) pp. 23-54 and *Ecological Ethics and Politics*, (Totowa, NJ: Rowman and Littlefield, 1983) pp. 62-70; Phillip Montague, "Two Concepts of Rights," *Philosophy and Public Affairs*, 9, 4 (1980) pp. 372-84.

3. Other philosophers who have appealed to autonomy to undermine the animal liberation position incude: Michael A. Fox, "Animal Liberation: A Critique," *Ethics*, 88, 2 (1978) pp. 106-18; Bonnie Steinbock, "Speciesism and the Idea of Equality," *Philosophy*, 53 (1978) pp. 247-56; Aubrey Townsend, "Radical Vegetarians," *Australasian Journal of Philosophy*, 57, 1 (1979) pp. 85-93.

4. Montague (1980) p. 384.

5. McCloskey (1979) p. 26.

6. Mary Anne Warren, "The Rights of the Nonhuman World," in Robert Elliot and Arran Gare (eds) *Environmental Philosophy: A Collection of Readings* (St. Lucia: University of Queensland Press, 1983) p. 110. See also Rosalind Godlovitch, "Animals and Morals," in R. Godlovitch, S. Godlovitch and John Harris (eds) *Animals, Men and Morals* (London: Gollancz, 1972), pp. 163-64.

7. Montague (1980) p. 374.

8. James Rachels, "Do Animals Have the Right to Liberty?" in Peter Singer and Tom Regan (eds) *Animal Rights and Human Obligations* (Englewood Cliffs, NJ: Prentice-Hall, 1976) pp. 205-23.

9. Montague (1980) p. 375.

10. Ibid., p. 375.

11. Ibid., pp. 376-77.

12. Peter Singer, "Utilitarianism and Vegetarianism," *Philosophy and Public Affairs* (1980) p. 327.

13. Tom Regan, "Utilitarianism, Vegetarianism and Animal Rights," *Philosophy and Public Affairs*, 9 (1980) p. 323.

14. Rachels (1976) p. 231.

15. Regan (1980) p. 308.

16. Montague (1980) p. 378.

17. Ibid., p. 379.

18. Ibid., p. 382.

19. Ibid., p. 382.

20. McCloskey (1979) p. 28.

21. Ibid., p. 29.

22. Ibid., p. 31.

23. Ibid., p. 35.

24. Ibid., p. 39.

25. See for example Peter Singer, *The Expanding Circle: Ethics and Sociobiology* (New York: Farrar, Straus and Giroux, 1981) and Mary Midgley, *Beast and Man: The Roots of Human Nature* (Ithaca, NY: Cornell University Press, 1978).

26. McCloskey (1979) p. 41.

Denise Réaume*

INDIVIDUALS, GROUPS, AND RIGHTS TO PUBLIC GOODS†

Are there any rights to public goods? Can they be claimed by individuals? Recent literature has elided these two questions and reached a sceptical conclusion. Joseph Raz, for example, thinks that it is at least unlikely that an individual can successfully claim a right to some sorts of public goods,[1] while Neil MacCormick has argued that legal rights secure individuals in the enjoyment of individual goods but not in that of collective goods such as clean air.[2] I shall argue that this oversimplifies the issue. One particular feature of public goods is wrongly isolated as rendering implausible a claim of individual right. In fact, the difficulty lies elsewhere. It is true that there is no individual right to some public goods, but not for the reasons given by Raz and MacCormick. Rather, the difficulty flows from the inherent nature of what I shall call 'participatory goods.' However, the key feature of such goods is not confined to pure public goods, nor is it present in all public goods. This means that there may be individual rights to some public goods, but only non-participatory ones. I shall also argue that any rights to participatory goods must be held by groups rather than individuals.

A complete analytic account of rights must consist of at least three facets. The first involves an elucidation of what a claim of right embodies. One might argue, for example, that a right is a claim to the protection of certain choices,[3] or certain kinds of interests,[4] or perhaps to the

* Faculty of Law, University of Toronto

† I am grateful to the Connaught Programme in Legal Theory and Public Policy of the University of Toronto and the Human Rights Fund of the Department of Justice of Canada for their generous support of the larger project on language rights of which this article is a part. Needless to say, the views expressed are my own and not necessarily those of either the government of Canada or the University of Toronto. An earlier draft of this paper was read at the Centre for Criminology and the Social and Philosophical Study of Law at the University of Edinburgh. I am grateful to the participants for their helpful comments. I would also like to thank Les Green, Joseph Raz, Wayne Sumner, Jeremy Waldron, and the members of the Law and Philosophy discussion group at the University of Toronto.

1 Right-based moralities, in Waldron (ed.) *Theories of Rights* (1984) 182, at 189–90

2 Taking the 'rights thesis' seriously, in MacCormick *Legal Right and Social Democracy* (1982) 126, at 143. See also MacCormick, Rights in legislation, in Hacker and Raz (eds) *Law, Morality, and Society* (1977) 189.

3 See, e.g., Hart, Legal rights, in Hart *Essays on Bentham* (1982) 162, and Wellman *A Theory of Rights* (1985).

4 See, e.g., Bentham's theory as reconstructed by Hart in 'Legal rights'; also Raz, On the nature of rights (1984) 93 *Mind* at 194.

satisfaction of certain needs. This involves both a discussion of that which is protected and the form or extent of the protection.[5] Recent literature has focused primarily on this aspect of the theory of rights, and it is clear that this is crucial to any analysis. However, such discussions are often insufficiently sensitive to two other aspects of the theory and to the independent impact they may have on the analysis of particular rights. A complete theory must also consider the nature of the right-holder and that of the good to which a right is claimed. That the common preoccupation with the first of these aspects has obscured the importance of the others can be illustrated by the dominant approach to the problem of rights to public goods. As we shall see, the argument that such rights are untenable flows from a theory of what a claim of right embodies. I hope to expand this analysis by attending more carefully to the kind of good that is the object of the purported right. My primary concern here is with the nature of the good claimed rather than with the qualifications for the status of right-holder, but the former will have an impact on who, if anyone, can claim certain rights. In the same way, one's analysis of what kind of claim a right is may influence what sort of entity can claim it. For example, the view that rights protect choices rules out certain entities, such as animals, as right-holders. In this way the three ingredients in a complete account of rights are interconnected.

The Right to Public Goods

Can there be rights to public goods? I will argue that a complete answer cannot ignore the nature of the good at issue. However, this question has usually been approached in a different way. Joseph Raz, for example, has addressed it tangentially in developing his general theory of rights.[6] I will use Raz's comments as a starting point for my own analysis because he is one of the few writers to discuss the issue in any detail, and because his views help illuminate the different, but not entirely incompatible, approach taken here. For convenience, let us refer to his as an 'interest theory' of rights. In Raz's formulation one has a right only if one's well-being or interest is sufficient reason for holding some other person(s) to be under a duty.[7] This definition is primarily concerned with the first of the three dimensions of a complete theory of rights outlined above. It specifies that a right is a claim to the protection of one's interests, and that this is accomplished by imposing obligations on others to act or refrain

5 E.g., Dworkin's trump theory is chiefly concerned with the second of these two issues – that is, what form the protection takes. See *Taking Rights Seriously* (1977).
6 Raz, supra note 1, supra note 4
7 Supra note 4, 195

from acting so as to secure some benefit for the right-holder. It also implies something about the nature of the interests that are protected: they must be important enough to justify the imposition of duties on others. Therefore, not just any interest will be capable of grounding a right.

Although Raz acknowledges the other two necessary aspects of a theory of rights, they are not his central concern. He offers a definition of the capacity to have rights, but declines to enter into a detailed discussion of whether this capacity inheres uniquely in individuals.[8] He raises the question of rights to public goods, but in order to make a point about the plausibility of a right-based moral theory rather than for the sake of providing an analysis of the kind of goods which can be the object of rights. As a result, the issue of whether individuals can have rights to public goods is filtered through his analysis of the type of claim a right is rather than treated as an independent issue. The question of the nature of group rights to such goods is treated similarly. This leads, as I hope to show, to a distortion in the analysis and to a failure to clarify an important aspect of individual and group rights.

Raz contends that valid individual rights to public goods are unlikely. Again, his starting point is the analysis of a right as the existence of an interest capable of justifying the imposition of obligations on others. He then argues that it is unlikely that any single individual's interest could justify the imposition of the duties which would be required in order to achieve the provision of a public good.[9] The argument acknowledges the two sides of the equation defining the existence of the right: the importance of the claimant's interest, and the magnitude of the imposition it requires on others. Raz seems to be arguing that an individual's interest in the provision of a public good is usually not very weighty and the burden that would have to be imposed on others is usually extremely large. These two factors combine to yield the conclusion that the individual is unlikely to have a right to a public good.

What is it about public goods that makes this plausible? Raz defines public goods as those goods from whose benefits no member of society can involuntarily be excluded.[10] If the good is provided at all everyone will

8 Ibid. 204

9 Supra note 1, 186–90

10 Ibid. 187. There is a further defining characteristic of a public good, namely that it be non-rival in consumption: it must be the case that consumption of the good by one individual does not reduce the level of consumption by others. Although an important feature of public goods, this characteristic does not affect the argument about whether there can be rights to such goods, and therefore I shall concentrate exclusively on the non-excludability feature. If anything this feature may even make it easier on substantive grounds to make out a claim to a right to a public good because one source of competing consideration – the enjoyment of the good by others – is eliminated.

be able to benefit from its enjoyment. For brevity's sake, we may refer to this as the non-excludability criterion. But note that this feature tells us nothing about the interest of any particular claimant in receiving the good or about the weight of the burden on others. Although Raz does not explicitly identify it, I think the relevant feature which makes his argument plausible for at least some public goods can be discerned in his examples. Consider, for instance, the case of a cultured society. In what sense is it a non-excludable good, and how does this affect the viability of an individual right to it? There are many possible ways of excluding people from the enjoyment of a certain good, and if the non-excludability criterion is given too strong an interpretation the concept of a public good evaporates entirely. In starkest terms, it is always possible to exclude someone from the benefit of any good by simply killing him.[11] More specifically, to take examples which are standardly considered public goods, some can be excluded from the benefits of national defence by being forcibly handed over to a hostile government, and exclusion of some from the benefits of a smallpox-free society can be accomplished by injecting them with smallpox virus. But, of course, we all have an independent right not to be murdered, or deported without reason, or assaulted, which independently protects us from exclusion by certain means. Clearly then, the notion of excludability takes for granted a background framework of rights and duties.[12] Given that one has certain basic rights which prohibit some means of exclusion, a public good is one from which one cannot otherwise be excluded.

Against such a framework of basic rights we can see how the existence of a cultured society is a public good in at least some respects. A cultured society is a very complex good, or cluster of goods, some of which may indeed fail to meet the non-excludability criterion. For example, it is possible to exclude some from libraries and art galleries and therefore from some aspects of the good of a cultured society. In referring to a cultured society as a public good, Raz cannot mean these aspects. Rather he has in mind 'the more diffuse [benefits] deriving from the general character of the society' as one which is cultured;[13] for example, a generally higher level of concern for the aesthetic side of life and richer

11 This point is made by Buchanan, An economic theory of clubs (1965) 32 *Economica* 1, at 14, and Barry and Hardin (eds) *Rational Man and Irrational Society* (1982) 182–3.

12 It also frequently takes for granted practical and economic infeasibility of exclusion. A good may be non-excludable in the sense that we do not yet have the technological capability to exclude people (although scientists are working on a means to do so) or in the sense that it is prohibitively expensive to exclude others. See Barry and Hardin, supra note 11, 182–3; Peston *Public Goods and the Public Sector* (1972) 17–18; and Laver *The Politics of Private Desires* (1981) 31.

13 Raz, supra note 1, 187

and more diverse opportunities for self-expression. In this very general, minimal sense in which it is simply better for everyone to live in a society which is cultured than in one which is not, the existence of a cultured society is a public good. Enjoyment of these general benefits cannot be denied to any member of the society. Of course, as Raz notes, someone can be excluded by being expelled from the society altogether, or by being confined permanently to a prison cell without any contact with the outside world, but these forms of exclusion would be prohibited by the background framework of rights.

This example helps to elucidate Raz's scepticism about the likelihood of an individual right to such a good. A cultured society requires the existence of a certain 'critical mass' of individuals who create and enjoy rock videos, read and write literature, compose, perform, and listen to music, paint and sculpt, and so forth. If no such critical mass existed, one who claimed the right to a cultured society would be claiming that her interest justified the imposition of a duty on others to create such a body. This would mean that a certain number of people would be required to take up an interest in the arts, devote their energies to culture, and otherwise alter their commitments and life-plans. This is the real nerve of Raz's argument, for it is difficult to see how one person's desire to live in a cultured society could justify such an imposition on so many others. The ultimate answer to this question will depend upon substantive moral arguments about the weight and urgency of the various interests at stake, but it is Raz's intuition that substantive arguments capable of justifying such a right will not be forthcoming.

There are two possible grounds upon which this intuition could be based, and it is unclear whether Raz is relying on one or both. Firstly, one might think such a claim of right is implausible because of the *number* of people who must be burdened in order to provide it. Typically, public goods of social importance require the co-operation of large numbers. Therefore the individual's interest would have to be great enough to justify such a large-scale imposition of burdens. Secondly, the difficulty in such a claim could be thought to arise out of the kind of burden which must be imposed on others, even if only a few need bear it. It may be that the necessary obligations would involve interference with important choices about how to live one's life and would therefore constitute a serious violation of individual autonomy or other prized values. It is arguable that such an imposition on even a single person would be unjustifiable. The provision of a cultured society carries with it both of these difficulties, but there are other goods (including public goods) which involve only one or the other. For example, acid rain would be an insignificant problem if the emissions of a few main contributors were halted, but this would cost these few companies hundreds of millions of dollars. Conversely, litter on the streets can be eliminated only if virtually everyone makes the small sacrifice of refraining from littering. Ultimately, the relevance of either the size of the burden or the numbers affected to whether the claimant's interest justifies the imposition of the necessary obligations is also a matter of substantive moral argument.

This discussion reveals that Raz's argument does not centrally turn on the kind of good a public good is, or even on the kind of interest one can have in its provision, but on the relative importance of an individual's interest and the onerous duties imposed on many others. This means, however, that whether an individual can have a right to a public good does not depend upon anything peculiar to public goods. Not all public goods require either the imposition of duties on large numbers of people or peculiarly onerous duties. For example, in making improvements to residential property, a single individual provides a good for all the other residents of the immediate neighbourhood – their property values may increase or, at the very least, they have the benefit of a more attractive home nearby making the neighbourhood more pleasant. Nor is being required to improve one's property – by keeping the front yard tidy, for example – such an onerous burden that its justification can be eliminated out of hand. Conversely, there are instances of private goods that require either onerous undertakings of others or the participation of many. For example, the gourmet meal that one consumes in a restaurant requires considerable talent and exertion from the chef, and the building of an office tower requires the co-operation of a great many workers. Thus Raz's argument against the existence of an individual right does not apply to all public goods, or only to public goods. In fact, the argument which defeats the individual claim is just the same as that which defeats a right to any other kind of good – the interest at stake simply is not sufficiently weighty. The only difference between the two cases is that public goods are more likely to defy a claim of right because they more commonly require particularly onerous burdens and widespread co-operation in order to bring them about. Nor does Raz pinpoint any other feature of public goods which necessarily makes a claim of individual right untenable.

For present purposes I need not quarrel with Raz's judgment that on substantive moral grounds an individual's interest in a cultured society is unlikely to be strong enough to justify imposing the required duties on many people. But I do want to probe this example a little deeper to see if there is something else in the nature of goods such as a cultured society which renders inappropriate a claim of individual right before we even get to the level of substantive moral argument. Secondly, I want to question whether this feature is present in all public goods so as to rule out individual rights to them. I hope to show that the features of public goods which Raz has pointed out are not in themselves sufficient to defeat a claim of individual right, but that they point us in the direction of another feature of some goods which does render an individual right conceptually impossible. This feature is a structural aspect of certain goods rather than an aspect bearing on the substantive question of how much we may expect of our neighbours. I will conclude that there are some cases in which no individual right is possible no matter how important the interest in its enjoyment is, and that there are other in which such a claim is possible despite the fact that the provision of the good requires widespread and onerous co-operation.

Individual rights

We can provide a better explanation of why an individual right to a cultured society is untenable by examining more closely the nature of that good and the way it is enjoyed. In my view, such an investigation reveals a preliminary conceptual question which turns on whether the interest in the enjoyment of a good is one that an individual can have *as an individual.* To see what I mean, we must distinguish between the production of a good and its enjoyment. To ask whether an individual can have a particular good is ambiguous as between these two ideas. If one needs the help of others in order to produce a good, which is the case with many public goods, there is a sense in which the individual, as an individual, cannot have that good – he cannot bring it about by himself. But there is a deeper sense in which one can be said to have a good as an individual: when the good is *enjoyed* by someone as an individual, when it is of value to the individual as such. To flesh out this idea and fully understand its importance we need to consider what sort of claim a right is. Although there are competing theories about the essential features of rights, the one I have in mind is central to all such theories. In the most general terms, a right is an interest which claims special protection or has special importance. Raz's definition, noted above,[14] that a right exists when one's interest is sufficient reason to justify imposing an obligation on others provides a useful general definition as it is designed to encompass various competing theories of rights. Although there is great controversy about which interests have such importance, theorists are generally agreed on this structural aspect of a claim of right. It is a claim that certain interests take precedence over at least some other sorts of considerations which go

14 Supra p. 2

towards justifying action. This is what Dworkin has called the 'trumping' power of rights, and what lies behind his definition of a right as an 'individuated political aim': 'An individual has a right to some opportunity or resource or liberty if it counts in favor of a political decision that the decision is likely to advance or protect the state of affairs in which he enjoys the right, even when no other political aim is served and some political aim is disserved thereby, and counts against that decision that it will retard or endanger that state of affairs, even when some other political aim is thereby served.'[15] The intuitive idea is that some interests are so important that they should be satisfied even if no one else benefits from the exercise of the right and even if it requires some sacrifice of others.

To apply this idea to the question of whether an individual can have such a claim we need only stress the potential conflict between the individual human being and the rest of society.[16] An individual right is a claim which a single human being is entitled to assert even if the exercise of that right makes things worse for everyone else. Therefore such a right can be claimed only with respect to goods or opportunities that can be individualized, that is, a good in which one's interest can be distinguished from, and possibly opposed to, that of others. The right to physical security will serve to illustrate the point. One may exercise this right by demanding freedom from torture even if everyone else would be made better off by the silencing of a dangerous enemy of the government if torturing him were permitted. This form of protection signifies that the interest at stake is one that is of importance to the person considered as an isolated individual.

Whether one can have a right as an individual to any good depends upon whether it is one which is individualizable in the above sense, that is, whether it is a good the enjoyment of which should, and therefore can, be satisfied even at the expense of some interest of everyone else. This condition can be met in the case of some public goods. Consider, again, the example of clean air. Although, as we have seen, clean air cannot be produced individually, it can nevertheless be enjoyed individually. It is a good which an individual can enjoy even if no one else does. Therefore it might sensibly be the object of a claim to its enjoyment whether or not others enjoy it. The individual's enjoyment derives from the fact that it is beneficial for *her* health, just as medical supplies or a proper diet are, whether or not they benefit others. The good is valuable for a completely individualizable aspect of one's being. This is what makes it conceptually

15 Dworkin, supra note 5, 91
16 Wellman, supra note 3, makes a similar point.

possible for there to be an individual right to some public goods. At this stage of the argument it may still be that an individual's claim of right to an individualizable public good will fail for something like the reason offered by Raz, viz., that the individual's interest is not sufficiently weighty. However, as Raz recognizes[17] (although MacCormick seems to deny it),[18] it is not necessarily the case that all such individual claims will fail. Imagine, for example, the public good of controlling a highly contagious and very dangerous disease such as cholera. Although this may involve the imposition of a duty on many to submit to confinement or to intrusive medical treatment, it is arguable that the interest of a single individual in avoiding the horrible effects of such a disease could justify such imposition. This is obviously not a complete argument in favour of the existence of such a right. It merely shares the same intuitions on which Raz relied, about the importance of the interests at stake, to suggest the plausibility of a claim of individual right to some public goods.

We can now see that, in so far as it points to the difficulty of justifying the imposition of duties on many others, Raz's argument relies on the fact that public goods usually cannot be individually produced. Although this may be relevant at the stage of substantive argument, it ignores the prior structural condition for a sound claim of individual right that the good be individually enjoyable. This condition can be met in the case of some public goods, such as clean air or freedom from contagion. But there are others in which it cannot, so that there cannot be an individual right to such goods regardless of the substantive arguments assigning importance to the competing interests.

This structural condition better explains why there is no individual right to a cultured society. I have said that a cultured society is a complex package of goods. But the package has a core upon which all other aspects of a cultured society are dependent. These core aspects of culture are such that each individual needs others in order to enjoy them, not merely in order to produce it. If we could provide the trappings of culture for a single individual – through Nozick's experience machine or by magically conjuring up theatres, cinemas, art galleries, and museums of which he was the sole beneficiary – we would not have satisfied the claim of right. The fact that we have to postulate an experience machine or the ability to produce culture by magic in order to provide it for a single person indicates that culture is a jointly produced good, but this is not what defeats the claim of individual right. These theatres and galleries would be empty trappings of culture, incapable of providing the most significant

17 Raz, supra note 1
18 MacCormick, Taking the 'rights thesis' seriously, Rights in legislation, supra note 2

benefits we associate with life in a cultured society. By far the greatest value in a cultured society inherently involves the presence of others who have similar interests and with whom one can interact and share that culture. The value of such a good is partly constituted by a particular kind of participation. Such goods, which I shall call 'participatory goods,' involve activities that not only require many in order to produce the good but are valuable only because of the joint involvement of many. The publicity of production itself is part of what is valued – the good *is* the participation.

This participatory nature of these core aspects affects the analysis of a right to the diffuse benefits of a cultured society which are the focus of Raz's discussion. These benefits are not themselves inherently participatory. However, as by-products of the participatory activity which is the core of culture, they are parasitic upon it. Unless the active creation and appreciation of culture takes place, there can be no diffuse benefits produced even for those who do not participate. Hence, one can have a right to the diffuse benefits of a cultured society only if one can have a right to the core goods of culture. I have argued that no individual right exists to participatory goods such as the participatory aspects of culture. A fortiori there can be no individual right to the sorts of benefits with which Raz is concerned. It is worth noting, however, that many of these goods may also be privately or individually enjoyed to a certain extent. In this respect they may have an individual aspect which is conceptually capable of grounding an individual right – although one which may be unlikely to succeed for substantive reasons such as those suggested by Raz. This aspect is less important, though, because it does not begin to capture the full value of culture. Further, there may be other individual rights that are parasitic on the existence of the participatory good. For example, if the good is created through voluntary efforts, there may then arise an individual right to an equal chance to participate in the good. This, however, is simply a particular instance of the right to equality of opportunity, which is an individualizable good.[19]

In an important respect, these goods are distinguished from many public goods because of their participatory nature. Owing to the free-rider problem, publicity is frequently a problematic rather than valuable aspect of the good. Participatory goods avoid this problem because they unite production and consumption. A cultured society is not a set of artefacts – plays, paintings, films. The good does not consist in some end product, such as clean streets, which, once in existence, is only externally related to its enjoyment as means to ends; it consists in

19 I am grateful to Michael McDonald for bringing this point to my attention.

participating in the production of those artefacts which constitute a cultured society. But there is no end product because, in a sense, these artefacts are never completed but are continuously reinterpreted and re-created by each generation. This process is the essence of a cultured society and can only take place *through*, not simply *because* of, the involvement of many. Unlike clean air, its enjoyment cannot be separated from its production.

An individual cannot have a right to such an activity because it cannot be enjoyed as an individual. If it could be provided to a single person it would be worthless to him. Sharing cultural experiences is the most important part of the benefit of having them. Another way to make the same point is to say that to individualize the right in this case would be to change it. The right to clean air is a right to the same thing whether one or one thousand people enjoy it. But the right to have works of art provided for one to admire is not the same as the right to a cultured society. Therefore Raz's argument that a single individual's interest is unlikely to be important enough to justify imposing burdens on others, even if sound, is misguided. The important point is that the individual has no interest as an individual in the most important aspect of these goods, not that his interest is a weak one.

This is not to deny that when such goods are provided it is individuals who enjoy them. But individualism in that weak sense is common not only to certain right-based theories but also to aggregative welfarist theories such as the varieties of utilitarianism which wholly reject the concept of fundamental moral rights. Thus weak individualism cannot be a sufficient conceptual condition of an individual right. It is not necessary for the purposes of this argument to decide whether all goods derive their status as goods from their capacity to benefit individuals, or whether there are corporate entities that have an existence independent of their members. If there are goods which are valuable but benefit groups as such rather than individuals, presumably these too would not be individually enjoyable and therefore could not be the object of an individual right. My argument depends not on what kind of entities there are but on how goods are enjoyed. Whether or not all goods are enjoyed by individuals, not all are individually enjoyed.

This shows that it is not the non-excludability criterion, as normally understood, which makes pure public goods unsuitable as the object of individual rights. It is not because everyone is affected that there can be no individual right to them, nor is it simply because widespread co-operation is required to produce the good. There is no individual right to a cultured society not because it is a pure public good, to the extent that it is so, but because it depends on a participatory good. Nevertheless, while not pure public goods, participatory goods do share certain elements of publicity. First, they are publicly produced, that is, their production requires many participants. While not technically a criterion of pure public goods, this is a feature characteristic of many of them. Second, they exhibit non-rivalness of consumption, which is one of the necessary features of public goods. Any one person's enjoyment of culture does not restrict the level of enjoyment of anyone else. This feature, too, is a matter of degree.[20] Some aspects of culture, such as the appreciation of public buildings, are purely non-rival, while others, such as attendance at a popular exhibit, are susceptible of crowding and therefore are non-rival only to a certain extent. Finally, they exhibit a limited degree of non-excludability. To return once more to the example of a cultured society: although it is impossible to exclude any from the most diffuse benefits of culture, it is easy to exclude many from the participatory aspects of culture by restricting access to museums and art galleries and the means of learning to appreciate culture. On the other hand, although some may be excluded from these core benefits, not everyone can be. If the good is to exist at all there must be more than one person sharing its benefits. I cannot provide such goods for myself without necessarily providing them for at least some others because the good itself is partly constituted by our participation in a common activity. How many others must be included in the circle of benefit depends upon the good at issue. In the example of culture, although many can be excluded, a large number of people must also be included for the product to be of any value.

At the other extreme the limiting case of a participatory good might be friendship. If I am to reap the benefits of friendship for myself, I must also provide them for at least one other person, although we can exclude everyone else in the world from our friendship. An example on a scale between culture and friendship is a typical game. I cannot enjoy the benefits of a game of hockey unless at least eleven other people do too. Everyone else in the world can be excluded, but there must be at least a small number of others besides myself who benefit. This is clearly not non-excludability in the pure form, but it is a degree of non-excludability. It also shares a significant feature with Raz's inherent public goods. The non-excludability of a certain number is not simply a matter of technical infeasibility or prohibitive cost. Since participation is constitutive of the good itself, the degree of non-excludability exhibited is among its essential features. The important point is that this degree of non-excludability makes these goods, and any others derivative from them,

20 Laver, supra note 12, 30

inappropriate objects of individual rights. Of course, the fact that its provision cannot exclude everyone does not guarantee that the good will in fact be provided – we can have an uncultured society, and I can decide to have no friends or not to play hockey at all. Similarly, to say that if we have clean air everyone will be able to enjoy its benefits does not guarantee that the good will be produced.

This analysis also more clearly reveals the proper significance of the fact that public goods sometimes require the imposition of onerous duties. It is true that participatory goods are very demanding, but in a way that is slightly different from that envisaged by Raz. It should be clear by now that these participatory goods require a special kind of participation. In order to achieve a cultured society, for example, it is necessary that there be many who take an active and genuine interest in the arts, among other things. Everyone need not participate, but a substantial number must. It is impossible, however, to speak of there being an obligation to take such an interest. While it is true that an obligation does not necessarily require actions that are against one's wishes or interests, that conflict must at least be possible. To say someone has an obligation is to say that even if it is against his interest to do as required, his duty still stands. A right to a cultured society might require that some members take a genuine interest in something in which they have none. In most standard cases satisfaction of a right requires only conformity of behaviour. But here behaviour and attitude cannot be easily separated. It is not enough that people go through the motions of enjoying the artefacts of culture; they must really do so in order to make the required contribution to creating and developing the culture. This combination of behaviour and attitude cannot be the subject of an obligation, not because it would be too harsh on the bearers of the obligation, but because it may be impossible. It may require the compulsion of that which cannot be compelled, namely willing participation. Again, because the diffuse public goods arising out of culture are parasitic on its participatory aspects, this problem tells against the viability of an individual right to the diffuse benefits as well.

Collective rights

We have seen, then, that there are some goods, not necessarily pure public goods, which inherently involve collective activity as part of their value and thus cannot be the object of an individual right. Does it follow, though, as Raz and MacCormick argue, that this is therefore an area of morality beyond the reach of rights? Or could there be 'collective' rights? The idea of a collective *right* is ill-suited to securing participatory goods. To begin with, if the collectivity which claims the right includes all members of a society, there would seem to be no need to make such a claim. Again, a right exists only when an interest is sufficient to justify the imposition of duties on others. If the interest at issue is that of everyone in a good which requires participation to give it value, there will be no division between those who provide the good and those who benefit from it. One cannot benefit unless one participates in its production; one cannot share in the production of the good without benefiting. The interest at stake is that of everyone in this participation. Therefore there will be no one against whom the right needs be claimed; no one upon whom obligations will have to be imposed. The idea of a collective right seems to have no point in such a situation.

This is because the free-rider problem, which does plague the production of many public goods, has no application here. It has sometimes been argued that this phenomenon could be overcome, in the public good context, if a norm existed placing everyone under a duty to co-operate.[21] Commonly, the difficulty arises when the provision of the public good has the structure of a Prisoners' Dilemma (PD) in which each member of society has an incentive to defect from the co-operation required to achieve the good and yet prefers universal co-operation to universal defection. In such situations coercion is required to ensure that each bears his share of the burdens. Clean air, unlittered streets, and national defence provide standard examples of this kind of public good. For instance, each member of society would benefit if the streets are kept clean; but for each it is worst if she refrains from littering while others do not and best if others refrain and she does not. It is therefore in each person's interest, whatever the others do, to litter, and the good will not be provided unless people are compelled to do their share. If a right to such goods existed, this would mean that the interest in this co-operation is important enough to ground an obligation on others.

But the very nature of the PD makes this impossible as an account of how a collective right could arise because it is impossible for the provision of a good which consists in participation in a group activity to be a PD. The PD model requires that the relevant interests that are ranked be individualizable. Only if the good in question is something which could be individually enjoyed could the individual defect –that is, abstain from participating in its production – and still enjoy the benefit. But here we are considering a good whose value to the individual lies partly in participating; if one did not participate the good would be of little value to one. This explains why the production of a cultured society cannot be a PD. Since the core good of a cultural society lies in participating at least in

21 Ullmann-Margalit *The Emergence of Norms* (1977)

the public appreciation and interpretation of culture, the full benefit which we associate with the existence of such a society would not accrue to someone who merely passively 'consumes' works of art. This is not to argue that there are no respects in which the achievement of a cultured society gives rise to PD problems. There are ways of contributing to this achievement which may be necessary, but from which the enjoyment of culture can be divorced. For example, it may be that financial support for the arts is instrumentally necessary in order to have a cultured society. However, the enjoyment of art is not intrinsically connected to the process of financial contribution to it. One can listen to public radio without paying, in the hope that others will contribute enough that one's own free-riding will make no difference. Financial support is merely an instrumentally necessary condition for the existence of culture, not part of the good itself.

This highlights an interesting feature of this kind of good. It avoids the PD problem because it exhibits pure jointness of production,[22] but in an unusual way. It is not simply that many people must co-operate in order to produce the good which only then can be consumed by these same people, but that production and consumption are one process. An attempt to consume is also a contribution to production. This means not that the collective action problem can be solved in these cases, as it can in others, but that it cannot possibly arise because of the nature of these goods. The good itself intrinsically unites consumption and production.

There is one further problem in the production of public goods which might give rise to a claim of right to ensure that the good is provided. It might be argued that it also applies to participatory goods, so as to ground a claim of collective right. This problem arises when, for a significant number of people, there is a divergence between one's interest in the good and one's overall interest. For example, it might be in my interest, in common with everyone else, to breathe clean air, and yet be in my greater interest as an industrialist to reduce my production costs by polluting. Thus my net interest is in pollution. In such a situation, if the public good is to be provided, those whose greater interest lies in not participating must nonetheless be required to do their share. The difference between this case and the PD is that although in both cases the agent recognizes clean air as a good, here she simply prefers that everyone should be permitted to pollute – because of the benefits that will accrue to her from polluting – over what is the first choice in the PD, mutual co-operation in abstaining from polluting. We might call this sort of case one of conflicting goods. This same problem can arise in the context of

22 Laver, supra note 12, 34–5

participatory goods as well, but when it does it raises another sort of doubt about whether a claim of collective right could be justified.

Imagine a society in which most members belong to a particular religious group. Although in some respects their relationship with God may be capable of individual enjoyment, there are also many aspects of their religious practice, including communal worship and celebration of sacred events, which require the joint participation of others to make them valuable. No one person can have the good unless at least some others also enjoy it. Part of the meaning, and therefore part of the value, of these events would be lost if each member of the community celebrated them privately. Now suppose that this community has a weekly day of religious observance which requires abstinence from one's usual regime and participation in a communal service. Suppose, further, that some members of the community have a private interest in not participating in this practice. They may have a greater financial interest in working on that day. If this competing interest affected enough of the members of the community it could begin to threaten the viability of the practice. If the numbers participating in this religious practice dwindles, it may lose its vitality and begin a spiralling descent into oblivion. The question may then arise whether the collectivity has a right that its members who have competing interest in working forgo that private benefit for the sake of the interest of the group.

The possibility of this sort of problem demonstrates another important feature of this kind of good. Although not everyone may be involuntarily excluded from participating in and therefore enjoying the good, individuals may exclude themselves from that enjoyment. Thus it lacks a minor feature commonly associated with public goods, non-optionality.[23] This is present whenever people cannot voluntarily control whether they will consume the good. Because people can opt out of the enjoyment of participatory goods this gives rise to the possibility that too few people will want the good to make its production possible. The assertion of a collective right in such a case is problematic. On the one hand we might conceive of the right-holder as the entire society including those who, as individuals, do not want the good. This right would be held against individual wayward members. However, on this scenario one might well argue that the occurrence of such a crisis within the society, rather than giving rise to a collective right, would constitute the disintegration of the collectivity so that the right could no longer be claimed collectively. If, instead, the collectivity is confined to those who do want the good and they claim the right to force non-members to join them, a different problem

23 Ibid. 30–1

arises. This claim may be conceptually possible, but it is likely to run into grave difficulties at the level of substantive justification, especially given the kind of participation which is required to produce participatory goods. Any such claim of right would constitute a serious infringement on the autonomy of those against whom the right is asserted, and may also run into the problem discussed above of requiring that which cannot be compelled, namely, willing participation. However, it is beyond the scope of this paper to decide whether such a right can ever be successfully defended; our concern is with the structure, not the content, of right-based moral theories. There is one sort of situation, however, in which this problem may be overcome. It may be possible to speak of a collective right of the members of a society against its government.[24] The state, as such, has no right to autonomy. Therefore, no substantive impediment to the recognition of society's right exists here.

Group rights

Thus far we have only indicated that it is difficult to make out a collective claim against individual members of the collectivity. There is, though, another context in which a certain kind of collective claim to a participatory good is more plausible and more likely to arise. I have in mind a claim of right made on behalf of a group which constitutes only part of the society, perhaps even a very small part. Its claim is that the rest of society should somehow accommodate or support some practice of the group even though it conflicts with that of the majority. The claim, then, is not against recalcitrant members of the group but against those who are not members at all. It does not require non-members to participate fully in the group's activity; it merely requires them to make it possible for the members to do so. I propose to distinguish this kind of case from the ones previously discussed, which I labelled 'collective rights,' by calling this a claim of group right.[25]

We can best examine this idea of group rights to participatory goods through an example. One which has attracted a great deal of political and legal attention in Canada recently is the claim of a minority linguistic community to the provision of public services in its language. Such a claim has recently been entrenched in the Canadian Charter of Rights and

24 Raz raises this possibility in a revised version of Right-based moralities, which appears as chapter 8 of his book *The Morality of Freedom* (1986), at 209.

25 Another example Raz offers of what he calls a collective right, that of Palestinian self-determination, fits better under the rubric of group rights. It is a claim by Palestinians as a group against the rest of international society or some portion of it. Ibid. 208.

Freedoms.[26] The Charter includes the right to receive governmental services and publicly provided education in either French or English. Here, I will concentrate on the right to a bilingual educational system which provides education in French for Francophone children and in English for Anglophone children. Such a system, like a cultured society, is a very complex cluster of goods. At the core it is a participatory good, but it also has many public aspects. Like the public goods which surround the core good of a cultured society, the public aspects of a bilingual education system are parasitic upon the provision of a core participatory good. Since there can be no individual right to the central participatory good, none of the surrounding goods can be the object of an individual right either. Therefore if there are any rights to this cluster of goods they must be held by a group.

There are many benefits which can arise out of a bilingual education system, from very general ones to very specific. These benefits also exhibit varying degrees of publicity. It is commonly recognized that whether a benefit is a public good is a matter of degree.[27] Although economists usually choose examples of pure public goods in order to examine various public choice problems, they also recognize that life is seldom this clear-cut. Not all public goods are pure ones. At the level of the most diffuse benefits, a bilingual education system is a pure public good in the same way that a cultured society is one: it increases the range of cultural experience generally available through the participation of its graduates in society. Perhaps it also even contributes towards a higher general level of tolerance for ethnic diversity. These are non-excludable benefits for everyone, whether or not one actually uses these schools.

But there are also benefits arising out of the provision of a bilingual education system that apply only to a narrower group. The existence of a French school system in a predominantly English province is a good for the entire French community in a way that it is not for everyone else. For example, the school system strengthens the language community by ensuring that the language is passed on to each new generation and contributes to the community's sense of identity. These things are good for this community, even those members who do not benefit directly by having children in the school system. But they are goods restricted to this community. They need not benefit the rest of society; they may even impose costs on everyone else. It is possible to exclude some from membership in a language community, and therefore from these benefits

26 Part I, Constitution Act, 1982, schedule B, Canada Act, 1982, c. 11 (U.K.), s. 23

27 See, e.g., Buchanan, supra note 11, 3, where he speaks of a 'conceptual public-private spectrum.'

of an education system in that language. Therefore, from the point of view of Canadian society at large these aspects of a bilingual education system cannot be considered public goods. However, in a more limited sense they are public goods. This brings out another aspect of the definition of publicity usually taken for granted in the standard economist's examples.

The designation of a good as public requires a prior delineation of the body or group for whom it is public.[28] Clean air, for example, is a public good for everyone on earth because it surrounds the entire planet and therefore affects everyone. Other goods, however, such as an unpolluted lake, are good only for a more limited number. All Canadians and Americans benefit in non-excludable ways from a healthy Great Lakes system, but everyone else in the world can be excluded from those benefits.[29] Furthermore, some public goods apply to groups which are conventionally rather than naturally defined. National defence is a public good for all Canadians, but we can and do exclude anyone not resident in the region politically defined as 'Canada.' Who is to be included in the group is defined by social rules, not natural facts. Just as national defence can usefully be considered a public good in a given state, despite the fact that it excludes most of the inhabitants of the world, so too there is an important degree of publicity in some goods within a national society from which some of its members are excluded. Such goods are public only for those who are members of an independently defined group. These might be called 'partial public goods,' and the more standard examples that apply to all members of a given society might be renamed 'universal public goods.' On this taxonomy the more general, diffuse benefits of a bilingual education system that I examined first are universal public goods, while the ones which apply only to a specific language community are partial ones. The admission of this distinction greatly expands the range of goods which can be treated as public, but this can be useful provided we are clear about the boundary between those for whom the good is public and those for whom it is not.

Partial public goods might be defined by reference to natural facts or positive rules. An example involving a naturally defined group (and which is also not a participatory public good) might be the control of a contagious disease to which only one segment of the population has a

28 Buchanan, ibid. 1, explicitly recognizes this in elaborating a theory 'that will include as a variable to be determined the extension of ownership-consumption rights over differing numbers of persons.'

29 Peston, supra note 12, 17, raises the example of the good of watching colour television, before it became common to own one's own, in a public house. Since some can be excluded from the bar, the good is public only for those inside.

genetic susceptibility. For those who are not susceptible, there is no benefit from the provision of this good, but providing it for some of those who are – through vaccination, for example – will provide it for all those susceptible by lessening the likelihood of each falling victim to the disease. An example of a rule-defined group would be a private club. For all those who are members, the club's facilities are a public good, though they are not public for all those who do not meet the membership criteria.[30] Cases involving rule-defined groups may present the further issue of the justifiability of the criteria for inclusion in the group. For any given good it might be argued that the group should be expanded or contracted. This normative question may be very important, but it does not change the public nature of the good. To treat something as a public good presupposes some previously defined group for whom it is a good; but it is an independent moral question whether that definition is justified. This can be illustrated by another aspect of the good of a bilingual education system.

A more specific good included in a bilingual education system is access to and ability to use the school facilities in which French is the language of instruction. It should be obvious in the light of the previous discussion that this can only be a partial public good. It is designed for the use of only a section of the society – in fact only a section of the Francophone community, that is, those of school age. In the Canadian context, the definition of those who are to be provided with this good is specified in section 23 of the Charter. This group excludes many who might well, in fact, benefit from minority language education. It is not the case that any Canadian can send his child to the linguistic school of his choice. Parents whose mother tongue is other than English or French must send their children to whatever is the majority language school system in the province. Even amongst French and English speakers the Charter draws distinctions. Someone from France moving to Canada has no right to send her children to a French school in Ontario, nor is a Briton guaranteed a place for his children in an English school in Quebec. The criteria for access to the good are designed roughly to protect the indigenous minority language group within each province. However, within each of these groups no one may be excluded from the benefit of an education for their children in their mother tongue. Because the criteria which define the groups here are not natural, but positive legal rules, they are of course subject to moral scrutiny. It can be and has been argued that all speakers of English should be guaranteed access to English schools and all Francophones to French schools. I do not propose to join this debate here.

30 I am indebted to Wayne Sumner for this example.

The important point is that once we know the boundaries of the group, we know for whom the good is public, and this group may not include the entire society.

Rules or norms may also have an even more significant role in an analysis of public goods. They may not only define the group for whom a good is public; they may also turn a private good into a public one. This possibilty relies upon a refinement of the distinction, already recognized in the literature,[31] between inherent and contingent public goods and extends the idea that a good can be characterized as public only against a backdrop of rights and duties. An inherent public good is one from which it is logically impossible to exclude anyone. The diffuse benefits arising from an open and tolerant society provide an example. A contingent public good is one from which it is logically possible to exclude some, but because of additional, contingent constraints this is not a practical possibility. The examples of contingent public goods usually offered involve some sort of technical or economic constraint – for example, the city water supply system from which everyone benefits only because engineers have not yet invented a way to control the water supply to each individual house, or because any such method is too expensive.

Public goods which are created by rules are contingently public in a different way. If the rule did not exist the good would not be public because the physical or technological means to exclude people exist. However, the rule creates a normative barrier to using them.[32] An example will help to clarify. A rule which says that wage rates must be uniform for each job category within a company turns the negotiating abilities of each of the workers into a public good.[33] This is not naturally public, because in the absence of the rule each employee would theoretically be able to negotiate a pay raise for herself alone. The existence of the rule, however, means that if any worker does negotiate a raise, all the other employees will benefit as well. In requiring that everyone must receive the same wage, the rule constitutes a normative bar on excluding anyone from any pay increase. It does so because implicit in

31 See Green, *The Authority of the State* (forthcoming) and Raz, supra note 1.

32 That rules can create public goods is commonly recognized in the context of the basic rules of a legal system such as the rules of contract which make an enforceable system of agreements a public good. See, e.g., Buchanan, Public goods and natural liberty, in Wilson and Skinner (eds) *The Market and the State: Essays in Honour of Adam Smith* (1976) 271–86. The analysis here extends this idea to cover rules which extend to only a segment of a political society and, for this reason, are partial rather than universal public goods.

33 This is a variation on an example used by Barry and Hardin, supra note 11, 33: '[I]f the law says that wage rates in a factory must be uniform for each job category, non-union workers cannot easily be excluded from enjoying the benefits of union negotiated wage increases.'

any rule is the requirement of formal equality – of treating like cases alike. It is not logically or physically impossible to exclude a particular employee from the pay raise: it is not even technologically or economically infeasible to do so. Because of the rule it is normatively impossible. With this rule in place, adding to the background framework of rights and duties, a new public good is created.

Similarly, the good of being able to attend a minority language school is made public by the existence of section 23 of the Charter. It is easy to see that it is not an inherent public good. It is possible to prevent access for some members of the rule-defined group by differentially charging or by physically preventing them from entering school property. But if we assume, for the sake of argument, that the definition of the group in this case is justified, it would be legally and morally wrong to refuse access to anyone who falls within that description. Once the group is defined, to allow access to some and exclude others would be to violate the moral injunction to treat likes alike. This injunction also has legal force, since any public official who discriminated in this fashion would be found to be acting ultra vires. This principle has now been constitutionalized in section 15 of the Charter, but in the simple form I am using here it has always had legal force.[34] Because section 23 is counted as part of the framework of rights, these school facilities become partial public goods.

At this stage someone might argue that the right to be treated with formal equality is usually regarded as an individual right. And, since this is what makes the good of access to school facilities public, the right to these must itself be individually held.[35] On the contrary, formal equality has no content upon which to base a judgment as to whether or not an individual can claim a right to it. It depends for its substance on some independent norm which determines the criteria for likeness and the good thereby guaranteed. We cannot know what formal equality provides a right to without this other norm. If there is a norm guaranteeing the provision of school facilities, formal equality provides that no one who falls within the qualification criteria may be excluded from the benefits of that good. Of course, if that rule is violated, it will be the individual who has been denied access who will bring a legal claim. But this is not enough to establish that the right is an individual one. Whether the formal right to equal access to the school facilities is an individual or a group right

34 Section 15 guarantees 'equality before and under the law,' among other things. Many people think that these equality provisions can be used much more ambitiously to pursue substantive equality. I do not dispute these uses. My argument is the modest one that whatever else these provisions may be interpreted to mean, they at least guarantee formal equality.

35 I am grateful to Wayne Sumner for raising this point.

depends upon the nature of the substantive good thereby guaranteed. If access to the physical facilities of the school were considered on its own, this could be the object of an individual right because under some description this good could be individually enjoyed. However, I hope to show that this good is meaningless unless tied to the core good of a bilingual education system which cannot be so enjoyed. This changes the complexion of the good of access to school facilities and therefore of its equal provision.

The final and most important aspect of the good of a bilingual education system is what actually takes place through the process of minority language education itself. This core good is participatory. It involves an activity which, at least in part, requires a group both for its provision and for its enjoyment. Although there are aspects of education which can be individually enjoyed, the main objective of providing education in a particular language, especially a minority language, has little to do with these. All educational systems aim to teach children certain basic skills and knowledge (such as reading, writing, and arithmetic) which are of value to the students as individuals. A minority language educational system shares these objectives. But in addition it aims to provide an important source of support for the linguistic community by giving members the opportunity to develop their capacity for communication in that language with other members of that community. From this perspective, there would be little point in going to school in one's mother tongue by oneself, or in providing minority language children with interpreters or translation devices in a majority language school. Part of the process of growing up within a particular linguistic community involves receiving one's education and initiation into its culture in that language. And one ultimate objective is to prepare these children to be able to participate fully in a particular language community and thereby contribute to its growth and development. The school system is a part of the group's social life. The good it provides can be enjoyed only as a member of the group, through the participation of many others. In so far as it is participatory, this core aspect of the good of a bilingual education system loses part of its publicity. It is possible for some of those whose participation is necessary to refuse to participate with selected others. However, as noted above, if the good is to be provided at all it must be provided for more than one person. Further, if such an educational system is to be successful it must be provided for a significant group of children.

The participatory nature of the core good of a bilingual education system must colour our understanding of the other aspects of the good previously discussed. Access to the physical facilities, the furtherance of the larger group's linguistic identity, and greater cultural diversity depend for their existence on the health of an activity which inherently requires participation. Therefore the key question must be whether a right to this core good is tenable. Without entering into the substantive justifications for any such rights, I have argued that an individual cannot claim a right to a participatory good. For these reasons there can be no individual rights to any of the package of goods which make up a comprehensive education system in a minority language. Since the core good is good only for a group, any right to a bilingual education system can be held, if at all, only by a minority language group. Further, if we assume that the two minority language communities in question have sufficient vitality that there are enough children to justify providing schools and enough teachers to staff them, there is no need for duties to be imposed upon some members of the group itself. Rather, because the claim is to publicly funded education in these two languages, it is a claim against the linguistic majority to make this participatory activity possible. Again, this does not mean that the majority must participate, but it may require that it support the activity through taxes.

If, then, there are any non-individual rights, they are likely to be group rights rather than collective ones. In such cases the right cannot be an individual one because it is a claim to a participatory good, and it is a group right because it is a claim to a public good which applies only to a segment of society and must be claimed as against the rest. It might now be argued that to call such a right a group right is misleading because such rights can be subsumed under the ordinary concept of individual rights.[36] In setting up an opposition between a minority language group and the rest of society, one is merely treating the linguistic minority as an individual in the same way that a corporation is treated as an artificial person. There is a sense in which this is true. However, there is also good reason for separating such rights from the usual sorts of individual rights. Although the group can be treated as an individual, it cannot be treated as an individual human being would be. The interests of the group, because they are interests in the maintenance and development of a participatory good, cannot be reduced to a set of individualized interests. The group's interest in the existence of a thriving educational system in its language is not the same as that of an individual person in being taught in that language. The substance of the right, the obligations which it will require of others, will be different than they would be in the context of a right held

36 Jeremy Waldron's discussion, in an unpublished paper entitled Rights, public choice and communal goods, has helped clarify my thinking on this issue. See also Wellman, supra note 3, 193–4.

by an individual person. For example, its own school system may be important to the continued existence of the community as a community. This requires that the system provide a comprehensive educational experience in the group's language, and perhaps that the community itself have a measure of control over curriculum. By comparison, an individual may be able to claim that it would further his career prospects to be able to speak this language, but this may not require either the comprehensiveness or the control that satisfaction of the group's right would require. These kinds of differences seem important enough to justify distinguishing this kind of right by labelling it a group right.

This account of the group quality of these rights differs significantly from that of Raz. Whereas my account of why there can be no individual right to such a good complements rather than competes with his, our respective approaches towards group rights are not similarly compatible. Raz does not explicitly distinguish between group and collective rights. Instead, he applies the same analysis to both, asking whether the claimant's interest is likely to be strong enough to justify the imposition of obligations on others. He therefore argues that if there is any sort of collective right to any inherently public good it is because the combined interest of all of the members of the collectivity is powerful enough to justify the imposition of duties although the interest of a single individual would not be.[37] Although the interest of a single Francophone, for example, is not sufficient to warrant the imposition on others of the duty to provide French education, the cumulative interest of a number of Francophones may be. Raz then rather mysteriously claims that 'though the existence of the right does not depend on the size of the group its weight or strength does.'[38] Now, it is easy to see how the strength of the right would vary with numbers if its strength depends on aggregating the interests of all who are members of the group. But for the same reason the existence of the right should also depend on numbers, on Raz's analysis. If the obligations required in order to secure the good are very onerous, it is conceivable that a group consisting of a small number of members could not claim a sufficiently weighty interest to have a right to that good. If, however, the group were to expand its membership, the interests of the extra members could just push the group's cumulative interest over the necessary threshold. This analysis makes the group's 'right' sound more like an aggregative consideration than a distributive one.

Although I agree that numbers count in the establishment of a right, I think that they count for different reasons. Furthermore, I dispute Raz's

37 Raz, supra note 1, 193–4
38 Ibid. 194, footnote 13

interpretation of the significance of numbers to the strength of the right. I would argue that numbers count in the first instance because we are concerned with the provision of goods which inherently require participation amongst members of the group both for the provision of the good and for its enjoyment. The sorts of goods which fit this description tend to be things like the communal practice of a religion or a language which are complex group practices requiring a certain number of members in order to be viable at all. This is most obvious in the case of a language. Linguistic demographers have long realized that the survival of a language requires a certain critical mass of speakers. It seems likely that the same is true of religious, cultural, and ethnic groups. Under these circumstances there can be a group right only if there is a group – that is, enough participants to make the group practice a viable one.[39] This constitutes an important difference between group and individual rights – the latter are often thought to be so valuable precisely because the number of those who share one's interest is irrevelant to whether it ought to be protected. However, although numbers are important to group rights in this respect, I would argue, against Raz, that they have no further relevance. If the group meets the viability test, numbers are irrelevant in establishing the weight of its right. They go towards the existence condition for a group (as right-holder), but not to the weight of its interest. As long as the group is viable it does not matter whether it has one hundred or one million members. Rather, the strength of its claim depends on how important the continued existence of the group is to its members. This does not vary with the number of participants.

Conclusion

Despite this disagreement, my argument ultimately supports one of Raz's most important claims – that any right-based moral theory which focuses exclusively on the claims of individual human beings must be inadequate as a moral theory.[40] Raz arrives at this conclusion by arguing that individuals cannot have rights to what he calls 'collective goods' such as a cultured society, but that nevertheless such goods are inherently valuable, and that a theory which cannot account for an important form of intrinsic good must be incomplete. My argument extends this criticism in two ways. Firstly, the concepts of partial public goods and rule-defined public goods expand considerably the scope of goods which may be subject to Raz's

39 A similar argument is made by Michael McDonald, Collective rights and tyranny (1986) 56 *Rev. de U. d'Ottawa* 115, at 121–2.
40 Ibid.

substantive argument. Secondly, it points out that the feature of Raz's collective goods which makes them unsuitable to a claim of individual right is instantiated in certain group activities, such as the maintenance of a linguistic or religious community. If such activities are intrinsically good, and I think they are, they constitute another phenomenon of which a complete moral theory must be able to take account.

I have argued that a right-based theory can only do this if it takes seriously the idea of group rights rather than confining the status of right-holder to individual persons. The tendency of Raz's argument is to try to steer us away from right-based theories altogether on the assumption that, although perhaps not intrinsically individualistic, they have an unwelcome tendency towards individualism. My conclusion is more modest. I do not seek to attack right-based theories per se, but only those which hold that only individual persons can have rights. If the areas of life covered by group activities of the sort discussed above are added to the terrain of rights theory it will be able to encompass an important and substantially wider range of moral phenomena. Right-based theories may still be incomplete,[41] on other grounds, but they may nevertheless help us to understand more of the moral issues we face than could a highly individualistic theory.

My aim has been to illustrate that there are certain goods – participatory goods – to which a claim of individual right is untenable because they are not individualizable. I have also argued that a subset of these goods – those which involve a claim by one group within society against the rest – can give rise to a claim of a group right. This argument does not finally settle the issue of whether there are, in fact, any group rights – that is, whether any such claims are valid – although I have suggested that minority language rights are plausible candidates. It examines only the nature of certain goods and argues that a right to them can be held only by a group, if at all. A complete account of group rights would require the consideration of issues such as the moral status of groups – are there other necessary conditions for them to be right-holders? – as well as substantive issues about the nature and value of particular group activities. But it is important that this further debate be conducted in the appropriate context, and that requires both attention to the complexity of the sort of goods which may be involved and the avoidance of a blanket categorization of right-based theories as inherently individualistic.

41 Supra note 24, 207–9.

OBLIGATION AND MORAL AGENCY

LUCIUS GARVIN

AN EXAMINATION of the philosophical literature of the last ten to fifteen years seems to reveal that in ethical discussions of determinism and indeterminism, the determinists have had the larger part, if not the better, of the argument. Defenders of libertarianism have been relatively scattered and relatively unaggressive, whereas exponents of the determinist doctrine of moral freedom have been numerous and, on the whole, bold and confident in their representations.

If there is reason to regard this situation as marking an even temporary retreat on the part of the libertarians before a militant wave of very "determined" determinists, it may be timely to assess the nature of the ethical position adopted by the latter group. To what extent, for example, does the relinquishing of the libertarian standpoint entail also a relinquishing of those fundamental moral concepts traditionally bound up with the question of freedom?

It is certainly the claim of most of the determinists that, whereas no defensible, or even intelligible, doctrine of moral freedom and responsibility can be based on indeterminist or libertarian conceptions, determinism is consistent with and essential to a view of moral agency and accountability that is adequate to the strictest requirements and presuppositions of moral discourse. And most of the determinists have been at considerable pains to exhibit how, from their viewpoint, it is possible to preserve the significance of such notions as guilt, desert, blameworthiness, responsibility, and freedom.

There is, however, one idea, ordinarily accorded a fundamental place in ethical discussions, which determinists have in most cases avoided: whether as offering special difficulties or as being something deliberately to be exorcised. This is the idea of "oughtness" or moral obligation.

It may, of course, be said that the concepts of guilt, remorse, and responsibility, which the determinists are fully prepared to expound, entail the concept of obligation; and doubtless many determinists would like to absorb the notion of obligation within the framework provided by their special definitions of freedom and responsibility. But it may well be argued that this cannot be done without sacrificing some of the significance inseparably connected with the idea of obligation. A brief examination of the determinists' position will indicate how this difficulty may be supposed to arise.

Freedom has usually been described by the determinists as belonging to any agent with respect to any act whose performance (or nonperformance) depends on his choice—so that, other factors providing the necessary conditions, his choice constitutes the sufficient condition for the performance of the act. The agent is regarded as responsible for the act in the sense that he produces it through his choosing—a choosing that flows out of his nature or character. The qualities of praiseworthiness and blameworthiness are then interpreted, not as characters belonging to the acts in virtue of their own value or disvalue, but as predicates to be applied to those acts which it is expedient or justifiable to praise or blame. A person, that is to say, is described as deserving blame to the extent that, on the usual teleological or utilitarian premises, blaming him will be productive of better consequences than the withholding of blame.

Because many determinists have been ethical teleologists, they have usually maintained, along with this doctrine of deserts, the view that actions are right or wrong in terms of the comparative value of their consequences. The difficulty of this position, however, has been that the obligation which is supposed to lie on moral agents to do the right and not the wrong has not seemed clearly consistent with the determinist view of moral agency. For that view allows only for what Broad calls "conditional substitutability."[1] It does not permit us to say categorically that an agent might have substituted another act for the one he performed but only that he could have done so if he had chosen; and, in turn, it does not permit us to say categorically that he might have chosen differently than he in fact did but only that he could have chosen differently if he had been motivated differently, and so on. But obligation, in its full moral sense, is categorical, Broad says, and hence requires a categorical, and not merely a conditional, substitutability such as determinism provides.

In order, perhaps, to avoid such strictures as Broad has set up, some recent exponents of determinism have sought to modify the usual teleological conception of the nature of moral judgments, by interpreting them according to the categories of praise and blame referred to above; so that such a judgment as "You ought not to do so-and-so" is to be regarded as correct, not in terms of the value or disvalue of the consequences of the act judged, but in terms of the efficacy of the judgment itself in controlling future conduct. Accountable acts are, on this view, distinguished from the non-moral acts of physical forces, not in virtue of their being (in contradistinction to the latter) undetermined, but in virtue of their being the sort of entities to which praise or blame, punishment or reward, may relevantly be applied. Such relevance arises only where moral criticism can, by controlling future choices, control thereby future actions. So that moral responsibility, like punishment and reward, is to be judged teleologically in terms of the effects of the judgment of responsibility and not in terms of an examination of the act or agent judged responsible.

What we are being offered, perhaps, is a schematism for a new kind of teleological ethics—an ultra-teleological ethics, as it were.[2]

But this analysis, valid and useful as it may be in its application to the general doctrine of responsibility, will still be criticized as missing the idea of the obligatoriness of acts on actors, usually carried by the phrase, "You ought." It is this failure to provide for what he calls "categorical obligability" that leads

[1] C. D. Broad, *Determinism, Indeterminism, and Libertarianism* (London: Cambridge University Press, 1934).

[2] I pass over, here, the question which will naturally occur—whether the judgment of the desirability of reward or punishment does not either presuppose a straightforward teleological criterion as determining the value of that judgment (in which case it may appear an inconsistency to withhold such a criterion in the case of the act judged) or require itself to be judged by a kind of "meta-judgment" as to the value of praising or blaming it (which meta-judgment, in turn, will require to be judged . . . . etc., *ad infinitum*). I should add that I do not know that any of the proponents of the view under consideration have actually stated their position in exactly the foregoing manner. But this formulation of the view may be said to be implicit, at least, in what many spokesmen for this interpretation of moral judgments have had to say.

Broad to conclude that either the doctrine of determinism or that of the "categorical ought" must be surrendered. And, since Broad is equally unable to accept the libertarian explanation of moral agency as a basis for obligation, he feels compelled to regard the notion of categorical obligation as probably a delusive one.

Now it is the thesis of this paper that Broad is demanding too much and that the advocates of what we have called the ultra-teleological view are requiring too little in their treatment of the idea of categorical obligability. We shall argue that there is, within the conceptual framework of teleological ethics, a meaning of obligation, which, though it is in a good sense categorical, does not require more than a conditional substitutability and which is at the same time predictable of moral agents directly rather than in the devious fashion required by the "ultra-teleologists." The meaning in question is the same idea of oughtness which G. E. Moore appears to have had in mind[3] when he spoke of our obligation to do the right act, where the latter is defined teleologically, as the act which, of all those open to the agent, will produce the best actual consequences. Most of the expositors of teleological ethics since Moore's discussion of the topic (including Russell, Broad, and Laird) have agreed in rejecting as untenable this notion of right, as well as the notion of "ought" connected with it. Others have accepted Moore's definition of rightness but have insisted that obligation or oughtness must be conceived in relation, not to actual, but to probable consequences, or perhaps not in relation to consequences at all, but only to the agent's intentions.

It is our suggestion that Moore's proposal about oughtness and rightness has been too easily dismissed and that those who have rejected it have usually been prompted by deontological considerations inadmissible within a strictly teleological system. We shall restate this sense of moral obligation in our own terms and then proceed to its explication and defense in relation to the problem of human choice and moral agency.

Moral obligation is present in any situation involving (*a*) an act which, under the circumstances, is the best act open to an agent (or, better, an act whose consequences are not intrinsically less valuable than the consequences of any of its alternatives) and (*b*) an agent who is bound, by reason of the value of the act, to its performance.

Notice that obligation is never with respect to an act taken as an isolated event but is always also with respect to a specific agent and, of course, a specific situation. One might describe oughtness very generally as occurring whenever there is value realizable because an agent is able to accomplish that realization. The value itself is the ground—the only "moral" ground—of the agent's obligation to act with reference to that value.

For this reason, oughtness as here conceived is categorical and not hypothetical. Whether it is categorical in Broad's sense of that term will be considered below, but there are, at any rate, certain senses in which oughtness has been held to be hypothetical, which are here rejected.

It is clear, for example, that oughtness, as just described, is not hypothetical in the sense proposed by Stace,[4] who, looking for an "empirical" interpretation of

[3] *Ethics* (New York: Henry Holt & Co., 1912), chap. v.

[4] W. T. Stace, *The Concept of Morals* (New York: Macmillan Co., 1937), pp. 254 ff.

obligation, suggests that when we say that we ought to do so-and-so, we mean that, if we want (as he believes everyone does want) to be happy, then we ought to do so-and-so. That is, general duties are universalized by being placed under a condition which, Stace feels, is a universal human demand, the desire for happiness; and the construction put on "ought" is that it is logical, rather than, in a strict sense, moral. The conception of "ought" we are proposing, on the other hand, is "moral" in the sense that the source of the obligation is found in value rather than in an allegedly universal human desire. Obligation, that is, is made categorical in our meaning, in virtue of the fact that its ground is placed in the value pole of the relation rather than in the agent pole. To be sure, obligation exists only if there is value capable of being realized, but the existence of obligation is not contingent upon the agent's desiring certain things, or upon his being, perhaps, any particular kind of agent at all, except a possible agent. Kant, for example, wishing to avoid the kind of hypothetical "ought" that Stace has defended, elected to put duty out of relation to the agent's desires but nevertheless put it in relation to something else, namely, the agent's rational nature. By so doing he sacrificed the very thing he hoped to save—the categorical "ought." For he placed oughtness under a condition: the condition that only in so far as an agent acts in accord with his reason—and a "reason" rather specially conceived, at that—can he be said to do what he ought to do.

Here the objection may be forthcoming that Kant, in restricting obligation to rational agents, was, however much more he may have wished to assert, at any rate conforming to a generally accepted principle of ethics—a principle that might be supposed to be implicit also in the description of obligation we are opposing to his. For, it may be held, our description of obligation, in limiting obligation to those acts the agent is capable of performing, involves that "ought implies can" and hence entails reflective moral competence on the part of the agent, since only agents who are rationally capable of deliberating over alternatives and discerning and discriminating among values are properly moral agents at all.

It must, of course, be granted that the term "moral agent" is commonly used to mean an agent capable of, if not actually engaged in, moral reflection. But it is our contention that it is not of the essence of obligation that it should be restricted in its application exclusively to agents that are moral in this sense. Rather, the obligation to perform certain acts falls upon agents capable of performing those acts, whether or not these agents are in a position to apprehend the value of the acts or are morally concerned to perform them. And if the question should be raised how agents, thus unconscious of or thus undisturbed about the values of acts they have it in their power to perform, differ, after all, with respect to moral obligation, from natural objects such as trees or mountains, our reply should be that, were there any good sense in which trees or mountains could be said to be capable of right acts (as above defined), then there would be nothing about the idea of obligation to preclude its applying to them. For the crux of our position is that even when potential actors are unaware of the moral significance of the actions open to them, obligation is already present, lurking, if you like, behind the scenes of consciousness; it is there to be significant for anyone capable of discovering it; its *esse* is not *percipi*. Duty, that is, may exist where the sense of duty does not.

Once the import of our position is seen, the irrelevant and delusive character of the objection most commonly raised against it will be apparent. That objection is to the effect that it is unconscionable and repugnant to suppose that anyone should be obliged to do something whose value he did not—and perhaps could not—appraise; that, while in legal affairs ignorance may be no excuse, in moral matters there can be no real obligation on the ignorant—any more than on a stone. Such an objection, however, involves the importation into our description of obligation of meanings that are actually quite foreign to it. Among the meanings invoked, probably, are the ideas of what we should expect of an agent in such circumstances, of what we should give such an agent in the way of advice, of what we should praise or blame him for. But these considerations do not, from a strict teleological standpoint, form any part of the principle of obligation, so that to introduce them into that principle is to be guilty of a defection from the teleological position and very likely of an implicit appeal to deontological conceptions.

This is not always apparent and would probably be denied by such writers as, for example, Laird, who doubtless supposed himself to be formulating a teleological definition when he said that what *ought* to be done is that act which is "*probably* productive of the maximum good that can be effected volitionally by any agent capable of responding to the good that he sees."[5]

Yet is it not clear that the modification of the definition of oughtness which substitutes probable results for actual ones and which introduces the requirement of moral sensitiveness on the part of the agent can have no justification unless there be something intrinsically valuable about moral sensitiveness or the possession of the sense of duty as such? If these have no value except as instruments in promoting the good, then it is difficult to see why any teleologist should be tempted to regard as obligatory an act which, though performed with all moral earnestness and after a precise appraisal of the available evidence, produced something less than the best possible results.[6] All the qualifications that one might wish to make concerning the agent's intentions and limitations can be stated in terms of our strict interpretation of oughtness (including the exposition of the paradox that the agent would, in the circumstances, have done better if he had violated his moral desires and chosen to do that act which, though he regarded it as wrong, was actually right). For, apart from deontological considerations, there is nothing to justify the claim that agents "ought" to do what, according to their best lights, they believe they ought to do, except the probable truth of the empirical generalization that the best results are likely to be achieved when rational beings conduct themselves under conscious moral controls. Or, to put the point in another way, one might state the obligation to be morally good (i.e., to act according to one's best moral and rational judgment) in the hypothetical proposition, "If one wishes to pursue that course of action which will, under ordinary circumstances, most probably be that which he ought to pursue, then he ought to be morally good." It is clear that the "ought" which occurs in the

[5] *International Journal of Ethics*, XXXVII (July, 1927), 339. (My italics.)

[6] Where, of course, such results included those that were consequent upon the presence of the moral concern that prompted the act.

consequent of this proposition is a logical, and not a moral, "ought."

In any event, it remains possible that there may be occasions when what are ordinarily our best weapons—reason and conscience—will play us false. When they do, it will be true that we ought not to have used them, though it will often also be true, by the same (teleological) token, that we ought not to be criticized or dispraised for using them.

Our position is strengthened if we note the tendency on the part of many moralists (not a few of whom are of the teleological persuasion) to qualify even further the description of obligable acts. Unable, apparently, to swallow even that definition of oughtness which is formulated in terms of the probably best consequences (since, as they point out, few agents can be expected to arrive at a rigorously exact interpretation of evidence), some moralists would define oughtness in terms of those consequences supposed, even if incorrectly calculated, by the agent to be probable. Others, noting that the human mind can err not only in its estimation of what an act's consequences will be, but also about the value of those consequences, have introduced still further complexities into the analysis of oughtness—so that we find Broad, for example, discussing the question whether our judgment should be in terms of the actual value of the probable consequences or the probable value of the actual consequences or the probable value of the probable consequences.[7] Ostensibly, the fundamental consideration underlying these speculations is simply the agent's ability to perform an act. Actually, it is the agent's ability to perform the act, if he is to do so with moral insight and integrity. For it is only the desire to invest the agent with such insight and integrity that can make it appear necessary to consider at all these modifications of the strict teleological position. It is, perhaps, what seems to be the absurdly arbitrary nature of these intermediate positions that has led so many writers to embrace the frankly deontological conclusion that all an agent can ever be under obligation to do is to act from a sense of duty.

It will be clear that the progressive narrowing down of the kinds of acts that "moral" agents are supposed to be capable of performing is not only a process by which obligation comes to be defined less and less in terms of the intrinsic value of consequences and more and more in terms of the intrinsic value of moral devotion, but that it is also a process of decreasing the area within which obligability may be considered to exist. And the ultimate terminus of the reasoning which throws further and further limitations on the number and kind of obligable actions may naturally be held to be the complete abolishment of such actions altogether. Such, no doubt, is the annihilation of moral choice that, according to the libertarians, is the accomplishment of determinism.

It is, of course, possible to interpret the attempt to qualify with increasing rigidity the area of responsible moral choice as an effort to avoid the deterministic "compulsions" of a view of obligation that might seem to leave us at the mercy of uncontrollable circumstances. On such an interpretation, it may appear natural to place the kernel of obligation in the simple act of choosing to obey one's sense of duty.

In any case, it is plain that, on the view of obligation defended in this paper obligability does not, to be categorical,' entail the categorical substitutability of

[7] *International Journal of Ethics*, XXIV (April, 1914), 303–6.

acts. On the contrary, the hypothetical substitutability of determinism is all we require in order that we may be able to say that agents who can choose and act rightly ought to do so. Such hypothetical substitutability is also all we require when we say of an agent who has chosen and acted wrongly that he ought to have done otherwise.

On the other hand, such a statement would not be, as the "ultra-teleologists" would have it, simply a means of controlling future conduct or an elliptical way of commenting on the desirability of punishing acts of that sort. For it would be a straightforward statement that the agent had performed an act which was less good than some other act he would have performed if he had chosen or desired or felt differently than he did; that he had therefore failed to do the best possible act; and that it was that act which he ought to have done.

Oberlin College

RESPONSIBILITY, UNDERSTANDING, AND PSYCHOPATHOLOGY*

I

Philosophical discussions of the conditions of moral agency typically are confined to various aspects of the age-old free will-determinism controversy. Important as the issues raised in the controversy are, they will not be my concern. Instead, I will try to show that, quite apart from whether moral agents must have "free will," they must meet two other conditions. First, moral agents must have a minimal understanding of the moral concepts applicable to them. I will refer to this as "moral understanding." Second, they must have some tendency to experience moral sentiments. Examples of moral sentiments are feelings of guilt, remorse, shame, and resentment, as well as genuine concern to treat others with fellow-feeling and due regard for their interests and well-being.[1] I will try to show that these two conditions are not independent of one another, in that the first condition cannot be satisfied unless the second is as well.

This emphasis on moral understanding and moral sentiments is not common in discussions of moral agency and responsibility. This may be because philosophers tend to concentrate on adults who, it is assumed, do have the requisite understanding and concern. But if we turn to the moral responsibility of children, questions about understanding and concern must be faced. We are concerned with the transition of children from nonresponsibility to responsibility, and it is very important that they be provided with an environment that encourages them to understand and care about moral

* I wish to express gratitude to Western Michigan University for a research fellowship supporting the completion of this paper.

1. Following John Rawls, I use the expression "moral sentiments" to refer to fundamental moral attitudes and feelings such as these. For a fuller discussion see: John Rawls, "The Sense of Justice," *Philosophical Review*, 72, No. 3 (July 1963); and, more recently, John Rawls, *A Theory of Justice* (Cambridge: Harvard Univ. Press, 1971).

matters. This at least poses practical problems. Does it pose any philosophical ones?

One might think not. After all, we know what counts as understanding moral concepts and what it is genuinely to care about moral matters—and that understanding them is one thing, caring about them another. And we know what relevance each has to the question of whether someone is morally responsible for what he or she does. Or do we? Consider the following:

> The psychopath is asocial. His conduct often brings him into conflict with society. . . . The psychopath is highly impulsive. He is a man for whom the moment is a segment of time detached from all others. . . . He can commit the most appalling acts, yet view them without remorse. The psychopath has a warped capacity for love. His emotional relationships, when they exist, are meager, fleeting, and designed to satisfy his own desires. These last two traits, guiltlessness and lovelessness, conspicuously mark the psychopath as different from other men.[2]

What are we to say of such persons, seemingly devoid of moral sentiments? Are they moral agents, albeit irresponsible ones? Or do they, like small children and animals, fall outside the sphere of moral responsibility altogether?

The issue is complicated by the fact that most psychopaths are able to converse very intelligently about moral matters, making all the distinctions one would expect from a moral agent. So, can it be denied that they have the requisite understanding? If we conclude that they do not lack understanding, we are faced with the following alternatives. On the one hand, we could hold that since psychopaths understand moral concepts but lack moral concern, they are a paradigm of moral irresponsibility. On the other hand, we might maintain, as does Herbert Fingarette, that caring about morality also is a necessary condition for moral agency.[3] Hence psychopaths would be nonresponsible (amoral) rather than irresponsible (immoral).

I believe that neither alternative is attractive. I will argue that Fingarette is right in rejecting the first alternative and that he is

2. William and Joan McCord, *Psychopathy and Delinquency* (New York: Grune & Stratton, 1965), p. 14.

3. See Herbert Fingarette, *On Responsibility* (New York: Basic Books, 1967), Chap. 2.

right in insisting that caring about morality is a necessary condition for moral agency. However, I will try to show that he can argue for this successfully only if he questions whether the psychopath has the requisite moral understanding. Basically, I will maintain, Fingarette's mistake is to try to keep separate the concepts of understanding and caring. In the sense of 'understanding' relevant to moral agency understanding *is* a kind of caring.

II

Since much of morality is interpersonal, it is important to ask what makes possible meaningful moral communication between moral agents. For some this might suggest the question of what makes it possible for moral agents to come to moral agreement about something. Paradoxical as it may seem, the answer to this question is the same as the answer to the question of what makes moral *dis*agreement possible. Let me explain.

Suppose I believe that abortion laws should be liberalized, and I ask my daughter if she thinks so too. If she answers, "No," does it follow that she and I morally disagree? Not if she is only four years old. What is missing here is something essential to all disagreement in opinion—a common understanding in terms of which that disagreement can be articulated. This seems to be what Wittgenstein has in mind when he refers to the importance of a shared "form of life":

> "So you are saying that human agreement decides what is true and what is false?"—It is what human beings *say* that is true and false; and they agree in the *language* they use. That is not agreement in opinions but in form of life.
>
> If language is to be a means of communication there must be agreement not only in definitions but also (queer as this may sound) in judgments.[4]

To take a simple example, my wife and I might disagree about the dimensions of our living room. But if our four-year-old offers a third estimate, she does not add to the disagreement. To disagree with us, she must first share our concepts of measurement. Evidence of such sharing would be her making judgments similar to ours on other occasions. Disagreement (in opinion) presupposes prior

4. Ludwig Wittgenstein, *Philosophical Investigations* (New York: Macmillan Co., 1953), Sections 241, 242.

agreement (in "form of life").[5]

Learning a language is an essential part of children coming to share the kind of understanding that makes it possible for them to agree or disagree in opinion with others. However, as Wittgenstein insists, learning a language is not merely learning how to use words. It is also learning how to think, perceive, feel, relate to others, and practically engage in the world. It is because of this that Wittgenstein says, "to imagine a language is to imagine a form of life." [6]

What kind of prior understanding (or "agreement") is presupposed by agreement or disagreement in moral opinion? It is tempting to say that all that is necessary is that each person display a minimal ability to engage in intelligent moral conversation. I will refer to this as "intellectual understanding." As seen in the psychopath, it is possible for someone without moral concerns or commitments to have this kind of understanding. It is precisely because of this possibility that I believe it mistaken to give in to this temptation; as I hope to show, intellectual understanding is not enough.

It must be borne in mind that morality is inextricably bound up in the practical, and not merely the theoretical, affairs of human beings. So, for there to be anything recognizable as morality, there must be persons with certain practical concerns, along with moral competence to bring to bear on these concerns. But what counts as moral competence? Certainly there must be some ability to reflect intelligently on moral problems. But if this is all there is to it, it would not be necessary to bring this competence to bear on practical concerns. One could still have an attitude of practical indifference. But, since morality is more than simply an exercise in thought, it is necessary that there be practical concern as well.

There are many ways in which this concern can be shown. In addition to taking action in behalf of moral concerns there are, for example, the tendencies to experience feelings of guilt, remorse, shame, and resentment. These are examples of what P. F. Strawson calls "participant attitudes." [7] Contrasted to these are "objective

5. This point is developed by Peter Winch in his "Nature and Convention," *Proceedings of the Aristotelian Society*, 60 (1959-60), 231-32.

6. Wittgenstein, Section 19.

7. P. F. Strawson, "Freedom and Resentment," in *Studies in the Philosophy of Thought and Action*, ed. P. F. Strawson (New York: Oxford Univ. Press), 1968.

attitudes," which are primarily concerned with social policies designed to control, treat, or manipulate the behavior and attitudes of others. Someone with an objective attitude might make use of his or her knowledge of the tendencies people have to experience participant attitudes. But in such a case the participant attitudes would be regarded from a third person perspective. In contrast, Strawson's participant attitudes are "essentially natural human reactions to the good or ill will or indifference of others towards us, as displayed in their attitudes and actions." [8]

Fingarette agrees with Strawson's view that participant attitudes play an essential role in morality, but he does not attempt to connect the understanding of moral concepts with moral sentiments. Strawson, on the other hand, says:

> Only by attending to this range of attitudes can we recover from the facts as we know them a sense of what we mean, i.e., of *all* we mean, when, speaking the language of morals, we speak of desert, responsibility, guilt, condemnation, and justice.[9]

After considering Fingarette's views in some detail, I will try to show why Strawson is right in saying this.

III

Fingarette claims that a person is not morally responsible for what he or she does until showing signs of genuine acceptance of responsibility. He notes that we do not begin to hold children morally responsible until we think they are able to accept that responsibility. Such acceptance may be shown in inner moral conflict, self-restraint, remorse, guilt feelings, and positively taking care of that for which one is held responsible. And what if the child shows none of this? Then, says Fingarette, we have chosen the wrong moment; we must wait. But what if the child grows into adulthood never displaying such concerns? Fingarette devotes the bulk of his essay to answering just this question. He does this by considering at great length the characteristics of psychopaths. Unlike small children, psychopaths can carry on quite intelligent moral conversations, and they are capable of very persuasively feigning guilt feelings

8. Ibid., p. 80.

9. Ibid., p. 94.

and intentions to fulfill responsibilities or change their ways. Yet, they, like small children, lack genuine moral sentiments.

It is important to notice that Fingarette is not interested in *why* psychopaths think and act as they do. Finding out, for example, that they suffer from brain damage or lack of parental affection would only add other reasons for judging them nonresponsible. But there already are sufficient reasons. So, he is not interested here in any questions related to the free will-determinism controversy, nor in related areas of concern such as mental disease or insanity. Instead, says Fingarette, quite apart from these matters, those who think and act as psychopaths do, for whatever reason, have made it pointless to consider or treat them as morally responsible for what they do.

Why does Fingarette draw this conclusion? His main argument seems, at first glance, to be one of social utility, focusing on the "incorrigibility" of psychopaths. Presumably, someone who is incorrigible is incorrectable, intractable, unmanageable, or unresponsive to the suggestions and proddings of others. So, Fingarette might be saying that the pointlessness of regarding psychopaths responsible for what they do is that they will never be convinced in any way that counts that they have certain responsibilities; at most there will be "intellectual" assent. Certainly all of this seems to be true of psychopaths, with their typical pattern of impulsiveness, unreliability, and repeated confrontations with penal and mental institutions.[10]

But psychopaths are not the only "incorrigibles." Nothing seems to dissuade serious protestors such as Gandhi and Russell from violating laws in the name of various causes.[11] Yet, such persons are often thought to be paradigm cases of responsible persons—and by virtue of their incorrigibility. Also, there are always hard-headed persons we know will never change their minds (about racial, political, or religious matters, for example). Are they, like psychopaths, to be exempted from responsibility in these areas—on grounds of

10. This is well documented by Hervey Cleckley, *The Mask of Sanity*, 4th ed. (St. Louis, Mo.: C. V. Mosby Co., 1964).

11. I owe the example of Gandhi and Russell to Vinit Haksar's valuable paper, "Aristotle and the Punishment of Psychopaths," in *Aristotle's Ethics*, ed. James J. Walsh and Henry L. Shapiro (Belmont, Calif.: Wadsworth Publishing Co., 1967). Haksar has some especially helpful suggestions about this example on p. 94.

intractability? Given its pervasiveness, incorrigibility alone does not seem to be a sufficient ground for exempting persons from responsibility. In fact, it is often a person's incorrigibility on certain matters that is criticized.

However, there is a passage in Fingarette suggesting something very special about the incorrigibility of a psychopath:

> If an individual will not play a game with us, we can still fall back on the intelligible framework of everyday life outside that game. But what if he will not enter life's fray itself in the spirit in which we enter it? To face such a person, such a reality (and not merely to think it) is to experience a deep anxiety; a queasy helplessness moves in our soul.[12]

Here we see that the psychopath is not merely intractable or hard-headed. It is as though we have nothing in common with such a person, even though we use the same words, and perhaps even the same gestures. There is nothing familiar and shared that we can fall back upon to ease this anxiety. This is not someone like Gandhi or Russell with different moral ideals than most, or someone with different information or a different moral interpretation of a situation. No, the psychopath is more radically different than this. How should this more radical difference be characterized?

Fingarette characterizes it in terms of the psychopath's total indifference to responsibility. This, it seems to me, is right. But it cannot clearly be seen to be right unless one makes a move resisted by Fingarette. He resists linking up the concepts of understanding and caring, on the grounds that:

> It de-emphasizes acceptance and care by placing them in the shadow of that glamorous hero of the philosophic tradition, "Knowing." This, in effect, reinforces the previously mentioned tendency to neglect accepting and caring; it hinders us from seeing them as essential, distinguishable things we must do in order to achieve responsibility.[13]

The problem with this is that, although it does overcome the neglect of the concepts of accepting and caring, it does so at the price of distorting those concepts. It forces one to reject the notion that in

12. Fingarette, p. 37.
13. Ibid., p. 22.

many fundamental instances understanding something *is* caring about it. Further, to say that sometimes understanding something is a way of caring is neither to neglect caring nor to fall into the philosophical tradition to which Fingarette is opposed. It does not neglect caring because the point being made is that excluding caring from understanding is to view understanding too narrowly. And, for the same reason, it does not reinforce that philosophical tradition; rather, it breaks new ground in philosophical discussions of human knowledge and understanding.[14] What I hope to show is that, by maintaining that psychopaths do lack the kind of understanding (as caring) essential for moral agency, one can see more clearly why it is appropriate to say, as Fingarette himself wishes to say, that psychopaths do not share with others the relevant "form of life." To develop this thesis I will consider Arthur Murphy's concept of practical understanding.[15]

IV

Murphy, too, argues that those lacking moral concern are not morally responsible for what they do. Like Fingarette, he emphasizes the pointlessness of trying to deal with such persons in terms of responsibility. However, unlike Fingarette, he maintains that what they lack is "practical understanding." In explaining why it is understanding that they lack, Murphy considers how children learn moral concepts.

On his account, moral reasons are to be understood as justificatory grounds for action. As such, they are practical reasons, reasons for doing something rather than merely thinking about something. How do children learn to relate competently to such reasons?

> Training here is prior to significant argument, logically as well as temporally, since without this working basis of normative concern

14. This, I take it, is part of what Gilbert Ryle is trying to do in "On Forgetting the Difference Between Right and Wrong," in *Essays in Moral Philosophy,* ed. A. I. Melden (Seattle: Univ. of Washington Press, 1958). Also, as Richard Schmitt has recently shown, this is a major concern of Martin Heidegger in *Being and Time.* See Schmitt's *Martin Heidegger on Being Human* (New York: Random House, 1969), especially Chaps. 2 and 5, for an analysis of the concept of understanding that I find very suggestive in this regard.

15. I am referring to Arthur Murphy's *Theory of Practical Reason* (LaSalle, Illinois: Open Court Publishing Co., 1965), especially Chap. 5.

> and competence—the concern and competence to get things right —all our talk of practical reasoning, would, as Wittgenstein has put it, "hang in the air," and we should have no common ground on which to stand.[16]

Children can be encouraged to develop normative concerns either by deliberate prompting or by examples set by those who already have normative concerns. Although the particular details may vary extensively, there are a number of commonplaces. Children are encouraged to share, to take turns, to have regard for the interests and feelings of others, to keep their word, and to take proper care of that which has been entrusted to them. They are exposed to examples of fellow-feeling, sympathetic concern, mutual trust and helpfulness, as well as to moral criticism and the full range of morally reactive attitudes and feelings.[17]

Children are not exposed to moral contexts as mere observers. They are encouraged to share the attitudes and concerns of others. Typically, as objects of these attitudes and concerns themselves, they gradually become participants in the ways of life of those surrounding them. Their responses to these ways of life can vary. At first there may be the indifference of one who simply does not notice or discriminate. Then there may be various degrees of acceptance, rejection, resistance and puzzlement. The point to be made here is that the original acquisition of moral concepts is not an exclusively (or even primarily) theoretical or intellectual accomplishment. The world of a child is not a world of science and theory; it is a world of practical endeavor.

The acquisition of attitudes and concerns of a participant in a moral form of life is not to be confused with a blanket acceptance of the conventional. Since much of what children see is unresolved tension and conflict, some questioning and puzzlement is to be expected. Further, although one can learn from examples, examples provide one with only a starting point from which one can go on to deal competently with novel instances. So, Murphy is not neglecting the importance of criticism and growth in practical

16. Ibid., p. 10.

17. For fuller accounts of conditions that encourage moral development see Rawls, "The Sense of Justice" and *A Theory of Justice.* Rawls bases much of his account on Jean Piaget's *The Moral Judgment of the Child* (New York: Macmillan Co., Free Press, 1965).

understanding. His point is only that this understanding must begin somewhere, and this is in particular communities of persons with normative concerns.

As a result of moral training, virtually everyone acquires some kind of sense of justice, or fair play. One might think that having a sense of justice requires having only some conceptual mastery concerning matters of justice. But John Rawls seems to be right when he says, paraphrasing Rousseau, "The sense of justice is no mere moral conception formed by the understanding alone, but a true sentiment of the heart enlightened by reason. . . ."[18] Since a sense of justice is a blend of reason and sentiment, it is important that neither aspect be slighted. But what is especially to be noted here is that, whatever rational features of a sense of justice are cited, they are inadequate to capture what Rawls has in mind unless they are connected with moral sentiments such as fellow-feeling, resentment or indignation at injustices done by others, and feelings of guilt, remorse, or shame at one's own unjust acts. Underlying these sentiments is a respect for persons that objects to their being treated merely as means to another's ends; this would be a violation of their dignity.[19]

The connection between having a sense of justice and moral understanding can be seen by drawing an analogy. Consider what is involved in having a sense of humor. This includes having some ability to identify situations as being humorous. But someone with a sense of humor must also emotionally respond to these situations by finding them laughable, hilarious, or simply amusing. That is, one must genuinely laugh, be in a mood of hilarity, or be amused.

We could imagine a very observant person who lacks a sense of humor, but who closely studies others in humorous situations. Conceivably he could acquire a knack at determining what is regarded humorous by others. He might even be able to write humorous books. (Imagine him as a straight-faced comedian.) Further, he could mimic the laughter of others. Despite this, he still would not have a sense of humor. His responses would be completely parasitic upon the responses of others. What he lacks is a full understanding of humor. Although he does not lack any "informa-

18. Rawls, "The Sense of Justice," p. 282.

19. I have considered this more fully in my "Human Dignity and Justice," *Ethics* (July 1972), 299-313.

tion" or "data" that others have, he does not see what they do.

Both a sense of humor and a sense of justice require certain kinds of cognitive abilities and dispositions to respond emotionally. Drawing an analogy to someone lacking a sense of humor, we could imagine someone lacking a sense of justice studying the behavior of those with a sense of justice. If he is sufficiently observant and cautious in his behavior, he might acquire a reputation as an astute judge of issues of justice. He might learn very well what others count as relevant in settling these issues. He could feign guilt feelings or act apologetic when criticized for acting unfairly. He could appear indignant when injustices are done to others by others and resentful when they are done to him. And he could put on a show of other-regard and positive concern to be just. Still, since all of this is only mimicry, he would lack a sense of justice. And, although he would not lack "information" or "data" that others have, he would not see what they see.

Speaking of morality in general, Murphy says that persons who in this way cannot "see" what is there are not moral agents. This is because they lack both concern and competence. A person like this, says Murphy,

> could "regard an action as a duty" in the sense of recognizing, perhaps with complete practical indifference, that it had the traits by which an action is socially identified as "right". . . . What he could never in this way "see" is how such rightness bound him as a moral agent to the performance of the action in question, . . . He could not understand why he ought to do it.[20]

No matter what remarks such a person might make about his "responsibilities," he does not take them seriously, and this is because he does not *see* (i.e., *understand*) why he should take them seriously.

This is related to the perennial question, Why be moral? How this is answered depends upon the degree of moral commitment one already has. The implication of Murphy's view is that it is the psychopath's lack of commitment that prevents him from seeing what is there. In a slightly different context Peter Winch expresses Murphy's point very well:

20. Murphy, p. 126.

> I think the situation is something like this. If one looks at a certain style of life and asks what there is in it that makes it worthwhile, one will find nothing there. One may indeed describe it in terms which bring out 'what one sees in it', but the use of these terms already presupposes that one does see it from a perspective from which it matters. The words will fall flat on the ears of someone who does not occupy such a perspective even though he is struggling to attain it. If one tries to find in the object of contemplation that which makes it admirable, what one will in fact see is the admiration and applause which surrounds it. So one will see oneself perhaps as a prospective object of such admiration. And then what one is aiming at is to be such an object of admiration. 'What was internal becomes external.'[21]

There is evidently something circular in this. One must already be morally committed to something to see its moral value. But, although this is so, this is what we should expect if morality is viewed as having an integrity of its own. It may be true that there are nonmoral reasons for being moral. But it is important to insist that there are moral reasons for being moral as well, and that these should be regarded as sufficient. That this is already a moral 'should' indicates the circularity. But this is not a serious objection unless one is trying to present an "external" justification of morality.

The danger of insisting on "external" justifications of morality, while rejecting "internal" accounts because of circularity, is that the significance of the integrity of moral agents is thrown into question as well. A fundamental problem in moral training is to get children to appreciate the "internal" perspective of morality, rather than regarding moral claims merely as threats, arbitrary decrees, handy devices for manipulating others, or simply obstacles to be avoided if possible. It is only if these attitudes are overcome, or avoided, that we can begin to speak of a person's moral integrity. So, granting the importance of encouraging the development of moral integrity in children, being able to provide "internal" reasons for being moral is essential.

V

Summing up, it cannot be denied that psychopaths have some kind of understanding of moral concepts. However, since they are

21. Peter Winch, *Moral Integrity* (Oxford, England: Basil Blackwell, 1968), p. 24.

devoid of moral sentiments, they can at best be said to have an "intellectual" understanding. This is to be contrasted with the "practical" understanding of those with moral sentiments. For moral agents, indignation, guilt feelings, and concern for the suffering and well-being of others *are* ways in which they understand wrongdoing, guilt, and the need others have for assistance. In these cases there is no gap between understanding and caring.

Still, one might want to say that, since there is a sense in which one can understand without caring, caring must be different from understanding. But what must be kept in mind is that caring is always about something; it has an object. Further, caring about something is in many instances the most fundamental way in which I regard it. In such cases it is not that I have a certain understanding of that something and then, superadded as it were, I also care about it in a certain way. I may not regard it in a detached, observing sort of way at all. For example, I do not first "observe" my son's wound—registering the "information"—and then, as a result of this perception, have some sort of concern for his plight. Rather, I perceive what has happened to him as a *wound,* and my recognition of it as a wound is seen in the immediate concern I have to help him. Were I to react at first in a detached, observing way to his wound, this would indicate some kind of failure of recognition. "Don't you see that he is *hurt?*" What I would need is a jarring back into reality—the reality that I share this world with my son, who is in need of my help. It is when care or concern is an essential feature of the way in which one perceives a situation that we have what Murphy calls "practical," and not merely "intellectual," understanding.

But even if psychopaths lack this "practical" understanding of morality, why should this make us experience Fingarette's "queasy helplessness"? It is that, despite appearances, there is no genuine meeting of minds between psychopaths and others on moral matters. Among those who take morality seriously there is a common concern to be justified in what one does. Although there might be serious disagreement about what specific responsibilities one has, at least the parties take the idea of responsibility seriously. But there seems to be no shared ground to fall back upon when confronted with psychopaths. It is as though they are from another world, another "form of life." The queasiness comes, not from feeling that they will never be convinced of our point of view (an everyday matter), but from the realization that they do not even share normative concern. It is as though there is at best mimicry or mockery, not mutual understanding. Quite aside from the question of whether one can get psychopaths to change their ways, there is the prior question of what one should even *say* to those who "will not enter life's fray itself in the spirit in which we enter it." And it is not merely that they do not understand our "form of life;" we do not understand theirs. As Wittgenstein says in another context:

> We also say of some people that they are transparent to us. It is, however, important as regards this observation that one human being can be a complete enigma to another. We learn this when we come into a strange country with entirely strange traditions; and, what is more, even given a mastery of the country's language. We do not *understand* the people. "And not because of not knowing what they are saying to themselves." We cannot find our feet with them.[22]

What is misleading about saying psychopaths are nevertheless morally responsible for what they do is that it suggests that mutual understanding is not lacking. But using the same words and copying gestures is not enough. Again, Wittgenstein says, "If a lion could talk, we could not understand him." [23] As Murphy points out, moral reasons are not addressed to everyone. They are for a moral agent only:

> It is *for* such an agent that they are practical reasons, i.e., reasons for doing something, not merely for thinking or believing that something is the case, and as in this way practical that they have a normative function in our conduct.[24]

But moral reasons *can* be practical only for those who are to some extent morally concerned. If justificatory reasons are to be practical reasons, they must be capable of being motivating reasons as well.

This is not to deny that justifying reasons sometimes do not motivate. Moral agents have other concerns as well, concerns that tempt them to ignore, suppress, rationalize away, or be indifferent

22. Wittgenstein, p. 223*.
23. Ibid.
24. Murphy, p. 123.

to moral considerations. Self-deception, too, is an ever present possibility. But, as Murphy points out, the very presence of moral self-deception indicates a concern to be justified.[25] Both Murphy and Fingarette connect self-deception with a concern to maintain some kind of integrity. Since psychopaths have no moral integrity to protect, if they are capable of any kind of self-deception, it is related to some other kind of integrity.

It should be noted that it is not being claimed that one's only moral responsibilities are those one has explicitly acknowledged. As Fingarette insists, much of the substance of our moral lives is coming to discover the responsibilities one has implicitly accepted by virtue of accepting the status of moral agency. It is because one is a certain kind of person (a moral agent), and not because there are certain acts one has performed, that one has moral responsibilities. Particular acts can alter one's responsibilities (promising, for example), but one cannot divest oneself of a responsibility simply by becoming indifferent to it, or by failing to acknowledge it.

Still, one might object, "This makes things much too easy. All one has to do to relieve oneself of the burdens of moral responsibility is to rid oneself of moral concerns—to become an amoralist." The short reply to this is: Easier said than done. First, relieving oneself of moral responsibility does not leave one free to do whatever one pleases. This surely is not our attitude toward small children, those with serious mental deficiencies, and animals. (And the more dangerous the animal, the more protection is provided.) Second, to divest oneself of all moral concern is an enormous undertaking for most. One would have to rid oneself of fellow-feeling, hardening oneself to the joys and sufferings of others. One would have to cease to be aroused by the injustices done to others and no longer resent injustices done to oneself. One would have to eliminate all feelings of guilt, shame, remorse, regret, or apology when treating others in objectionable ways. I should think that none of this would be easy for those who have moral sentiments, nor is it clear that they could reflectively consider it desirable even to try.

But if this is all that can be said, can morality be given a solid enough foundation? On this view, how is morality to be "justified"? I think Strawson has the right answer to these questions:

25. See Murphy's Chap. 6. See Fingarette's *Self-Deception* (London: Routledge & Kegan Paul, 1969).

> Inside the general structure or web of human attitudes and feelings of which I have been speaking, there is endless room for modification, redirection, criticism, and justification. But questions of justification are internal to the structure or relate to modifications internal to it. The existence of the general framework of attitudes itself is something we are given with the fact of human society. As a whole, it neither calls for, nor permits, an external 'rational' justification.[26]

He compares this to our commitment to induction, which he says is "original, natural non-rational (not *ir*rational), in no way something we choose or could give up."

To have no recourse to a view outside our moral commitments from which we might display the rationality of morality and irrationality of amorality might seem to be a defeat of rationality. But, as Bernard Williams says of something similar, this would be a defeat for humanity, not rationality.[27] To point out that morality is contingent upon the extent to which human beings are capable of a shared "form of life" that includes moral sentiments is to point out its fragility. However, given the increasing difficulty and danger of human beings trying to live in moral isolation from each other, it makes clear the responsibility of those who do have moral concerns to extend as far as possible the limits of this shared understanding. Nothing I have said is intended to support moral skepticism or relativism. But it is intended to indicate upon what moral "objectivity" is ultimately dependent, indicating at the same time that this "objectivity" has no a priori guarantee. In this sense, it is true that morality is what we make of it.

MICHAEL S. PRITCHARD

WESTERN MICHIGAN UNIVERSITY

---

26. Strawson, p. 94.

27. Bernard Williams, *Morality* (New York: Harper & Row, 1971). Williams discusses indifference to morality in his first chapter.

American Philosophical Quarterly
Volume 16, Number 3, July 1979

II. COLLECTIVE ACTIONS AND SECONDARY ACTIONS

DAVID COPP

I CONTEND that collectives can and do perform actions. Nation-states wage wars, corporations change their price schedules, and charitable organizations solicit funds. Even relatively unorganized and impermanent collectives perform actions. The Paris mob stormed the Bastille, for example. The large body of recent work in action theory contains little on the subject of collective action, despite the recent interest in issues connected with the attribution of moral responsibility and obligations to collectives. In what follows I attempt to provide an account of collective action, to relate this account to theories of the actions of persons, and to make suggestions for further study of the issues in moral philosophy.

It is plain that collectives do not act independently of the actions of persons.[1] Under certain circumstances, the action of a person, or the actions of a number of persons, are "the basis for attributing" an action to a collective. For example, certain actions of a head of state may be the basis for attributing to his country the action of declaring war. In this paper, I consider the following question: What is the relation between the action of a person, or the actions of a number of persons, and the action of a collective when the former is the basis for attributing the latter action to the collective? Below, I define a relation which I call "the constitution relation," and I claim that this relation holds between the action of the collective and the action of the person in these cases. The action of the collective is "constituted" by the action of the person or the actions of the persons in question.[2] I will also suggest that one can give a systematic account of the relations between many sorts of actions in terms of the constitution relation. If I am right, this relation is of general interest in the theory of action.

I. Secondary Actions

There are cases where persons may properly have actions attributed to them on the basis of actions of other persons. For example, if Jones gives someone power of attorney and orders him to purchase a certain building for him, then, if the attorney buys it for Jones, Jones has bought it. Jones has not signed any purchase document himself, but he is obliged to meet the terms of sale and he has acquired the rights of an owner. The action of buying the building is attributable to Jones on the basis of his attorney's actions. Cases of this sort bear a striking similarity to many cases of collective action, such as cases where corporations purchase property. I will call actions of these types "secondary actions." An agent's action is a secondary action if, and only if, it is correctly attributable to this agent on the basis of either an action of some other agent, or actions of some other agents. The account I will present of collective actions can be used to give an account of all secondary actions.

However, some would object that the occurrences I have called "secondary actions" are not actions at all. Clearly there are important differences between these occurrences and the occurrences which we would all agree to be actions and which I will call "primary actions." In particular, as I shall claim, the "secondary actions" of an agent are, but the primary actions are not, "constituted" by actions of *other* agents. However, there are also important similarities between "secondary actions" and primary actions. Like primary actions, "secondary actions" of an agent can be done intentionally by him, can violate obligations he has, and can fulfil his commitments. For example, in the property purchasing case, Jones ordered the attorney to purchase the building for him. He intended to purchase the

[1] I assume throughout that no collective is a person. If it is thought that a collective may be a person, read "person which is not a collective" where I write "person." Also, I treat omissions as actions. If an agent omits doing something, refrains from doing something or fails to do something, I will write that he performs an action, regardless of whether his omission is intentional.

[2] For the sake of brevity, I shall frequently omit repeating the point that the actions of more than one person may be involved.

building and intended to purchase it in the way he did purchase it, by having the attorney sign the appropriate documents. He purchased it intentionally. Also, the sequence of events and actions which occurred would have been sufficient for Jones' fulfilling any commitment he might have had to purchase the building. And if he had had an obligation not to purchase it, for whatever reason, he would have been as responsible for purchasing it in this case as if he had signed the papers personally. I choose to emphasize these similarities between primary and secondary actions by thinking of "secondary actions" as actions.

Joel Feinberg objects to this choice ([8], p. 227). He says it is "dangerously misleading" to say that "the very actions of agents themselves, and not merely their normative consequences, are directly ascribable to their principals." He suggests that it is also misleading to attribute any action to a principal on the basis of the actions of an agent. For example, if *A* has *B*'s power of attorney and the right to sign *B*'s signature, and if *A* signs *B*'s name to a cheque payable to *C*, then the "pecuniary consequences" are exactly as they would have been had *B* himself signed his name. Yet *B* ". . . did not act—*A* acted for him." But while it would be incorrect in this case to say that *B* signed the cheque, it would be correct, and it need not be misleading, to say that *B* paid *C* the money. What it would be misleading to say depends, in part, on the situation one is in, and on what is in question in the situation. If *B* had owed *C* the money, and if it was in question whether the debt had been paid, it would not be misleading to report that *B* had paid *C* the money. In fact, in this case, it would be both misleading and incorrect to deny this. Feinberg is wrong, then, to think that it is always misleading to attribute an action to one agent on the basis of an action of another agent. Still, Feinberg's case demonstrates that when an action is attributable to a principal in a situation on the basis of the acts of an agent, it need not be the case that *every* action performed by the agent in that situation is itself attributable to the principal.

Some would wish to deny, in particular, that it is possible for a collective to perform an action (see Margolis [13], p. 254; compare Kelsen [10], p. 97). However, claims of this sort are typically unaccompanied by arguments. Of course it is true that collectives do not have bodies and cannot perform bodily movements. But it needs to be shown that this debars them from performing actions. It might be thought that a collective cannot perform any "basic actions." But, if so, then the claim that being capable of acting requires being capable of performing basic actions needs defense as much as does the original claim that a collective cannot perform any actions.[3] Perhaps the common intuition here is one which underlies the doctrine we might call "explanatory individualism." A collective, one might say, could not have any "immediate impact" on the world, but can only have impact "through" the actions of persons. Alleged actions of collectives can always be explained ultimately in terms of the actions of persons. The question here, of course, is why should we regard this as showing that collectives do not act, rather than merely as showing how their actions can ultimately be explained?

It might be held that it is not possible for a collective to have an intention, that for this reason it is not possible for a collective to act intentionally, and that whatever cannot act intentionally cannot act at all. But it is possible for a collective to have an objective and to do something in order to achieve that objective. It is possible for a collective to do something for a reason. Many nations share the goal of preventing a nuclear war and the belief that preventing the proliferation of nuclear technology is necessary to prevent this. For this reason, these nations have signed various treaties. But a sufficient condition of an agent's performing an action intentionally is that it perform the action for a reason.[4] This example shows that collectives can act for reasons. It is apparent, for example, that the cell of le front de libération du Québec which kidnapped James Cross did so intentionally. It must have if it kidnapped Cross, for it is not possible for a kidnapping to be unintentional. The cell kidnapped Cross with the intention at least of obtaining the release of certain prisoners. Thus, it seems possible for a collective to do something intentionally.

There is no theoretical gain merely from denying

[3] On "basic actions," see, for example, Danto, [2] and [3], and Goldman, [9], pp. 24, 63–72. Davidson contends that all "primitive actions" are bodily movements ([5], pp. 11–14), and moreover that bodily movements are "all the actions there are" (p. 23). It would follow that there are no actions of collectives, for collectives do not perform any bodily movements. However, Davidson's argument shows, at best, that any primary action of a person is identical to some bodily movement. Davidson does not consider the possibility that there are secondary actions or that collectives perform actions.

[4] This is suggested, for example, by Anscombe in [1], §12, 13, 16, 22.

that occurrences such as this kidnapping were actions performed by collectives. What is needed is an account of these occurrences which enables us to understand their relation to actions of persons and their differences from primary actions of persons. In certain theoretical contexts, it might be useful to emphasize the differences between primary and "secondary actions" and to restrict the term "action" to primary actions of persons. My view is that, at least in moral philosophy, it is fruitful to emphasize the similarities which are here and to think of "secondary actions" as actions. I hope the theory which results confirms this view.

II. The Constitution Relation

In cases where an action is attributable to one agent on the basis of actions performed by another agent, what is the relation between the secondary action of the one agent and the relevant actions of the other agent? For example, the country of Exemplar, a constitutional monarchy, declared war on Germany in 1939. This action is attributable to Exemplar on the basis of the Prime Minister's, Mr. Dux's, action of issuing an appropriate formal proclamation. What is the relation between these actions? Below, I define a relation which I call the "constitution relation." I contend that the one action "constitutes" the other.

To begin with, it needs to be seen that the actions were not identical. Suppose that Exemplar's declaring war was caused by German military actions in Europe. We may suppose that Dux's issuing the proclamation was not caused by this. Dux opposed the war despite German actions. His issuing the proclamation was caused by his knowledge that he would lose his position if he did not follow the instructions of the majority in Parliament. We may suppose that Dux's issuing the proclamation actually cost the treasury very little. However, even if we suppose this, we may suppose that there was a significant cost to the treasury incurred in Exemplar's declaring war. There was a special session of Parliament to debate the issue and the cost of the session was not negligible. Thus the two actions had different causes and effects. It follows, I claim, that Dux's issuing the proclamation and Exemplar's declaring war were not identical. I assume here, without argument, that the contexts created in this example by the phrase "was caused by," for example, are not referentially opaque. Davidson supports this assumption (in [6]). And Davidson argues that *events* are not identical if they have different causes or effects, and he thinks that actions are events ([7], pp. 231, 217; [4], p. 699; [5], p. 4). In any case, it would be particularly implausible to claim that the actions in question were identical given that they were performed by different agents.

Moreover, the relation holding between these actions is not causation. Dux's issuing the proclamation did not *cause* Exemplar to declare war. It is possible then that one agent's action should be the basis for attributing an action to a second agent even if it did not cause the second agent to perform that action. And, on the other hand, it is possible that one agent's action should cause another agent to act even if it is not the basis for attributing this action to the other agent. For example, consider a case where a policeman's writing a parking ticket caused the recipient of the ticket to curse. The recipient's action was a reaction prompted or caused by the policeman's action, but it was a primary action. It is not attributed to the recipient on the basis of the policeman's action. Thus, the causal relation must be distinguished from the relation that holds between secondary actions and the relevant primary actions.

Nevertheless it does appear that when the relation in question holds between one action and a second, the first is sufficient under the circumstances for the second. And the first is necessary for the second in that, roughly, the second would not have taken place but for the first. In the declaration of war case, given the content of the proclamation, given that Dux was Prime Minister of Exemplar and had been authorized to issue a declaration of war, given that the proclamation was in fact published, and so on, Dux's action was a sufficient condition of Exemplar's declaring war. It is not possible that he should have issued the proclamation under circumstances similar in all relevant respects, yet it not have been the case that Exemplar declared war. Moreover, war would not have been declared but for Dux's action, assuming roughly that no agent would have done anything else sufficient for Exemplar's declaring war if Dux had not issued the proclamation. My definition of the "constitution relation" is very complex, but underlying it is the relatively simple idea just sketched.

I begin by stating the following definition:

D1: S_2's doing A_2 is, under the circumstances C, a sufficient condition of S_1's doing A_1 if, and only if, there are "C-R relevant" facts about the circumstances in which S_2 does A_2, such that it is not possible, given these facts (facts C), that S_2 should do A_2 yet it not be the case that S_1 does A_1.

In what follows, I will explain which of the facts about the circumstances in which given actions are performed are "C-R relevant"—relevant to the obtaining of the constitution relation between the actions in question. The notion is that an action performed by one agent may be a sufficient condition of an action performed by a second agent *regardless* of certain facts, but *given* certain other facts. It may be a sufficient condition of an action of a second agent *regardless* of facts which would merely render it causally sufficient for the action of the second agent, which facts would not be "C-R relevant", but *given* the "C-R relevant" facts, which include facts about the law and about the constitution of, or patterns of interpersonal interactions within, given organized or unorganized collectives. I shall explain this in more detail.[5]

Clearly not every fact about the circumstances in which an action is performed can be allowed to count as "C-R relevant". Consider that for *any* two actions that are performed, one might say that it is a fact about the circumstances that these actions both occur. But it is not possible, given this fact, that the first action be performed but the second action not be performed. Thus, if this fact were "C-R relevant", the first would be "sufficient under the circumstances" for the second, and by similar reasoning any action which is performed could be shown to be "sufficient under the circumstances" for any other action which is performed. Thus, the fact that S_1 did A_1, and the truth of any propositions entailed by "S_1 did A_1" or entailing this within propositional logic are not relevant to whether S_1's doing A_1 is constituted by any other action. Thus, the truth of the material conditional "if S_2 did A_2, S_1 did A_1" is not relevant, nor is the truth of the proposition "S_2 did A_2 and S_1 did A_1".

Moreover, facts which "render" one action causally sufficient for another are not relevant to the obtaining of the constitution relation between these actions. That is, suppose A_1 was caused by A_2, and suppose that if it had not been the case that *p*, then, other things being equal, it would not have been the case that A_2 caused A_1. Then the fact that *p* is not relevant to the obtaining of the constitution relation between these two actions. This restriction permits my account to distinguish the constitution relation from the causal relation. My account will allow that one agent's action may be causally sufficient for another agent's action even if it does not constitute the other agent's action, and vice versa. In the parking ticket case, for example, psychological facts about the recipient of the ticket are not relevant to whether his cursing was constituted by the policeman's action because these facts rendered the policeman's action causally sufficient for the recipient's cursing. For this reason, facts about the psychological or motivational nature of an agent typically are not relevant to the obtaining of the constitution relation between an action of that agent and any other actions.[6]

Which facts about the circumstances in which an action is performed are relevant to the obtaining of the constitution relation between that act and some other act or acts? First, these will include all facts about the constitutional rules or laws, laws and by-laws of organized collectives. Thus, in the declaration of war case, the "C-R relevant" facts include that Dux was Prime Minister; that Parliament had passed a resolution asking that war be declared; that the King of Exemplar had approved the declaration of war; and that according to the constitution, a declaration by the Prime Minister with the authority of the monarch is conclusive in making it the case that the country declares war. It is not possible, given these facts, that Dux should have published the proclamation but Exemplar not have declared war.

Second, the "C-R relevant" facts about a situation may also include facts about the composition and dynamics of, or patterns of interpersonal relations within, given unorganized collectives. Despite the previous restriction against causal facts, facts about the causal dynamics of unorganized collectives, such as mobs, may be relevant. Facts about causal relations between actions of persons in the collective may be relevant provided they do not render the actions of the persons concerned causally sufficient for the action of the collective which is in question. For example, consider a case where a mob lynched a scoundrel. Suppose that the action of the citizen who personally did the execution did not cause the mob to lynch the man. And facts about the causal relations between this citizen's action and other persons' actions did not render the former causally sufficient for the mob's action. Then, these facts may be relevant to whether this citizen's actions constituted the mob's action. On the other hand,

[5] I was helped with what follows by the criticisms of Nicholas Sturgeon, Steven Davis, and the referee for this journal.

[6] However, as Steven Davis pointed out, such facts may be made relevant by a law or rule of some collective. For example, a law could provide that one person retains the power of attorney of another only as long as both parties are sane.

suppose a demagogue's demanding the scoundrel's execution is what caused the mob to act. In this case, the fact that the mob tends to be caused to act by speeches of demagogues would be ruled irrelevant to the obtaining of the constitution relation between the demagogue's act and the mob's. This is because this fact rendered the former causally sufficient for the latter.

One action's being a sufficient condition, under the circumstances, of a second is not enough for it to constitute the second. For example, suppose Exemplar's system of government were such that Exemplar's declaring war in 1939 was sufficient under the circumstances for Dux's issuing the proclamation. Even on this supposition, Dux's action did not *depend on* Exemplar's declaring war in the way in which Exemplar's declaring war depended on his issuing the proclamation. And Dux's action was a primary action. It is not attributed to Dux on the basis of Exemplar's declaring war. For this reason, we need to add a second clause to the definition of the constitution relation.

The idea is that if one action constitutes a second, then the second depends on the first in that, roughly, if the first action had not occurred, neither would the second have occurred. It is clear that this way of explaining the dependence of the second action on the first is incorrect as it stands. Exemplar still might have declared war even if Dux had not issued the proclamation he did in fact issue. On the one hand, Dux could have issued a different but similar proclamation instead. And if Dux had not issued the proclamation, the King could have issued the proclamation himself. On the other hand, Exemplar's declaring war could have been doubly ensured by actions of Dux. He could have both issued the proclamation and sent Hitler a threatening postcard. In this case, again, even if he had not issued the proclamation, it still would have been the case that Exemplar declared war. Thus, if there are several ways in which a secondary action could have been brought about, it will not be true that it would not have occurred had the action which is actually its basis not occurred. And, if a secondary action is multiply ensured by actions of other agents, then again it will not be true that it would not have occurred if an action which is one of its bases had not occurred. There is a simple way of avoiding these two types of problem cases in stating a sense in which an action must depend on any other action which constitutes it. We say, in effect, that assuming that neither of these sorts of problem arises in the case in question, then, if the one action had not occurred, neither would the secondary action have occurred.

This idea is expressed as follows: S_1's doing A_1 is constituted by S_2's doing A_2 only if, had S_2 not done A_2, then it would not have been the case that S_1 did A_1, assuming, perhaps counter-factually, that (i) there was no S_3 and A_3 such that S_3 did *not* do A_3 but *would* have done A_3 had S_2 not done A_2, and S_3's doing A_3 in the circumstances would have been sufficient for S_1's doing A_1, and (ii) there was no S_3 and A_3, where S_3 is not identical to S_1, but where S_3 *did* A_3 and S_3's doing A_3 in the circumstances would have been a sufficient condition of S_1's doing A_1 even if S_2 had not done A_2. This requires some explanation.

This second clause is satisfied in the Exemplar case if, and only if, had Dux not published the proclamation, then on two assumptions, it would not have been the case that the country declared war. What are these assumptions? On the first, there is nothing which any agent did *not* do but which it would have done had Dux not issued the declaration and which would have been sufficient in the circumstances for Exemplar's declaring war. The King did not bypass the Prime Minister, so we are assuming here that if the Prime Minister had not published the declaration, the King still would not have bypassed him. We are also assuming here that the Prime Minister would not have performed some *other* effective action if he had not published the proclamation. Roughly, the first assumption in this case is that, even if Dux had not issued the proclamation, Exemplar's action would not have been brought about by someone's doing something *else* to bring it about. On the second assumption, no agent *other than Exemplar* did anything which would have been sufficient for the declaration of war even if Dux had not issued the proclamation. We are assuming here, for example, that Parliament's passing the resolution asking that a declaration of war be sent would not have been sufficient for Exemplar's declaring war even if Dux had not published the declaration. Roughly, the second assumption is that there was nothing taking place which would have ensured the declaration of war even if Dux had failed to issue the proclamation. On these two assumptions, there was no "insurance" against Dux's failing. The second clause is satisfied in this case just in case, had the Prime Minister not issued the proclamation, then on these two assumptions, it would not have been the case that Exemplar declared war. But this is so in our example. Therefore this second clause is satisfied.

This clause shows a sense in which Exemplar's declaring war depended on Dux's issuing the proclamation, but Dux's action did not depend on Exemplar's declaring war. On the relevant assumptions, it would not have been the case that Exemplar declared war if Dux had not issued the proclamation. But consider whether Dux would have issued the proclamation if Exemplar had not declared war. Assume that the only way for Exemplar to declare war is for the Prime Minister to issue a proclamation. Exemplar's declaring war was sufficient under this circumstance for Dux's action. But now make the two required assumptions. On the first, there is nothing which any agent did not do but would have done had Exemplar not declared war and which would have been sufficient for Dux's issuing the proclamation. This assumption leaves Dux's actual actions intact. On the second assumption, no agent other than Dux did anything which would have been sufficient for Dux's action even if Exemplar had not declared war. This also leaves Dux's actual actions intact. Now, even on these assumptions, it is not true that if Exemplar had not declared war, Dux would not have issued the proclamation. Admittedly it is difficult to evaluate this counter-factual. But there is a possible situation, not very different from the "actual" situation, in which the antecedent is true but the consequent is false.[7] Thus, there is a possible situation in which, even given our assumptions, and even given that Dux issued the proclamation, Exemplar did not declare war. In this situation, Dux merely lacked the Parliamentary authority necessary to make his actions effective. The possibility of this situation shows that it is *not* the case, even given the two required assumptions, that if Exemplar had not declared war, Dux would not have issued the proclamation. But it *is* true, given the corresponding assumptions, that if Dux had not issued the proclamation, it would not have been the case that Exemplar declared war. In this sense, Dux's action did not depend on Exemplar's action, but the latter did depend on Dux's issuing the proclamation. This is reflected in the fact that in the case at hand, and according to the definition I will now state, Exemplar's declaring war was constituted by Dux's issuing the proclamation. But it is not the case that Dux's action was constituted by Exemplar's action, even if the latter was sufficient under the circumstances for the former. Clause (c) of the definition is not satisfied.

The following is a definition of the constitution relation:

D2: For agents S_1 and S_2 and actions A_1 and A_2, S_1's doing A_1 was constituted by S_2's doing A_2 if, and only if,

(a) S_2's doing A_2 was, under the circumstances C, a sufficient condition of S_1's doing A_1, but

(b) neither the obtaining of C, nor S_2's doing A_2, was itself a sufficient condition of S_1's doing A_1, and

(c) if S_2 had not done A_2, then it would not have been the case that S_1 did A_1, assuming, perhaps counter-factually, that there was no S_3 and A_3 such that either

(i) S_3 did not do A_3 but would have done A_3 had S_2 not done A_2, and S_3's doing A_3 in the circumstances would have been a sufficient condition of S_1's doing A_1, or

(ii) where $S_3 \neq S_1$, S_3 did A_3 and S_3's doing A_3 in the circumstances would have been a sufficient condition of S_1's doing A_1 even if S_2 had not done A_2.[8]

It should be noted that on D2 an action of a collective may be constituted by each of a number of distinct actions. This is because a secondary action may be multiply ensured by actions of other agents. Thus, if the King and the Prime Minister had both issued individually effective proclamations, then Exemplar's declaring war would have been constituted both by the King's issuing his proclamation and by Dux's issuing his proclamation. If this seems counter-intuitive, the problem is entirely terminological. It would be solved by our saying in cases where a secondary action is multiply ensured by actions of other agents that these actions are "minimally sufficient constituents" of the secondary action, and that the secondary action is constituted, not by each of these, but by the set containing all of its minimally sufficient constituents.[9] This being noted, I will not make the terminological change.

[7] See the discussion of counter-factuals in Lewis [11].

[8] This analysis is modelled, to a large degree, after Goldman's analysis of "level generation" in [9], pp. 38-44. Clauses (a), (b) and (c) of my analysis are mutants of Goldman's clauses (3a) and (3b). My clause (c), however, also is meant to do the sort of work done in Goldman's analysis by his clause (3c). and to solve a problem analogous to one Goldman admits that his analysis fails to handle (pp. 43-44). I was led to this sort of analysis, in part, by J. L. Mackie's analysis of "INUS conditions" in [12].

[9] I was helped here by suggestions of David Lyons and Nollaig MacKenzie.

An action performed by a collective may also be constituted by several agents' performing actions. For example, a legislature's adopting a given bill would be constituted by several members' voting in favour of that bill, perhaps together with several other members' refraining from voting against the bill. Similarly, a group's pushing a bus up a hill would be constituted by several individuals' pushing the bus. The definition D2 needs to be generalized to cover such cases. Moreover, to avoid certain problematic examples, a fourth clause needs to be added to the generalized analysis. The analysis together with the fourth clause allows that, even if *ninety-nine* members of a one hundred member legislature which operates on a simple majority decision rule happened to vote in favour of a given bill, still those ninety-nine members' together voting in favour of the bill would constitute the legislature's approving the measure. On the other hand, the analysis rules out the possibility of entirely irrelevant actions' being constituents of a collective's action. It rules out the possibility, for example, of our getting the result that those ninety-nine members' voting in favour of the bill, and my mowing the lawn on my twelfth birthday, together constituted the legislature's approving the measure. I state the generalized definition D3 in a footnote.[10]

The definitions I have stated in this section are designed to capture the idea that when one action is attributed to an agent on the basis of an action of another agent, the former is both sufficient for the occurrence of the latter and necessary for this in the sense that the latter would not have occurred but for the occurrence of the former. Despite the complexity of these definitions, the underlying idea is, I believe, simple and plausible.

III. Collective Actions, Secondary Actions, and the Constitution Relation

I am now in a position to state an answer to the question with which I began this paper. When an action performed by a person is the basis for attributing an action to a collective, the collective's action is constituted by the person's action. Moreover, a necessary condition of a collective's performing an action is that some person perform an action which constitutes the collective's action, or that some persons perform actions which constitute this. In this sense, the actions of collectives are constituted by actions of persons and a collective is not a self-sufficient agent. I advance these claims as hypotheses whose plausibility is supported, I contend, by the examples already discussed.

Let us consider some putative counter-examples to this thesis. Gerald Massey has suggested ([14], p. 96) that the actions of collectives which are mereological sums of persons, such as +(Tom, Dick, Harry),[11] may not be explainable on the model which explains actions of collectives such as families or nations. Consider, then, Tom, Dick and Harry's carrying the piano upstairs. Is this action constituted by actions of the three men? I claim that it is. Clause (a) of D3 is satisfied. Each of Tom, Dick and Harry helped carry the piano upstairs, and given that no-one else helped, their actions were sufficient for Tom, Dick and Harry's carrying the piano upstairs. Also, clause (b) is satisfied. The

[10] The generalized and amended analysis is as follows:

D3: For agents $S_1, S_2, \ldots S_n$ and actions $A_1, A_2, \ldots A_n$, S_1's doing A_1 was constituted by S_2's doing A_2, S_3's doing A_3, and S_n's doing A_n if, and only if,

(a) under the circumstances C, S_2's doing A_2, S_3's doing A_3, ... and S_n's doing A_n was a sufficient condition of S_1's doing A_1, but

(b) neither the obtaining of C, nor the performing of $A_1, A_2, \ldots A_n$ by agents $S_1, S_2, \ldots S_n$ respectively was sufficient by itself for S_1's doing A_1, and

(c) if it had not been the case that (S_2 did A_2, or S_3 did A_3, ... or S_n did A_n), it would not have been the case that S_1 did A_1, assuming there was no $S_{n+2}, \ldots S_{n+r}$, and $A_{n+2}, \ldots A_{n+r}$, such that either
 (i) it was not the case that S_{n+2} did A_{n+2}, ... and S_{n+r} did A_{n+r}, but this *would* have been the case had it not been the case that (S_2 did A_2, ... or S_n did A_n), and, under the circumstances, S_{n+2}'s doing A_{n+2}, ... and S_{n+r}'s doing A_{n+r} would have been sufficient for S_1's doing A_1, or
 (ii) where $S_{n+i} \neq S_1$, for all $2 \leq i \leq r$, it was the case that S_{n+2} *did* A_{n+2}, ... and S_{n+r} did A_{n+r}, and under the circumstances, this would have been a sufficient condition of S_1's doing A_1 even if it had not been the case that (S_2 did A_2, ... or S_n did A_n), and

(d) $\{\langle S_2, A_2\rangle, \langle S_3, A_3\rangle, \ldots \langle S_n, A_n\rangle\}$ is the union of sets $\varnothing_1, \varnothing_2, \ldots \varnothing_m$, *each* $\varnothing_i (1 \leq i \leq m)$ of which is such that,
 (i) letting $\varnothing_i = \{\langle S_j, A_j\rangle, \langle S_{j+1}, A_{j+1}\rangle, \ldots \langle S_{j+p}, A_{j+p}\rangle\}$, S_j's doing A_j, ... and S_{j+p}'s doing A_{j+p} was a sufficient condition of S_1's doing A_1, under the circumstances C, but
 (ii) it is *not* the case that there is a proper subset of $\varnothing_i$, $\{\langle S_k, A_k\rangle, \langle S_{k+1}, A_{k+1}\rangle, \ldots \langle S_{k+q}, A_{k+q}\rangle\}$, such that, under the circumstances C, S_k's doing A_k, ... and S_{k+q}'s doing A_{k+q} was a sufficient condition of S_1's doing A_1.

In Massey's terminology ([14], p. 92), D3 ensures that "constitute" is a "multigrade predicate".

[11] The terminology and symbolism are explained in Massey [14]. His paper contains references to the classic works on "mereology," or the "logic of individuals".

fact that no-one else helped, that is, that anyone who helped carry the piano was either Tom, Dick or Harry, is not itself a sufficient condition of Tom, Dick and Harry's carrying the piano. And Tom's helping, Dick's helping and Harry's helping also is not itself sufficient for Tom, Dick and Harry's carrying the piano upstairs. I will not discuss clauses (c) and (d) but I think it can be seen that this action of a mereological sum of persons is constituted by actions of persons. I would claim that all actions of sums of persons are constituted by actions of persons. It should be noted that some putative counter-examples to this claim may be cases involving a sum of actions of persons rather than an action by a sum of persons.[12]

Another putative counter-example to my thesis involves "computer actions." Perhaps a collective's actions will not be constituted by actions of persons in some cases involving computer technology. In certain circumstances, for a computer to send a bill to a customer of a corporation would be for the corporation to bill that customer. Suppose then that the Hudson's Bay Company sent me a bill for twenty-five dollars. The billing procedure is fully computerized, let us say. No person instructed the computer to send me the bill. However, some persons once programmed the computer, informed the computer of my charge account and informed it of my purchases. The Bay's sending me the bill was subsequent to these actions of its employees, but despite appearances, was it constituted by these actions of its employees? Let us make the case more difficult. Suppose the company once decided to forgive a certain proportion of the customers' debts. The computer was programed and fitted with a randomizer with the result that bills are sent to customers selected at random.[13] In this case, it appears that the employees' earlier actions cannot plausibly be supposed to have been sufficient, even under the circumstances, for the company's billing me. Thus, the company's action was not constituted by actions of persons. However, I will claim that even in this case, despite appearances, the employees' actions were sufficient under the circumstances for the company's action. The programer's action of programing the computer to bill all and only customers whose names are selected by the randomizer, and the other employees' relevant actions, were sufficient for the company's billing me. That is, they were sufficient for this given that the computer's randomizer selected my name, that the computer was reliable, and so on. I think that even in this case the company's action is constituted by actions of its employees.

This case suggests some interesting issues. Is it possible for a computer or an automaton to perform an action? Is it possible for a computer to be a person? Is it possible for a computer which is not a person to perform an action? These issues would have to be considered in a full defense of my thesis.

These examples have suggested some possible problem areas for my thesis about collective action, but they have not shown that the thesis needs to be modified. I hypothesize not only that all collective actions are constituted by actions of persons, but also that all secondary actions of an agent are constituted by actions of other agents. If an action is correctly attributable to one agent on the basis of actions of other agents, then the action of the first agent is constituted by these actions of these other agents. Consider a secondary action performed by a person, such as in the property purchasing case discussed above. In this example, it could be shown that Jones' purchasing the building was constituted by his attorney's signing the appropriate documents.

Primary actions of persons are at the foundation of all secondary actions. All actions of collectives are constituted by actions of persons. These are either primary or secondary actions. If they are secondary actions, they in turn are constituted by actions of other agents which again may either be primary or secondary actions. In the end, following this procedure, we will find a foundation of primary actions, and these must be actions of persons, for any action of a collective is of course a secondary action. That is, if we assume the truth of the above hypotheses, then, since the constitution relation is transitive, we must suppose that all secondary actions are constituted by primary actions of persons.

IV. Primary Actions, Level Generation and the Constitution Relation

Primary actions of an agent differ from secondary actions in that they are not constituted by actions of *other* agents. It has been thought by a number of philosophers, however, that any primary action of an agent either is, or stands in some "nice" relation to, a "basic action" of that agent. (See Danto, [2] and [3]). Alvin Goldman proposes a systematic

[12] The distinction between sentential conjunction and phrasal conjunction would be appealed to in explaining this. See Massey [14], p. 94.

[13] This complication was suggested by the referee for this journal.

theory of the relation between an agent's primary and basic actions. On his view, all primary actions are "level generated" by basic actions. He proposes an account of basic actions and a definition of the relation of level generation.[14]

It could be shown that if all primary actions are, or are level generated by basic actions, then all primary actions are, or are constituted by basic actions. The constitution relation is a generalization of the relation of level generation. Not every pair of actions related by the constitution relation is related by level generation. This is because, trivially, if A_1 level generates A_2 then A_1 and A_2 are actions of the *same agent*. More important, as the computer billing example shows, it is possible for one action to be constituted by other actions even if it occurred subsequently to those actions. But it is a necessary condition of one action being level generated by another that neither action be subsequent to the other ([9], p. 43). Therefore, one action may constitute another which does not level generate it. But, it could be shown, if one action generates another then it constitutes the other. If this is right, and if all primary actions are generated by basic actions, then all such actions are constituted by basic actions.

The result is that, on several hypotheses, basic actions are the foundation of all action. Any non-basic action is constituted by basic actions. The relevant hypotheses are that there are basic actions, that the actions of collectives are constituted by actions of persons, that all secondary actions are constituted by primary actions of persons, and that any primary action either is or is constituted by basic actions. If these claims are correct, then we can state a systematic theory of action in terms of the constitution relation.

V. The Constitution Relation and Moral Philosophy

These results have important implications for certain areas of moral philosophy, and in particular, for studies of the moral agency of collectives. I have argued that a necessary condition of a collective's performing an action is that some person or persons perform an action or actions which constitute the collective's action. In this sense, the actions of collectives are constituted by actions of persons, and a collective is not a self-sufficient agent. Not being a self-sufficient agent, moreover, it follows that a collective is not a self-sufficient *moral* agent. That is, simply, the actions of a collective cannot accord, or fail to accord, with the requirements of morality unless some person performs an action which constitutes the collective's doing so.

It should not be assumed, however, that "moral attributes" simply transfer across the constitution relation. It should not be assumed, for example, that if a collective is blameworthy for something it has done, where its doing this was constituted by a given action of an individual, then that individual is blameworthy for this given action. More generally, as I shall try briefly to illustrate, it is not the case, if S_1's doing A_1 is constituted by S_2's doing A_2, that if S_1 is blameworthy for A_1, S_2 is blameworthy for A_2. Moreover, it is not the case, if S_2's doing A_2 would constitute S_1's doing A_1, that if S_1 has an overriding moral obligation to do A_1, then S_2 has an overriding obligation to do A_2. This is because, where S_1 and S_2 are different agents, S_2 may be in a more complicated moral position than is S_1.

It appears that where a primary action of a person is constituted by another action he performs, moral attributes may transfer across the constitution relation, but perhaps only in one direction. For example, if S's doing A is constituted by S's doing B, then if S is blameworthy for A, S is blameworthy for B. But it is not in general true that if S is blameworthy for B, S is blameworthy for A. Suppose that I am blameworthy for giving a superstitious Smith a two dollar bill, and suppose my doing so constitutes my paying Smith the two dollars I owe him, still I need not be blameworthy for repaying Smith (see Goldman [9], p. 4).

Where a secondary action of one agent is constituted by an action of another agent, moral attributes may not transfer because one of the agents may be in a more complicated moral position than is the other. Suppose that Jones is blameworthy for suing his elderly poverty-stricken uncle, and suppose his doing so was constituted by his lawyer's suing the uncle for him. Still, it need not be the case that the lawyer is blameworthy for what he did. The lawyer may have had a contract he was bound to honour. The lawyer may have had excuses not available to Jones. It is possible, for these reasons, that the lawyer is not blameworthy even though his actions constituted Jones' suing his uncle and even though Jones is blameworthy for this. Similar cases show that it is possible for a collective to be blameworthy

[14] Goldman [9], pp. 20–48, 63–72. Goldman holds all actions either to be or to be generated by basic actions, but he does not consider that there might be secondary actions (pp. 45–46, but see p. 226).

for doing something even though the person whose action constituted the collective's action is not blameworthy for what he did. Suppose it is a corporation which wrongfully sues Jones' uncle. It is also possible for a collective to have an overriding obligation to do something even though an individual, an action of whose would constitute the collective's fulfilling its obligation, does not have an overriding obligation to perform that action.

However, this does not show that nothing at all follows about the moral positions of persons from facts about the moral responsibility borne by, and the moral obligations had by collectives. In this paper, I have attempted to state and support an important premise in an argument I have used elsewhere to show the implications of collective responsibility and collective obligations for individuals.[15] This is the claim that the actions of collectives are constituted by actions of persons.[16]

Simon Fraser University

Received March 28, 1978

REFERENCES

[1] G. E. M. Anscombe, *Intention* (Ithaca, N.Y., 1969).

[2] Arthur Danto, "Basic Actions," *American Philosophical Quarterly*, vol. 2 (1965), pp. 141–148.

[3] Arthur Danto, "What We Can Do," *The Journal of Philosophy*, vol. 60 (1963), pp. 435–445.

[4] Donald Davidson, "Actions, Reasons and Causes," *The Journal of Philosophy*, vol. 60 (1963), pp. 685–700.

[5] Donald Davidson, "Agency," in Robert Binkley, *et al* (eds.), *Agent, Action and Reason* (Toronto, 1971), pp. 3–25.

[6] Donald Davidson, "Causal Relations," *The Journal of Philosophy*, vol. 64 (1967), pp. 691–703.

[7] Donald Davidson, "The Individuation of Events," in N. Rescher, *et al* (eds.), *Essays in Honor of Carl G. Hempel* (Dordrecht, 1969), pp. 216–234.

[8] Joel Feinberg, "Collective Responsibility," in his *Doing and Deserving* (Princeton, 1970), pp. 222–251.

[9] Alvin J. Goldman, *A Theory of Human Action* (Englewood Cliffs, N.J., 1970).

[10] Hans Kelsen, *General Theory of Law and State* (Cambridge, Mass., 1945).

[11] David Lewis, *Counterfactuals* (Cambridge, Mass., 1973).

[12] J. L. Mackie, "Causes and Conditions," *American Philosophical Quarterly*, vol. 2 (1965), pp. 245–264.

[13] Joseph Margolis, "War and Ideology," in Virginia Held, Sidney Morgenbesser and Thomas Nagel (eds.), *Philosophy, Morality and International Affairs* (London, 1974), pp. 246–265.

[14] Gerald J. Massey, "Tom, Dick, Harry, and All The King's Men," *American Philosophical Quarterly*, vol. 13 (1976), pp. 89–107.

[15] In "Individuals, Collectives and Moral Agency," my unpublished Ph.D. thesis (Cornell University, 1976).

[16] I would like to thank Richard Boyd, Steven Davis, Raymond Jennings, Nollaig MacKenzie, David Lyons, Lennart Nordenfelt, Nicholas Sturgeon and the referee for this journal for their helpful suggestions and comments.

American Philosophical Quarterly
Volume 16, Number 3, July 1979

V. THE CORPORATION AS A MORAL PERSON

PETER A. FRENCH

I

In one of his *New York Times* columns of not too long ago Tom Wicker's ire was aroused by a Gulf Oil Corporation advertisement that "pointed the finger of blame" for the energy crisis at all elements of our society (and supposedly away from the oil company). Wicker attacked Gulf Oil as the major, if not the sole, perpetrator of that crisis and virtually every other social ill, with the possible exception of venereal disease. It does not matter whether Wicker was serious or sarcastic in making his charges (I suspect he was in deadly earnest). I am interested in the sense ascriptions of moral responsibility make when their subjects are corporations. I hope to provide the foundation of a theory that allows treatment of corporations as members of the moral community, of equal standing with the traditionally acknowledged residents: biological human beings, and hence treats Wicker-type responsibility ascriptions as unexceptionable instances of a perfectly proper sort without having to paraphrase them. In short, corporations can be full-fledged moral persons and have whatever privileges, rights and duties as are, in the normal course of affairs, accorded to moral persons.

II

It is important to distinguish three quite different notions of what constitutes personhood that are entangled in our tradition: the metaphysical, moral and legal concepts. The entanglement is clearly evident in Locke's account of personal identity. He writes that the term "person" is "a *forensic* term, appropriating actions and their merit; and so belongs only to *intelligent agents*, capable of law, and happiness, and misery."[1] He goes on to say that by consciousness and memory persons are capable of extending themselves into the past and thereby become "concerned and *accountable*."[2] Locke is historically correct in citing the law as a primary origin of the term "person." But he is incorrect in maintaining that its legal usage somehow entails its metaphysical sense, agency; and whether or not either sense, but especially the metaphysical, is interdependent on the moral sense, accountability, is surely controversial. Regarding the relationship between metaphysical and moral persons there are two distinct schools of thought. According to one, to be a metaphysical person is to be a moral one; to understand what it is to be accountable one must understand what it is to be an intelligent or a rational agent and vice-versa; while according to the other, being an agent is a necessary but not sufficient condition of being a moral person. Locke holds the interdependence view with which I agree, but he roots both moral and metaphysical persons in the juristic person, which is, I think, wrongheaded. The preponderance of current thinking tends to some version of the necessary pre-condition view, but it does have the virtue of treating the legal person as something apart.

It is of note that many contemporary moral philosophers and economists both take a pre-condition view of the relationship between the metaphysical and moral person and also adopt a particular view of the legal personhood of corporations that effectually excludes corporations *per se* from the class of moral persons. Such philosophers and economists champion the least defensible of a number of possible interpretations of the juristic personhood of corporations, but their doing so allows them to systematically sidestep the question of whether corporations can meet the conditions of metaphysical personhood.[3]

III

John Rawls is, to some extent, guilty of fortifying what I hope to show is an indefensible interpretation of the legal concept and of thereby encouraging an

[1] John Locke. *An Essay Concerning Human Understanding* (1960), Bk. II, Ch. XXVII.
[2] *Ibid.*
[3] For a particularly flagrant example see: Michael Jensen and William Meckling, "Theory of the Firm: Managerial Behavior, Agency Costs and Ownership Structure," *Journal of Financial Economics*, vol. 3 (1976), pp. 305–360. On p. 311 they write, "The private corporation or firm is simply one form of legal fiction which serves as a nexus for contracting relationships . . ."

anthropocentric bias that has led to the general belief that corporations just cannot be moral persons. As is well known, Rawls defends his two principles of justice by the use of a thought experiment that incorporates the essential characteristics of what he takes to be a pre-moral, though metaphysical population and then "derives" the moral guidelines for social institutions that they would accept. The persons (or parties) in the "original position" are described by Rawls as being mutually self-interested, rational, as having similar wants, needs, interests and capacities and as being, for all intents and purposes, equal in power (so that no one of them can dominate the others). Their choice of the principles of justice is, as Dennett has pointed out,[4] a rather dramatic rendering of one version of the compelling (though I think unnecessarily complex) philosophical thesis that only out of metaphysical persons can moral ones evolve.

But Rawls is remarkably ambiguous (and admittedly so) regarding who or what may qualify as a metaphysical person. He admits into the category, in one sentence, not only biological human beings but "nations, provinces, business firms, churches, teams, and so on,"[5] then, perhaps because he does not want to tackle the demonstration of the rationality, etc., of those institutions and organizations, or because he is a captive of the traditional prejudice in favor of biological persons, in the next sentence he withdraws entry. "There is, perhaps, a certain logical priority to the case of human individuals: it may be possible to analyze the actions of so-called artificial persons as logical constructions of the actions of human persons . . ."[6] "Perhaps" is, of course, a rather large hedge behind which to hide; but it is, I suppose, of some significance that in *A Theory of Justice* when he is listing the nature of the parties in the "original position" he adds "c. associations (states, churches, or other corporate bodies)."[7] He does not, unhappily, discuss this entry on his list anywhere else in the book. Rawls has hold, I think, of an important intuition: that some associations of human beings should be treated as metaphysical persons capable on his account of becoming moral persons, in and of themselves. He has, however, shrunk from the task of exploring the implications of that intuition and has instead retreated to the comfortable bulwarks of the anthropocentric bias.

IV

Many philosophers, including, I think, Rawls, have rather uncritically relied upon what they incorrectly perceive to be the most defensible juristic treatment of collectivities such as corporations as a paradigm for the treatment of corporations in their moral theories. The concept of corporate legal personhood under any of its popular interpretations is, I want to argue, virtually useless for moral purposes.

Following many writers on jurisprudence, a juristic person may be defined as any entity that is a subject of a right. There are good etymological grounds for such an inclusive neutral definition. The Latin "*persona*" originally referred to *dramatis personae*, and in Roman law the term was adopted to refer to anything that could act on either side of a legal dispute. [It was not until Boethius' definition of a person: "*Persona est naturae rationabilis individua substantia* (a person is the individual subsistence of a rational nature)" that metaphysical traits were ascribed to persons.] In effect, in Roman legal tradition persons are creations, artifacts, of the law itself, i.e., of the legislature that enacts the law, and are not considered to have, or only have incidentally, existence of any kind outside of the legal sphere. The law, on the Roman interpretation, is systematically ignorant of the biological status of its subjects.

The Roman notion applied to corporations is popularly known as the Fiction Theory. Hallis characterizes that theory as maintaining that "the personality of a corporate body is a pure fiction and owes its existence to a creative act of the state."[8] Rawls' view of corporate persons could not, however, be motivated by adherence to the Fiction Theory for two reasons. The theory does not demand a dichotomy between real and artificial persons. All juristic persons, on the theory, are creations of the law. The theory does not view the law as recognizing or verifying some pre-legally existing persons; it argues that the law creates its own subjects. Secondly, the theory, in its pure form at least, does not regard any juristic persons as composites. All things which

[4] Daniel Dennett, "Conditions of Personhood" in *The Identities of Persons* ed. by A. O. Rorty (Berkeley, 1976), pp. 175–196.
[5] John Rawls, "Justice as Reciprocity," in *John Stuart Mill, Utilitarianism*, ed. by Samuel Gorovitz (Indianapolis, 1971), pp. 244–245.
[6] *Ibid.*
[7] John Rawls, *A Theory of Justice* (Cambridge, 1971), p. 146.
[8] Frederick Hallis, *Corporate Personality* (Oxford, 1930), p. xlii.

are legislatively created as subjects of rights are non-reducible or, if you will, primitive individual legal persons. (It is of some note that the Fiction Theory is enshrined in English law in regard to corporate bodies by no less an authority than Sir Edward Coke who wrote that corporations "rest only in intendment and consideration of the law."[9])

The Fiction Theory's major rival in American jurisprudence and the view that does seem to inform Rawls' account is what I shall call "the Legal Aggregate Theory of the Corporation." It holds that the names of corporate bodies are only umbrellas that cover (but do not shield) certain biological persons. The Aggregate Theory treats biological status as having legal priority and corporate existence as a contrivance for purposes of summary reference. (Generally, it may be worth mention, Aggregate Theorists tend to ignore employees and identify corporations with directors, executives and stockholders. The model on which they stake their claim is no doubt that of the primitive partnership.) I have shown elsewhere[10] that to treat a corporation as an aggregate for any purposes is to fail to recognize the key logical differences between corporations and mobs. The Aggregate Theory, then, despite the fact that it has been quite popular in legislatures, courtrooms, and on streetcorners simply ignores key logical, socio-economic and historical facts of corporate existence. [It might prove of some value in clarifying the dispute between Fiction and Aggregate theorists to mention a rather famous case in the English law. (The case is cited by Hallis.) It is that of *Continental Tyre and Rubber Co., Ltd.* vs *Daimler Co. Ltd.* Very sketchily, the Continental Tyre company was incorporated in England and carried on its business there. Its business was the selling of tires made in Germany, and all of its directors were German subjects in residence in Germany, and all but one of its shares were held by German subjects. The case arose during the First World War, and it turned on the issue of whether the company was an English subject by virtue of its being incorporated under the English law and independent of its directors and stockholders, and could hence bring suit in an English court against an English subject while a state of war existed. The majority opinion of The Court of Appeals (5–1) was that the corporation was an entity created by statute and hence was "a different person altogether from the subscribers to the memorandum or the shareholders on the register."[11] Hallis aptly summarizes the judgment of the court when he writes that "The Continental Tyre and Rubber Co., Ltd., was an English company with a personality at law distinct from the personalities of its members and could therefore sue in the English Courts as a British Subject."[12] The House of Lords, however, supporting the Aggregate Theory and no doubt motivated by the demands of the War, overturned the Court of Appeals. Lord Buckley wrote "The artificial legal entity has no independent power of motion. It is moved by the corporator. . . . He is German in fact although British in form."[13] This view has seen many incarnations since on both sides of the Atlantic. I take Rawls' burying of his intuition in the logical priority of human beings as a recent echoing of the words of Lord Parker who in the Continental Tyre case wrote for the majority in the House of Lords: ". . . the character in which the property is held and the character in which the capacity to act is enjoyed and acts are done are not *in pari materia*. The latter character is a quality of the company itself, and conditions its capacities and its acts and is attributable only to human beings . . ."][14]

In Germanic legal tradition resides the third major rival interpretation of corporate juristic personhood. Due primarily to the advocacy of Otto von Gierke, the so-called Reality Theory recognizes corporations to be pre-legal existing sociological persons. Underlying the theory is the view that law cannot create its subjects, it only determines which societal facts are in conformity with its requirements. At most, law endorses the pre-legal existence of persons for its own purposes. Gierke regards the corporation as an offspring of certain social actions having then a *de facto* personality, which the law only declares to be a juridical fact.[15] The Reality Theory's primary virtue is that it does not ignore the non-legal roots of the corporation while it, as does the Fiction Theory, acknowledges the non-identity of the corporation and the aggregate of its directors, stockholders, executives and employees.

[9] 10 *Co. Rep.* 253, see Hallis, p. xlii.
[10] "Types of Collectivities and Blame," *The Personalist*, vol. 56 (1975), pp. 160–169. and in the first chapter of my *Foundations of Corporate Responsibility* (forthcoming).
[11] "Continental Tyre and Rubber Co., Ltd. vs. Daimler Co., Ltd." (1915). K.B., p. 893.
[12] Hallis, p. xlix.
[13] "Continental Tyre and Rubber Co., Ltd. vs. Daimler Co., Ltd." (1915), K.B., p. 918.
[14] (1916), 2 A.C., p. 340.
[15] See in particular Otto von Gierke, *Die Genossenschaftstheorie* (Berlin, 1887).

The primary difference between the Fiction and Reality Theories, that one treats the corporate person as *de jure* and the other as *de facto*, however, turns out to be of no real importance in regard to the issue of the moral personhood of a corporation. Admittedly the Reality Theory encapsulates a view at least superficially more amenable to arguing for discrete corporate moral personhood than does the Fiction Theory just because it does acknowledge *de facto* personhood, but theorists on both sides will admit that they are providing interpretations of only the formula "juristic person = the subject of rights," and as long as we stick to legal history, no interpretation of that formula need concern itself with metaphysical personhood or agency. The *de facto* personhood of the Reality Theory is that of a sociological entity only, of which no claim is or need be made regarding agency or rationality etc. One could, without contradiction, hold the Reality Theory and deny the metaphysical or moral personhood of corporations. What is needed is a Reality Theory that identifies a *de facto* metaphysical person not just a sociological entity.

Underlying all of these interpretations of corporate legal personhood is a distinction, embedded in the law itself, that renders them unhelpful for our purposes. Being a subject of rights is often contrasted in the law with being an "administrator of rights." Any number of entities and associations can and have been the subjects of legal rights. Legislatures have given rights to unborn human beings, they have reserved rights for human beings long after their death, and in some recent cases they have invested rights in generations of the future.[16] Of course such subjects of rights, though they are legal persons, cannot dispose of their rights, cannot administer them, because to administer a right one must be an agent, i.e., able to act in certain ways. It may be only an historical accident that most legal cases are cases in which "the subject of right X" and "the administrator of right X" are co-referential. It is nowhere required by law, under any of the three above theories or elsewhere, that it be so. Yet, it is possession of the attributes of an administrator of rights and not those of a subject of rights that are among the generally regarded conditions of moral personhood. It is a fundamental mistake to regard the fact of juristic corporate personhood as having settled the question of the moral personhood of a corporation one way or the other.

V

Two helpful lessons however, are learned from an investigation of the legal personhood of corporations: (1) biological existence is not essentially associated with the concept of a person (only the fallacious Aggregate Theory depends upon reduction to biological referents) and (2) a paradigm for the form of an inclusive neutral definition of a moral person is provided: "a subject of a right." I shall define a moral person as the referent of any proper name or description that can be a non-eliminatable subject of what I shall call (and presently discuss) a responsibility ascription of the second type. The non-eliminatable nature of the subject should be stressed because responsibility and other moral predicates are neutral as regards person and person-sum predication.[17] Though we might say that The Ox-Bow mob should be held responsible for the death of three men, a mob is an example of what I have elsewhere called an aggregate collectivity with no identity over and above that of the sum of the identities of its component membership, and hence to use "The Ox-Bow mob" as the subject of such ascriptions is to make summary reference to each member of the mob. For that reason mobs do not qualify as metaphysical or moral persons.

VI

There are at least two significantly different types of responsibility ascriptions that should be distinguished in ordinary usage (not counting the lauditory recommendation, "He is a responsible lad.") The first-type pins responsibility on someone or something, the who-dun-it or what-dun-it sense. Austin has pointed out that it is usually used when an event or action is thought by the speaker to be untoward. (Perhaps we are more interested in the failures rather than the successes that punctuate our lives.)

The second-type of responsibility ascription, parasitic upon the first, involves the notion of accountability. "Having a responsibility" is interwoven with the notion "Having a liability to answer," and having such a liability or obligation seems to imply (as Anscombe has noted[18]) the existence of some sort of authority relationship either between people or between people and a deity or in some weaker versions between people and social norms. The kernel of insight that I find

[16] And, of course, in earlier times animals have been given legal rights.

[17] See Gerald Massey, "Tom, Dick, and Harry, and All The King's Men," *American Philosophical Quarterly*, vol. 13 (1976), pp. 89–108.

[18] G. E. M. Anscombe, "Modern Moral Philosophy," *Philosophy*, vol. 33 (1958), pp. 1–19.

intuitively compelling, is that for someone to legitimately hold someone else responsible for some event there must exist or have existed a responsibility relationship between them such that in regard to the event in question the latter was answerable to the former. In other words, "*X* is responsible for *y*," as a second-type ascription, is properly uttered by someone *Z* if *X* in respect to *y* is or was accountable to *Z*. Responsibility relationships are created in a multitude of ways, e.g., through promises, contracts, compacts, hirings, assignments, appointments, by agreeing to enter a Rawlsian original position, etc. The right to hold responsible is often delegatable to third parties; though in the case of moral responsibility no delegation occurs because no person is excluded from the relationship: moral responsibility relationships hold reciprocally and without prior agreements among all moral persons. No special arrangement needs to be established between parties for anyone to hold someone morally responsible for his acts or, what amounts to the same thing, every person is a party to a responsibility relationship with all other persons as regards the doing or refraining from doing of certain acts: those that take descriptions that use moral notions.

Because our interest is in the criteria of moral personhood and not the content of morality we need not pursue this idea further. What I have maintained is that moral responsibility, although it is neither contractual nor optional, is not a class apart but an extension of ordinary, garden-variety, responsibility. What is needed in regard to the present subject then is an account of the requirements for entry into any responsibility relationship, and we have already seen that the notion of the juristic person does not provide a sufficient account. For example, the deceased in a probate case cannot be held responsible in the relevant way by anyone, even though the deceased is a juristic person, a subject of rights.

VII

A responsibility ascription of the second type amounts to the assertion of a conjunctive proposition, the first conjunct of which identifies the subject's actions with or as the cause of an event (usually an untoward one) and the second conjunct asserts that the action in question was intended by the subject or that the event was the direct result of an intentional act of the subject. In addition to what it asserts it implies that the subject is accountable to the speaker (in the case at hand) because of the subject's relationship to the speaker (who the speaker is or what the speaker is, a member of the "moral community," a surrogate for that aggregate). The primary focus of responsibility ascriptions of the second type is on the subject's intentions rather than, though not to the exclusion of, occasions. Austin wrote: "In considering responsibility, few things are considered more important than to establish whether a man *intended* to do A, or whether he did A intentionally."[19] To be the subject of a responsibility ascription of the second type, to be a party in responsibility relationships, hence to be a moral person, the subject must be at minimum, what I shall call a Davidsonian agent.[20] If corporations are moral persons, they will be non-eliminatable Davidsonian agents.

VIII

For a corporation to be treated as a Davidsonian agent it must be the case that some things that happen, some events, are describable in a way that makes certain sentences true, sentences that say that some of the things a corporation does were intended by the corporation itself. That is not accomplished if attributing intentions to a corporation is only a shorthand way of attributing intentions to the biological persons who comprise e.g. its board of directors. If that were to turn out to be the case then on metaphysical if not logical grounds there would be no way to distinguish between corporations and mobs. I shall argue, however, that a *C*orporation's *I*nternal *D*ecision Structure (its CID Structure) is the requisite redescription device that licenses the predication of corporate intentionality.

Intentionality, though a causal notion, is an intensional one and so it does not mark out a class of actions or events. Attributions of intentionality in regard to any event are referentially opaque with respect to other descriptions of that event, or, in other words, the fact that, given one description, an action was intentional does not entail that on every other description of the action it was intentional. A great deal depends upon what aspect of an event is being described. We can correctly say, e.g., "Hamlet intentionally kills the person hiding in Gertrude's room (one of Davidson's examples), but Hamlet does not intentionally kill Polonius," although "Polonius" and "the person hiding in Gertrude's room" are co-referential. The event may be properly

[19] J. L. Austin, "Three Ways of Spilling Ink" in *Philosophical Papers* (Oxford, 1970), p. 273.
[20] See for example Donald Davidson, "Agency," in *Agent, Action, and Reason*, ed. by Binkley, Bronaugh, and Marras (Toronto, 1971).

described as "Hamlet killed Polonius" and also as "Hamlet intentionally killed the person hiding in Gertrude's room (behind the arras)," but not as "Hamlet intentionally killed Polonius," for that was not Hamlet's intention. (He, in fact, thought he was killing the King.) The referential opacity of intentionality attributions, I shall presently argue, is congenial to the driving of a wedge between the descriptions of certain events as individual intentional actions and as corporate intentional actions.

Certain events, that is, actions, are describable as simply the bodily movements of human beings and sometimes those same events are redescribable in terms of their upshots, as bringing about something, e.g., (from Austin[21]) feeding penguins *by* throwing them peanuts ("by" is the most common way we connect different descriptions of the same event[22]), and sometimes those events can be redescribed as the effects of some prior cause; then they are described as done for reasons, done in order to bring about something, e.g., feeding the penguins peanuts in order to kill them. Usually what we single out as that prior cause is some desire or felt need combined with the belief that the object of the desire will be achieved by the action undertaken. (This, I think, is what Aristotle meant when he maintained that acting requires desire.) Saying "someone (X) did y intentionally" is to describe an event (y) as the upshot of X's having had a reason for doing it which was the cause of his doing it.

It is obvious that a corporation's doing something involves or includes human beings doing things and that the human beings who occupy various positions in a corporation usually can be described as having reasons for *their* behavior. In virtue of those descriptions they may be properly held responsible for their behavior, *ceteris paribus*. What needs to be shown is that there is sense in saying that corporations and not just the people who work in them, have reasons for doing what they do. Typically, we will be told that it is the directors, or the managers, etc., that really have the corporate reasons and desires, etc., and that although corporate actions may not be reducible without remainder, corporate intentions are always reducible to human intentions.

IX

Every corporation has an internal decision structure. CID Structures have two elements of interest to us here: (1) an organizational or responsibility flow chart that delineates stations and levels within the corporate power structure and (2) corporate decision recognition rule(s) (usually embedded in something called "corporation policy"). The CID Structure is the personnel organization for the exercise of the corporation's power with respect to its ventures, and as such its primary function is to draw experience from various levels of the corporation into a decision-making and ratification process. When operative and properly activated, the CID Structure accomplishes a subordination and synthesis of the intentions and acts of various biological persons into a corporate decision. When viewed in another way, as already suggested, the CID Structure licenses the descriptive transformation of events, seen under another aspect as the acts of biological persons (those who occupy various stations on the organizational chart), to corporate acts by exposing the corporate character of those events. A functioning CID Structure *incorporates* acts of biological persons. For illustrative purposes, suppose we imagine that an event E has at least two aspects, that is, can be described in two non-identical ways. One of those aspects is "Executive X's doing y" and one is "Corporation C's doing z." The corporate act and the individual act may have different properties; indeed they have different causal ancestors though they are causally inseparable. (The causal inseparability of these acts I hope to show is a product of the CID Structure, X's doing y is not the cause of C's doing z nor is C's doing z the cause of X's doing y although if X's doing y causes event F then C's doing z causes F and *vice versa*.)

Although I doubt he is aware of the metaphysical reading that can be given to this process, J. K. Galbraith rather neatly captures what I have in mind when he writes in his recent popular book on the history of economics: "From [the] interpersonal exercise of power, the interaction . . . of the participants, comes the *personality* of the corporation."[23] I take Galbraith here to be quite literally correct, but it is important to spell out how a CID Structure works this "miracle."

In philosophy in recent years we have grown accustomed to the use of games as models for understanding institutional behavior. We all have some understanding of how rules in games make certain descriptions of events possible that would not be so if those rules were non-existent. The CID Structure

[21] Austin, p. 275.
[22] See Joel Feinberg, *Doing and Deserving* (Princeton, 1970), p. 134f.
[23] John Kenneth Galbraith, *The Age of Uncertainty* (Boston, 1971), p. 261.

of a corporation is a kind of constitutive rule (or rules) analogous to the game rules with which we are familiar. The organization chart of a corporation distinguishes "players" and clarifies their rank and the interwoven lines of responsibility within the corporation. An organizational chart tells us, for example, that anyone holding the title "Executive Vice President for Finance Administration" stands in a certain relationship to anyone holding the title "Director of Internal Audit" and to anyone holding the title "Treasurer," etc. In effect it expresses, or maps, the interdependent and dependent relationships, line and staff, that are involved in determinations of corporate decisions and actions. The organizational chart provides what might be called the grammar of corporate decision-making. What I shall call internal recognition rules provide its logic.

By "recognition rule(s)" I mean what Hart, in another context, calls "conclusive affirmative indication"[24] that a decision on an act has been made or performed for corporate reasons. Recognition rules are of two sorts. Partially embedded in the organizational chart are procedural recognitors: we see that decisions are to be reached collectively at certain levels and that they are to be ratified at higher levels (or at inner circles, if one prefers that Galbraithean model). A corporate decision is recognized internally, however, not only by the procedure of its making, but by the policy it instantiates. Hence every corporation creates an image (not to be confused with its public image) or a general policy, what G. C. Buzby of the Chilton Company has called the "basic belief of the corporation,"[25] that must inform its decisions for them to be properly described as being those of that corporation. "The moment policy is side-stepped or violated, it is no longer the policy of that company."[26]

Peter Drucker has seen the importance of the basic policy recognitors in the CID Structure (though he treats matters rather differently from the way I am recommending.) Drucker writes:

> Because the corporation is an institution it must have a basic policy. For it must subordinate individual ambitions and decisions to the *needs* of the corporation's welfare and survival. That means that it must have a set of principles and a rule of conduct which limit and direct individual actions and behavior . . .[27]

X

Suppose, for illustrative purposes, we activate a CID Structure in a corporation, Wicker's favorite, the Gulf Oil Corporation. Imagine that three executives *X*, *Y* and *Z* have the task of deciding whether or not Gulf Oil will join a world uranium cartel. *X*, *Y* and *Z* have before them an Everest of papers that have been prepared by lower echelon executives. Some of the papers will be purely factual reports, some will be contingency plans, some will be formulations of positions developed by various departments, some will outline financial considerations, some will be legal opinions and so on. In so far as these will all have been processed through Gulf's CID Structure system, the personal reasons, if any, individual executives may have had when writing their reports and recommendations in a specific way will have been diluted by the subordination of individual inputs to peer group input even before *X*, *Y* and *Z* review the matter. *X*, *Y* and *Z* take a vote. Their taking of a vote is authorized procedure in the Gulf CID Structure, which is to say that under these circumstances the vote of *X*, *Y* and *Z* can be redescribed as the corporation's making a decision: that is, the event "*XYZ* voting" may be redescribed to expose an aspect otherwise unrevealed, that is quite different from its other aspects e.g., from *X*'s voting in the affirmative. Redescriptive exposure of a procedurally corporate aspect of an event, however, is not to be confused with a description of an event that makes true a sentence that says that the corporation did something intentionally. But the CID Structure, as already suggested, also provides the grounds in its other type of recognitor for such an attribution of corporate intentionality. Simply, when the corporate act is consistent with, an instantiation or an implementation of established corporate policy, then it is proper to describe it as having been done for corporate reasons, as having been caused by a corporate desire coupled with a corporate belief and so, in other words, as corporate intentional.

An event may, under one of its aspects, be described as the conjunctive act "*X* did *a* (or as *X* intentionally did *a*) ε *Y* did *a* (or as *Y* intentionally did *a*) ε *Z* did *a* (or as *Z* intentionally did *a*)" (where $a =$ voted in the affirmative on the question of Gulf

[24] H. L. A. Hart, *The Concept of Law* (Oxford, 1961), Ch. VI.
[25] G. C. Buzby, "Policies—A Guide to What A Company Stands For," *Management Record*, vol. 24 (1962), p. 5ff.
[26] *Ibid.*
[27] Peter Drucker, *Concept of Corporation* (New York, 1964/1972), pp. 36-37.

Oil joining the cartel). Given the Gulf CID Structure, formulated in this instance as the conjunction of rules: when the occupants of positions *A*, *B* and *C* on the organizational chart unanimously vote to do something and if doing that something is consistent with, an instantiation or an implementation of general corporate policy and *ceteris paribus*, then the corporation has decided to do it for corporate reasons, the event is redescribable as "the Gulf Oil Corporation did *j* for corporate reasons *f*." (where *j* is "decided to join the cartel" and *f* is any reason (desire + belief) consistent with basic policy of Gulf Oil, e.g., increasing profits) or simply as "Gulf Oil Corporation intentionally did *j*." This is a rather technical way of saying that in these circumstances the executives voting is, given its CID Structure, also the corporation deciding to do something, and that regardless of the personal reasons the executives have for voting as they do and even if their reasons are inconsistent with established corporate policy or even if one of them has no reason at all for voting as he does, the corporation still has reasons for joining the cartel; that is, joining is consistent with the inviolate corporate general policies as encrusted in the precedent of previous corporate actions and its statements of purpose as recorded in its certificate of incorporation, annual reports, etc. The corporation's only method of achieving its desires or goals is the activation of the personnel who occupy its various positions. However, if *X* voted affirmatively purely for reasons of personal monetary gain (suppose he had been bribed to do so) that does not alter the fact that the corporate reason for joining the cartel was to minimize competition and hence pay higher dividends to its shareholders. Corporations have reasons because they have interests in doing those things that are likely to result in realization of their established corporate goals regardless of the transient self-interest of directors, managers, etc. If there is a difference between corporate goals and desires and those of human beings it is probably that the corporate ones are relatively stable and not very wide ranging, but that is only because corporations can do relatively fewer things than human beings, being confined in action predominately to a limited socio-economic sphere. The attribution of corporate intentionality is opaque with respect to other possible descriptions of the event in question. It is, of course, in a corporation's interest that its component membership view the corporate purposes as instrumental in the achievement of their own goals. (Financial reward is the most common way this is achieved.)

It will be objected that a corporation's policies reflect only the current goals of its directors. But that is certainly not logically necessary nor is it in practice true for most large corporations. Usually, of course, the original incorporators will have organized to further their individual interests and/or to meet goals which they shared. But even in infancy the melding of disparate interests and purposes gives rise to a corporate long range point of view that is distinct from the intents and purposes of the collection of incorporators viewed individually. Also, corporate basic purposes and policies, as already mentioned, tend to be relatively stable when compared to those of individuals and not couched in the kind of language that would be appropriate to individual purposes. Furthermore, as histories of corporations will show, when policies are amended or altered it is usually only peripheral issues that are involved. Radical policy alteration constitutes a new corporation, a point that is captured in the incorporation laws of such states as Delaware. ("Any power which is not enumerated in the charter and the general law or which cannot be inferred from these two sources is *ultra vires* of the corporation.") Obviously underlying the objection is an uneasiness about the fact that corporate intent is dependent upon policy and purpose that is but an artifact of the socio-psychology of a group of biological persons. Corporate intent seems somehow to be a tarnished illegitimate offspring of human intent. But this objection is another form of the anthropocentric bias. By concentrating on possible descriptions of events and by acknowledging only that the possibility of describing something as an agent depends upon whether or not it can be properly described as having done something (the description of some aspect of an event) for a reason, we avoid the temptation to look for extensional criteria that would necessitate reduction to human referents.

The CID Structure licenses redescriptions of events as corporate and attributions of corporate intentionality while it does not obscure the private acts of executives, directors etc. Although *X* voted to support the joining of the cartel because he was bribed to do so, *X* did not join the cartel, Gulf Oil Corporation joined the cartel. Consequently, we may say that *X* did something for which he should be held morally responsible, yet whether or not Gulf Oil Corporation should be held morally responsible for joining the cartel is a question that turns on issues that may be unrelated to *X*'s having accepted a bribe.

Of course Gulf Oil Corporation cannot join the

cartel unless X or somebody who occupies position A on the organizational chart votes in the affirmative. What that shows, however, is that corporations are collectivities. That should not, however, rule out the possibility of their having metaphysical status, as being Davidsonian agents, and being thereby full-fledged moral persons.

This much seems to me clear: we can describe many events in terms of certain physical movements of human beings and we also can sometimes describe those events as done for reasons by those human beings, but further we can sometimes describe those events as corporate and still further as done for corporate reasons that are qualitatively different from whatever personal reasons, if any, component members may have for doing what they do.

Corporate agency resides in the possibility of CID Structure licensed redescription of events as corporate intentional. That may still appear to be downright mysterious, although I do not think it is, for human agency as I have suggested, resides in the possibility of description as well.

Although further elaboration is needed, I hope I have said enough to make plausible the view that we have good reasons to acknowledge the non-eliminatable agency of corporations. I have maintained that Davidsonian agency is a necessary and sufficient condition of moral personhood. I cannot further argue that position here (I have done so elsewhere). On the basis of the foregoing analysis, however, I think that grounds have been provided for holding corporations *per se* to account for what they do, for treating them as metaphysical persons *qua* moral persons.[28]

University of Minnesota

Received May 16, 1978

[28] This paper owes much to discussions and comments made by J. L. Mackie, Donald Davidson and Howard K. Wettstein. An earlier version was read at a conference on "Ethics and Economics" at the University of Delaware. I also acknowledge the funding of the University of Minnesota Graduate School that supports the project of which this is a part.

American Philosophical Quarterly
Volume 17, Number 1, January 1980

V. ARE ANIMALS MORAL BEINGS?

S. F. SAPONTZIS

BY "moral being" I mean any being which meets both of the following conditions: it is capable of acting morally, and it merits moral rights, i.e., the rights to life, dignity, and a fulfilling life. Therefore, this paper is concerned with two questions: (I) are animals other than human beings (henceforth simply "animals") capable of acting morally, and (II) what are the implications of the answer to the previous question for animal rights and human obligations to animals? Part I of what follows is devoted to answering the first of these questions, Part II to answering the second.

I

Animals do many things which would ordinarily be considered moral actions if they were done by human beings. Seeing eye dogs and guard dogs show considerable self-restraint and responsibility, and there are numerous accounts of other, untrained dogs acting courageously, loyally, and compassionately. There are also accounts of porpoises and dolphins risking their lives to save the lives not only of members of their own species but also of human beings. Members of many species of animals show extended parental concern and devotion to members of their families. Thus, if moral evaluation were confined to the behavioral level of describing what was done and determining whether it sufficiently resembles paradigm cases of courageous, kind, responsible, etc. behavior, then it would be clear that many animals are capable of moral action. At the behavioral level a dog's pulling a child to safety is no less a moral action than a human's doing the same thing.

Nevertheless, animals are not considered moral beings. Setting aside religious dogmas about creatures with souls vs. those without, being created in God's image, etc., the traditional arguments to show that animals are not capable of moral action concern the relation between reason and morality. Basically, all these arguments have the following form:

A-1 Only rational beings can be moral.
A-2 Animals are not rational.
A-3 Therefore, animals cannot be moral.

Such arguments entail that the courageous, kind, responsible, etc. actions of animals can only appear to be moral, as parrots and radios only appear to speak.

Since this argument obviously is valid, questions about its soundness must concern the truth of its premises. Three such questions come quickly to mind: (i) what does "rational" refer to; (ii) why is rationality necessary for morality; and (iii) do animals really lack the rationality necessary for morality? The remainder of Part I will be devoted to answering these three questions.

i

In everyday morality and traditional moral philosophy "rationality" refers to normal, adult, human intelligence (henceforth simply "normal intelligence"). When Plato, Aristotle, Kant, Mill, and other philosophers who subscribe to versions of the above argument discuss practical reason, their examples show it is the reason of normal, human adults they have in mind. Their examples almost always concern normal adults, seldom children or geniuses, and almost never the retarded, insane, senile, brain damaged, or animals. Their references to common moral sense are inevitably references to the sensibilities and sensitivities of normal adults. Similarly, in everyday moral practice animals, children, and the retarded, insane, senile, and brain damaged are generally considered amoral. Because they lack normal intelligence, their morally undesirable actions are generally not considered criminal or immoral but merely regrettable, unavoidable consequences of their not knowing better. If a normal, adult human were to act in the same way, however, he would be considered immoral, for it is presumed he knows better. Finally, although solving a particularly complex moral problem may require a particularly wise or thoughtful person, such as Solomon or Socrates, the correctness of the answer, once discovered, is supposed to be apparent to all people of common sense, i.e., to all normal, human adults. Thus, both traditional moral practice and philosophy indicate that premise A-1 asserts that only beings of normal intelligence can be moral.[1]

[1] Common moral practice does provide some challenges to this conclusion, most notably our treatment of teen-age delinquents. However, these practices do not show that there is something else besides or instead of normal intelligence to which "reason" refers.

ii

Arguments showing that reason is necessary for morality fall into two groups. The arguments in the first group take the following form:

B-1 An action is moral only if the agent recognizes it is the moral thing to do and does it because it is the moral thing to do.
B-2 Only rational beings are capable of such recognition and motivation.
B-3 Therefore, only rational beings can act morally.

In order to avoid confusion in discussing this and the following argument we must clearly distinguish two aspects of morality. "Moral$_n$" will refer to the moral value of an action which is independent of the agent's relation to the action. Fulfilling a promise, preventing a murder, aiding someone in distress, caring for a child, etc. have a certain moral value no matter what the agent's reasons for doing them or whether he is even aware that he is doing these things. Ordinarily, kindness and honesty are morally preferable to cruelty and dishonesty regardless of the agent's motives or understanding of the situation. It is to this agent-neutral moral value of actions that "moral$_n$" will refer. "Moral$_a$" will refer to the moral value of the agent's understanding of the action and his motive for doing it. Thus, while an honest act done to impress a friend has equal moral$_n$ value with an honest act done because it is honest, the moral$_a$ value of the second action is superior to the moral$_a$ value of the first action. Finally, "moral" can be used in the ordinary, inclusive sense to refer to the moral$_n$ plus moral$_a$ value of an action.

Using these definitions we can reformulate argument B in the following way to avoid the appearance of circularity in premise B-1:

B-1′ An action is moral$_a$ only if the agent recognizes its moral$_n$ value and does it because of its moral$_n$ value.
B-2 Only rational beings are capable of such recognition and motivation.
B-3′ Therefore, only rational beings can act morally$_a$.

Although this formulation has a different conclusion than the original, "morally$_a$" having been substituted for "morally," this is not important here. It was acknowledged above that the reason why animals cannot act morally, if they cannot, is not to be found at the behavioral or moral$_n$ level; so it is solely the moral$_a$ aspect of morality that concerns us as we ask whether animals can act morally.

The traditional justification for premise B-1′ relies on the common sensical contrast between intentional, sincere moral$_n$ actions and actions which only accidentally effect some moral$_n$ good or are produced by ulterior motives unconcerned with moral$_n$ good. For example, the person who wrestles a would-be hijacker to the floor in order to prevent a crime is acting morally$_a$, while the person who trips and accidentally knocks the hijacker down and the person who jumps the hijacker to get a reward are not acting morally$_a$.

The traditional justification for premise B-2 emphasizes that moral$_n$ principles are universal, disinterested, and impersonal or that determining what is moral$_n$ requires understanding the consequences of actions and calculating how they will affect the general welfare. In either case reason, rather than sensation, instinct, emotion, or feeling, is the faculty required for such recognition and, therefore, for acting morally$_a$.

Turning to the second group of arguments supporting the necessity of reason for morality, these take the following form:

C-1 Only beings which are free to choose what they will do can act morally$_a$.
C-2 Only rational beings are free to choose what they will do.
C-3 Therefore, only rational beings can act morally$_a$.

There are two traditional justifications for premise C-1. First, moral$_a$ actions are something the agent is responsible for, and only a free being can be responsible for its actions. For example, a coin machine which gives the correct change is not responsible for this, since it could not choose to do otherwise. The serviceman who can choose to do a poor or an effective job of maintaining the machine is the one who is responsible for its performance. Second, moral$_a$ action is a sensitive response to a complex situation, including antecedent conditions and future possibilities, while a determined action is a blind response to an immediate stimulus. Therefore, only free beings can recognize and respond to the morality$_n$ of a situation. For example, a bird which

Normal intelligence is a condition which can be attained to different degrees and to varying degrees in different areas. While this make it difficult to determine whether someone is normal enough to be a normal adult, it does not refute the thesis that in everyday morality and traditional moral philosophy "reason" refers to normal intelligence.

tends its young only because they have a certain smell is not acting morally$_a$. Forced by instinct to respond to this morally$_n$ irrelevant part of the situation, the bird is not able to respond to the morally$_n$ relevant parts of the situation with a course of action chosen for its moral$_n$ value. Consequently, it is incapable of acting morally$_a$.

The traditional justification for premise C-2 is that only beings capable of "standing back" from the course of nature to reflect on it are free. Only reflective beings can develop concepts of how nature works and can be controlled. Therefore, only reflective beings are free, since being able to initiate action is at least a necessary condition for freedom and since "initiating action" means basing one's actions on his concepts of his environment and his relation to it.

Since both of these arguments obviously are valid, if there is any fault in them it must again lie in the truth of their premises. In each argument the first premise asserts a common sensical, necessary condition for moral$_a$ action, and the second premise claims that that necessary condition can be met only by beings of normal intelligence. Since animals lack normal intelligence, these arguments could be shown unsound by showing that the actions of some animals meet the conditions stated in premises B-1′ and C-1. This can be done without too much difficulty. Additionally, it can be shown that everyday moral practice does not confirm the reasons given to support premises B-2 and C-2. Thus, the following discussion will show both that there are counterexamples to premises B-2 and C-2 and that the reasons traditionally given to support these premises are false.

The common sensical idea underlying argument B is that in a moral$_a$ action the moral$_n$ value of the action is the basic reason for doing it. What everyday moral practice requires of a moral$_a$ action is that it be based on a recognition of some moral$_n$ good to be accomplished and a sincere effort to accomplish that good.

The moral$_n$ actions of many animals meet this common sensical condition. When a dog pulls a child from a fire, it is not acting blindly, like an insect reacting to a chemical mating stimulus, nor does it seem to have ulterior motives. If anything, animals seem to be much less deceptive than humans; the sincerity of their compassionate, courageous, etc. actions is seldom, if ever, an issue. The only real issue here is whether animals recognize the moral$_n$ goods and evils of situations and respond to them or whether they simply react on the basis of instinct or reflex conditioning.

When instinct and reflex conditioning are mentioned we usually think of cases like salmon compulsively swimming upstream in mating season and Pavlov's dogs salivating at the sound of a bell. If an act of courage or compassion is stimulated in either of these ways, it lacks moral$_a$ value. However, an action can be instinctual or conditioned yet still be a response to moral$_n$ goods and evils. When we morally educate children we attempt to instill in them the habits of responding to danger courageously and to need compassionately. Similarly, maternal instincts are responses to the needs of the young. A wolf's care for its young is not mechanical nor carried out inflexibly, without regard to the actual needs of the young in particular situations. Such instinctual and conditioned behavior is not like that of an ant following a chemical path without any comprehension of how its behaviour contributes to the welfare of its community. Maternal instincts and moral$_n$ habits are responses to the moral$_n$ goods and evils of the situation and are directed to accomplishing that good or alleviating that evil. Therefore, actions based on such instincts and habits meet the common sensical requirement that moral$_a$ actions be based on a recognition of the moral$_n$ goods to be effected by the action and be motivated by that recognition.

Furthermore, not all moral$_n$ actions of animals can be accounted for by instinct or conditioning. The cases of porpoises helping drowning sailors must be spontaneous acts of kindness. There is no reason to believe porpoises have developed an instinct for saving humans, and they certainly have not been conditioned to perform such acts through training or repetition. Other examples are not as striking, but unless one is predisposed to think animals always act on instinct or reflex, there is at least no more reason to think that a pet dog pulling a drowning child from a swimming pool is acting instinctually or reflexively than to think that a human doing the same thing is acting instinctually or reflexively. So, to the conclusion that some instinctual and conditioned behavior satisfies the conditions of premise B-1′ we can add that there are some non-instinctual, non-reflexive cases where animals recognize and respond to the moral$_n$ goods and evils of situations.

The only remaining question concerning whether or not some animal behavior meets the conditions for moral$_a$ action set forth in premise B-1′ is whether an animal acting kindly, for instance, recognizes that kindness is a *moral$_n$* good. There are really two questions here, which we shall treat in turn: what is really morally$_n$ good, e.g., Christian or samurai values, and what is the nature of a moral$_n$ value, as opposed to pragmatic, aesthetic, etc. values?

Answering the question about what really is moral$_n$ is the traditional job of moral philosophers. However, in everyday morality being able to answer this question is not a necessary condition for acting morally$_a$. Someone who intentionally, sincerely acts to prevent a robbery would be considered to have acted morally$_a$ even if he does not know how to demonstrate that stopping the robbery was the morally$_n$ proper thing to do. Justifications are commonly required only when an action does not accord with accepted moral$_n$ norms. For instance, while everyday morality requires that anyone maintaining that a robbery is moral$_n$ must be able to demonstrate this, it requires no such justification of the morality$_n$ of stopping a robbery. Therefore, even though animals are incapable of demonstrating the morality$_n$ of their actions, their intentional and sincere kind, courageous, etc. actions can be moral$_a$ actions, for they accord with accepted moral$_n$ norms and, consequently, do not require justification to be moral$_a$.

Turning to the second question, it asks whether animals distinguish moral$_n$ values from other kinds of values. Drawing such a distinction is a difficult task; philosophers have argued over it for centuries, and most non-philosophers would not have the slightest idea how even to begin to draw it. It is again a concern of moral theory, not of everyday moral practice. For example, if someone intentionally and without ulterior motives risks his life to save someone else, his courageous act would be considered moral$_a$ without any further question about whether he is able to distinguish moral$_n$ values from other kinds of values. Again, as long as one's action accords with accepted moral$_n$ standards, one does not have to be able to answer this theoretical question in order to act morally$_a$. Therefore, even if animals do not know how to distinguish moral$_n$ values from other kinds of values, as long as their actions accord with accepted moral$_n$ standards this inability cannot discredit the moral$_a$ value of their intentional and sincere, kind, courageous, etc. actions.

If being able to answer the questions of moral theory was a criterion for acting morally$_a$, then there would be few moral$_a$ actions. However, this conclusion is not confirmed by everyday experience, which would be a Hobbesian state of nature dominated by a terrible sense of anxiety if there were few moral$_a$ actions. So, people do not have to be moral theorists in order to act morally$_a$. Since it would be unfair to require animals to meet stiffer criteria of moral$_a$ action than are required of humans, it follows that being able to answer philosophical questions about morality cannot be used as a criterion to show that animals cannot act morally$_a$.

Thus, premise B-2 is false, and argument B is unsound. However, before proceeding to argument C let us consider the justification traditionally offered for premise B-2. Moral philosophers who subscribe to argument B usually link recognizing moral$_n$ values to employing some fundamental moral principle or principles. For example, Kantians hold that in order to act morally$_a$ one must determine what is morally$_n$ correct by employing the categorical imperative. Utilitarians hold that only those who base their actions on the principle of utility can know what is morally$_n$ good and sincerely attempt to accomplish that good. Thus, moral philosophers take the common sensical idea that moral$_a$ actions must be based on a recognition of what is moral$_n$ and a sincere effort to be moral$_n$ and tie it to some abstract, controversial, philosophical theory about the fundamental principles of morality.

However, it is doubtful that there is any link between that common sensical idea and those philosophical theories. People like Job and Cephalus, who never employ the categorical imperative, the principle of utility, or other such abstract principles, can and do intentionally and sincerely perform acts of kindness, courage, honesty, fairness, etc. They may be acting on the basis of sentiment, intuition, religious belief, tradition, or some other non-philosophical basis, but the kindness, fairmindedness, etc. of their actions is neither accidental to their intent nor merely a means for attaining some non-moral$_n$ goal. Philosophers who hold that nonetheless there is still something morally$_a$ lacking in their acts confuse morality with moral theory and being moral with doing moral theory. Such confusion is probably due to the desire of these philosophers not merely to describe but also to reform or at least refine everyday moral practice. However, although abstract reasoning and principles are necessary for constructing moral theories and might even improve moral practice, everyday moral practice indicates that they are not necessary for intentional, sincere moral$_n$ action, i.e., for moral$_a$ action.

Whatever their other problems, intuitionist accounts of morality are successful at describing the way moral$_n$ values are commonly recognized and determined in everyday moral practice. Although in complex situations or in attempts to convince ourselves to do what is right we may turn to something like the categorical imperative or the principle of utility, in most situations we simply perceive or feel what is the moral$_n$ thing to do and, if we are moral$_a$, do it. If such actions do not count as $moral_a$ actions, which according to the justification given for premise B-2 they do not, then $moral_a$ actions are as rare as dragon's teeth. I believe this is sufficient to discredit the traditional justification for that premise. $Moral_a$ action does not require any of the kinds of reasoning on which moral philosophers believe moral practice should be based.

Thus, the compassionate, courageous, etc. actions of some animals meet the common sensical condition for $moral_a$ action asserted in argument B, and the justification for linking reason and $moral_a$ action in premise B-2 is faulty. Consequently, the argument that animals are incapable of $moral_a$ action because normal intelligence is required for recognizing $moral_n$ values and motivating $moral_a$ action is unsound.

Turning to argument C, it maintains that freedom is necessary for $morality_a$ and that only rational beings are free. According to the justification for premise C-1 freedom is necessary for $morality_a$ in order that fixing responsibility may be a sensible practice and that the agent may recognize and respond to complex situations. The second of these reasons pertains to the issue of $moral_n$ sensitivity vs. instincts and conditioning and, therefore, has already been discussed. Freedom vs. mechanical instincts and conditioning is not a dichotomy but a continuum, and many animals have instincts or dispositions which are sufficiently flexible and responsive to the $moral_n$ goods and evils of a situation to qualify them as $moral_a$ agents on this ground.

Turning to the other reason, if only free beings can be held responsible for their actions, everyday practice indicates some animals must be free, since they are commonly held responsible for many of their actions.[2] The common activity of housebreaking a dog, for example, presupposes that certain of a dog's activities are not entirely determined by instinct or canine nature and that praise and punishment can be non-arbitrarily meted out to dogs. Thus, dogs can be sensibly and fairly held responsible for certain of their actions. Similarly, when dealing with animals we distinguish free acts from accidents, compulsions, and acts based on misunderstanding or coercion. For example, a cat may freely choose to take a vitamin pill offered to it, have the pill forced down its throat, or take it unknowingly when it is hidden inside a meatball. Thus, in everyday practice certain animals are not treated like machines or natural phenomena which cannot sensibly be held responsible for what they do. These animals are treated as responsible beings free to choose what they will do. Therefore, since these animals lack normal intelligence, premise C-2 is false, and argument C is unsound.

As for the traditional justification for premise C-2, that only reflective beings can initiate action, since "reflective ability" here refers to having normal intelligence, that justification is clearly false. Many animals are capable of initiating action. They recognize and respond to complex situations, solve practical problems, adjust their behaviour to overcome obstacles to their endeavors, and so forth. For example, dogs learn, without being taught, to push open screen doors; deer find new paths around landslides; and wild chimpanzees use leaves to get at water they could not otherwise reach. Normal intelligence is needed to control and reconstruct nature, something animals do not do, but such reflective ability is not needed to be sufficiently free of the mechanical clutches of nature to initiate action.

Thus, both traditional arguments to show that only rational beings can act $morally_a$ fail. Many animals are sufficiently free and sensitive to the $moral_n$ goods and evils of situations to be moral beings. Nonetheless, there is still something about the courage, kindness, etc. of animals which distinguishes them in a $morally_a$ relevant way from the moral virtues of human beings. Although the traditional argument concerning freedom, reason, and $morality_a$ is a failure, it does incidentally indicate where this distinction lies: humans do, but animals do not, try to control and reconstruct things, including themselves.

iii

One of the defining characteristics of $morality_a$ is that $moral_a$ actions are dedicated to the fulfillment of an ideal way of life. It is because $morality_a$ requires dedication to an ideal that simply acting in accordance with $moral_n$ principles, even intentionally, is not sufficient to qualify one's actions as $moral_a$. Ulterior motives, e.g., fear of punishment or desire to impress one's friends, undermine the $moral_a$ value of one's honest, dutiful, etc. actions because such motives are felt to be demeaning, pedestrian, uninspired, and uninspiring. Such motives make honest, courageous,

[2] "Freedom" will be left undefined here, for it is not necessary to define it in order to refute argument C. That freedom, whatever it may be, is a necessary condition for responsibility, as is claimed in traditional justifications of premise C-1, provides a sufficient basis for showing that premise C-2 is false. Trying to avoid this problem by reformulating that justification in terms of some special kind of "moral responsibility" will not work. "Moral responsibility" does not refer to a special kind of responsibility but to being responsible in $moral_n$ matters in just the same way one may be responsible in economic or professional matters.

etc. acts means to mundane ends; however, to be $moral_a$ actions they must be motivated by the belief that such an action is part of what is required for a respectable, dignified, honorable, superior way of life.

Effectively pursuing ideals requires taking control of and reconstructing things, since ideals are conditions which will not naturally or effortlessly come to pass. These things include oneself, especially in morality. The literature of morality is dominated by stories, counsels, slogans, images, and other devices to inspire us to take control of those forces around and inside us which lead away from the moral ideal and either to suppress them or to redirect them in ways conducive to attaining the ideal moral life. Depth psychology, too, emphasizes that the formation of an ego ideal is an essential part of the development of a moral personality. Whether one is dedicated to a life of love or one of duty, a life dominated by the sentiments or by reason, as a moral being one has to screen the psychological and social forces which influence his actions and seek to remake society and his personality in a way which maximizes good and minimizes evil.

Animals do not try to control and reconstruct their world or themselves. Rather than trying to reconstruct their environment to better fulfill their needs, animals simply fit in with, adjust to, or get along with what they are given. Although they have social orders, there is no evidence they have social reformers. Although they can be trained and disciplined, they do not seem to engage in self-directed programs of training, discipline, or self-development. Although they are curious, they are not dedicated to increasing their knowledge or perfecting their methods of learning. This lack among animals of dedication and striving to fulfill ideals through control and reconstruction is the truth behind the old idea that while the human world is progressive, nature is repetitive. Although nature evolves, animals do not initiate change in an attempt to attain a better way of life.

Consequently, animals are not moral beings, in spite of their many admirable acts. They are not moral beings because these actions are not part of an attempt to fulfill an ideal way of life. The goods and evils they respond to are not so evaluated because of their relation to an ideal life, and their good deeds are responses to the situation at hand rather than part of a program of fulfilling an ideal. Adopting the following terminology will help to describe the situation here: kindness, courage, honesty, etc. are "virtues"; intentional, sincere acts of kindness, courage, etc. are "virtuous acts"; and "moral acts" are virtuous acts which are done as part of fulfilling an ideal way of life. Thus, many animals are virtuous, but none are moral.

If reason or normal intelligence is what is needed to project and dedicate oneself to ideals, then it will be correct to say that only rational beings can be moral beings. Thus, we can formulate the following argument to justify premise A-1, that only rational beings can be moral:

D-1 An action is moral only if the agent does it because he believes it will contribute to attaining an ideal way of life.

D-2 Only rational beings can project and dedicate themselves to ideal ways of life.

D-3 Therefore, only rational beings can be moral.

This argument seems to be sound. Although many animals possess sufficient reason, sensitivity, or intelligence to recognize virtues and to do virtuous deeds, they seem to lack the ability to lead a dedicated moral life. This is the truth underlying the contention in argument B that animals cannot recognize the morality of $moral_n$ values. While many of their actions are virtuous, animals are not moral beings because these actions are not part of a moral life.

II

As noted at the beginning, there are two conditions for being a moral being. So far we have discussed only the condition of being able to act morally. The other condition is being the object of moral respect or rights. According to this condition a moral being is one whose basic interests must be respected, a being with rights to life, dignity, and a fulfilling life, or a being who must be treated as an end and never as merely a means to satisfying the needs and desires of others. We may call this the condition of receiving moral respect, as the first condition is that of acting out of moral respect. Thus, a moral being must be both a moral agent and a moral recipient.

These two conditions are not independent. It is commonly maintained that it is because a being is capable of acting morally that it merits respect. According to Kant, for example, it is because rational beings are capable of acting morally, which is an end in itself, that they must be treated as ends in themselves.[3] Similarly, that animals are not capable of acting morally, while humans are, has traditionally been cited to justify treating animals, but not humans, merely as means to satisfying human needs and desires. Does the above analysis of why animals are

[3] *Foundations of the Metaphysics of Morals* (New York, 1959), pp. 46–47.

not capable of acting morally support this inference that they do not merit moral rights?

Any inference from having (or lacking) certain capabilities to meriting (or not meriting) rights encounters the "is"/"ought" problem. Having (lacking) the abilities necessary for acting morally is a factual condition; that one's life, dignity, and other basic interests must (need not) be respected is a prescription; and a prescription cannot be deduced from a description. However, let us set aside this difficulty by assuming that we are concerned to make the world the best place we can and that if beings acted morally that would do more than anything else to make the world a better place. In the context of that intention and that evaluation prescriptions can be deduced from descriptions concerning the ability to act morally.

Having set aside this general, logical problem we can consider the merits of the particular inference under discussion here. The peculiarity of the animals' condition is that although they act virtuously they cannot act morally. They do good deeds but they are not dedicated to doing better. This condition is not unlike that of being holy, as Kant understands this, or being kind-hearted. According to Kant, God is not a moral being because He does not have to be commanded to do good. Being purely rational He does not have to overcome the temptations or inertia of a sensuous nature and does good without conflict, strife, or effort. God always acts virtuously, but He is not striving to fulfill an ideal way of life and, therefore, is not a moral being.[4] Similarly, someone who is kind-hearted or otherwise disposed by temperament or sentiment to do good will act virtuously without striving to do so. Such a person treats others kindly not because he recognizes any imperative to do so, believes it his duty, or judges kindness to be part of a better way of life for humankind. He acts kindly because his immediate response to the needs of others is a feeling of sympathy and a desire to help them out. Thus, such spontaneous, sentiment-inspired acts are also virtuous but not moral, and in so far as someone is capable of such acts he is capable of acting virtuously but not morally.

Are the holy and the kind-hearted worthy of respect? God is certainly considered worthy of respect. Since God fulfills the ideal for which moral beings are striving, it would be strange, indeed, if He did not merit respect. God is, then, a being who merits respect even though He cannot act morally. Even as just a thought experiment the idea of the holy shows that it is conceptually possible for something not to be a moral agent yet still be a moral recipient. Even if being a moral agent is a sufficient condition for being a moral recipient, the case of the holy shows it is not a necessary condition.

The case of kind-hearted people is a bit more clouded, at least in the history of moral philosophy. The Kantian tradition holds that such people do not merit respect for their kind hearts. Such people just happen to do good; it is a fortunate accident that their inclination ordinarily accords with the dictates of reason.[5] However, common moral practice does not confirm this Kantian evaluation. Kind-hearted, generous, compassionate, etc. people are not commonly considered less worthy of respect than those who act virtuously out of a sense of duty. Indeed, they are considered more worthy; a sense of duty is commonly considered of secondary value, something which those who unfortunately lack virtuous dispositions must fall back on to do good. The loving parent, for example, is considered superior to the dutiful parent, and saints are not people who recognize obligations to their fellows but who love them. The person who wants to do the right or good thing is considered more estimable than the person who does not want to do it but does it out of a sense of duty. Finally, as the discussion of instincts and conditioning showed, and as common experience readily confirms, a person who is kind by disposition is not ignorant of the goodness of acting kindly. The virtue of a kind act is that it is kind, and a person who is kind by disposition does kind deeds because they are kind. Therefore, kind-hearted people do kind deeds knowingly and purposely, and their actions in no way resemble accidental good deeds. Consequently, the common practice of respecting good dispositions is justified, even though actions motivated by such dispositions are virtuous but not moral.

God and the kind-hearted show that a being is worthy of respect because it acts virtuously. Even if a being cannot or is not acting morally, it still merits respect if it does good deeds intentionally and without ulterior motives. Although animals are not in exactly the same situation as those of God and of kind-hearted people, many animals are in a a morally significantly similar situation: they act virtuously. Therefore, these animals qualify as beings who must be respected. They are beings who must be accorded rights to life, dignity, and a fulfilling life by those who are concerned to create a more virtuous world, i.e., by moral beings.

[4] *Ibid.*, pp. 30–31.

[5] *Ibid.*, pp. 14–15.

Even though they are not moral agents, animals who act virtuously should be moral recipients. What prevents these animals from acting morally, i.e., not striving to fulfill an ideal way of life, is, as in the cases of the holy and the kind-hearted, not a sufficient reason to justify beings who can act morally treating these animals merely as means to satisfying needs and desires. In order to create a better world, one in which virtue is always encouraged and respected, all beings capable of acting virtuously must be treated as ends in themselves.

California State University/Hayward

Received December 15, 1978

Philosophy and Phenomenological Research
Vol. XLV, No. 2, December 1984

The Psychopath as Moral Agent

ROBERT J. SMITH
University College, University of Maryland

The psychological literature dealing with the psychopath[1] is mainly concentrated on psychiatric case histories of antisocial depredations, or with measurement of this diagnostic category via physiological,[2] attitudinal,[3] and familial correlates.[4] Recently, however, philosophers have shown increasing interest in the psychopath as a paradigm case in examining value theory, moral responsibility, and even rationality. The psychopath is a direct challenge to these realms of discourse because, while judged psychologically ill by some clinical authorities, s/he is not recognized by these same authorities as distinguished by irrationality; may therefore possess a perfectly consistent set of values, and even behave responsibly within this framework. By examining these issues of rationality, responsibility, and valuation as they relate to psychopathy, philosophical analysis permits us a more objective perspective on this fascinating entity.

---

[1] My use of the term corresponds to the classical primary psychopath as described for example by Cleckley (1976). For identification purposes I use the following criteria generally agreed on by clinicians and researchers: (1) beguiling; (2) guiltless; (3) manipulating; (4) cynical; (5) primitive egocentricity; (6) unempathic; (7) professes conventional values; (8) unperturbed; (9) restless; (10) oriented in present.

[2] See H. J. Eysenck, *Crime and Personality* (Boston: Houghton Mifflin, 1964); R. D. Hare, *Psychopathy: Theory and Research* (New York: Wiley, 1970); D. T. Lykken, "A Study of Anxiety in the Sociopathic Personality," *Journal of Abnormal and Social Psychology* 55 (1957): 6-10; and H. Quay, "Psychopathic Personality as Pathological Stimulation Seeking," *American Journal of Psychiatry* 122 (1965): 180-83.

[3] See N. L. Berg, "Self-concept of Neurotic and Sociopathic Criminal Offenders," *Psychological Reports* 34 (1974): 622; A. F. Campagna and S. Harter, "Moral Judgment in Sociopathic and Normal Children," *Journal of Personality and Social Psychology* 31 (1975): 199-205; and R. J. Smith and J. E. Griffith, "Psychopathy, Machiavellianism, and Anomie," *Psychological Reports* 42 (1978): 258.

[4] See A. H. Buss, *Psychopathology* (New York: Wiley, 1966) and B. A. Maher, *Principles of Psychopathology* (New York: McGraw-Hill, 1966).

Often, however, accounts by philosophers ignore important clinical and social manifestations of psychopathy, dealing with this entity as if it were a discrete, all-or-none category encompassing narrow defining criteria. The intent of the present article is to summarize the issues philosophers have recently raised concerning psychopathy, critique them from a clinical and social perspective, then attempt to set this concept in an appropriate socio-cultural frame. Although I divide the issues of responsibility and rationality of psychopathic behavior for the purposes of discussion, they are obviously interdependent concepts.

Philosophical Considerations

Responsibility

Haksar[5] has focussed on the question of the responsibility of the psychopath for his/her behavior. Unlike cases of outright psychosis, the psychopath usually passes traditional tests of legal responsibility, e.g., M'Naghton-like decisions requiring only that the individual be able to cognitively distinguish right from wrong. Wootton[6] has nicely demonstrated the circularity of the argument (or its converse) that the psychopath is mentally ill, therefore not responsible, because s/he commits antisocial acts; an argument all too often invoked by mental health authorities. Legal decisions such as *Durham vs. The United States*, however, where a psychiatric diagnosis of mental illness has served as the criterion of responsibility independent of the defendant's cognition regarding right and wrong illustrate Wootton's point, since the psychopath shows none of the traditional criteria of psychic disturbance, e.g., marked anxiety, disturbed reality contact, or hallucinations; and therefore is a poor candidate for the charge of being mentally ill.

Haksar attempts to break out of these logical difficulties by suggesting that there are independent criteria for judging the psychopath to be not responsible. He notes several such from psychology/psychiatry that he believes can break the vicious circle of defining psychopathy as mental illness merely on the criterion of antisocial behavior. From the former he selects the cortical immaturity hypothesis[7] wherein psychopaths are alleged to show electroencephalographic (EEG) patterns not unlike those seen in children. From the latter discipline he examines psychiatrist Cleck-

---

[5] See V. Haksar, "Aristotle and the Punishment of Psychopaths," *Philosophy* 39 (1964): 323-40 and V. Haksar, "The Responsibility of Psychopaths," *The Philosophical Quarterly* 15 (1965): 135-45.

[6] B. Wootton, *Social Science and Social Pathology* (London: Allen & Unwin, 1959).

[7] Hare, op. cit.

ley's sixteen criteria for diagnosing psychopathy, and especialy Cleckley's observation that the psychopath, unlike an everyday criminal, behaves so recklessly as to suggest at least obscure motives for this behavior, if not some sort of deep-seated mental illness. That is, the psychopath appears to be oriented to the most immediate of gratifications, is unconcerned about future goals, and therefore "throws away" health, family, job, etc. However, Haksar[8] raises the very legitimate question, commonly ignored by clinicians, of whether or not the psychopath's "present" rather than "future" orientation is any less legitimate a value than those goals others of us build toward. Whatever the answer, he notes that the psychopath is not totally unconcerned about the future and may hold a job, avoid getting killed, and show purposive behavior, in the overall pursuit of pleasurable gratification.

Haksar[9] also raises the issue of the extent to which we could expect the psychopath to be able to get rid of criminal values once acquired. This the psychopath does not seem able to do, he argues, and thereby illustrates psychological sickness. For Haksar values are not relative, but objective; to be discovered in concrete reality (nature). Still the person, including the psychopath, may recognize discoverable objective truths in moral matters but choose not to adopt them; a point also made by Fingarette,[10] to underscore that such recognition — even if only illustrated in going round communal morality — speaks for adequate reality contact and an intact ego.

Haksar[11] argues that there is a meaningful distinction relevant to psychopathy between moral insanity and moral sickness. Even if one *did* subscribe to moral relativism, the morals recognized by a given group could also be recognized by the psychopath, but because of moral sickness, s/he could not follow them. Moral sickness would involve not the *inability to see* moral facts, as in insanity, but the *inability to choose* moral values. Although aware of moral facts, it is this incapacity to choose that Haksar believes is sufficient to excuse psychopaths from responsibility. For Haksar, then, the psychopath is not insane but morally ill.

Murphy[12] has also addressed the issue of psychopathic responsibility, concentrating on the seeming lack of conscience of the psychopath. Particularly in the sense of the psychopath's apparent inability to be con-

---

[8] Haksar, art. cit. (1965).

[9] Haksar, art. cit. (1964).

[10] H. Fingarette, *The Meaning of Criminal Insanity* (Berkeley, California: University of California Press, 1972), p. 111.

[11] Haksar, art. cit. (1964).

[12] J. G. Murphy, "Moral Death: A Kantian Essay on Psychopathy," *Ethics* 82 (1972): 284-98.

cerned about the rights of others, thereby, Murphy argues, forfeiting his/her own rights. Since one such right is the right of being judged responsible by one's fellows, the psychopath cannot claim this right, and therefore is "dead" as a moral person; hence liable to even the most strenuous therapeutic intervention efforts. Indeed, Murphy suggests that the psychopath from the moral point of view, is best judged an animal, and cannot be wronged.[13]

Pertinent to the issue of responsibility is the question of whether the psychopath behaves voluntarily or acts from compulsion or irresistible impulse. Arrington poses the philosophical and indeed forensic dilemma of how the seeming irrationality of psychopathy, for example his/her penchant for carelessly getting caught, could at the same time be the product of a mind ". . . intelligent, knowledgeable, and logically acute."[14] He observes that philosopher Flew holds the psychopath responsible because the latter is not under inner compulsion nor external constraint, but acts "in character," that is, there seems little conflict within the psychopathic personality. Therefore, if the psychopath should be laboring under an irresistible impulse, it cannot be an irresistible impulse of like nature to that of, e.g., the kleptomanic, who is "out of character" and desires to reform.

Rationality

Duff uses the psychopath as a paradigm case to show ". . . how the inadequacies of traditional empiricist accounts of the notions of understanding and rationality in moral and emotional contexts may hinder the recognition of this kind of disorder."[15] Two capacities he identifies as essential for a rational human life are: (1) the intellectual capacity for reasoning about the empirical features of one's environment, one's actions, and consequences; (2) the capacity to control one's actions, and resist contrary impulses in the light of one's rational purposes. Duff credits Haksar's[16] point that the psychopath may have values that are simply different from ours (society). Perhaps the psychopath is merely unconvinced by our arguments for our values, rather than being rationally incapacitated and thus disordered. A rebel against conventional values would

[13] Of note here for my subsequent argument is Murphy's parenthetical observation that a purely "Hobbesian Man," motivated solely by egoistic desire and self-preservation, would be prima facie a psychopath.

[14] R. L. Arrington "Practical Reason, Responsibility and the Psychopath," *Journal for the Theory of Social Behaviour* 9 (1979): 73.

[15] A. Duff, "Psychopathy and Moral Understanding," *American Philosophical Quarterly* 14 (1977): 190.

[16] Haksar, art. cit. (1965).

be precisely such a case, and we would not feel obliged to label this psychopathy.

Suppose we argue that rationality can only be decided on objective, factual criteria (à la Haksar) and a consistent relation to one's own wants or values. Here the psychopath, who negotiates well his/her social environment and above all relates consistently to values held, passes the test of rationality and thus is indistinguishable from a principled rebel, such as Mahatma Ghandi or Bertrand Russell. But Duff finds these objective criteria for rationality insufficient. He believes it is the psychopath's failure of empathy — his or her lack of ". . . love, remorse and concern for others"[17] — that is the key to the psychopath's irrationality.

In trying to achieve a more adequate criterion, Duff examines the case of Camus'[18] stranger, Meursault. Duff takes a cue from the moral philosophy of M. S. Pritchard, holding that it is not only intellectual recognition of criteria for moral judgments, but a *concern* for such values that is decisive. This concern would be expressed from the fact that the subject person comes out of a background of shared experiences, e.g., childhood, with some form of moral and emotional life that includes values and emotions logically connected to those s/he is presumably trying to understand. "Logical" for Duff here means tracing the connections between "our" moral values and "theirs." It is here that Meursault fails. Meursault's life is psychopathic because ". . . he has never come to share in a common form of moral or emotional life, and thus can neither understand these dimensions to the lives of others, nor develop them in his own life."[19] "Understanding" in Duff's sense means sensing emotional and moral connections, for example, between various uses of the term "hurting another." A person must not only be able to enumerate the criteria for defining "hurting another," and state that this is wrong, but be able to see how the term could be extended to new cases not falling on a prescribed list. The psychopath fails here because s/he can only parrot rigid, stereotyped moral applications, and thus cannot understand what dishonesty or injury are as kinds of human action.[20] S/he participates in no relevant set of values beyond his/her own immediate egoistic desires. It is not that conventional values are rejected, as is the case with a principled rebel, but the psychopath ". . . has never come to understand, or to share in, this dimension of human life."[21]

---

[17] Duff, art. cit., p. 191.

[18] A. Camus, *The Stranger*, trans. S. Gilbert (New York: Knopf, 1960).

[19] Duff, art. cit., p. 198.

[20] Ibid., p. 196.

[21] Ibid., p. 192.

In addressing the issue of rationality, Arrington[22] poses such questions as: Does the psychopath do things he or she would prefer not to do? Would the psychopath act differently if there were good reasons for it? The answer to the latter question may depend on whose "good reasons" we accept. If we accept what the "typical man" accepts, we mark the psychopath off as abnormal, but the principled rebel is also caught on this criterion, as on many issues s/he also will not be typical. Utilizing these criteria we would be merely serving the prejudices of the many. What reasons has the psychopath for his/her behavior, then? Or are there only irrational causes? Arrington, following Fingarette,[23] suggests defining rationality as acting to further one's own values, irrationality then being the performance of acts that would not lead to realization of one's goals or values. The psychopath seems to pass this test of rationality, since s/he is one who ". . . schemes and cunningly organizes his efforts to obtain his goals, who knows what he is doing. . ."[24] Next Arrington investigates the form of the psychopath's goals. He argues that values that can be raised to a standard or maxim, and that are not just a product of desire but of reasoned willing, might be classed as rational goals. And this seems not to be the case for the psychopath, whose goals are particularistic and do not transcend the here and now. The seeming unprincipledness of the psychopath, irrespective of principles verbalized, may be used to count him/her as irrational: "His values are just *given*, the products of feelings and impulses."[25]

However, even psychopathic egoism, particularistic in its aim, could be raised to a maxim if it were vouched for everyone, i.e., became universal egoism. On the basis of this egoism the psychopath does not resist impulses, thinking it foolish to do so; s/he feels no guilt or shame, for s/he is doing nothing conceived of as wrong. For Arrington, then, deciding about the rational status of the psychopath is a matter of what lies behind the egoistic values. We *could* view this egoism as principled, therefore as potentially correct for all of us. The psychopath's alleged lack of drive and motivation may be only true from the standpoint of those holding "prudential" values. S/he may be acting on a consistent principle, even if it is an undesirable principle. Which interpretation psychopathy gets — principled or unprincipled egoism — is an empirical, not philosophical issue, argues Arrington.

---

22 Arrington, art. cit. (1979).

23 Fingarette, op. cit.

24 Arrington, art. cit., p. 72.

25 Ibid., p. 86, italics in original.

Summary

Haksar makes the important suggestion that underlying the orientation to the present of the psychopath may be as legitimate a set of values as any other, such as future-oriented ones. The legitimacy alone of this question (without solution) challenges a common set of criteria for excusing the psychopath from responsibility: failure to learn from experience, failure to follow a life plan, and unreliability. However in further consideration, Haksar concludes that while not insane in a traditionally legal sense, the psychopath may be excused from responsibility because of an inability to choose moral values and is thus morally ill. Murphy's position agrees with this in that he sees the psychopath as morally dead without even the right to punishment, which is reserved for a responsible agent.

On the rationality issue, Duff[26] finds the psychopath irrational because of a failure to share and to be able to logically extend in a principled way, values that spring from distinct moral and emotional precedents, as argued in the case of Camus' Meursault. Arrington,[27] while claiming the issue is ultimately empirical, finds the psychopath potentially irrational for much the same reason as Haksar and Murphy find him/her irresponsible — his/her goals are egoistic and thereby particularistic. If the psychopath is not capable of raising his/her goals to the level of a maxim after the fashion of a Kantian principle applying to everyone in the society, then their purveyor is by Arrington's definition irrational.

Critique

Continuity vs. Type

Underlying all of the foregoing philosophical analyses is the conception of the psychopath as a case apart, as a qualitatively different phenomenon from the nonpsychopath.[28] While this assumption might facilitate logical analysis, its truth value is questionable on two fronts. On the clinical, the influential philosopher/psychiatrist Jaspers[29] has ordered psychopathy to those disorders characterizable as differing from the normal personality only in their behavioral manifestations. For him, psychopathic behavior is seen as only an exaggerated extension of the normal

---

[26] Duff, art. cit.

[27] Arrington, art. cit.

[28] Even when, as with Murphy (1972, p. 296), it is acknowledged that ". . . all the actual cases may be neither black nor white, but various shades of gray."

[29] J. Zubin, "Classification of the Behavior Disorders," *Annual Review of Psychology*, ed. P. R. Farnsworth, O. McNemar, and Q. McNemar (Palo Alto, California: Annual Reviews, 1967).

personality, and is not discontinuous with it. Diagnosing such problematic cases involves more the extent of the symptomatic behavior than the presence or absence of symptoms. With, e.g., organic brain syndrome symptoms, or schizophrenic hallucinations, we are on much safer ground to project symptoms as categorical, because these disorders more clearly involve physiological or internal psychic events. The clinician Karpman has noted that the psychopath "has no conflict;"[10] an observation that inevitably questions a traditional diagnosis of psychological illness, and Arrington[11] has noted that the psychopath seems to have little desire to change — again a consistent clinical finding.

Psychophysiologically, there is also little evidence known to this writer for viewing the psychopath as a type. One may take EEG records as a prominent example. No specific brain wave pattern has emerged among samples diagnosed as psychopathic. Gale[12] estimates that as high as 25 percent of unselected youth samples show atypical EEG patterns, and that such patterns are common among other psychiatric disorders. In addition, he notes that it would be paradoxical to accuse the young psychopath of being cortically immature (because of slowed EEG activity in a laboratory environment) when s/he is usually especially mature on, for example, behavioral measures. Slow wave form cortical activity may decrease with age — as does psychopathic acting out — but Gale views it as gratuitous to impute causation to this correlation, since so many other factors may be operative. While there is some evidence that extraverts as a class may seek stimulation because of underarousal,[13] and while psychopaths show some features of this group, there is little consistent psychophysiological evidence on which to "typecast" them; a view that the researches of Schachter[14] and Schmauk[15] also reflect. deFundia, Draguns, and Phillips[16] argue, not unlike Jaspers, that pathological behavior in general represents merely the caricatured extreme of culturally shared modes of behavior, and this would be particularly the case for psychopa-

---

[10] B. Karpman, "The Myth of the Psychopathic Personality," *American Journal of Psychiatry* 104 (1948), p. 525.

[11] Arrington, art. cit.

[12] A. Gale, "Can EEG Studies Make a Contribution to the Experimental Investigation of Psychopathy?" Paper presented at the Advanced Study Institute on Psychopathic Behavior, Les Arc, Bourg St. Maurice, France (September, 1975).

[13] Eysenck, op. cit.

[14] S. Schachter, *Emotion, Obesity and Crime* (New York: Academic Press, 1971).

[15] F. J. Schmauk, "Punishment, Arousal, and Avoidance Learning in Sociopaths," *Journal of Abnormal Psychology* 76 (1970): 325-35.

[16] T. A. deFundia, J. G. Draguns, and L. Phillips, "Culture and Psychiatric Symptomatology: A Comparison of Argentine and United States Patients," *Social Psychiatry* 6 (1971): 17-20.

thy because of the social nature of the symptoms.

The Nature of Values

The philosophical analyses presented accept the dichotomy of values into "normal" and "psychopathic"; even where, as in Haksar, neither perspective is judged necessarily superior to the other. Thus living for the present moment is contrasted with a more future-oriented perspective presumed shared by the many; and empathy with values socially given is vouchsafed as basic for human adjustment. But a legitimate question raises itself here: are in fact the values of the psychopath so remarkably different from ours as is casually assumed? Are such characteristics as having empathy, following a life plan, feeling guilt — the values of those of us who are not designated psychopathic? I submit that such a view of "our" values is idealized if not socio-culturally naive, and misrepresents the actual state of affairs where those values practiced are concerned.

It is necessary, in my judgment, to make a distinction between (a) those values certain societies idealize and would like to think are practiced; and (b) those which widely prevail. A society where Kantian values were significantly actualized, e.g., act to treat humanity as an end in itself and not as a means, would obviously find psychopathic behavior mystifying and unregenerate. Related *a* values inconsistent with psychopathy include: altruism and empathy in human relations, a premium on truthfulness and sincerity, and pointing toward the future (which includes gratification delay). However, there is considerable literature within the field of empirical psychology alone indicating that many modern societies[37] are quite seriously in violation of Kantian maxims and homely virtues. Such societies are, in Murphy's[38] terms, significantly Hobbesian, even Machiavellian. Machiavellian values include: manipulating others, showing little affect in interpersonal relations, and showing low conventional morality (read type *a* values). The reader will note the similarity of such values to criteria for psychopathy, and statistically significant correlations have related them.[39] Christie and Geis[40] have found that scores to their Mach Scale (based on Machiavelli's writings) increased markedly among U. S. college students between 1955 and 1964 samplings, and they

---

[37] I focus my discussion on the (capitalistic) society I know best; the critique should hold less for socialistic societies, which ostensibly at least, foster other values — and thereby perhaps other psychological problems.

[38] Murphy, art. cit.

[39] Smith and Griffith, art. cit.

[40] R. Christie, and F. Geis, *Studies in Machiavellianism* (New York: Academic Press, 1970).

see Machiavellianism on the increase in "modern society."

Block[41] contrasted the choices of ideal masculine and feminine adjectives made by college students from the U. S. and six Western European lands. The U. S. students of both sexes, compared with their Western European counterparts, significantly preferred the adjectives: self-centered, self-confident, adventurous, assertive, and ambitious. The U. S. men added restless and competitive, the U. S. women, practical and shrewd, to their respective lists. Bakan[42] has related such *agentic*, individualistic (as opposed to *communal*) adjectives to capitalistic societies. The values reflected in these adjectives show considerable overlap with psychopathic criteria; related examples are by no means rare.[43]

The philosophical discussions of psychopathy have in the main proceeded as if only type *a* values were at issue in considering the psychopath. Several of these authors,[44] have fastened on Camus' stranger as a prototypical psychopath because of his obliviousness to values of type *a*. While acknowledging that Camus was himself not attempting to portray a psychopath, for Duff, Meursault's indifference is the key to his psychopathy; he seems to share none of our idealized *a* values, e.g., he evinces little emotion at the death of his mother. At the same time, however, he is not very interested in those of type *b* either. In my judgment Camus frames his central figure precisely as he does in order to underscore the absurd situation in which one finds oneself when banal versions of type *a* values are brought to bear by society. Duff is not unaware of this perspective:

> Meursault has *seen through* the illusory concern with which others surround and support themselves: it is honesty, not incomprehension which explains his failure to act as others expect.[45]

Still Duff rejects permitting Meursault to wear the mantle of a "rational rebel" because Duff feels he does not comprehend any values, even self-serving ones. But with this observation Duff has created a profile of the psychopath quite at odds with clinical experience, where self-serving plays a major role. If we return to our list of typical symptoms of psychopathy as compiled by clinicians (footnote 1), we find a substantially agreed-on number that are not shared by Meursault but are highly self-serving: manipulating; beguiling; primitive egocentricity; professes conventional values. The only criteria which Meursault would seem to share

---

[41] J. H. Block, "Conception of Sex Role: Some Cross-Cultural and Longitudinal Perspectives." *American Psychologist* 28 (1973): 512-26.

[42] D. Bakan, *The Duality of Human Existence* (Chicago: Rand McNally, 1966).

[43] R. J. Smith, *The Psychopath in Society* (New York: Academic Press, 1978).

[44] See Murphy, art. cit. and Duff, art. cit.

[45] Ibid., p. 193.

with diagnostic symptom lists are: (1) guiltlessness, and (2) unempathic. But invoking the first would seem precluded in his case because he does not do a great deal that would call forth guilt. Even the murder he commits has no plan about it nor potential gain for him — it is an existentially absurd event. Thus only unempathic survives as a damning criterion, but looms rather small for the making of a diagnosis.

Clinically, the psychopath seems quite another kind of animal from Meursault, as a brief foray through any abnormal psychology text will quickly demonstrate. They are almost invariably engaging, manipulating, restless pleasure seekers. A common subtype of psychopath, for example, is the impersonator who casually adopts the personality of a particularly valued person or poses in a highly desirable role, such as that of priest or physician. In a society where one is rated on what one possesses, rather than one's humanness per se,[46] the impersonator is the extreme case of a person who "becomes" by literally stealing the identity of another. Thus a social unknown, therefore a "nothing," becomes "something." It is no accident that the identity stolen is not just any other, but that of someone who has "more" personality (read social recognition) than the thief. This reflects the conventional albeit type *b*, values of the psychopathic impersonator. Comparison with cultural heroes such as sport or "media personalities" to his/her disadvantage drives the impersonator to this most extreme of thefts — literally a caricature of a common social motif where one is valued on the basis of one's reflected image. One is reminded that it is in America where the image industry was born and thrives.

A classic example, of identity thievery is that of Ferdinand Demara who impersonated various professionals, including doctors of both psychology and medicine, carring out the functions of both careers. Paradoxically, Demara became famous in his own right as an "identity thief," and successded in having a Hollywood film made about his life — which illustrates parenthetically how society and psychopathy may intertwine. Having become a "something," Demara could then afford to "settle down." It has been suggested that he has done so.[47]

I would argue that the psychopath is not so much interpersonally alienated — for people find him/her attractive — as existentially alienated, seeking desperately after a fixed identity. The psychopath is a relatively empty self, seeking realization through alluring type *b* values aimed at self aggrandizement, rather than being a creature with no or even nihilistic values. With the psychopath we have a focus on individual differences

---

[46] E. Fromm, *To Have or To Be?* (New York: Harper & Row, 1976).

[47] J. C. Coleman, *Abnormal Psychology and Modern Life*, 4th ed. (Glenview, Illinois: Scott, Foresman, 1972).

with a vengeance; but the press to stand out from one's fellows is inherently parasitic, and societal pressure as a whole in this direction leads to the sort of excesses that psychopaths commonly perpetrate. Philosopher Cherry[48] has designated such competition among selves as a "Guinness Book of Records" philosophy. In societies where Being is validated only for those who stand out — are noticed — the person who does not attain this, i.e., most of us, and who is at the same time sufficiently enculturated, is faced with serious challenges regarding self definition.

If there is one problem Meursault does not have, it is this pathetic, social drive for recognition. Meursault, then, is a poor example, of the psychopath, either clinical or subclinical. He is fully indifferent to society. The psychopath, however, practices society's type *b* values (again even while professing type *a*) — and manipulates others so as to achieve them as painlessly as possible. Meursault lacks the unbridled egoism that the psychopath displays, wherein others are used merely to serve the self. Let me illustrate this more dramatically by contrasting Meursault's murder of an Arab with an actual case of a more typically psychopathic murder.[49]

An American soldier, M,[50] (age 29) found himself assigned to an overseas location where he was very unhappy and wished to return to America. A planned fake desertion of him by his wife was considered to achieve this end, but was not carried out. Then a further disappointment created rage in M: an anticipated reassignment to America with his wife went awry. He learned that this promised trip was to be for him only a temporary visit.

M was aware that crimes committed by U. S. military personnel in foreign lands are not locally prosecuted, the perpetrator being simply hustled back to America. With his wife, whom M much later said he had threatened to shoot along with their two children if she failed to cooperate, he put in practice a scheme they had at various times discussed. Mrs. M went to the local enlisted men's club where she sought out a black soldier (the couple were white) whom she took to the family apartment. There the victim was to be seduced then shot as a rapist. The shooting was carried out by the returning husband, who quickly disappeared while the wife broke in on neighbors to announce that a dead intruder lay on her bedroom floor. M had originally set the stage so that his wife would be seen as the murderer, believing that she would not be tried and the whole family

---

[48] C. Cherry, "How Differences Make a Difference," *Philosophy and Phenomenological Research* 41 (1980): 64-92.

[49] Although I agree with Cleckley that murder is uncommon among psychopaths.

[50] This account is based on a variety of sources including discussions with the prosecution, court testimony, and on the soldier's confession as reported in several newspapers.

would be returned to America. She later denied having shot the victim. When Mrs. M was in fact tried locally as a civilian, and perhaps since he was already sentenced to life imprisonment by a military court as the mastermind of the plot, M eventually confessed to the crime itself. In the course of his confession, the soldier referred authorities to the game "rapo" from Eric Berne's book *Games People Play*. Part of Berne's description of this reads:

> Here White leads Black into compromising physical contact and then claims that he has made a criminal assault or has done her irreparable damage. In its most cynical form White may actually allow him to complete the sexual act so that she gets that enjoyment before confronting him. The confrontation may be immediate, as in the illegitimate cry of rape, or it may be long delayed, as in suicide or homicide following a prolonged love affair. If she chooses to play it as a criminal assault, she may have no difficulty in finding mercenary or morbidly interested allies, such as the press, the police, counselors and relatives. Sometimes, however, these outsiders may cynically turn on her, so that she loses the initiative and becomes a tool in their games.[51]

The truly psychopathic elements of this act are evident. First there was M's rage at authority for thwarting an egocentric wish. Then there is the superficially clever but erratic plan based on what seem only partially thought through — but not psychotically irrational — expectancies (of achieving reassignment).[52] Then a response (murder) out of all proportion to the thwarted egoistic wish (return to U. S.). There is also the total disregard of the other — the black soldier's unlucky role as object — when the immediate gratification of the self seemed at hand. The wife, insofar as she was an unwilling accomplice, was also manipulated into the status of an object for her husband's aim. Finally, the literal and bizarre playing out of a macabre, cynical script, which presumably had fascinated both parties to the crime.

This murder has little in common with Meursault's of the Arab. The Arab and his companion had followed Meursault and his party because of a grudge against Meursault's acquaintance, Raymond, and there had been a fight among them prior to the shooting. Then Meursault, alone on the beach, encountered the Arab again. In the heat and sweat of an Algerian summer day, the Arab raised his knife threateningly to Meursault, who shot him with Raymond's gun; taken previously from Raymond so that he, in his anger at the Arab, would not deliver a shot. There is no thwarted ego, no manipulation of others or situation, no immediate gratification, no macabre script. There is merely perfunctory self-protection, with perhaps confusion and mild dissociation created by the heat

---

[51] E. Berne, *Games People Play* (New York: Grove Press, 1964), pp. 126-27.

[52] An informal IQ estimate on the soldier — known to the writer from the college classroom — would be in Wechsler's "Bright-Normal" range.

and sweat dazzling Meursault. An absurd, but not psychopathically absurd, killing.

I do agree with Duff[53] that to make a life intelligible — whether Meursault's or a garden variety psychopath's — the beliefs and values obtained for the individual must "form an intelligible extension, development, or modification of concepts and values within a tradition we share with him."[54] This the psychopath in fact does. S/he has merely radically extended the already widely practiced values of type *b*, and so seen represents a reasonable perspective on the society as it exists — an extra — rather than antisocial personality. Thus the "typical man" in American society is encouraged from childhood in the direction of individualism and aggressive competing, which are qualities implicit or explicit in virtually any clinical case of psychopathy one chooses of those offered by clinicians. The psychopath well understands the interests of others, the reasons for their actions (contrary to Duff's argument[55]), precisely because s/he shares — again in desperate, caricatured form — these same type *b* values. It is this sharing of motivational expectancies that permits the psychopath to be such a skillful manipulator of others.

Rationality

Arrington[56] addresses the concept of practical rationality elaborated by Fingarette,[57] which includes conduct, norms, even emotional elements. It is thus quite removed epistemologically from the rationalist tradition of Plato, Descartes, Spinoza, or Kant. Practical rationality involves essentially optimizing one's own goals and is perforce tinged with varying emotional input, since many goals are undergirded by primary drives such as hunger and sex, even aggression, and may be quite separate from, if not opposed to, intellect per se. Indeed, it sounds more like some sort of Benthamist hedonic calculus than traditional rationalism. But if rationalism is so defined, it would seem to easily encompass the psychopath because "He seeks the same things ordinary people seek — money, glory, adventure; . . ."[58] These are clearly values of type *b*, and the psychopath is commonly assiduously at work actualizing them.

A further criterion Arrington proposes to distinguish practical rationality involves being able to extend a principle of action to all other agents

---

[53] Duff, art. cit.

[54] Ibid., p. 193.

[55] Ibid., p. 198.

[56] Arrington, art. cit.

[57] Fingarette, op. cit.

[58] Arrington, art. cit., pp. 81-82.

in similar circumstances. In the case of the psychopath, he asserts, this could be "principled egoism." I see no reason why the psychopath could not accept universal egoism as such a principle, and therefore qualify as practically rational on this criterion. The psychopath, I believe, already *assumes* that others are motivated, if only covertly, just as s/he is by type *b* values — and there is ample evidence to confirm this assumption in the mass media. Recently, for example, I have heard that an American journalist won a Pulitzer Prize for a story presented as fact but existing as fiction. The values provoking deception of this nature become part of the belief system of any incipient psychopath growing to maturity in a society which, at some level, encourages them.

Arrington cites[19] six common psychopathic characteristics (Table 1) which he believes may be seen either as: (1) expressions of a general egoistic principle ("live for today, for tomorrow we may die") with which the psychopath's behavior is consistent, hence rational; or (2) as values the psychopath could not process to the extent that one could say s/he were a committed egoist. As argued above, I do not believe the psychopath would gainsay others responding as s/he does, thus being able to qualify as a principled egoist. The issue is perhaps empirical, as Arrington would have it, but I know of no instrument currently in use to test it.

Table 1

Psychopathic Characteristics with Corresponding

b Values

Characteristic	*b Values*
1. Inability to resist impulse or temptation of the moment	1. "Fly now — pay later"
2. Limited affect, or lack of love and affection for others	2. "Look out for number one"
3. Aggressiveness	3. "Sell yourself"
4. Lack of shame, regret, or sense of guilt	4. "Do your own thing"
5. Inability to learn from experience	5. "Live for today for tomorrow we may die"
6. Lack of drive or motivation	6. ———————

[19] Ibid., p. 84.

But the crux of the matter lies more concretely with the values implicit in the six presumed psychopathic characteristics of Table 1. The adjacent matching slogans, very familiar to the "typical American," show clearly that there are important social values which are vigorously propagated and that are psychopathic in nature.

From the psychopathic characteristics of Table 1 coupled with corresponding *b* values, one sees how the psychopath may be quite a good fit to certain societies. Thus one is encouraged to give in to impulse, aggressively project the self at the expense of others, and let the future take care of itself. (While characteristic 6 has no corresponding value it also seems a doubtful criterion of psychopathy, and dependent for its validity on a type *a* value orientation to the future.)

Although the psychopath may have socially undesirable values from a Kantian, altruistic perspective, from the perspective of the socio-cultural values not idealized but met in daily practice, the psychopath reflects quite the rationality that clinicians (e.g., Cleckley,[60] Sheldon)[61] have at times grudgingly ascribed. To this extent — and it is no small one — the psychopath is acting ". . . as the reasons of a typical person would dictate."[62]

Conclusion

The aim of the present analysis has been to examine the views of the psychopathic personality coming from philosophical analysis, in the light of clinical practice, and to move on to consider this diagnosis from the neglected perspective of cultural determinants. Although psychopathy may be a disputed diagnosis world-wide, at least Anglo-American clinicians have shown reasonable agreement about major symptoms (as Arrington also notes).[63] Philosophers have generally accepted the description of the psychopath presented in clinical writings. What the philosophers have added to the clinical picture is probing questions about psychopathy rather than unique answers. While pointing out that some of the clinician's favorite criteria for confirming psychopathy, e.g., orientation to the present, primitive egocentrism, are value judgments that may conceivably be as reasonable as any other given set, they arrive at much the same judgment as the clinician: the psychopath is morally ill because of inability to process what are called here type *a* values. Even where recognizing as Murphy does that society may have a hand in producing psychopathy, the emphasis is on the failure of the individual to develop, to

---

[60] H. Cleckley, *The Mask of Sanity*, 5th ed. (St. Louis: C. V. Mosby, 1976).

[61] W. H. Sheldon, *Varieties of Delinquent Youth* (New York: Harper, 1949).

[62] Arrington, art. cit., p. 86.

[63] Ibid., p. 87.

become other than a "mere child,"[64] rather than on any inherent qualities within the society itself that may foster psychopathy. Thus the psychopath remains an "antisocial personality" for many philosophers.

My analysis stresses that the psychopath is not ill nor even seriously out of phase when functioning within a society where *b* values are both practiced and legitimated in the marketplace.[65] In extreme cases the psychopath may overstep convention by caricaturing these values and thus anger authorities who idealize *a* values, thereby risking being locked away. This fate is particularly likely to befall the socio-economically underprivileged. Yet the psychopath knows that the day of release will come and s/he can return to the "real world" where *b* values "make things tick." Is it any wonder that efforts at clinical treatment of psychopaths to date have uniformly failed[66] and that the psychopath "fails to learn from experience" (in jail or hospital)? Insofar as the prevailing values of a society continue in the *b* direction, then the psychopath has indeed learned from experience and is an important source of moral agency for that society — is a heavily socialized, not antisocial personality.

---

[64] Murphy, art. cit., p. 297.

[65] A logical question following on my analysis is whether societies at least ostensibly committed to other values — for example, cooperation at the expense of individual competitiveness — actually produce fewer cases of psychopathy. The question is vexed for at least two reasons: (1) countries differ in ordering cases to the category of psychopath; (2) it is not clear if a society fostering psychopathy would be more tolerant of such cases, thereby diagnosing fewer, or — while creating more — inevitably have more of them to be locked away. Indirect evidence suggesting fewer psychopathic-like behaviors are observed in communal societies may be found in Smith (1978).

[66] Cleckley, op. cit.

AMERICAN PHILOSOPHICAL QUARTERLY
Volume 34, Number 1, January 1997

ASCRIPTIONS OF RESPONSIBILITY

Marina A. L. Oshana

JUDGMENTS OF RESPONSIBILITY

The question I wish to address in this paper[1] is this: When we judge a person to be morally responsible for her character, her choices, her actions or omissions, what are we expressing by that judgment? One view, currently quite popular, is that when we say a person is responsible we mean that the person has invited, through her behavior, a response on the part of others marked by attitudes such as gratitude and resentment, and that the person is an appropriate object of such attitudes in light of certain conditions for agency that she has met.[2] But another possibility is that, in judging a person responsible, we are saying the person is accountable for her behavior, in the sense that we think it appropriate that the person offer an explanation of her intentions or beliefs about her behavior.

I will call these the reactive-attitudes analysis and the accountability analysis of responsibility ascriptions, respectively. The second part of this paper addresses the reactive-attitudes analysis while part three concerns the accountability view. I will argue that the account of responsibility ascriptions offered by the reactive attitudes analysis — viz., that these are constituted by the attitudes we take to others in reaction to their behavior—falls short as an explanation of judgments about responsibility. Instead, the reactive-attitudes analysis does two things. One, it offers an account of the emotional dynamics at play where decisions about responsibility occur. Two, it invites speculation about the conditions for responsible agency. Both functions are interesting in their own right. That a person is subject to certain attitudes and practices might give us reason to consider her a free agent, and as good or bad, praiseworthy or blameworthy. Additionally, an account of responsible agency might be extrapolated from the attitudes and practices persons visit upon the putative agent in response to her behavior.

But the judgment that an agent is responsible is not equivalent to the responses we register to the conduct of moral agents. Responsibility ascriptions are not expressions of our treatment of others, although insofar as we do regard an agent as responsible we tend to treat him accordingly. Nor are they reducible to the gamut of emotions we display toward others in light of the good or ill will they visit upon us by their actions and attitudes. Nor, in charging a person with moral responsibility, are we first and foremost expressing the view that the person is a free agent, although this condition is presumed as a legitimating condition for such charges.

I will begin with some general observations about responsibility claims.

Obligation claims versus Agency claims

A good place to begin is with the observation that judgments about responsibility are ambiguous. In claiming "Alice is responsible for keeping her temper in check," we may be saying that Alice maintained her temper as a result of some effort on her part. But more likely, we are expressing the belief "Keeping her temper in check is something Alice has a duty to do." Here, the judgment "*X* is responsible for *Y*" is intended as a statement to the effect that *X* *has* certain responsibilities to others: tasks, duties, or obligations pertaining to *Y*, usually in light of *X*'s station. Thus, parents are responsible for overseeing the well-being of their children, adult wage earners are responsible for paying taxes, attorneys are responsible for respecting the confidentiality of their clients, and so forth.[3]

But to be morally responsible is not, prima facie, to have or to owe obligations to another.[4] In investigating the meaning of responsibility ascriptions, we are not primarily concerned with the notion of having responsibilities. What we are interested in is the idea of *being* responsible. This is a sense of responsibility concerned, very generally, with responsible agency.

The minimal form of agency is causal. According to a causal agency analysis, responsibility ascriptions credit a person (or a thing) with a role in bringing about an event or state of affairs, and nothing more. Ascribing causal responsibility consists in identifying the factor that must actually operate in order for an event to transpire.[5]

Thus, when we say "Alice is responsible for the fact that baby Bernie ingested the wrong medicine" we mean, at the very minimum, that Alice caused Bernie to ingest the medicine; that she brought about, directly or indirectly, events either wanted or unwanted. In performing this action (or allowing the action to transpire), Alice may have been discharging — or may have failed to discharge — some duty or obligation. But whether the act was in some sense obligatory is not of importance.

I suspect that our primary interest in ascribing responsibility is to claim that an agent's acts can be credited to him in a deeper way than is granted by a mere causal connection.[6] In particular, three factors render the minimal causal sense of responsible agency insufficient for our purposes.

First, affirming that someone is a causal agent responsible for some event or state of affairs does not enable us to say that the agent can be *held* morally responsible, or can be responsible to someone. We do not hold young children, or animals, responsible for the events they caused. Nor must a person be causally responsible for all those acts she is held morally responsible for. For example, parents are vicariously responsible, both morally and legally, for at least some of the acts of their non-adult children.[7] When we *hold* a person such as Alice responsible to someone (Bernie's parents, perhaps) for giving Bernie the medicine, it is in light of certain expectations we have of Alice, given a maturity we assume of her, given what we have reason to believe she knew herself to be doing, and given the circumstances that led her to act.

Second, the kind of responsibility attributed to one who is identified as merely a causal agent does not allow for moral evaluation. That the agent is causally responsible is not, in and of itself, a reason to judge the agent a good or bad, praiseworthy or blameworthy, person as a result. But we want an account of agency that makes moral approval or disapproval possible. Even if the act for which we deem a person responsible is morally neutral — the sort for which moral evaluation is unwarranted — we want to have room to appraise the person for her action if need be.[8]

Three, since causal responsibility can be ascribed to events, things, non-human animals and to irrational or under-developed humans as well as to fully mature, rational persons, it does not single out a class of things that might properly be described as moral agents, or members of a moral community. We might blame the collapse of a building on faulty construction, or the car crash on faulty brakes, but these things aren't *blameworthy* because they aren't moral agents.

Given that we have in mind a more robust sense of responsible agency, the question posed at the outset remains: When we judge a person to be morally responsible for her character, her choices, and her actions, what are we expressing by that judgment? What do ascriptions of moral responsibility amount to?

Being a Responsible Agent and Being Held Accountable

Generally speaking, when we describe someone as a morally responsible agent, we mean that the person is someone whom we recognize as bearing characteristics of the sort that make him a member of the moral community. He is someone with whom morally relevant relationships are possible, and he is a fitting subject of moral appraisal.

Accounts of responsible agency require that a responsible agent satisfy certain epistemic conditions and certain conditions of control. The epistemic conditions guarantee that the responsible agent is self-aware, that he is rational, that he is not ignorant of the circumstances in which he acts, that he is cognizant of and is able to act within established moral guidelines, and that he is responsive to reasons to adjust or amend his behavior in light of these guidelines. The control conditions ensure that the agent acts freely and has authority over his acts; he is not hostage to neuroses, he is capable of deliberate, intentional behavior, the causal history leading up to his action is free of coercion, manipulation, intimidation, etc.

Absent some of the epistemic and control conditions, a person will be a less likely candidate for responsible agency. The satisfaction of some set of these will mean that the person is a responsible agent, someone we can legitimately hold accountable when the need to do so arises. There is obviously a threshold that decides when a person is a moral agent, but it is not within the scope of this paper to explore the specifics of the threshold. Let it suffice to say that the responsible agent is someone who acts knowingly and freely, and the actions and characteristics for which he is responsible are "his own."

Attributions of moral responsibility that move beyond ascriptions of causal agency may take either of two forms. One may focus on the phenomenon of holding an agent responsible for his actions; this is the accountability analysis to which I will return in part three. On the other hand, the reactive-attitudes account will use the fact that an actor met certain conditions for responsible agency to anchor an account of responsibility ascriptions in which *being* responsible just amounts to *being* an a suitable candidate for certain kinds of treatment. Thus, "X is responsible for Y" will amount to the claims that X did (or is) Y, that X possesses the qualities of a responsible agent, and that X is rightly subject to the counteractions of others as a result. The reactive-attitudes account enjoys current favor, and it is to this account that I now turn.

Reactive Attitudes as Judgments about Responsibility

The view that judgments about responsibility are best construed as claims about the attitudes and treatment appropriate to moral agents was raised by Peter Strawson in "Freedom and Resentment."[9] Strawson attempts to explain the intelligibility of ascriptions of moral responsibility given the possibility of causal determinism. Strawson notes, first, that the truth of determinism would not entail that the typical excusing conditions for responsibility (e.g., the agent was acting in ignorance, or under hypnosis, neurosis, coercion, or physical compulsion) held true of *all* agents. Conditions such as these lead us to excuse a person from responsibility, and, clearly, such properties cannot be predicated of every causally determined individual.

But the ingenious element of the paper lies in Strawson's charge that the truth or falsity of determinism plays very little, if any, active role in the judgments human beings make about agent-responsibility. Rather, whether we call persons responsible or not is decided by the attitudes we take toward one another in response to behavior and traits of character. These attitudes include gratitude and indignation, perhaps feelings of confidence and mistrust, and are accompanied by practices such as punishing and rewarding, praising and blaming. These "reactive" attitudes, believes Strawson, *constitute* ascriptions of responsibility — having such attitudes is what ascriptions of responsibility amount to. To regard a person as responsible *just is* the predisposition to react to the person in certain ways; to explain the phenomenon of responsibility ascriptions *just is* to give evidence of this reactive or responsive stance. There does not exist an additional, perhaps more fundamental, ground or justification for responsibility ascriptions independent of this range of attitudes. Responsiveness to the behavior of others does not merely serve as a starting point for an analysis of responsibility; it completes it.

Some controversy has arisen as to whether Strawson's view is that we cannot renounce the reactive attitudes even when the truth or likelihood of determinism would entail excusing conditions from moral responsibility sufficient to make these attitudes irrational. The bulk of his readers subscribe to this interpretation, making much of Strawson's "rationality argument"[10]. If we are determined, Susan Wolf charges, and "if this implies, as a matter of metaphysical fact, that we are not free or responsible beings,"[11] such attitudes might strike us as inappropriate. The value we place on "living in accordance with the facts" may compel us to replace the reactive attitudes with an objective stance more fitting our metaphysical status. But even if an objective stance could be sustained, it is arguable that the social costs of "getting the metaphysical facts straight" about ourselves and others would be far greater than the cost of self-deception. Determined or not, "it is an absolutely fundamental natural fact about us that we are deeply and perhaps unrenounceably committed to the reactive attitudes and practices."[12] So natural and fundamental a part of human life are these attitudes and practices that they cannot be renounced. Thus, it may be more rational to retain the reactive attitudes than to forsake them, and suffer a loss of some part of our humanity, given the deep and incommensurable role they play in human life.

It is not Strawson's view, as it is Wolf's, that determinism implies that we are neither free nor responsible. Too much, as well, may be made by Strawson's readers of the rationality argument. Strawson might simply be saying that to be morally responsible or to be exempt from responsibility is wholly and rightly decided by the fact of being open to the reactive attitudes. The reactive attitudes are what anchor moral responsibility; since we have these attitudes, and since they cannot be threatened by causal determinism, causal determinism makes no difference one way or another to our status as responsible creatures.

Whatever reading of Strawson one prefers, both sides recognize that the propriety of these attitudes turns on the truth of the belief that people are, in some sense, responsible for what they do. In utilizing the Strawsonian account, John Martin Fischer contends that an agent is morally responsible for an action to the extent that the agent is an *appropriate* subject of, or is "rationally accessible to," certain reactive attitudes and practices, such as moral reward and punishment, as a result of performing these actions.[13] Says Fischer,

> A theory of moral responsibility sets the conditions under which we believe that an individual is a *rational candidate* for praise or blame on account of his behavior. [Such a theory] explains rational accessibility to the pertinent attitudes and practices.[14]

Fischer's interest is in analyzing these conditions. His reasoning can be reconstructed as follows: To say that a person is morally responsible is to say that the person is the kind of agent in virtue of which the reactive attitudes and attendant practices are fitting. The reactive attitudes are justified when the subject meets certain epistemic and control conditions for responsible agency. Thus, explaining why an agent is a fitting subject of the reactive attitudes involves offering a theory of responsible agency — a theory that focuses on the conditions that make a person a rational candidate for the reactive attitudes. What judgments of responsibility amount to, then, are judgments of free agency.

It is natural that philosophers such as Fischer, who embrace the reactive attitudes as an inescapable and distinctive component of human life, will make the conditions required for the correct application of these attitudes and practices of paramount importance. For Fischer, the emphasis on articulating the conditions under which the concept of moral responsibility may be properly applied raises issues of the sort with which he is most concerned (namely, the compatibility of causal determinism and divine foreknowledge with moral agency, and the freedom or "control" conditions that make moral agency possible).

But it is a mistake to use the reactive attitudes and practices as a launching point for a theory of responsibility and responsibility ascriptions. Certainly these attitudes are not *constitutive* of responsibility, or even an essential part of responsibility ascriptions, as Fischer and other Strawsonians maintain.[15] While it may be *natural* to judge a person morally responsible only if the person is an appropriate subject of the reactive attitudes, a person isn't responsible *because* she can be praised, anymore than she is held accountable *because* she is appropriately subject to certain types of reactive attitudes. How we naturally act toward persons we believe are responsible offers evidence of just that—behavior to which we are arguably predisposed and nothing more. But why should the fact (if it is a fact) that we are committed to these attitudes justify a belief that people are responsible for their acts? We do not call a person responsible simply because she meets certain conditions for free moral agency, nor because others regard her as if she were a free agent anymore than we call an emerald priceless because we value or desire it. Rather, we call a person an appropriate subject of the reactive attitudes because the person is responsible. And that judgment, I shall argue, is explained by the fact that the agent is accountable.

An example may clarify my position. Suppose you are the chairman of my department, and the time has come to evaluate my teaching performance. As a junior member of the department, I have been occupied by an array of academic duties. You suspect I might be less than stellar in the classroom, but you are inclined to be lenient in your assessment of my teaching. To your surprise, my teaching secures strong reviews. When you ask me to explain how I have managed to juggle the stresses of the year with apparent success, and I reply that hard work was the key, you might feel admiration (or envy) toward me; but then again, you may feel nothing. What expresses your belief that I am responsible for this situation is to be found in the fact that you believe I am in a position to explain the actions and motives that lead to my success. The fact that you may respond to me with certain feelings is not implicit in the fact that I am responsible, although these feelings may reflect that fact.

Thus while being an appropriate object of the reactive attitudes provides evidence of moral agency, and offers insight into how we behave toward responsible persons, more than the fact that a person is rightly subject to the attitudes is needed if we are to make sense of responsibility ascriptions. The reactive attitudes account is best construed as offering a way of getting at a description of responsible agency, i.e., of being the right kind of subject for these attitudes. Insofar as we can establish that persons are responsible agents, the phenomenon of responsiveness, of evaluating and reacting toward a person in light of the person's choices, conduct, and characteristics is legitimate. But as the preceding example shows, that a person can legitimately be praised, blamed, resented, envied, esteemed, and the like, even if it captures a person's standing as a responsible agent, doesn't appear to explain the content of responsibility ascriptions.

Let me summarize the discussion of this section. First, while Fischer's account of responsible agency is useful in that it sketches out the characteristics one must have in order to be held responsible or to be regarded as a fitting subject of certain social attitudes and practices, an account of responsible agency doesn't provide a sense of what ascriptions of responsibility involve. If we agree that the concepts of accountability and agency are distinct, an answer to the question "What does it mean to hold an entity responsible?" will call for something other than an analysis of the conditions for free agency.[16]

Even if being responsible meant in part that others regarded one in a certain way, the reactive-attitudes and practices are clearly not adequate to signal responsibility. Responsibility cannot be exhausted by the attitudes persons assume in response to the behavior of others, for these feelings and practices might miss the mark; we might, that is, be mistaken in directing them to inappropriate subjects. Equally, while the subject may be appropriate, the attitude may not be.

In light of this I think it is sensible to say that these attitudes are the collateral effects of a belief that an entity is a responsible agent and is to be held responsible for some act. Contra Fischer, I do not think it is the purpose of a theory of responsibility to explain the propriety of the reactive attitudes and practices. When we say that someone is responsible for his actions — however ascriptions of responsibility are cashed out—we mean to convey something other than the thought that we regard the agent in a special responsive way.

Holding agents accountable

In attributing an agent with responsibility we may not be especially interested in the fact that he meets the conditions for responsible agency. Instead, we may be pronouncing some expectation we have *of* him as a moral agent. We may be saying that we *hold* him responsible for his actions, his character, intentions, the outcome of these, and the like — for the things he does (or is), and for those he is expected to do (or be). On this view, the judgment "*X* is responsible for *Y*" will express the beliefs "*X* did *Y* (or is *Y*), *X* possesses the qualities of a responsible agent, and *X* is accountable or answerable for *Y*".[17]

On this view, when we say a person is morally responsible for something, we are essentially saying that the person did or caused some act (or exhibits some trait of character) for which it is fitting that she give an account. In judging that an account ought to be given, we presume that the individual from whom an accounted is expected has (a) antecedently met the requirements of responsible agency, and (b) has performed some act (or has exhibited some characteristic) of the sort subject to certain accepted standards of morality and, (c) typically has fallen short of these standards.[18] The accountability interpretation assumes the actor possesses and is able to exercise certain capacities—rationality, self-awareness, an ability to appreciate and reply to telling questions, and the like.

I will formulate the accountability interpretation as a biconditional: a person is responsible for an act if and only if it ought to be the case that the person account for her behavior, where doing so involves giving some statement of the person's beliefs or intentions regarding the act. Thus "*X* is accountable for *Y*" can be unpacked as "It is appropriate that *X* explain her intentions in doing (or being) *Y*".

The process by which a person is deemed "account-responsible" involves a number of (usually sequential) components. Consider the claim "Clarence is responsible for the explosion in the chemistry lab." According to the accountability approach, when we judge that Clarence is responsible for this event, we are expressing the belief that Clarence caused the explosion through some action of his own, *and* that it is appropriate that Clarence give an account of having caused the explosion. Whether Clarence actually gives an account is not the issue; we are only claiming that it is appropriate that he give an account. Assuming Clarence is not a Robinson Crusoe, but a member of society, the judgment "Clarence is responsible for the explosion" might, following Baier, be analyzed as follows:

1. Clarence is accountable to others in the sense that it is fitting that he explain his role in the action leading up to the explosion; Clarence is "answerable-responsible".

2. If the explanation fails to excuse or exonerate Clarence on moral grounds, he is "culpable-responsible".

3. Others are in a position to take rectifying or corrective measures against Clarence.

On a Baier-type model, holding persons responsible is part of a social practice of ascribing responsibility, first by making clear any moral expectations we have of persons *vis á vis* behavior and character, and then by having in place certain social instruments that ensure adequate redress where necessary.[19] Making moral expectations clear presumes the existence of a normative moral system against which actions and traits of character are assessed. Note that the practice of reacting to an actor in light of his behavior does not demonstrate that such a normative system is in place.

Must an Account Be Given to Affirm Responsibility?

Of course, situations exist in which it seems sensible to claim that a person is responsible for her behavior even where that person is, for reasons other than an absence of moral agency, in no position to give an account of her behavior. Four such situations come to mind: 1. Cases involving subsequent incapacitation; 2. Cases of extreme evil; 3. Cases of private moral failure;[20] 4. The Robinson Crusoe case. Let us examine each of these in turn.

1. Suppose I have slandered you but have subsequently become insane, or have died. We might wish that an account could be given in these circumstances; we might hope for an account that would explain, excuse, or justify my conduct. But, of course, no account can be produced by me. (Let us assume that accounts by proxy are not an option.) In what sense, then does it remain appropriate that an account be provided?

2. Imagine that an act of gross wickedness has been perpetrated, such that no account would be meaningful.[21] If Alice maliciously tortures baby Bernie in order to obtain from his parents a greater baby-sitting wage, any expectation we have that she account for her behavior seems beside the point. The act is so abominable that merely to ask for an account suggests a potential for justification the act does not possess. The ready answer in this case, of course, is that Alice fails to meet the requisite criteria for moral agency (she is plainly imbalanced). But let us assume Alice is not so imbalanced as to be ignorant of what she is doing; she appreciates fully the measure of her evil, but embraces it nonetheless. The fact that no account would be comprehensible in these circumstances, and anything presented as an attempt would seem hollow, does not appear to lessen the burden of responsibility Alice bears for her conduct. If characterizing a person as responsible means that an account is expected and appropriately forthcoming from the person, is Alice not responsible?

3. There are moral failures that are the concern of none but the actor alone. Suppose you are a spiteful person. You resent the fact that your arguably more deserving colleague has been awarded a promotion. As a result, you refuse to include her in social gatherings at which she might meet persons who would be instrumental in furthering her career. Surely it is correct that you are morally responsible for your action. But, it is not obvious that anyone may appropriately ask for an account of that action. Since some moral failures may be nobody's business, an account needn't be forthcoming in order for ascriptions of responsibility to be warranted.

4. Imagine Robinson Crusoe, alone on his island (or in the company of the mute Friday) slandering you most bitterly. What force is there to the claim that, in calling Crusoe responsible for this act we are claiming an account is owed us? To whom is Crusoe able to give an account? Does it make sense to say an account ought to be given if there is no one present to receive it?

In each of these cases, the intuition is that the actors are responsible for their behavior, and that their inability to account for this behavior does not alter this responsibility in the slightest. Although each performs an act for which it seems appropriate that an account be forthcoming, the circumstances insulate the agent from accountability. So, it seems, in calling a person responsible, we must be expressing something other than the view that an explanation or account is expected and fitting.

Moreover, while such cases appear to present a stumbling block for the accountability interpretation, the responsiveness account can, it seems, explain why individuals whose moral failures are "private" are responsible. These individuals are appropriate targets of the reactive attitudes. Does this show that the responsiveness account is better equipped to explain responsibility ascriptions?

Certain cases of the first, second, and fourth varieties can be handled by the accountability approach at least as easily as they can by alternative accounts. It makes as little sense to react with resentment or indignation to the actions of an insane person as it does to expect an account of him. If it is meaningful to treat evil Alice as an agent toward whom reactive attitudes and conduct are appropriate, then it is equally meaningful to regard her as someone who can and ought to account for her actions. Finally, although Crusoe lacks an audience, he is a moral agent who in typical circumstances would be asked for an account of his conduct (an account that would, variously, minimize the harm, redress, or justify the act that has been done).

Moreover, it is meaningful to say in cases of the third sort that the propriety of an account from the jealous colleague explains the fact that we ascribe responsibility to him or her, although in this case no *right* to demand or exact an account exists. After all, neither does a right exist to respond to the moral failures of others. The apparent ease with which the reactive attitudes analysis deals with cases of private moral failures is due to the fact that it bypasses the idea of requiring a right to intervene in private affairs; attitudes emerge, right or no right.

The central point is that the concept of accountability — the idea that it is fitting that the agent explain her intentions — enables us to charge a person with responsibility even where she fails to explain her behavior. The accountability analysis of responsibility ascriptions does not insist that the person *in fact* give an account to someone, or that there be someone (or some institution) to whom the agent must deliver the account, or that the account elicit a response.

It is most important that the merits of the two accounts be appraised for the usual run of cases. And, in the usual cases, it would be inappropriate (or unnecessary) to take a reactive attitude toward one from whom we did not first have cause to expect an account. We regard a person as a suitable candidate for the reactive attitudes, and we take these attitudes to the person, because we think the person is accountable for his or her behavior. The person who fails to offer an account is open to criticism or reproach because of this failure.[22] Also, in the usual cases, it would not be unreasonable to expect an account from one whose behavior elicited no reaction from us to speak of. We can think of the person as accountable even if we never assume a responsive stance towards him — responsibility ascriptions can be "attitude neutral".

Is accountability limited to undesirable acts?

One might protest that the accountability interpretation makes sense only with respect to untoward actions or traits of character, as the second stage of evaluation makes explicit.[23] After all, it is unlikely we would think it appropriate that the agent who has done nothing untoward supply an account of her behavior; to give an account is to give something like a defense, or a justification. Hence Baier's charge that "accountability" is reserved for cases of liability and the need to decide moral sanctions.

In general, moral evaluation will occur because someone has performed an undesirable action, or has failed to follow through with a task, or has exhibited a substandard character. But the fact that our concern in attributing responsibility is primarily to decide cases of moral violation does not mean that the general function of responsibility judgments isn't to seek accountability. The accountability approach works for the usual run of cases (those involving blameworthy conduct), and explains responsibility for morally neutral actions as well. Morally neutral cases do not as a rule call for an account, but it may still be appropriate that the actor state his or her point of view about the action he or she has performed.

THE MERITS OF THE ACCOUNTABILITY APPROACH

Construing judgments about moral responsibility as judgments about accountability is preferable for a number of reasons. One reason is that the accountability approach focuses on the activity of the agent whose responsibility is at issue—the subject himself— rather than inviting and then extrapolating responsibility ascriptions indirectly, by way of the feelings, attitudes, and punitive or rewarding practices of others. These signal that someone other than the agent believes the agent to be responsible, but accountability places the burden squarely upon the actor, whether or not others assume certain attitudes and practices of a responsive sort. The expectation of an account from an actor signals a straightforward regard of him as a responsible, autonomous agent; deriving his responsibility from the stance taken to him by others does not.

Second, a theory of responsibility ascriptions built upon the notion of accountability explains the propriety of our reactive attitudes. We can't properly react to someone unless the person is one from whom an account is expected. It would be improper to resent the actions of a small child, or a dog, or a senile friend since these are creatures incapable of appreciating, no less than explaining, their reasons for action in a way that makes the action comprehensible for the purpose of moral evaluation.

A third advantage of the accountability approach is that, as a rule, our interest in determining whether an agent is free or not arises only if the agent has done something that gives us reason to seek an account from her. It is only fair to expect an account of a person if the person in fact acted freely (the belief that someone is a free agent is implicit in our belief that the person is someone we hold accountable), and so free agency is a condition upon which accountability rests. But the condition of freedom is one in which we take an interest after we have cause to hold the person accountable for her behavior; that a person may have been lacking in freedom is typically noticed in the context of asking for an excuse.[24] Thus, questions about accountability are epistemically prior to concerns about agent freedom.

CONCLUSION

I have defended the view that what we mean when we say "*X* is responsible for *Y*" is that *X* has done (or caused, or is) *Y*, and that it is fitting that *X* account for doing (or causing, or being) *Y*. A theory of moral responsibility spelled out in terms of the conditions for responsible agency, or in terms of the having of responsibilities, or in terms of responsiveness, is of explanatory value only where there first exists some reason to think the individual accountable for her actions. This calls for a prior sense of what it means to hold a body responsible. Hence, the accountability view offers a general answer to the question of what is meant by ascriptions of responsibility.

California State University, Sacramento

Received September 20, 1996

NOTES

1. This paper was developed during a 1995 NEH Summer Seminar for College Teachers in Boulder, Colorado. I am grateful to John Martin Fischer, Peter French, Gale Justin, and Michael McKenna for their comments on previous versions of the paper.

2. This view originates with Peter Strawson, and is detailed in his influential paper "Freedom and Resentment," *Proceedings of the British Academy,* 48 (1962), pp. 1-25. Reprinted in John Martin Fischer and Mark Ravizza, eds., *Perspectives on Moral Responsibility,* (Ithaca: Cornell University Press, 1993), pp. 45-66. All references are to the latter text.

3. Although his classification of types of responsibility differs somewhat from my own, I have appropriated, with modifications, some of Kurt Baier's categories in this discussion. The idea of having responsibilities is analogous to Baier's notion of "task-responsibility," or the "forward-looking aspect" of agent-responsibility. In its forward-looking sense, agent-responsibility consists in being socially entrusted, on either customary, legal, or moral grounds, with a specified event, state of affairs, or duty. See Baier, "Types of Responsibility," in Peter A. French, ed., *Individual and Collective Responsibility,* (Cambridge, MA: Schenkman Publishing, 1972). Reprinted in *The Spectrum of Responsibility,* ed. Peter A. French (New York: St. Martin's Press, 1991), pp. 117-122. References are to the latter text. See also Baier's "Moral and Legal Responsibility," in Siegler, Mark et. al., eds., *Medical Innovation and Bad Outcomes: Legal, Social and Ethical Responses,* (Ann Arbor: Health Administration Press, 1987), pp. 101-129.

4. While a person may be held accountable for those things she had an obligation to do, the things for which a person can be held accountable are not restricted to things the person had an obligation or a responsibility to do. I can be accountable for my slovenly habits, or for my acts of bravery, where neither of these attends the discharging of an obligation. Equally, the fact that an act is one I am obliged to perform does not decide whether I am accountable for performing it or for failing to do so.

5. Actual causal control differs from what John Martin Fischer calls "regulative" control in that the latter involves the power to alter the mechanism of action; to do otherwise than one actually does. Regulative control has metaphysical implications bearing on determinism whereas causal control *simpliciter* does not. Fischer pursues this distinction in "Responsiveness and Moral Responsibility," in *Responsibility, Character, and the Emotions: New Essays in Moral Psychology,* ed. Ferdinand Schoeman, (Cambridge University Press, 1987), pp. 81-106.

6. Of course, the judgment "X is responsible" might capture both the idea of *having* responsibilities and the idea of *being* agent-responsible, just as it might convey the ideas of causal agency and of accountability. For example, the claim "Exxon Corporation is responsible for cleaning up the oil spill" might express a combination of the following three propositions:

i. Exxon has a duty to clean up the spill (is task-responsible).

ii. Exxon causally brought about the spill.

iii. Exxon is accountable for cleaning up the spill.

7. In what follows, I will ignore cases of vicarious responsibility, and will speak as if being the actual cause of an act or event is a presupposition of responsibility ascriptions.

8. Judith Jarvis Thomson's distinction between "Blame 1" and "Blame 2" captures this idea. See her "Morality and Bad Luck," reprinted in Daniel Statman, ed., *Moral Luck,* (Albany: SUNY Press, 1993), pp. 195-215.

9. Among the best of a huge body of literature on Strawson's account are: A.J. Ayer, "Free-will and Rationality," in *Philosophical Subjects: Essays Presented to P.F. Strawson,* ed. Zak van Straaten, (New York: Oxford Clarendon Press, 1980); John Martin Fischer, "Responsiveness and Moral Responsibility," op. cit.; Fischer, *The Metaphysics of Free Will,* (Cambridge, MA: Blackwell Publishing, 1994); Galen Strawson, "On 'Freedom and Resentment'" in his *Freedom and Belief,* (Oxford University Press, 1986); R. Jay Wallace, *Responsibility and the Moral Sentiments* (Cambridge, MA: Harvard University Press, 1994); and Susan Wolf, "The Importance of Free Will," *Mind* 90 (1981): 386-405. The articles by G. Strawson and Wolf are reprinted in Fischer and Ravizza (1993).

10. Peter Strawson, "Freedom and Resentment," section IV, p. 55.

11. Wolf, "The Importance of Free Will."

12. Galen Strawson, "On 'Freedom and Resentment.'"

13. Fischer contends that the morally responsible agent is "rationally accessible" to these attitudes because the mechanism from which the agent acts (e.g., the will) is "weakly reasons responsive." Moreover, the agent possesses some degree of "guidance" control over those things for which she is held responsible. See his "Responsiveness and Moral Responsibility," and *The Metaphysics of Free Will.*

14. Fischer, "Responsiveness and Moral Responsibility," op. cit., p. 81.

15. I take the phenomenon of responsiveness to be incidental to responsibility ascriptions. This is a stronger view than one which regards the reactive attitudes as part of, but not the whole of, what is essential to being morally responsible.

16. Nothing about Fischer's position is incompatible with a theory that explains holding people responsible. Fischer might agree that showing what is true of persons such that they are proper candidates for the reactive attitudes calls for a discussion of accountability. But such an account is incidental to Fischer's primary interest.

17. The sense of accountability I have in mind is something of an amalgam of the concepts of "accountability" and "answerability" as Baier distinguishes them. On his version, one who is accountable is socially required to discharge a certain task *and* must give an account to some specified person of whether or not the task has been discharged. By contrast, one is answerable where one has *failed* to discharge a given social requirement. Answerability "is the logical consequence...of a failure to discharge a social requirement of any sort." However, no excuse or explanation needs to be given for this failure unless there is some specific person to whom one is "task-responsible" for providing such a report. (Baier, "Moral and Legal Responsibility," note 7, p. 126-7; p. 113). I do not insist that an agent fail to discharge a task in order to be answerable, although I concede we look for answers more frequently when something goes wrong than we do when all is well. Nor is a person only held to account to a specific person, as Baier requires. Nonetheless, Baier's notion of answerability as the "backward-looking aspect" of agent-responsibility is largely analogous to "accountability" as I envision it. When we say that a person is responsible for something, we mean that the person did something that is recognized as morally relevant, and for which it ought to be the case that the person give an account.

18. I follow D.E. Cooper and Lionel Kenner here. Both contend that what we normally expect of people sets the standard in deciding assignments of responsibility as well as degree of blame (or praise). See Cooper, "Collective Responsibility," pp. 255-264, and Kenner, "On Blaming," pp. 189-197, in French (1991). Since the accountability analysis isn't restricted to cases of moral shortcoming or failure, "having fallen short" is only the typical case where accounts are appropriate.

19. Baier, "Types of Responsibility," p. 118; "Moral and Legal Responsibility," p. 102.

20. Michael McKenna brought the second and third class of cases to my attention.

21. Gary Watson explores such cases in his "Responsibility and the Limits of Evil: Variations on a Strawsonian Theme," in Schoeman (1987), pp. 256-286. Reprinted in Fischer and Ravizza (1993), pp. 119-148. All references are to the latter text.

22. In this manner the Strawsonian approach may retain a role in the accountability picture.

23. Baier, "Moral and Legal Responsibility," p. 112. Note that the same charge could be levied against the responsiveness account.

24. J. L. Austin raised the idea that questions about freedom arise when we have reason to consider whether an agent might be excused from bearing some degree of responsibility for his actions. Austin notes that the tendency in ordinary language to think of excuses as a way to avoid responsibility rather than to deny freedom is somewhat misleading since, strictly speaking, one need not avoid responsibility by pleading an excuse. The excuse may mitigate responsibility, or it may bring forgiveness, while an acknowledgment of responsibility remains. See Austin, "A Plea for Excuses," in J.O. Urmson & G.J. Warnock, eds., *Philosophical Papers,* (Oxford: Oxford University Press, 1961; 1970). Reprinted in French (1991), pp. 39-54.

PUBLIC AFFAIRS QUARTERLY
Volume 12, Number 1, January 1998

MORAL AGENCY, INDIVIDUAL RESPONSIBILITY, AND HUMAN PSYCHOLOGY

N. Ann Davis

It is both a credo of common sense and an axiom of the social and behavioral sciences that experiences early in life have a profound influence on a person's psychological, social, and moral development. We need not take a stance on the nature vs. nurture debate to acknowledge that—whatever cards we may be dealt in the genetic lottery—how we are raised, the environment in which we grow up, and the events that befall us in childhood strongly affect how we develop as individual human beings, and what sorts of moral beings we become.

Experiences in infancy and early childhood are not merely influential, but formative. What happens early in our lives—how our caregivers respond to our needs, and how we as individuals are affected by the larger social context in which we are raised—are not simply events in our lives, or mere background conditions, but things that may be fulcral in making us the sort of human beings we become. When we add to this an appreciation of some of the other powerful influences of childhood—such things as family dynamics, cultural and educational context, and socioeconomic circumstances—we reach similar conclusions. These conditions and vicissitudes contour the basic shape, if not the precise details, of our personal and moral identities as adults. They affect how we see ourselves, how we construe our options, and how we perceive and respond to the needs of other human beings.

These claims are not obviously controversial. People generally profess to acknowledge both the causal impact and moral relevance of childhood experiences, and the importance of the larger educational, social, political, and economic context in which a child is raised. But it is not clear that, as a society, we have really come to grips with the broader moral implications of such an acknowledgment, or really thought through how it should influence our thinking in the policy domain. There is a deep tension between what the social and behavioral sciences reveal about human beings' psychological development—and often enough, what we can learn simply by using common sense and attentive observation—and some of our views about moral assessment in general, and about moral responsibility in particular. Since our views about moral assessment and moral responsibility also color our normative views on policy-related issues, as well as our views about the proper approach to policy formation, the failure to effect coherence between the received wisdom of the social sciences and our views about moral accountability has implications that extend far beyond the realm of theory.

In this essay, I explore some aspects of the tension between the revelations of the social and behavioral sciences and our (insufficiently well-scrutinized) views about the proper basis of attributions of moral accountability. I shall also sketch some of the problems we face if we continue to endorse practices and implement policies that presuppose (what I shall argue are) deeply flawed views about moral agency, individual responsibility, and personal accountability.

I

Most reflective people would readily concede that an individual's coming to be a responsible moral agent is something that has both psychological components and developmental preconditions. The connections between these components and preconditions and the achievement of agency have both logical and empirical dimensions. On the one hand, we believe that there are tight conceptual connections between the notions of agency and responsibility themselves, and thus between seeing someone as a moral agent and thinking that he or she is properly held accountable for chosen deeds and their consequences. Attributions of responsibility presuppose belief in the individual's general moral competence: if we think that someone does not actively possess the sort of general moral competence we associate with moral agency, we think that he or she *cannot* plausibly be viewed as responsible for his or her actions.

On the other hand, we also recognize that physical, emotional, and environmental factors play complex and important causal roles in an individual's moral development. Most notably, perhaps, we recognize that they can function as barriers or impediments. At the limit, they can effectively preclude an individual's developing the sorts of skills and abilities that form the basis of our attributions of general overall moral competence.

Together these observations support some broad normative conclusions. Though philosophers do not agree on either the interpretation or the details of the view that "'Ought' implies 'can'," there is, nevertheless, broad agreement both on the truth of some such doctrine and on its general relevance. We recognize that individuals who lack the skills and capacities that are central to the exercise of agency cannot reasonably be expected to meet the sorts of demands that we visit upon those who are fully moral agents, and we believe that only the conduct of individuals who are agents can fairly be assessed in robust moral terms. If possessing the sort of general moral competence we view as constitutive of moral agency is a precondition of being properly viewed as morally responsible for one's actions, then an individual who did not, in fact, develop such competences cannot reasonably be held morally responsible for his or her actions, or fairly subjected to moral censure for them. It is thus problematical to suppose that the conduct of such individuals is properly subjected to the sorts of moral criticism, social sanction, or legally enforced punishments that we routinely visit upon individuals whose moral agency is not in question. And it is even more problematical for us to propose and implement social policies that embody such presumptions. We shall shortly revisit the notion of agency in somewhat greater detail. But there are, it appears, some observations that we can make at the outset. As individuals who are participating members of the moral community, we both attach importance to the possession of moral agency and agree, at least in general terms, on what it is to possess the general moral competence we associate with agency. We view a moral agent as an individual with a complex psychology whose manifestations are contingent on aspects of the individual's development and personality. The conduct of human moral agents exemplifies a range of integrated cognitive abilities and affective capacities, ones that both constitute and reflect the individual's particular personality and psychological history.[1]

I think that there is broad agreement on what it is for a human being to be a moral agent. But attempts to formulate precise characterizations of the notion of agency, definitive lists of the preconditions for moral responsibility, or catalogues of just what sorts of cognitive and affective capabilities attributions of agency presuppose quickly become cumbrous and technical, and thus inaccessible to individuals who cannot or will not navigate the twists and turns of the fine-grained accounts that academics often favor. This is a pity, for the notions of moral responsibility and agency are not just technical philosophical constructions or psychological constructs, but notions that play a central role in our understanding of our own moral identities and our interpretations of other persons' behavior. As such, they also color our views about what policies are efficacious and which sorts of policy are morally defensible. An investigation of (what I will call) our working understanding of agency and responsibility may be unable to yield the precision that academics like; the observations that emerge are likely to be fraught with the sorts of incoherences and ambiguities that vitiate their usefulness in rigorous theorizing. Still, I think that there is enough broad agreement on the core of these notions to support the modest claim that I wish to make here: that the development of moral agency in a human being can readily be seen to be dependent upon the circumstances of his or her early physical and psychological development. Even that modest claim, I shall argue, has some powerful implications for theorists and policy-makers.

II

At the core of our working understanding of the notion of moral agency lies the picture of an individual who is an *Effective, Rational, Sympathetic Actor* (or *ERSA*): someone who possesses an integrated combination of cognitive skills and coherent affective responses, and both enough intelligence and fixity of purpose to draw upon those skills and feelings in formulating plans of action. Among these skills is that of being able to make reasonably informed projections about the consequences of acting (or not acting) in various ways; this is something an individual must be able to do if he or she is to be able to understand the relationship between a means and an end, or compare one proposed means to its rivals. And both ERSAs' projections of consequences and their assessments of the merits of competing options must reflect some appreciation of the fact that their conduct has an impact on other human beings. Though they recognize that different individuals express their intelligence, physical power, and feelings in different ways, ERSAs understand that, as human beings, they share deep intellectual, physical, and emotional similarities. Finally, though ERSAs may sometimes suffer from bouts of weakness of will or other disconnections between deliberation and action, a being who could not generally follow through on his or her deliberations (etc.) is one whose status as an ERSA would be seriously in question. Effective, Rational, Sympathetic Actors must thus be able to take action in light of their projections, deliberations, values, and assessments in a significant range of circumstances.

This is only a partial and simplified characterization of the skills that are requisite for human moral agency, and of the background conditions that must be met for an ascription of responsibility to be justifiable in a particular set of circumstances. But it is clear and contentful enough for us to be able to see that the realization of an individual's potential for becoming a moral agent depends, in salient respects, on how things were for him or her early in life. If a child's upbringing was not 'good enough', then the child may not develop the relevant skills, understanding, and empathy, or be able to exercise them effectively.[2] If, for example, a child's primary caregiver was abusive, neglectful, wildly inconsistent, or simply unresponsive, the child may grow up unable to perceive or respond to other people's needs, and unable to understand or respond to other people's demonstrations of affection.[3] (Attachment disorder is an extreme instance of this.[4]) If the caregiver did not provide the young child with a nutritionally adequate diet, or the environment itself was toxic (e.g., there was a high concentration of lead-based paint dust in the child's home, or heavy metals contamination of the water), then the child's brain and central nervous system may be damaged, and his or her intellectual development seriously impaired. In extreme cases, the child may simply be unable to achieve the cognitive sophistication needed to be an Effective, Rational, Sympathetic Actor. If even the rudiments of a basic education were missing, then both the child's capacity to make intelligent informed projections of consequences and his or her ability to envision alternative possibilities may be seriously limited. This obviously affects both the child's ability to understand his or her causal power and his or her ability to appreciate its moral implications.

A child's maturing into an Effective, Rational, Sympathetic Actor involves the acquisition of skills and competences whose development may be compromised by a number of contingent factors. Appreciating the fact that early childhood experiences are formative thus not only involves acknowledging that such experiences play a significant causal role in a child's becoming the sort of person he or she becomes, but also our understanding that—at the limit—such experiences may make or break the child in moral terms. We do not need to articulate a detailed technical account of the concept of moral agency or produce a complete catalogue of the subtle presumptions and preconditions of responsibility ascriptions to appreciate that the circumstances of infancy and early childhood may affect a child in ways that bear on his or her potential to become an Effective, Rational, Sympathetic Actor.[5]

Though I think that both our moral theorizing and our formation of social policies must take account of the facts of human development and vulnerability, our vulnerability must not be exaggerated. Human beings do not all become moral agents in the same way, or at the same age, and even individuals who are clearly classifiable as ERSAs may possess different constellations of skills, or possess those skills to differing degrees.[6] Nor is serious psychological damage or physical impairment in childhood something that makes the achievement of true moral agency impossible. Some people are more resilient than others, and some kinds of damage that occurs in early childhood may be reparable, or effectively compensable.[7] An individual's early experiences do not rigidly determine the parameters of moral possibility for him or her;

generally, what they do is make certain kinds of success or failure more or less likely. Still, not all of the damage done to a child may be remediable. And for a particular child in a particular set of circumstances, the needed correctives—including early intervention and diagnosis, and the provision of effective therapy, oversight, and support—may be unavailable. There are things that befall some children that effectively foreclose the possibility of their becoming sufficiently effective, rational, or compassionate, and that thus foreclose the likelihood of their being able to have meaningfully open moral futures: futures as moral agents in a community with other agents.

Again, I think that these observations are likely to seem uncontroversial, perhaps even banal. It is clear that the conditions of a human being's early life can affect him or her profoundly, and it is clear after reading even a few case histories that children subjected to serious abuse or neglect in early life often have serious difficulties later on.[8] Though there is of course a great deal of variability of expression (partly depending on such factors as class and gender), the sort of difficulties these individuals experience exhibit some broad patterns. For example, children who engage in behavior that strikes us as incomprehensible in its coldness and violence are often ones who themselves received little love and attention in early life.[9]

But the ways that we often go about making moral assessments and ascribing moral responsibility are in important respects at odds with psychological wisdom and moral common sense. Both the testimony of experts and the anecdotal observations of sympathetic non-experts should make us appreciate how vulnerable children are, and how fragile are some of the links that must be solidly forged if the child is to become an Effective, Rational, Sympathetic Actor. Nevertheless, we often seem to treat the development of moral agency, and associated moral capacities—and, in many instances, psychic capacities more generally—as if they were transcendent, even transcendental, capacities or skills. Even when we know that, as a child, an individual suffered poverty, deprivation, neglect, and abuse, we often speak as if both the moral evaluation of the individual's acts as right or wrong, and the attribution of moral responsibility for them, were straightforward and unproblematical.

The invocation of the rhetoric of individual responsibility, which often figures in people's views about proper public policy, provides evidence of the prevalence of such thinking. We shall consider more subtle examples later on; for now I shall focus upon a couple of the more familiar popular instances of the use of this rhetoric in a broad policy context.

III

One popular example of the invocation of the rhetoric of individual responsibility can be found in the advocacy of a "Just say 'No'" approach to the attempt to prevent teen-age pregnancy and deter the use of illegal drugs.[10] Though many of the people who employ this rhetoric undoubtedly know that a significant number of the adolescents who use illegal drugs or become pregnant in their early teens have spent their lives in environments in which drug use is rampant and teen-age pregnancy the norm—and one in which violence, poverty, ignorance, and despair often orchestrate the character of children's lives well before birth—they do not appear to accord much moral weight to such facts.[11] Except in cases in which a child was overtly coerced into using illegal drugs or engaging in unprotected sexual intercourse, proponents of the "Just say 'No'" approach think that the child's conduct is a proper object of robust moral scrutiny. When the conduct was voluntary (in this narrow sense), it is thought to be both appropriate to assign the children full responsibility for their choices, and fair to allow them to bear the brunt of the predictable consequences that result from their actions: (e.g.) poverty, violence, poor health, and social marginalization. The predictably untoward consequences that stem from a girl's choice to engage in unprotected, uncontracepted sexual intercourse, or a youth's choice to use illegal addictive drugs, are thought to be avoidable. As the slogan suggests, whether or not a particular child actually does avoid them depends on what the child chooses to do, on whether or not he or she chooses to "Just say 'No'."

The implication is that the source of (e.g.) a pregnant teen-ager's putatively immoral behavior and its untoward consequences lies in her failure to have made the right choices. And her failure to have made the right choices is thought to be a moral failure, one that stemmed from her refusal to will herself to do things that were unequivocally identifiable as right (or avoid doing things that were unequivocally identifiable as wrong). The presumption is that both the ability to will oneself to do the right thing and one's psychic strength generally are essentially unaffected by the actual vicissitudes of one's life. Certainly there has been a great deal of publicity about the harshness of life in the inner city, and the psychological effects of early neglect and abuse, and of experiencing or witnessing violence, are well documented. Yet proponents of the "Just say 'No'" approach to the problems of teen-age pregnancy and illegal drug use invoke the rhetoric of individual responsibility even in such grim circumstances. They see the conditions in which a child makes a 'choice' to engage in unprotected sexual intercourse or use illicit drugs—conditions that may include poverty, ignorance, emotional deprivation, violence, abuse, and relentless manipulation by the media—as essentially irrelevant to the moral assessment of the choice or its makers.

Certainly not all of those who embrace the "Just say 'No'" approach to social problems possess the blend of coldness, intellectual shallowness, and lack of imagination that characterized Nancy Reagan's pronouncements on the subject. Nevertheless, the view that problems like teen-age pregnancy and illicit drug use stem largely from an individual's weak will, or weakness of character, remains a popular one. We cannot presume either that the explanation of the popularity of invocations of the "Just say 'No'" approach to evaluating the predicament of even the most deprived inner city children lies in its proponents' utter lack of information about the character of the children's environment. It thus seems reasonable to conjecture that it is not simply ignorance, lack of imagination, or sheer indifference that lies at the root of the popularity of invocations of the rhetoric of individual responsibility, and the belief that appeals to take responsibility for one's actions should form the core of social policies aimed at reducing teen-age pregnancy and the use of illicit drugs. Views about agency and responsibility seem also to be playing a large part. Many people regard the strength of a person's will or character as a proper object of moral assessment, and view it as one that is deeply independent of the circumstances in which the person—and hence his or her will, and character—developed. By their lights, it is thus legitimate for us to seek to prevent social ills by imprecating those who fall prey to them to set themselves to strengthen their character.

Dubious views about the nature of agency and responsibility also seem to underlie people's current enthusiasm for lowering the age at which children who have committed especially heinous acts may be tried as adults. Even in the face of data that strongly suggest that the most flagrantly antisocial 'youthful offenders' were usually themselves the victims of abuse and neglect as young children, and developmental data that indicate that even untraumatized older children do not possess the package of cognitive, behavioral, and affective properties that individuals must possess to be able to exercise judgment and self-control, people persist in invoking the rhetoric of individual responsibility in defense of harsh punitive practices. Thus it is thought justifiable for us to try and punish a 12-year-old as we would try and punish an adult.[12] Both at the state and at the federal level, enthusiasm for harsher punishment of violent children seems to have overcome people's awareness that it is children, i.e., beings who are not yet fully Engaged, Rational, Sympathetic Actors, who are the target of their anger.

Though the trend to lower the age at which individuals may be tried as adults is nationwide, it is difficult to feel confident that one has understood the reasoning behind such proposals. As people who have read much of anything about child development—or simply spent some time with 12-year-olds—can attest, even 'normal' 12-year-olds are not like adults in cognitive or affective terms. They cannot predict consequences or project options as adults can, nor can they exercise adult-level impulse-control or prudence. How, then, can it be thought to be either reasonable or morally defensible to urge that the legal system should treat violent 12-year-olds like violent adults? Though some people undoubtedly mean to invoke social protectionist reasons in defense of proposals to remove violent children from the community, reasons of that sort clearly do not justify the practice of punishing such children as adults. It is, I think, plausible to conjecture that what drives such proposals is deeper: an amalgam of moral outrage and fear, couched in the rhetoric of individual responsibility. Only if the child is appropriately held responsible for such deeds can it be thought just to inflict severe adult punishment upon him or her. Those who champion the practice of trying violent children as adults seem to construe the heinousness, violence, or senselessness of a child's acts as providing grounds for believing that it is appropriate to hold the child fully responsible for his or her deeds.

The rationale for holding children morally and criminally responsible for their violent acts seems to be that, since the acts in question are so very horrible, the wrongness of acting in such a way must have been obvious to them, even though they are children. And if a child's awareness of the wrongness of the act can be presumed, then his or her acting in the wrongful way can be seen as vicious and willful: thus the child can appropriately be held responsible for committing a violent crime.[13] The child should thus not have been tempted to act in such a way, or—if, somehow, he or she had in fact been so tempted—then the child can be justly faulted for not having exercised appropriate restraint. Once again, he or she could have "Just said 'No'."[14] The presumption is that the effective exercise of will lies within the power of virtually all individuals, even children as young as 12. It is something that is unfettered by the vicissitudes of an individual's upbringing and experience, and something whose moral force is in effect early in life. The power of will emerges intact, even from the most dreadful of personal circumstances, and forms the basis for attributions of responsibility and fault even before the onset of the age of reason.[15]

IV

The objections to invocations of the rhetoric of individual responsibility in these contexts—the attempt to prevent illegal drug use and teen-age pregnancy among inner-city children, and the trying and punishing of children as adults—are both clear and powerful. First, and most obviously: If our moral assessments of a human being's conduct are to be meaningful and fair, then they cannot properly ignore the human context in which the conduct has taken place. We possess strong evidence that abuse, neglect, and deprivation affect, and can strongly impair, a child's psychological and moral development.[16] Though the adolescent whom such an impaired child becomes is not, of course, literally powerless—i.e., he or she can utter the word 'No,' and sincerely mean not to do the thing in question—he or she may be effectively unable to follow through on this resolve.[17] It is thus clearly problematical to make appeals to the individual's possession of the ability to say 'No' the cornerstone of policies aimed at the prevention of antisocial behavior, or policies that articulate its proper punishment. Advocating that we continue to do so is at odds both with moral common sense and with our working understanding of the notions of agency and responsibility.

Second, the achievement of maturity and effective moral agency are gradual processes, not all-or-nothing, precisely datable and locatable events. Though neither is fully an Effective, Rational, Sympathetic Actor, other things being equal, an older child is further along in the process of becoming one than a younger child is, and an older child is thus properly held morally responsible for a greater range of things. But progress down this path is not linear, and its details are not fixed: human beings mature psychologically and morally in different ways and at different ages.[18] Not all children of the same age are properly assigned the same sort of moral or legal responsibility or moral fault; a child who has suffered neglect or persistent abuse cannot fairly be subjected to the same standards as a child whose parents and environment were 'good enough'.[19] Any serious attempt at assessing a child's psychological maturity and capacity for responsibility must be informed not only by an understanding of human psychological development in general, but also by awareness of this particular child's particular history.

We could, of course, decide that it is too difficult for us to make accurate assessments of whether a child's environment was 'good enough' for him or her to be able to develop the skills and capacities we associate with moral agency, and thus propose that our social policies invoke (something like) a strict liability standard, or—supposing that it is not an oxymoron—a modified strict liability standard. Thus we might propose (e.g.) that we assess a child's conduct against the standard of a 'reasonable child of ordinary prudence', or some such thing. But such a proposal clearly has very little to recommend it. Whatever advantages we think might accrue from adopting this sort of standard to assess the criminality of adults' conduct, the application of such a standard to children is patently unreasonable: it flies in the face of our recognition that they are children. Though most 14-year-olds might be capable of exercising judgment and control in a particular sort of situation, anyone who has dealt with children and adolescents is aware that there is tremendous individual variability. The paths to psychological and emotional maturity are many, not one, and different children mature in different ways. Invocations of the standard of 'the reasonable child' may be useful in some contexts—e.g., if one wants to figure out whether a particular textbook is suitable, or a particular movie is too graphic. But it clearly cannot reasonably be invoked to rebut the charge that this particular child could not fully understand the complexities of the situation, or effectively control his or her response to it.

Finally, though determinations of legal innocence and guilt are based on the application of clearly-defined criteria, this is clearly not the case in the moral arena. In legal contexts, judgments of guilt and innocence have a verdictive character, and the notions of guilt and innocence are ones that are technical, and defined exclusively. One is either guilty of a specific offense, or not guilty of it. Moreover, the absence of legal guilt must be presumed, and can be rebutted only when specific sorts of evidence and testimony allow for its rebuttal. In addition, though factors about a child's early environment and psychological maturity may not be thought to negate the propriety of convicting the child of a crime, such factors are allowed to enter into the determination of appropriate punishment. They are deemed highly relevant at the sentencing phase, and in at least some cases, they may effectively nullify many of the material consequences of having been found guilty.

But in the moral arena, offenses—i.e. putatively wrongful acts—are not so narrowly or unequivocally defined as they are in the legal arena, and there are many possible gradations of guilt and innocence. In actual moral practice, we treat the notions of guilt and innocence both as relative (to this agent, in this context, regarding the performance of this sort of act) and slippery. If we understand both that the achievement of moral agency is closely tied to an individual's psychological development, and that such development is a subtle and variable process, we should be willing to acknowledge that people in general—and minor children in particular—can be more and less morally responsible, and more and less at fault. Since, in the moral context, there is no sentencing phase to take the sting out of the finding of (moral) guilt, it is reasonable to expect our moral verdicts—i.e., our moral judgments—to be both cautious and informed: tempered by a rich awareness of the psychological and developmental factors that affect a child's effective exercise of (incipient) moral agency.

When we combine the three objections, I believe their overall effect is powerful, and thus that we can see that it is both intellectually and morally problematical for people to invoke the standard legalistic, verdictive framework to evaluate and assess the conduct of a 12-year-old whose life history is a harrowing tale of neglect, extreme deprivation, and abuse. Even more problematical is the claim that it is justifiable to invoke such a framework as a basis for punishing such a child as if he or she were an adult. The criminal justice system is supposed both to be empirically informed and constrained by moral concerns. Though it is legitimate for people to be concerned about the removal of violent individuals from general society, this hardly justifies our espousing practices that offend both justice and common sense. Social policies that mandate punishing 12-year-olds as adults are thus clearly prima facie morally objectionable. They can justly be enacted only if those who would apply them can argue persuasively that the 12-year-old in question possessed the sorts of capacities and competences we associate with moral agency. But, in fact, children of 12 are not likely often to meet such criteria. Given what we know about the life circumstances of individuals who perpetrate the sorts of violent deeds that those of standard moral sensibilities find horrific, it is hard to believe that 12-year-old youthful offenders will meet them more frequently than their age cohort.

Reflection on the problem of abused, deprived, or neglected children highlights some of the consequences of our failure to harmonize our moral assessments (including responsibility ascriptions) with psychological and developmental wisdom in a particularly poignant way, and it enables us to formulate what I believe is a powerful moral objection to certain sorts of social policies. But the problem is certainly not a local or isolated one. Our failure to examine the moral implications of the fact that childhood experiences are formative is not unique or idiosyncratic, but a symptom of our more general unwillingness to address the moral implications of psychic events in people's lives, and our more general failure to formulate moral perspectives that adequately reflect the complexities of human beings' psychological nature.

V

There are, in fact, other sorts of situations in which the failure to integrate psychological wisdom and moral practice allows people to continue in postures that are both normatively and theoretically objectionable, and to endorse public policies that are deeply morally problematical. Morally relevant, psychologically significant events—ones that may dramatically affect individuals' cognitive skills or affective equilibrium, or their ability to effectively integrate thought, feeling, and deed—are not confined to infancy and childhood. There is abundant evidence that, though it is, of course, much more pronounced in infancy and childhood, human psychological vulnerability does not cease with the end of childhood. Individuals who experience traumatic events later in life may be profoundly, even permanently, affected by them. The effects are variable, but they exhibit salient commonalities. The term 'post-traumatic stress disorder' (*PTSD*) has been used to identify a range of symptoms associated with the individual's impaired response to such events, events like rape, domestic violence, serious threats to life (including accidents, crimes, and natural disasters), divorce, and the death of one's spouse or partner.[20] Some of the problems associated with PTSD include depression, physical illness (headaches, stomach complaints, hypertension, sleep disorders), rage (either at individuals who are thought to have been responsible for the trauma, or at those who managed to escape its effects), intrusive thoughts or imagery (reliving the trauma; nightmares), feelings of isolation, alienation, powerlessness and vulnerability, and confusion about one's values, or loss of a sense of the meaning of life.[21]

There are obviously a vast array of possible trauma-producing events, as well as a wide range of possible reactions to them. Though not all the individuals who experience them will be seriously or irreparably affected, events like earthquakes, fires, floods, serious automobile accidents, violent crimes, and terrorist incidents can have profound effects on an individual's physical and psychological well-being. Not everyone who survives an incident in which others are violently killed (e.g.) will be permanently, traumatically affected by it in ways that significantly affect his or her ability to be an Effective, Rational, Sympathetic Actor, and not everyone who is permanently traumatically affected by such an event will be affected in the same way. It is reasonable, too, to believe that how severely a person is affected by the occurrence of a traumatic event bears some relation to his or her psychic state prior to its occurrence. But—as even a brief perusal of the daily newspaper attests—the occurrence of traumatic events cannot be deemed a rarity, nor can the psychological effects of such experiences be explained (away) as the consequence of prior pathology. People may disagree about the etiology and treatment of different expressions of PTSD, and about its legal implications, but its general moral significance seems undeniable. It is hard to see how someone could suffer multiple, long-lasting virulent symptoms of the sort associated with PTSD and yet have his or her agency—the capacity to be a Effective, Rational, Sympathetic Actor—unimpaired, or his or her conduct fairly appraised within the familiar parameters of moral assessment.

When we reflect on the physical, psychological, and moral vulnerability of a developing human being, and on the fact that even someone who had an unremarkable and untroubled upbringing may yet experience traumatic events that at least temporarily compromise his or her ability to exercise the capacities we associate with being an Effective, Rational, Sympathetic Actor, we come to several important realizations.

One of these is that we need to rethink the ways we make attributions of responsibility—and more globally, the ways we view the practice of morally assessing people's conduct. As a minimum, our practices should be modified to reflect a more sophisticated appreciation of human psychological development, and a livelier awareness of the fact that things can happen to human beings that seriously affect their ability to reason, feel, respond, and act in the ways that we take to be necessary for us to attribute moral agency to them (as a general capacity), and moral responsibility to them for particular deeds. We thus need to encourage greater attention to information about human psychological development, and a more robust appreciation of human vulnerability: a more robust appreciation of the psychological and moral consequences of a person's experiencing damage or trauma. Clearly, both philosophical theories that seek to offer accounts of agency and more informal proposals of criteria for moral practice and assessment need to accommodate such information. So, of course, does any social policy we seek to advance as morally defensible rather than merely expedient.

VI

The details of an adequate accommodation are undoubtedly both controversial and complex; the claim that we should either assign the attribution of responsibility a much smaller role in our overall scheme of moral assessment or insist upon the necessity of more informed attributions has far-reaching implications. But it seems reasonable to suppose, even at this point in the undertaking, that we would benefit from a willingness to draw upon and apply (something like) the notions of psychological and moral damage. The invocation of notions of damage can serve to remind us both that the experiences of infancy and early childhood are formative, and that certain ways of things going wrong in a person's life can have profound effects on whether he or she will be able to develop and exercise the capacities we take to be fundamental to the possession of moral agency.

Even in such a vague and promissory form, the observation is important, for it reminds us both that a person's moral identity is not properly understood as a sort of template conferred at birth, and that moral agency is not properly seen as the manifestation of a faculty or talent that is directly responsive to some inherently powerful and effective psychic organ, viz., the individual's will. Though children who have not been seriously damaged generally develop the ability to recognize things as right and wrong and to draw upon such notions in their deliberations, the acquisition of action-affecting moral sensitivity is not the expression of an inborn tropism or moral sense. Nor is it something that manifests itself through the exercise of a special power—the will—whose development is unaffected by the individual's environment. The wrongness of certain sorts of conduct may be obvious to individuals whose care and environment have been 'good enough', but not to one who has been the victim of abuse and neglect; such a person may have significantly impaired cognitive capacities, and skewed perceptions.[22] Even when a damaged child is aware at some level that a contemplated course of action is wrong, this awareness may not exercise the sort of powerful action-governing effects that it does for a normal person. In cases of serious neglect and abuse, an individual's rage and frustration may eclipse more subtle motivations and intellectual appreciations that the desired course of action is wrong. A teen-age girl who was herself neglected and abused as a young child may be more moved by her burning need to have someone in her life who loves her unconditionally than by the dim and inchoate awareness that having a baby at 14 will negatively affect the quality of her life—and her baby's life—in dramatic and pervasive ways.

Both the formation of a human's moral identity and the individual's moral efficacy—an individual's moral agency—depend upon a variety of contingent factors. And the basic shape of an individual's personality has implications regarding the nature of his or her identity as an ERSA. Together, the acknowledgment of our psychological vulnerability and the invocation of the notion of damage can provide an effective reminder that some of the things that happen to human beings may not be reparable, or even compensable. Though we are wonderfully adaptable beings, we are not purely plastic or entirely malleable. The basic shape of our personality is formed early in life; try as we might, we cannot go back to square one, or change our spots for stripes.[23] And it is a reminder that even if some sorts of damage are (at least in part) theoretically reparable, this does not mean that this damage is reparable here and now, for this particular individual: some individuals are simply more vulnerable than others. Moreover, even if some sorts of damage are theoretically remediable when there is early intervention and careful oversight by a trained, involved, and compassionate interlocutor, this does not provide enough moral counterweight to the reasons we have for withholding the attribution of full agency and responsibility to someone who was badly damaged as a child. Often enough, the very circumstances that contributed to the damage also result in the failure to implement measures to ameliorate it. The damaged child remains in the sort of familial, social, and economic environment in which the damage occurred, and goes on to pass a sorry legacy to his or her own children. As the proposal to treat violent 12-year-old offenders as adults suggests, a society that is reluctant to shoulder the financial costs of providing effective education and real economic opportunity to the child's parents, or adequate assistance to children unlucky enough to be born into conditions of poverty, abuse, and neglect, is not likely to be willing to shoulder the considerably larger burden of providing effective therapy and oversight for the damaged children in later life.

It is here, I think, that we find one of the deeper unacknowledged sources of support for the popularity of the invocation of individual responsibility in social policy contexts, and the prevalence of the "Just say 'No'" mentality as a response to teen-age pregnancy, illegal drug use, and the criminalization of violent children. It is both morally easier and cheaper to blame an individual for his or her willful failure to do the right thing than it is to acknowledge that the sources of much moral misconduct lie in factors—like poverty, ignorance, and violence-saturated media—that lie within the purview of societal control and responsibility. And it is clearly easier for us to react with anger and outrage at the senseless violence of youthful offenders than it is to act with sympathy and compassion. Outrage preserves the distance between us, and emphasizes the difference between us, while compassion demands that we draw close enough to try to understand what it is that might motivate a child to act so badly. Disavowing the "Just say 'No'"-based approach to public policy and the individual responsibility rhetoric on which it trades opens us up to the challenge of rethinking our understanding of the bases of individual entitlement and desert, and the meaning of our membership in the moral community. We would do well to question whether our moral energies are better spent charting the contours of individual fault—by, e.g., continuing to concern ourselves with the details of assigning fault and responsibility—or working to effect a redistribution of both our material resources and our psychic energy.

VII

I have thus far been arguing for three modest claims. First, I have argued that what befalls a child early in life may have profound effects on his or her psychological development, and thus affect the child's prospects of becoming an Effective, Rational, Sympathetic Actor. Second, I have tried to show that, though there may be a variety of competing technical accounts of the notion of agency, we can presume widespread agreement on the core of the notion: it is (something like) the capacity to become an Effective, Rational, Sympathetic Actor that forms the kernel of our understanding of the notion of general moral competence, or moral agency. Putting these two points together, we can see that individuals whose early lives are fraught with neglect, abuse, and deprivation may thus be not only materially and psychologically damaged by the circumstances that lie beyond their control, but also morally damaged by them, perhaps irreparably.

I have also argued that it is problematical to assume that damaged individuals can be fairly and reasonably held morally responsible for their choices and their foreseeable consequences, problematical to apply to them the same tests of awareness and control that we apply to persons who have not sustained such damage. At least some of our familiar moral practices and patterns of moral assessment—most notably those that draw upon the rhetoric of individual responsibility—appear to be seriously at odds with an honest accommodation of what we know about human psychological vulnerability and moral development. It is thus clear that, since the moral defensibility of some of our social policies is predicated on the soundness of these practices and patterns, there is reason to question whether they are, in fact, morally defensible. I have focused on some of the more egregious sorts of cases of reliance on these views in our formation of public policy, the "Just say 'No'" approach to the problem of teen-age pregnancy and illicit drug use, and the move toward prosecuting and punishing younger and younger children as adults. But with a little imagination, we can see that the problems with reliance on the rhetoric of individual responsibility do not stem only from clear instances of its misinterpretation or its unsympathetic application, e.g., to the deeds of abused, neglected or severely deprived children. They are quite general problems, and deep ones as well, and they have potentially broad implications both for moral theorizing and for policy formation. This is an important claim, and one that is less modest than the previous three. The remainder of the essay will be devoted to its development.

VIII

One natural response to the problems with the application of the rhetoric of individual responsibility to the problems of teen-age pregnancy and illegal drug use among inner city children, or the criminalization of violent children, is to point out that it is objectionably unsympathetic, and to advocate its tempering by a system of excuses and exemptions. One might do this by pointing out (e.g.) that a child who grew up in the hopeless and violence-filled climate of the inner city has suffered damage that his or her middle-class counterpart did not, and claiming that it is thus appropriate to judge this child, and this child's (putatively) immoral conduct, less harshly.

But a little reflection will expose some of the problems with this suggestion.[24] First, it is not simply inner-city children, or children whose parents are poor and uneducated, who suffer abuse and neglect. The steady stream of cases described by the media remind us that sexual abuse happens even in families with education, money, and social position.[25] And both the clinical observations of mental health professionals and responses to surveys suggest that, though more common and perhaps more damaging to children from lower socioeconomic strata, abuse and neglect occur throughout the social spectrum (particularly when we include such things as psychological abuse, and the child's exposure to parental violence).[26] Nor is post-traumatic stress disorder narrowly confined to a specific group of particularly vulnerable individuals. Though one may wish to maintain that applications of the strategy of excuse-and-exemption are appropriate only in cases of extreme psychological damage—and hence that moral agency and moral responsibility are properly attributed to individuals who meet a fairly low threshold of competence—such a response is fundamentally wrong-headed.

When we reflect on the implications of human psychological vulnerability, and on the moral implications of pervasive psychological damage to a child, we see that the problems with the rhetoric of individual responsibility are not confined to egregious cases, nor are they a consequence of overzealous invocation of such rhetoric. It is the presuppositions that underlie that rhetoric that are problematical; they bear on its tenability in broad terms.

The picture that underlies the rhetoric of individual responsibility is one that heavily emphasizes the conscious, cognitive, and self-consciously ratiocinative element of human deliberations and actions. A course of action is (putatively) identifiable as wrong, and hence an individual knows, or can be got to admit, that it is wrong; this is supposed to provide sufficient ground and sufficient incentive for the individual's not doing it. But a little thought suggests that this is not an accurate representation of the behavior of individuals who have experienced damage or trauma, or of human beings in general. In according so much weight to explicit moral reasoning and other conscious and self-conscious dimensions of assessment, it presents an incomplete and inaccurate picture of human action. Most notably, perhaps, it treats questions about an agent's motivation in action—and other unconscious sources of action—as secondary, simple, or morally inconsequential. This is a mistake on several fronts.

Though it is reasonable to assume that healthy mature adults are able both to articulate plausible moral principles and to understand the importance of setting themselves to act in accordance with such principles, even a sane and healthy adult is a human being who has had a particular psychological history, and who carries around some psychic baggage in consequence. As human beings, we have complex, often conflicting, motivations, only some of which we are able consciously to acknowledge. We are selectively aware of empirical data and detail, and prone to emotionally-driven distortions of the facts, and to misconstruals of our own contribution to our lives being as they are. It is reasonable to think that most people will acknowledge that they have blind spots and biases, and to expect that sophisticated adults will be at least somewhat psychologically astute and critically self-aware: enough, at least, to acknowledge the moral importance of scrutinizing their motives and questioning their interpretations of the facts. However, while this provides a dimension of depth for agents' conscious moral reasoning, it is not reasonable to think that the achievement of physical maturity or the attainment of effective moral agency resolves, or negates, underlying human psychological complexity and motivational confusion. There are elements of our own psyches that are not transparent to us, even when we direct careful and honest attention to the task.[27] And there are mechanisms of defense that humans regularly and reliably draw upon, emotionally driven, unconsciously acquired, and unacknowledged distorters of information and significance.

As humans, our attention is both selective and biased. We are especially prone to tune out things that are painful or damaging to our conception of ourselves, or to our interpretation of the world. When the stakes are high, and we are faced with the necessity of trying to find an appropriate response to an emotionally charged and morally complex situation, this penchant for denial is both deeper and less visible to us.

Examples abound. A forty-year-old woman who has just been told that her mammogram is problematical may tell herself that there was a mix-up at the doctor's office. Since she does not happen to recall any pre-menopause-onset breast cancer in her family, and she does occasional perfunctory self-examinations, there really cannot be a problem, she thinks; the doctor must have misread her mammogram, or mistaken someone else's films for hers. Confronted with his spouse's declaration that she is desperately unhappy and wants to get out of the marriage, a man may be inclined to reinterpret previous evidence that all is not well, or to deny its significance. Thus he may tell himself that it is just his spouse's middle-age restlessness that is the problem, or that things will be better when the children are a bit older. As those who have experienced cancer diagnoses (and cancer scares) and marital turbulence can attest, reactions of this sort are not unusual, nor are they in themselves deeply pathological. Though they may appear to involve a sort of denial that is different in scope and subtlety from the sort we expect to find in individuals who are emotionally immature or suffering from severe pathology—e.g., an angry teen-ager's denial that she is pregnant until she is too far along to contemplate abortion, or an alcoholic's insistence that he can quit drinking any time he wants to, and that 'the few beers' he drinks have no appreciable effect on his driving—they are contiguous with such behaviors, not different in kind.

Denial is, of course, not the only distortion to which human beings are prone. In order to protect ourselves from having to credit strong evidence of our own irrationality or immorality—from having to accept a picture of ourselves that squares poorly with our image of ourselves as decent and reasonable people—we engage in rationalization, a process whereby we present a distorted or dishonest picture of our own reasoning. Thus an instructor with unacknowledged sadistic tendencies may represent his penchant for making caustic comments and giving low grades as a strategy for trying to get students to improve their work; he may not know, or be able to acknowledge, that part of his motivation for imposing such 'high standards' stems from his taking pleasure in asserting his power over the students, and being able to use his position of authority to hurt and humiliate them.

Closely related to rationalization is projection, our imputation of our own unattractive motives and reasons to another person. A rock-climber involved in a serious accident may offer an unconsciously exaggerated picture of her partner's carelessness and inattention in order to deflect attention—her own and other people's—from her own negligence and guilt. A man who has been taught that it is wrong to express 'negative feelings' may be inclined both to deny his own feelings of anger, and to attribute such feelings to his spouse or his boss when a more disinterested assessor would take a different view. Again, the difference between the instructor, the climber, and the angry spouse, and the five-year-old who insists that he locked his little sister in her room to help her stay out of trouble, is a difference in degree, not in kind. Even when we have attained emotional and moral maturity—i.e., we are unquestionably Effective, Rational, Sympathetic Actors—we are still subject to ambivalences and distortions in reasoning, and prey to the workings of deep, unacknowledged motivations.

People also 'forget' things that are emotionally difficult; repression serves the general purpose of protecting us from painful knowledge, or self-knowledge, and enabling us to represent our own reasons as congruent with each other: coherent with other reasons whose force we acknowledge, and consistent with a world view we find defensible. A woman who has a brief encounter with a man she met while she was embroiled in a messy divorce may later be unable to recall the man's name, or even to remember many of the details of her involvement with him. Though such examples may seem too blatant and self-serving to be plausible, it is often a mark of repression that the things we 'forget' are precisely those we have good reason to remember, and a strong desire, and powerful need, to forget.

This is only a partial (and oversimple) list of the sorts of emotion-based distortions to which humans are prone.[28] The point of providing it is not to claim that—appearances to the contrary notwithstanding—there is no morally relevant difference between the conduct of an individual who is an Effective, Rational, Sympathetic Actor and one who is not, or between the sorts of moral assessments that are appropriate in each instance. It is rather to remind us that the achievement of moral competence is a matter of degree. Someone who is an ERSA is not free from the sorts of vulnerabilities that can vitiate the possibility of effective agency and undercut the propriety of assessments of responsibility, but is, rather, someone whose general moral competence is not compromised by his or her human vulnerabilities. A moral agent—one who is an Effective, Rational, Sympathetic Actor—is not free from the distorting effects of denial, rationalization, projection, repression, and other mechanisms of defense. Rather, a moral agent is someone whose emotionally-driven cognitive distortions are not so great that (cumulatively) they result in a systematic inability to interpret reality, or so powerful that they frequently overpower the individual's ability to act in accord with his or her deliberations and choices.[29] Moral agency is something we express through our human psychology, not something that enables us (somehow) to transcend it.

This bears on the tenability of the suggestion that we might try to mitigate policies that invoke the rhetoric of individual responsibility by availing ourselves of the sort of excuse-and-exoneration strategy I sketched above. If what I have been saying is plausible, then, though we may be able to separate the most blatant cases of general moral non-competence from the others, it is not reasonable for us to suppose that we can do a great deal more than this. There is no bright line separating those who are Effective, Rational, Sympathetic Actors from those who are not, those whose conduct is (thus) properly assessed by the use of the rhetoric of individual responsibility, and those conduct is not. There is a large, morally muddy, middle ground.

IX

When we reflect on the far-reaching effects of an individual's particular developmental history, on the motivational and psychological complexity of human beings, and on the virtual universality of humans' employment of thought-and-emotion-distorting defense mechanisms, we are in a position to understand why schemes of moral assessment that offer superficial blanket assessments of individuals' conduct are implausible, and why social policies that trade upon such schemes are morally problematical. For example: the invocation of the rhetoric of individual responsibility in the context of teen-age pregnancy trades on the presumption that it is reasonable for us to regard the descriptors 'teen-ager', 'unmarried', and 'pregnant' as picking out a group of young women with a relevantly similar moral profile, and reasonable for us to see that profile as providing the basis for interpreting and assessing the conduct of the individuals who fit it. But—as we have seen—such an approach is problematical in many ways. It ignores, or misrepresents, the deep importance of psychological context and individual developmental history. In so doing it distorts both the point and the character of moral assessment.

Though the frequent invocation of the rhetoric of individual responsibility might lead one to think otherwise, we cannot sensibly regard our moral assessments as verdicts to be delivered *sub specie aeternitatis.* They are, rather, patterns of interpretation to help us make moral—and psychological—sense of ourselves and other human beings. To formulate such an interpretation of someone's conduct, we must have some understanding of the sorts of conditions under which he or she has acted, and some appreciation of what it means to act in the psychic space created by those conditions and constraints. We cannot understand such things if we dismiss the individual's interpretation of his or her own behavior, or if—more generally—we treat questions of motivation as only tangentially relevant to the interpretation and assessment of the person's acts. Moral assessments must be informed by an appreciation of the mechanisms of human motivation, not merely the metric of conscious deliberation. Because our motivations are not directly accessible to us—or unproblematically accessible even to an educated and disinterested third party—acknowledging the centrality of motivation to the enterprise of moral assessment involves admitting that moral assessment is both fallible and limited. And this should make us wary of adopting social policies that seem to carry the presumption that such moral assessments are generally straightforward and unproblematical.

The attribution of motives and beliefs to another person is an act of interpretation, one that we are not justified in undertaking unless we have detailed knowledge about the individual in question, and significant psychological sophistication. It is not the stuff of simple observation, based narrowly on the individual's own report about the discrete contents of his or her consciousness. To put the point (over)simply: since this is so, we cannot fairly rely on an excuse-and-exonerate strategy in any but the most straightforward instances.

The use of excuse-and-exonerate strategies is problematical in other ways as well. One person's interpretations of his or her own deeds are not unaffected by others' interpretations of them, or by the evaluative structures and norms used to assess them. Thus someone who has been 'officially' told (e.g.) that she cannot do certain things as well as other people—restrain herself, think clearly, or understand math—may interpret her own behavior differently than someone whose behavior has not received that sort of limiting response. To see the power of others' interpretations, one can watch children, read about the power of the self-fulfilling prophecy, or peruse the voluminous literature about self-esteem. Or one can look at some of the anomalous self-descriptions offered by defendants who have tried to get exonerated by invoking (e.g.) battered spouse defenses. The use of the categories of excuse and exoneration deeply affect—sometimes clearly distort—our perception of ourselves and our motivations.

X

Though my argument may appear to support a radical extension of the strategy of excuse and exoneration, that has not, in fact, been my intention. My suggestion is not that we try simply to articulate a more psychologically-informed understanding of the notion of moral agency, or a more stringent set of criteria for the application of the rhetoric of individual responsibility. The drift of my argument is rather that—once we acknowledge the necessity of formulating a notion of moral agency that is psychologically informed—we should be able to appreciate that the rhetoric of individual responsibility warrants (at best) a much smaller place in our moral world view, and that social policies that emphasize such rhetoric and accept its presuppositions are profoundly morally suspect. Judgments of responsibility—as we make them now—have an ineliminably verdictive cast: we view determinations of responsibility as necessary preconditions of assessments of fault and findings of guilt or innocence. But verdictive assessments are of limited benefit, and in fact can do much harm, in the moral arena. The notions of social control, deterrence, and procedural fairness do not and should not play the same sorts of roles in the moral domain that they do in the legal domain, and the same sorts of liberties and simplifications that go on as a matter of course on the legal front are not easily justifiable in moral contexts. There is no moral Supreme Court, and there is no mechanism for conducting the sort of scrutiny that trial attorneys conduct, or for achieving the sort of closure that goes along with the jury's determination of guilt or non-guilt. And there is nothing on the moral front that validates the presumption that arriving at a 'correct' moral judgment is necessary, or even possible, nothing that should lead us to suppose that it is justifiable for other agents to undertake a minutely-detailed investigation of a 'moral defendant's' life and deeds. There are no good grounds for supposing that moral judgments must be verdictive, and no clear ways to ensure that a moral verdict will be fair. There is thus good reason to think that we should avoid founding our social policies on moral practices that are so clearly problematical.

***

I have argued that more careful attention to the facts of human psychological development and a deeper appreciation of human psychological vulnerability should lead us to question both the tenability and fairness of some of our current moral practices and presumptions, and the moral defensibility of public policies that seem to presuppose the soundness of these moral practices. Both our understanding of what it is for us to be moral agents—Effective, Rational, Sympathetic Actors who are also human beings, engaging with others of our kind—and the social policies we design to govern ourselves must be firmly based in a solid understanding of what it is for us to be human beings in the first place.[30]

University of Colorado at Boulder

NOTES

1. This short nontechnical gloss attempts to capture the salient commonalities of more technical accounts of agency.

Though I describe and discuss only human moral agents in this context, I am not saying, and do not believe, that only members of the species *Homo sapiens* can be moral agents. The point is rather that we cannot understand the moral agency of human beings if we ignore important basic facts about the kinds of beings they are, both biologically and psychologically. The ways that human beings characteristically develop physically, psychologically, and socially—the ways they think, feel, respond, and interact—are relevant to our understanding of what it is for a human being to be a moral agent.

2. The expression 'good enough parent', is Bruno Bettelheim's (from *A Good Enough Parent* [New York: Vintage, 1988]). It is an extension of D. W. Winnicott's 'good enough mother'. According to Winnicott, the five basic needs of a child are these: (1) physical care and protection; (2) affection and approval; (3) stimulation and teaching; (4) discipline and control which are consistent and age-appropriate; and (5) the opportunity and the encouragement for the gradual acquisition of autonomy. (These are nicely and succinctly summarized in Dorota Iwanec, *The Emotionally Abused and Neglected Child* [Chicester: John Wiley and Sons, 1995].) They are discussed at greater length in D. W. Winnicott, *Collected Papers (*London: Tavistock, 1958).

3. " . . . the seriously rejected child has no opportunity to learn how to express love, because it [sic] has never known a loving parent after whom it can model its own behavior, and even though it may crave affection, it may have difficulty accepting it when it is offered. . . . the emotionally abused child becomes emotionally isolated, unable freely and openly to form warm, lasting, and intimate relationships with others. Its attachments tend to be troubled by emotional constriction or defensiveness; in addition, as a result of the psychological damage brought about by maltreatment, the child will have less tolerance of stress." Iwanec, op. cit., p. 66.

4. "There is a strong causal relationship between an individual's experiences with his [sic] parents and his later capacity to make affectional bonds." John Bowlby, *The Making and Breaking of Affectional Bonds* (London: Tavistock, 1979), p. 135. Also see Bowlby, *Separation: Anxiety and Anger* (New York: Basic Books, 1973), and Bettelheim, op. cit.

5. Thus it does not matter whether we favor a conception of agency that, like those of Hume and Mill, assigns a central role to our possession of the capacity for sympathy, or one that, like those of Kant and advocates of the natural law tradition, emphasizes reason, and thus does not take the possession of sympathy to be necessary either for understanding the difference between right and wrong or for being motivated to do right and avoid wrong. As is clear from the text, I do not favor a Kantian view; I believe that construing the possession of agency as something that enables us to transcend our human psychology is seriously—and dangerously—wrong-headed. But the line of argument I am developing here is one that applies whether one's allegiance is to Hume and Mill or to Kant. The point I am concerned to make is that a brutal upbringing will make a child insensitive to the needs and interests of others; whether one diagnoses this insensitivity as the expression of a weakened capacity for sympathy or as a failure of the child to see him or herself as a person in a community of other, equally important, persons, is immaterial in the present context. I am grateful to John Deigh for putting the point so clearly and succinctly.

6. As Louise Silvern reminded me, humans' development into agents can be viewed as exhibiting both what the systems development school calls multi-finality—i.e., beings who appeared similar at some one point in their development may not all ultimately wind up in the same place, or get there at the same time—and equi-finality: beings who were previously at different developmental stages may ultimately converge on the same one, in this instance, the possession of moral agency.

7. " . . . children differ, often dramatically, in their response to parental treatment; and the existence of 'stress-resistant children' suggests that harsh and even hostile environments can produce pro-social, competent children." Iwanec, op. cit., quoting Loourie and Stefano, "On Emotional Abuse," (1978).

8. Female children who have suffered both sexual abuse and physical maltreatment appear to be more likely to experience sexual abuse or physical maltreatment as adults. See, e.g., Tiffany Wind and Louise Silvern, "Type and Extent of Child Abuse as Predictors of Adult Functioning," *Journal of Family Violence*, Vol. 7, No. 4, 1992, pp. 261-281; p. 273. Even if children are not themselves directly the targets of violence, the experience of witnessing parental violence can produce traumatic responses. See Louise Silvern and Lynn Kaersvang,

"The Traumatized Children of Violent Marriages," *Child Welfare,* Vol. 68, no. 4. July-August 1989, pp. 421-436.

9. In general, boys and girls respond differently to abuse, including sexual abuse. Girls are more likely to experience 'internalizing' problems—e.g., guilt and depression; boys are more likely to experience 'externalizing' ones—e.g., violence and other forms of acting out. See, e.g., Jeffrey J. Haugaard and N. Dickon Repucci, *The Sexual Abuse of Children* (San Francisco: Jossey-Buss, 1989), especially chapter 4, "Consequences for Victims," pp. 60-100.

10. It is important to recognize that neither this sort of rhetoric nor its preconditions vanished from the scene with the departure of Reagan and Bush. Indeed, there are 'drug use prevention' programs currently being marketed to schools that exemplify the very sort of ideology being criticized here. The proliferation of 'abstinence only' programs of sex education provides further evidence that "Just say 'No'" thinking is alive and well.

11. If, while pregnant, the child's mother used contraindicated drugs or medications, or alcohol or tobacco in significant amounts, this may affect fetal development. If the child's mother was herself a growing teen-ager not receiving good care and attention—e.g., not consuming an adequate diet, or receiving competent prenatal care—this also affects the fetus. The poverty and the youth of the mother have been strongly implicated in low-birth-weight babies, and premature births.

12. In earlier drafts, I had written "14-year-old." But an article from the Boulder *Daily Camera* (2 April 1996; p. 1) caused me to revise my estimate down. Here are portions of the text of that article, entitled "12-year-olds could be prosecuted as adults."

> Juveniles as young as 12 who commit violent crimes could be charged as adults under changes in the Colorado Children's Code approved in the state House on Monday.
>
> Under existing law, the minimum age for such prosecution is 14. While some lawmakers favored dropping the minimum to 10 for crimes such as murder, that proposal was not attached to HB1005, the first of three bills dealing with juvenile justice." . . .
>
> The measure was proposed because of the rise in violent crimes involving youths in their early teens. . . . The bill allows 10-year-olds to be tried for juvenile offenses; the limit was previously 12. Ten- and 11-year-olds could be sentenced to a new facility called the Division of Youth Corrections, but only for a maximum of seven years for murder, five years for felony sex offenses and two years for other felony offenses. Those under 10 could not face criminal charges.
>
> Rep. Jeanne Adkins, R-Parker, said the bill should have no problem when it reaches the Senate. . . ."

Unfortunately, Rep. Adkins was right. Nor is Colorado alone in its zeal to treat 'youthful offenders' like adults. See Title XIV of HR 3355, the Violent Crime Control and Law Enforcement Act of 1994.

13. One could, of course, construe the very obviousness of the act's wrongness as providing presumptive evidence of the child's psychopathology, rather than

irrefutable evidence of the child's responsibility. For a popular discussion of some of the patterns of behavior associated with the commission of such crimes, see (e.g.) Ken Magid and Carole A. McKelvey, *High Risk: Children Without a Conscience* (Toronto: Bantam Books, 1987), Robert D. Hare, *Without Conscience: The Disturbing World of the Psychopaths Among Us* (New York: Pocket Books, 1993), and the classic, Hervey Cleckley, *The Mask of Sanity*, 5th edition (St. Louis: Mosby Books, 1976).

14. It is not accidental, I think, that such proposals seem often to be attractive to those who think that the corrective to children's commission of antisocial acts lies in the implementation of 'family values'. If a child has been taught the right values, the child would have known that the act was wrong. Then (the reasoning continues) all that would be needed to avoid it was the exercise of the child's will; once again, he or she could "Just say 'No'."

15. Someone might try to claim that the practice of punishing violent children as adults has deterrent value. But that claim, too, would depend heavily on the assertion that children possess both the emotional wherewithal and the cognitive sophistication to be deterred by the prospect of dreadful consequences. Once again, the "Just say 'No'" dictum seems to play a role. The way to teach children not to commit heinous acts is to show them that they will be severely punished if they commit them; they can then be expected simply to decide not to act in that fashion.

16. To say this is not to say that every child who experiences such horrors will grow up damaged. See note 6. Interestingly, variation in individuals' response to hardship forms one of the supports of the view that a person's will is (somehow) causally independent of his or her material circumstances. The reasoning seems to be that if it is possible for *some* children from the inner city to go on to lead 'pro-social and competent' lives, then we cannot say that the explanation for the fact that *this* child is antisocial and incompetent lies in the vicissitudes of his or her childhood environment. Such views betray a basic failure to understand the concept of a risk factor, and perhaps—more generally—an unwillingness to credit the essentially stochastic nature of predictions about human behavior.

17. Events that terrify or overstimulate the child and cause the child to feel powerless seem to lead to the development of post-traumatic stress disorder. See Wind and Silvern, op cit., p. 263, and Charles R. Figley (ed.), *Trauma and Its Wake: The Study and Treatment of Post-Traumatic Stress Disorder* (New York: Brunner/Mazel, Inc., 1985), and discussion in the text below.

18. See note 6.

19. See note 3.

20. See, generally, Figley (ed.), op cit. My partial list is drawn from John P. Wilson, W. Ken Smith, and Suzanne K. Johnson, "A Comparative Analysis of PTSD Among Various Survivor Groups," 142-172, p. 153; and from Bonnie Green, John P. Wilson, and Jacob D. Lindy, "Conceptualizing Post-traumatic Stress Disorder: A Psychosocial Framework, " p. 53-69.

21. Raymond M. Scurfield, "Post-trauma Stress Assessment and Treatment: Overview and Formulations," 219-256, in Figley (ed.), op cit., p. 233.

22. It is not clear at precisely what age children understand that death is permanent. Certainly we should expect different children to really grasp this at

different ages. We should also expect that a child who is neglected and uneducated may be slower to grasp this, particularly if the child is also heavily exposed to violence on a regular basis, either in his or her daily life, or on television. How could such a child be expected to witness perhaps dozens of murders in a day and view death with appropriate moral gravity?

23. The point is nicely put by Bettelheim, op. cit., p. 11: "Changes that may occur when we are older are likely to affect only limited areas of our personalities and our lives. The importance of early experiences thus rests on the fact that they set the stage for all that comes later, and the earlier the experiences are, the more emphatic their influence."

24. There is also the *ad hominem* point that it undercuts the move towards trying younger and younger children as adults. Though I do not wish to claim that every 12-year-old child who commits a heinous act has suffered serious neglect or abuse, or that every such child suffers from organic damage or cognitive impairment brought about by deficiencies or problems with the child's environment in early life, there are strong enough correlations to think that the majority of such children will be shown to have had problematical backgrounds (or the sort of problematical history that is taken to be indicative of psychopathy). (Here it is also important to bear in mind that child abuse and neglect have been linked with a whole range of parental behaviors and circumstances, including "poor marital relationships, social isolation, impulsive personalities, ill-health, poverty, chaotic life-style, psychosomatic problems, poor social and problem-solving skills, difficulties in social communication, neglectful and abusive backgrounds of parents, and a lack of knowledge of children's age-appropriate needs, as well as alcohol-, drug-, and substance abuse.") Iwanec, op. cit., p. 11.

25. See Haugaard and Repucci, op cit.

26. As a number of commentators point out, abuse and neglect may be more damaging to children of lower socioeconomic strata than it is to their better-heeled cohorts, either because such children are more likely to have other problems that exacerbate the effects of the abuse, or because they are less likely to have effective exposure to competent help and support.

27. This is one of the premises behind psychotherapy, and one of the pillars of support for depth psychological interpretations of human personality.

28. In order to avoid linking them to a specific account of the meaning or etiology of unconscious motivation, I have offered broad, general accounts of some of the more familiar defense mechanisms. See Anna Freud, *The Ego and the Mechanisms of Defense,* revised edition (Madison, CT: International Universities Press, 1966).

29. This is obviously not sufficient. To be an Effective, Rational, Sympathetic Actor, one must also have certain kinds of affective responses, and be able in some fairly robust way to act in accordance with one's choices. Someone with an impulse-control disorder may know that (e.g.) gambling can get him into serious trouble, and form a resolve to refrain from doing it. The problem is that when he feels the temptation to gamble, all his reasons do not have the motivational force to stop him.

30. I wish to thank John Deigh, Ben Rich, and Louise Silvern for their thoughtful discussions of earlier versions of this essay. I benefited also from the comments of Robert Holmes.

KANT ON DUTIES REGARDING NONRATIONAL NATURE

Allen W. Wood and Onora O'Neill

II—Onora O'Neill

NECESSARY ANTHROPOCENTRISM AND CONTINGENT SPECIESISM

ABSTRACT Kant's ethics, like others, has unavoidable anthropocentric starting points: only humans, or other 'rational natures', can hold obligations. Seemingly this should not make speciesist conclusions unavoidable: might not rational natures have obligations to the non-rational? However, Kant's argument for the unconditional value of rational natures cannot readily be extended to show that all non-human animals have unconditional value, or rights. Nevertheless Kant's speciesism is not thoroughgoing. He does not view non-rational animals as mere items for use. He allows for indirect duties 'with regard to' them which afford welfare but not rights, and can allow for indirect duties 'with regard to' abstract and dispersed aspects of nature, such as biodiversity, species and habitats.

It is a mixed pleasure to comment on a paper whose argument is acute, whose scholarship is deep, and which may leave little to be said. What I shall say will mainly endorse, and sometimes extend, many of Allen Wood's arguments and much of his interpretation of Kant. However, I shall set Kant's complex claim that rational nature has absolute and unconditional value in a rather different context, and indicate how it may bear on ways in which we may think that Kant's ethics is either anthropocentric or speciesist.

Despite some differences I accept most of Wood's conclusions. I too think that Kant's starting points are in a certain sense anthropocentric, but that both his starting point and his conclusions are less speciesist than is often supposed. More controversially, it seems to me unlikely, and certainly undemonstrated, that there is a plausible systematic approach to ethics whose starting point and conclusions are both less speciesist and less blind to the moral importance of abstract or dispersed aspects of nature such as ecosystems, habitats, species or biodiversity. This conclusion may surprise those who think that Kantianism must be the least promising basis for an account of proper relations between the human and the non-human worlds.

I

Logocentrism and Personification. Wood frames his central claim about Kant's views on the treatment of non-human animals using two not-quite Kantian terms. He begins with the thought that Kant's ethics is 'anthropocentric—or rather it is *logocentric*' meaning that 'it is based on the idea that rational nature, and it alone, has absolute and unconditional value' (AW 189).[1] The switch of terms reflects Wood's surely accurate view that Kant does not simply assume the privileged status of a particular animal species, namely humans. Even if Kant is a speciesist, he is not a human chauvinist who unthinkingly assumes the greater worth of the human species. Not only does he think that non-human rational natures, if any exist, will like humans 'have absolute and unconditional value', but he supports his logocentric claim with substantial arguments.[2]

Wood argues that the problem with Kant's views on non-human animals arises not immediately from logocentrism, which he broadly endorses, but from Kant's advocacy of a *personification principle* (AW 193), which is 'the idea that humanity or rational nature has a moral claim on us only *in the person of* a being who actually possesses it' (AW 193). The personification principle makes a claim about the beings who are on the receiving end of moral action, to whom duties may be owed, and who may in some cases be holders of rights: it implies that 'there can be no duties *toward* [non-human] animals, toward nature as a whole, or indeed toward *any* non-rational being at all' (AW 194; see esp. *MS* 6: 442–5).[3]

Nevertheless, as Wood points out, Kant in no way regards non-rational nature as a mere instrument for human use and

1. References to Wood's paper 'Kant on Duties Regarding Non-rational Nature', this volume pp. 189–210, will be parenthetical, as (AW 9).

2. Kant often mentions the possibility that there are other rational species in the universe. See, for example, *Anthropology from a Pragmatic Viewpoint*, where he speculates about rational beings who unlike us 'could not think in any way but aloud' (*VA* 7: 321), among whom face to face deception would presumably be impossible.

3. Reference to Kant's writing will be parenthetical using the same texts and abbreviations as Wood uses and sets out on AW 208; however *VE* will cover all the *Lectures on Ethics*.

despoliation. There are passages in a number of works where he claims that we have duties 'with regard to' irrational nature and in particular 'with regard to' non-human animals, and specifically that we ought to not be cruel to them. These duties are classified as indirect duties, and as following from our direct duties to promote our own moral perfection by cultivating a good disposition in ourselves (*MS* 6: 443–5). On the surface this latter thought seems curious: unless there are *independent* reasons for thinking that decent treatment of non-human animals is an element or source of moral perfection, why should we think that it promotes a moral disposition? The argument needs some further premise, for example a claim that a sensitive attitude to non-rational nature improves attitudes to (parts of) rational nature, or that we tend to transfer attitudes towards the former to the latter.[4]

Wood thinks that this rather unsatisfactory position is forced on Kant by the combination of his commitments to logocentrism and to the personification principle, and claims that by viewing decent treatment of non-human animals as an indirect duty to ourselves Kant at least makes 'the best of an extremely bleak situation' (AW 195). He admires him for making the best of this bad situation, but criticises the 'features of his ethical theory which forced a bad choice on him' (AW 195).

II

Kant on Absolute and Unconditional Value. Kant himself does not use the term 'logocentrism'. Wood introduces it with the claim that a position is *logocentric* if it 'is based on the idea that rational nature, and it alone, has absolute and unconditional value' (AW 189); a later formulation has it that logocentrism 'recognizes no value which is independent of the dignity of rational nature' (AW 195).

The introduction of the notion of *dignity* into the second formulation is, I think, a distraction. Kant introduces the notion of dignity *after* he has established the distinction between those things which are ends in themselves and those which are not. Things which are not ends in themselves may be used as mere means, so may be traded off for other things, and so can have a *price*. By

4. Kant suggests such arguments at *VE* 27: 710.

contrast, ends in themselves may not be used as mere means, so may not be traded, so will be beyond price and may be said to have *dignity*: '...an end in itself has not merely a relative value—that is, a price—but has an intrinsic value—that is, *dignity*.' (*G* 4: 435). Without the prior distinction of things with instrumental or conditional value and those with absolute, unconditional (intrinsic) value, which is the basis for distinguishing what may be traded off and what may not be, there would be no context for distinguishing price from dignity. The fundamental issue is whether and how a distinction between things with and without absolute and unconditional value is to be established.

Kant's strategy in introducing this distinction and arguing for the *Formula of Humanity* in the second Chapter of the *Groundwork* is perplexing. He notes that *if* there were something whose existence is in itself an absolute value, then it and it alone would be the ground of a possible Categorical Imperative (*G* 4: 428). But he does not immediately try to establish the antecedent of the conditional. Rather he insists bluntly that he cannot *show* but only *assert* that certain beings are ends in themselves and so of absolute value, in the words 'Now I say that man, and in general every rational being, *exists* as an end in himself, *not merely as a means* for arbitrary use' (*G* 4: 428). Nor is his next move a demonstration of this assertion. He notes that certain other sorts of things cannot be ends in themselves, and could at most have derivative or instrumental value (objects of inclination, inclinations themselves, the products of human action, natural objects). By contrast, rational natures *if any exist* might be ends in themselves (*G* 4: 429); if none such exist there may be nothing of absolute value.

Two gaps need filling. First, since Kant has in mind a particularly demanding view of what it is to be a rational nature, which he sees as a natural being with ability to act freely and to reason, one cannot simply take for granted that humans are rational natures in the relevant sense. Second, even if there are rational natures, among them human beings, Kant needs to demonstrate that they are ends in themselves. If he cannot, there may be *nothing* that should be viewed as an end in itself, and so *nothing* of absolute value, and accordingly *no* supreme principle for reason and morality.

Despite his lack of any demonstration in *Groundwork* II that human or any other beings are rational natures and ends in themselves and of absolute value, Kant starts his argument for the Formula of Humanity from the proposition: The ground [of the moral principle] is: '*Rational nature exists as an end in itself*' (*G* 4: 429). He then notes that we—we humans—think of ourselves in this way but confirms that this is no more than subjective, and states baldly in a footnote that the proposition that rational natures including humans are ends in themselves 'is put forward here as a postulate'. (*G* 4: 429, n., cf. *G* 4: 448 for the same strategy). This arresting tactic reminds one uncomfortably of Bertrand Russell's quip that the method of postulation has the advantage over the method of argument that theft has over honest toil.[5]

Unlike Wood, I am inclined to think that there is not and is not meant to be a complete argument for The Formula of Humanity in the second chapter of *Groundwork*, and to take seriously the footnote comment, to which Kant adds the remark that 'The grounds for it [the postulate] will be found in the final chapter' (*G* 4: 429, n.). I take this seriously because Kant has strategic reasons for postponing this essential step of his argument: the context of argument of *Groundwork* II, as of *Groundwork* I, does not have the resources to establish that we (or other seemingly rational beings) are rational natures in the required strong sense, or to show that human or other rational natures have absolute and unconditional value.

In *Groundwork* I Kant had also drawn a distinction between an unconditional good—the good will—and conditional goods—all the others. All the conditional goods were held to be of value only if their use was governed by good willing (*G* 4: 393–4). The sole unconditional good was identified as willing of a certain sort, achievable only by beings capable of free and reasoned action: such rational natures were said to be the only possible source and bearers of unconditional worth. However, in *Groundwork* I, as in *Groundwork* II, no satisfactory argument established that there are any such beings, or in particular that we humans are among them, or that such beings have absolute and unconditional worth. In the

5. Wood has offered a more kindly account of Kant's argument in *Groundwork* II in another recent paper: Allen Wood, 'Humanity as an End in Itself' *Proceedings of the Eighth International Kant Congress*, Vol I, Part 1, pp 301–319, Marquette University Press, Milwaukee, 1995.

last paragraph of Chapter I Kant noted that the framework of ordinary reason had not allowed him to establish 'the source of its own [moral] principle', and in the last sentence that we need 'a full critique of reason' to establish that principle (*G* 4: 405). He stresses just the same gaps in his argument when he points out, in *Groundwork* II, that the claims that human beings are rational natures and ends in themselves and of unconditional worth, is still no more than a postulate. And he is fully aware of the incompleteness of his argument when in the final paragraph of Chapter II he acknowledges that, despite all that has been said, morality may be 'a mere phantom of the brain' and insists in its last sentence that no more can be established without a critique of reason (*G* 4: 445). Kant clearly does not think it either surprising or avoidable that he had to make do with a promissory note in his initial sketch of an argument for the Formula of Humanity.

Kant seeks to complete his argument only in *Groundwork* III beyond 352, where the initial analytic procedure of a 'Metaphysic of Morals' is replaced by a compressed 'Critique of Practical Reason'. There he hopes to show that we humans cannot but assume both that we are parts of nature and that we are free and able to reason (in the required strong sense), in short that humanity *must* take itself to be (part of) rational nature.[6] The argument that the theoretical and practical standpoints are both indispensable but mutually irreducible is, as Kant insists, still less than a proof that humans are rational natures: there is no proof of human freedom, no refutation of scepticism about human freedom. Yet the argument if successful is a powerful strategy for showing that human reasoners must assume that they are rational natures in the required sense, in that it aims to show that if we are sceptics about our own freedom then we will have to be sceptics about our knowledge of the natural order as well.[7] The two standpoints stand and fall together, so calling into question positions which take it that knowledge of the natural order, hence of causal links, can be established independently and then used to argue against the

6. I have attempted a more extended discussion of the strategy of Kant's *Groundwork* and of the interpretation of the Formula of Humanity in 'Universal Laws and Ends in Themselves' and 'Reason and Autonomy in *Grundlegung* III', both in Onora O'Neill, *Constructions of Reason: Explorations of Kant's Practical Philosophy*, Cambridge University Press, 1989, pp 126–44; 51–65.

7. See 'Reason and Autonomy in *Grundlegung* III', esp pp 59 ff.

possibility of human freedom, and so against the whole Kantian moral vision.

The conclusion of *Groundwork* III, that we must take ourselves to be *both* free and reasoning beings *and* part of the natural order, is needed for Kant's to show that we must treat one another and ourselves as having 'absolute and unconditional value'. If human beings must take themselves to be rational natures, they must view themselves as standing in two distinct relationships to action. On the one hand they are agents whose free and reasoned actions bear on others, on the other hand they are parts of nature and so recipients, affected by others' action (and their own). The dual view of ourselves is the pivotal thought behind the Formula of Humanity (and, I would argue, behind other formulations of the Categorical Imperative[8]). Like other formulations of the Categorical Imperative, the Formula of Humanity assumes agency: hence the imperatival form. However, the Formula of Humanity also takes a quite explicit stance on the fact that human beings (or other rational beings) are on the receiving end of action, in that it specifies how they are to be treated.

There are then *two* distinguishable presuppositions of what Wood terms Kant's logocentrism. In the first place there is the indispensable anthropocentric claim that we are agents, to whom moral demands, indeed categorical imperatives, can be addressed. Secondly there is the recognition that we are not merely agents, but rational natures, that is beings who are on the receiving end of one another's action. The first, the indispensable anthropocentric claim, is not peculiar to Kant, although he has distinctive conceptions of freedom and reason. Some form of anthropocentrism is a necessary presupposition of any moral theory or moral discourse: no agents, no morality. Anthropocentric starting points are needed not only by Kant but by other forms of Kantian ethics, by utilitarians, by rights theorists, by virtue ethicists and by others whose conception of morality is not theoretically structured. Kant is distinctive on this point not because he assumes that morality requires agents, but because he has a strong and complex notion of what it is to be free and rational, and so an agent. This indispensable anthropocentrism neither assumes nor establishes any form of speciesist moral conclusions. It says

8. See 'Universal Laws and Ends in Themselves', note 3.

simply that morality requires agents, and leaves open who or what may be on the receiving end of the action that is to be morally regulated, and whether the ways in which they should be treated vary with their species.

The second presupposition of Wood's logocentrism is also widely shared: it is the claim that rational natures are not only agents but are on the receiving end of one another's action. This presupposition is not self evident: it holds only if rational natures lead connected lives, or (as Kant often puts it) 'share a world'. Kant, of course, also assumes that rational natures act on other, non-rational natural objects; however this broader claim is merely part of the background of logocentrism.

Only when both of these presuppositions are in place can the basis for the core of the logocentric claim, the view that rational natures have absolute and unconditional worth, be established. Rational natures who can affect one another by their action may destroy, damage or undercut one another, thereby destroying or damaging the agency that is needed for morality. Either then they must treat one another as ends in themselves, that is as beings with absolute and unconditional worth, or they will in effect reject the indispensable anthropocentrism which any practical reasoning and any moral action presupposes, thereby also undermining their view of themselves as rational natures. Rational natures cannot then coherently refuse to see one another and themselves as ends in themselves, so as beings with absolute and unconditional value: this is the core of logocentrism.

The implications of the view that rational natures have absolute and unconditional value is encapsulated in imperative form in the Formula of Humanity and is developed in the account of human duties which Kant derives from the Formula. If human beings, and perhaps other rational beings, are the only beings known to be capable of reasoned action, the preservation and indeed development of their capacities to act is a condition of there being any action of moral worth. However, since humans (and any other rational natures) can by their action destroy, damage or fail to sustain their own and one another's capacities for agency, their unconstrained action would undercut all moral worth. So if there is to be any morally worthy action, humans (and other rational natures) must accept certain constraints: they must view and treat one another not as mere means but as self existent ends (ends in themselves). Two sets of duties follow from the two parts of the Formula. The requirement not to use others as mere means underlies 'perfect' duties, which require rational natures not use one another (or themselves) as mere dispensable and disposable means that can be destroyed or damaged or deceived for arbitrary ends, so eliminating, eroding or by-passing agency. The requirement to treat others as ends in themselves underlies 'imperfect' duties: because human agents have fragile and undeveloped abilities and are always, and often intensely, physically and mentally vulnerable to one another, they must, if they are to ensure that moral action has a reliable place in their world, sustain human abilities by developing their own capacities for action (talents) and supporting one another's pursuit of (permissible) ends.

The account of duties presented in *Groundwork* II is evidently tailored to the human case: it is appropriate to rational natures who have a high degree of plasticity (their skills and talents are not naturally fixed but can be developed in many differing ways) as well as a high degree of mutual vulnerability and dependence (which other rational natures might not have). However, other types of beings could use the arguments of *Groundwork* III and supplementary empirical considerations to establish that they were rational natures in the relevant strong sense, and could use an accurate account of ways in which their abilities are plastic and in which they are mutually dependent, hence vulnerable, to establish an appropriate account of their duties. Presumably any population of rational natures must reach the conclusion that if there is to be anything of moral value, then the survival of rational natures is necessary, and hence that they must be committed at least to limiting mutual destruction and damage—the analogue of 'perfect' duties among humans. However, a population of rational natures whose capacities and abilities were fully formed throughout life, or who were less fragile, interdependent and mutually vulnerable than humans, might conclude that, while they were bound to refrain from mutual destruction, damage and deceit, they were not bound to extensive, or even to any, 'imperfect' duties of self-development or of mutual support and beneficence. Not every plurality of rational natures need have just the same duties as humans have.

III

Anthropocentrism and Personification. Logocentrism, as Wood defines it, comprises not only the core view that rational natures are ends in themselves, and of absolute value, but the claim that *only* rational natures are ends in themselves and of absolute value. However, the background arguments for the core of logocentrism do not show that rational agents, among them human agents, must accord unconditional and absolute value *only* to others of their own kind. Perhaps there are other beings, who are incapable of rational agency, but nevertheless have absolute and unconditional worth, or at least a lesser moral standing which all rational agents must recognize. These possibilities have been championed by a wide range of non-Kantian thinkers, many of them concerned about the moral status of human beings lacking rational capacities, of non-human animals and more broadly of the environment.

Although claims on behalf of non-rational beings are easy to state, they are hard to establish. Kant's distinctive argument to show that theoretical reason cannot stand alone, that beings who claim to know the natural order must take themselves to be free and rational in a strong sense, hence must see themselves and one another both as agents and recipients, hence as ends in themselves, and as having unconditional or absolute value, is not readily extended or supplanted.

Wood argues that Kant mistakenly thought that he could not establish any duties to non-rational beings because he also adopts the personification principle, by which every duty is a duty owed to some person or persons (AW 196). The personification principle adds to the logocentric claim that only rational nature has absolute and unconditional value and should be treated as an end in itself, an insistence that this requirement applies only to humanity (more generally: rational nature) *in someone's person.* Given Kant's narrow use of the term *person* this move has stark consequences: duties are owed *only* to rational natures. Even if in practice Kant thinks that there are duties to immature or impaired humans, who are not currently rational, he should not have done so, and he was correctly following the implications of the personification principle in denying that there are human duties to non-human animals, or to other parts of non-rational nature, or to supernatural beings. (AW 196–197, *MS* 6: 443–5) It is the personification principle rather than logocentrism which, as Wood views it, saddles Kant with speciesist conclusions. In Wood's view this move was unnecessary and mistaken: 'a logocentric ethics, which grounds all duties on the value of human or rational nature, should not be committed to the personification principle'. (AW 197) On the contrary, any logocentrist who is committed to respect for rational nature should also respect both *fragments* of rational nature and *necessary conditions* of rational nature (AW 198). Wood offers this extended view of the proper scope of moral concern as a 'reasonable interpretation' of the basic logocentric principle (AW 198).

The most convincing case for extending the scope of moral concern for rational natures is to those currently less-than-rational beings who are incipiently or nearly rational (who, in Wood's terms, exhibit 'fragments of rationality'), but are not currently persons in Kant's narrow use of the term. For example, extensions are commonly and convincingly argued in favour of human beings whose rational agency is either potential (infants) or temporarily reduced (in illness) or fading (the senile), or borderline (the severely retarded). Kant never in fact doubts that all of these are owed the duties that we owe to those humans who are in the maturity of their faculties: in this respect he was perhaps, and honourably, a speciesist.[9]

The same line of thought might be extended for any non-human animals who exhibit 'fragments of rationality', although Kant does not explicitly do so. Yet, as Wood notes, Kant does not seem to have drawn the conclusion that non-human animals are merely things for unrestricted human use, although he also does not regard them as ends in themselves. On his view, non-human animals should not be wantonly destroyed or cruelly misused, although they may be sold, used for labour (but not for excessive labour) and killed (painlessly) for food (*MS* 6: 442–3; *VE* 27: 434–5; 459–60).

Two sorts of question can be asked about Kant's views on non-human animals. A first, substantive question is whether Kant places sufficient or appropriate restrictions on human uses of non-human animals. I shall leave this question largely unanswered,

9. AW 198–199; Onora O'Neill *Towards Justice and Virtue: a constructivist account of practical reasoning*, Cambridge University Press 1996, Ch 4.

while noting that it would be very surprising if two centuries of increasing knowledge about non-human animals, centuries which include the Darwinian and genetic revolutions, and during which the place of non-human animals in systems of transport and production has been transformed, had no implications for Kant's substantive views of animal–human relations.

The second question is why Kant (as it may seem rather priggishly) classifies duties with regard to non-human animals as *indirect* duties falling under the imperfect human duty of self improvement. Even if Kant does not begin with speciesist assumptions, does not the fact that he establishes no direct duties to non-human animals mean that he reached unacceptably speciesist conclusions? This second basis for thinking that Kant reaches unacceptably speciesist conclusions is not that he sets no moral requirements on human treatment of non-human animals, but that these requirements do not arise either out of a right or claim of non-human animals to be treated as ends in themselves, but are indirect duties. The personification principle excludes non-persons from the status of right holders to whom duties are owed. Those who think that non-human animals have such rights dispute this exclusion. However, the claim that non-humans have rights cannot be established by mere assertion— any more than the claim that rational natures have duties and rights could be.

Evidently it would be hard to extend or adapt Kant's argument to show that rational natures have absolute and unconditional worth to fit the case of non-human animals, because it derives the moral status of humans from their capacities as rational natures.[10] If non-human animals are not agents, and have no duties, it will be hard to find a Kantian argument to show that they have rights, or that they are ends in themselves. The problem is one of burden of proof. Nothing in Kant's argument demonstrates that non-rational natures are not ends in themselves: but nothing shows that they are, and nothing suggests how it could be shown. It is wholly unclear how the argument for rational natures being ends in themselves could be extended to non-rational natures.

Given this situation it is not surprising that Kant concludes that there are no duties *to* non-human animals; it is perhaps more surprising that his conclusions are not more thoroughly speciesist,

10. See the discussion of *arbitria libera* as contrasted with *arbitria bruta*, *MS* 6: 213–4.

and that he views decent treatment of non-human animals as an indirect duty. It would evidently be implausible to view it as an indirect aspect of duties to seek others' happiness. By elimination Kant is left arguing that decent treatment of non-human animals contributes to our self improvement, and that without it we may become hard or callous to suffering in other humans. In taking up this line of thought Kant draws on the same considerations that have been crucial to many who urge the moral claims of non-human animals from other, including utilitarian, perspectives: the sympathy which we often feel to non-human but sentient animals.

The fact that Kant holds some substantive views about the importance of treating non-human animals decently suggests that, despite his rejection of the thought that they could be ends in themselves, he in fact seeks to mitigate the implications of the personification principle. It is true that he denies that non-human animals have rights (*MS* 6: 241), or that they can bind us to any duties, and that he never regards them as ends in themselves. Nevertheless, in allowing that harming non-human animals is an *indirect* violation of duties to humanity Kant endorses more or less the range of ethical concern for non-human animals that more traditional utilitarians allowed: welfare but not rights. The proximity of his substantive conclusions to those of utilitarians are easily missed because many contemporary utilitarians insist that decency to non-human animals requires more than Kant argues for: it should be more closely modelled on human welfare, and in particular non-human animals should not be farmed, killed or eaten. Earlier utilitarians might not have found Kant's substantive views on the treatment of non-human animals either unfamiliar or wholly inadequate.

The fact that there are indirect duties from which non-human animals ought to benefit is not a trivial protection. For Kant indirect duties matter: they are real duties that bind all who are capable of having duties. The objection that one may have to his position on non-human animals must then be not so much that agents are not required to have regard to them, but that the basis for these duties is not any right or claim of the non-human animal. This objection would be convincing if its proponents could show that non-human animals have fundamental (moral, natural) rights, and so that Kant was mistaken in thinking that human duties to non-human animals are only indirect duties. However, the burden of proof on those who think that non-human animals have such rights is severe. Kant found it hard enough to show that interacting rational natures must regard one another as having absolute and unconditional worth, so must treat one another not as mere means but as ends in themselves, so have duties to one another, and rights against one another. A corresponding argument to show that animals who are not agents must also be regarded as having unconditional worth, and should have rights without duties, would be even harder to construct, and would have to use an entirely non-Kantian approach to reach conclusions that mirror Kant's conclusions about rational natures.

Alternative ways of trying to show that non-human animals, even if not ends in themselves, still have rights are also demanding. All too often claims that there are animal rights look plausible only because the thought that non-human animals may have *positive* rights is entirely plausible: but this neither Kant nor utilitarianism nor any other account of ethics need dispute.[11] The elusive argument would need to show that non-human animals have, if not all the moral (natural, fundamental) rights that humans have, at least some of these rights and so that obligation bearers—humans—owe them at least some direct duties.

Typical arguments about the moral standing of non-human animals are much less ambitious. Many of them do not aim to show that non-human animals are ends in themselves, or even that they have moral rights, but only that they are sufficiently like human animals to have a somewhat analogous status. Appeals to analogy have well known strengths and weaknesses. Where the analogies are good, an argument may look quite convincing: for example the Great Apes have many fragments of the forms of rationality that we find in humans,[12] so we should accord them the same protection that we accord humans with analogous fragments of rationality, and should think that in doing so we are fulfilling duties to them. It is less clear that we can attribute fragments of rationality to all non-human animals who have desires, sentience and some capacities to initiate action; and indeed many champions of the

11. See Onora O'Neill, 'Environmental Values, Anthropocentrism and Speciesism', in *Environmental Values*, 6, 1997, pp 127–42, esp p 132.

12. Peter Singer and Paola Cavalieri, *The Great Ape Project*, Fourth Estate, London, 1993.

moral claims of non-human animals seek not to show that they are agents as humans are, but to simply emphasize the significance of their sentience.[13] Of course, those who view sentience as the basis of moral standing do not generally take it that all sentient beings are ends in themselves, or of absolute worth; many of them do not claim that sentient beings have rights.

The problem with extending the scope of moral concern to non-human animals is not that there are no or few analogies between human and non-human animals: it is that there are also so many areas in which analogies fail. Abilities to communicate, to transmit cultures, to develop technologies, to represent the past and the future are found (if at all) in very weak forms in all non-human species, and are absent in the vast majority of non-human species. Many, but not all, of the advocates of concern for non-human animals accept that the case for duties to non-human animals will vary with species, and few expect to show that analogical reasoning can establish much in the way of duties to, let alone rights for, species with little resemblance to humans. As analogies with humans weaken, as sentience rather than fragments of rationality are viewed as the analogous feature, as sentience itself fades or takes forms remote from human sentience, it is likely that non-Kantian approaches to moral concern for non-human animals will also have to regard certain duties to non-human animals as indirect duties. Even if there would be advantages in showing that some duties to non-human animals are direct duties, owed in virtue of moral standing and rights which those non-human animals have, this position may be inaccessible; even if it were accessible, indirect duties to non-human animals might still be important.

These issues may matter less than some friends of the non-human world fear. An approach which, like Kant's, emphasizes indirect duties may even have some advantages over approaches which emphasize the rights of non-human animals. An emphasis on animal rights is in effect an emphasis on a form of individualism that is not restricted to humans, and is not always hospitable to broader ethical claims about action that affects the environment. As has often been noted, concern to preserve all (sentient) animals, or to accord all of them rights, may be blind or even inimical to

13. Peter Singer, *Animal Liberation*, London, Jonathan Cape, 1976 gave great impetus to recent uses of this type of argument.

the importance of preserving other features or aspects of the environment such as species, habitats, or biological diversity, whose preservation may require action which kills or harms individual non-human animals, such as predators or parasites, or members of a successful species who are crowding out others. Yet there is little prospect of taking account of these concerns by showing, for example, that subspecies or biodiversity, or rivers and forests, have rights. In the end, positions in ethics that allow for duties of any sort will either have to take indirect duties seriously, or will overlook the importance of dispersed features of the biosphere such as habitats or food-chains, or of abstract features such as species and genetic diversity, or of inanimate parts of nature such as the gulf stream or the ozone layer, as well as the importance of what Wood refers to as 'the natural environment as a whole' (AW 202). Indirect duties must be part of any environmentally sensitive ethics.

Wood is, I think, right when he speaks of Kant's ethics as demanding that we see nature as a whole as a teleological system. However, a focus on indirect duties offers another, perhaps humbler, way of filling out the appropriate relations between the human and non-human worlds. Natural systems are the material basis for all human and non-human life, for human production and for human culture: if then we have duties not to destroy but to sustain one another, and indirect duties with regard to non-human animals, these will often have to be expressed yet more indirectly in efforts to establish and sustain productive ways of life, clean waters, fertile soils, non-polluting technologies and stable habitats for human and non-human animals, as well as preserving biodiversity.[14] These additional indirect duties form a system with perfect and imperfect duties to self and to others, and with other indirect duties. This way of extending a measure of moral concern to aspects of the natural order may strike some as inadequate, whether because it does not accord non-human animals fundamental rights, or because it does not explicitly make sentience the sole ground of moral standing. However it has, as Wood notes, the advantage that it provides a route for taking account not only of individual non-human animals but of natural systems.

14. O'Neill *Towards Justice and Virtue*, Chs 6 and 7.

IV

Some Conclusions. Moral reasoning, I have argued, is *necessarily anthropocentric.* It can be done and understood, accepted and rejected only by those with more or less human capacities to act—including, if such there be, rational aliens or non-human rational species of this earth. The fact that some form of anthropocentrism is necessary for all practical and moral reasoning, does not by itself entail that logocentrism, in Wood's sense of the term, is necessary for all moral reasoning. Logocentrism combines anthropocentrism (of a specific variety) with the claim that 'rational nature, and it alone, has absolute and unconditional value'. Anthropocentrism does not incorporate any substantive view about value, and is common ground for a large range of moral theories as well as for moral sceptics, nihilists and egoists, who defend no substantive account of moral value, but accept that there are forms of practical reasoning.

What is distinctive about Kant's ethics is the argument from (his version of) anthropocentrism, combined with the assumption that rational agents are the recipients of one another's action, to the central logocentric claim that agents must view one another as ends in themselves and so as having absolute and unconditional value. It is this thought that provides the basis for the Formula of Humanity and so for an account of direct and indirect human duties, including indirect duties with regard to non-human animals. This position can, as Wood argues, be extended at the margins to allow for direct duties to those with fragments of rationality, or with incipient rationality. However, since it also grounds at least some indirect duties with regard to a wider range of sentient animals, to whom we have attitudes and responses like those we have to humans, and other indirect duties that extend to abstract and dispersed aspects of the natural order, Kant's position is likely to lead to wider-than-human, but not indefinitely wide, view of the objects of moral concern. His position may be speciesist up to a point: it requires action that takes account of difference of species. It does not establish that non-rational beings of any species have rights, or that rational beings have direct duties to them. But Kant's position is not a straight and simple form of human chauvinism. No doubt there are other imaginable ethical positions whose view on the scope of ethical concern and the standing of non-human animals provides a wider, although probably not a complete, block to speciesist conclusions. What stands in the way of their acceptance is the continued lack of the necessary arguments.

Acknowledgments

Michael Tooley, "Abortion and Infanticide," *Philosophy & Public Affairs* 2 (1972), pp. 37–65. Copyright © (1972) by Princeton University Press. Reprinted by permission of Princeton University Press.

Mary Anne Warren, "On the Moral and Legal Status of Abortion," *The Monist* 57 (1973), pp. 43–61. Copyright © 1973, The Monist, Peru, Illinois 61354. Reprinted by permission.

Joel Feinberg, "The Rights of Animals and Unborn Generations," in *Philosophy & Environmental Crisis*, William T. Blackstone (ed.), Athens GA: University of Georgia Press, 1974 pp. 43–68. Reprinted with the permission of University of Georgia Press.

Francis C. Wade, "Potentiality in the Abortion Discussion," *Review of Metaphysics* 29 (1975), pp. 239–255. Reprinted with the permission of Catholic University of America.

Neil MacCormick, "Children's Rights: A Test-Case for Theories of Right," *ARSP* 62 (1976), pp. 305–316. Reprinted with the permission of Franz Steiner Verlag Stuttgart GmbH.

R. G. Frey, "Animal Rights," *Analysis* 37 (1977), pp. 186–189. Reprinted with the permission of the author. Appeared in *Analysis*.

Jeffrie G. Murphy, "Rights and Borderline Cases," *Arizona Law Review* 19 (1977), pp. 228–241. Copyright © (1977) by the Arizona Board of Regents. Reprinted by permission.

H. J. McCloskey, "Moral Rights and Animals," *Inquiry* 22 (1979), pp. 23–54. Reprinted from 'Moral Rights and Animals' by H.J. McCloskey, Inquiry (www.tandf.no/inquiry), Vol 22, 1979, pp 23–54, by permission of Taylor & Francis AS.

Annette Baier, "The Rights of Past and Future Persons," in *Responsibilities to Future Generations: Environmental Ethics*, Ernest Partridge (ed.), Buffalo NY: Prometheus Books, 1981, pp. 171–183. Reprinted with the permission of Prometheus Books.

Tom Regan, "Justice and Equality," Chapter 7 in Tom Regan, *The Case for Animal Rights*, Berkeley: University of California Press, 1983, pp. 232–265. Reprinted with the permission of University of California Press.

Carl Wellman, "The Growth of Children's Rights," *ARSP* 70 (1984), pp. 441–453. Reprinted with the permission of Franz Steiner Verlag Stuttgart GmbH.

Robert Elliot, "Moral Autonomy, Self-Determination and Animal Rights," *The Monist* 70 (1987), pp. 83–97. Copyright © 1987, The Monist, Peru, Illinois 61354. Reprinted by permission.

Denise Réaume, "Individuals, Groups, and Rights to Public Goods," *University of Toronto Law Journal* 38 (1988), pp. 1-27. Reprinted by permission of University of Toronto Press Incorporated.

Lucius Garvin, "Obligation and Moral Agency," *Ethics* 58 (1948), pp. 188–194. Reprinted with the permission of the University of Chicago Press.

Michael S. Prichard, "Responsibility, Understanding, and Psychopathology," *The Monist* 58 (1974), pp. 630–645. Copyright © 1974, The Monist, Peru, Illinois 61354. Reprinted by permission.

David Copp, "Collective Actions and Secondary Actions," *American Philosophical Quarterly* 16 (1979), pp. 177–186. Reprinted with the permission of the *American Philosophical Quarterly.*

Peter A. French, "The Corporation as a Moral Person," *American Philosophical Quarterly* 16 (1979), pp. 207–215. Reprinted with the permission of the *American Philosophical Quarterly.*

S. F. Sapontzis, "Are Animals Moral Beings?" *American Philosophical Quarterly* 17 (1980), pp. 45–52. Reprinted with the permission of the *American Philosophical Quarterly.*

Robert J. Smith, "The Psychopath as Moral Agent," *Philosophy and Phenomenological Research* 45 (1984), pp. 177–193. Reprinted with the permission of the International Phenomenological Society.

Marina A. L. Oshana, "Ascriptions of Responsibility," *American Philosophical Quarterly* 34 (1997), pp. 71-83. Reprinted with the permission of the *American Philosophical Quarterly.*

N. Ann Davis, "Moral Agency, Individual Responsibility, and Human Psychology," *Public Affairs Quarterly* 12 (1998), pp. 51-78. Reprinted with the permission of North American Philosophical Publications, Inc.

Onora O'Neill, "Kant on Duties Regarding Nonrational Nature," *Aristotelian Society Supplementary Volume* 72 (1998), pp. 211-228. Reprinted with the permission of The Aristotelian Society.